COLOR, CULTURE, CIVILIZATION

COLOR, CULTURE, CIVILIZATION

Race and Minority Issues in American Society

Stanford M. Lyman

UNIVERSITY OF ILLINOIS

Urbana and Chicago

Library of Congress Cataloging-in-Publication Data

Lyman, Stanford M.
    Color, culture, civilization : race and minority issues in
American society / Stanford M. Lyman.
        p.   cm.
    Includes bibliographical references and index.
    ISBN 0-252-02048-0
    1. Racism—United States.   2. Minorities—United States.
3. United States—Race relations.   I. Title.
E184.A1L95 1994
3.05.8′00973—dc20   93-17539
                                                                CIP

Contents

Preface

In "Pluralism and Its Discontents," an essay published in the fall 1992 number of *Contention*, and known to me only after I had completed writing this book, Henry Louis Gates, Jr.—whose work is the subject of the final chapter of this book—took note of the fact that American concerns about curricular reform, and indeed about society and culture in their entirety, "center around notions of representation, cultural equity, and self-esteem." So too does the argument of this book express my concerns about these notions. Indeed, analyzing pluralism and its discontents strikes me as the most important sociocultural problem of our time. If this book contributes more light and less heat on these subjects than do the news reports coming every day, I believe I shall have accomplished something.

Color, Culture, Civilization is a product of more than four decades of my work on the sociology of minorities and the analysis of race and ethnic relations. Over such a long period of time I have accumulated too many debts to repay in so short a space. For so many of the friends and colleagues who shall go unmentioned by name here, I hope this statement will be recognized as but a small token of the gratitude that I feel is owed to them.

Throughout most of my career I have benefited from working with and receiving advice and encouragement from Marvin B. Scott. Arthur J. Vidich has always given me the best of constructive criticism. Years ago, the late Horace Cayton me helped to understand the intricacies of Robert E. Park's ideas about race and culture. Cecil Greek, Peter Kivisto, and Ying-jen Chang served as an ever helpful audience during the formative phase of some of the essays contained in this book. Herbert Hill guided me through the thicket of laws and court cases affecting the lives of African Americans. At a critical juncture in the preparation of chapter 12 of this book, Mary Lydon corrected my misunderstanding of Derrida's conception of voice.

For more than forty years I have been a member of the Barons, a club composed of nisei men who not only opened home and heart to me but also provided me with diverse opportunities from which I could learn about the social character and subcultural personality of Japanese Americans. For even longer, the family and friends of my high school chum, Galen Chow, have shown me the various styles of life that make up the realities of Chinese life in the western United States.

Over the past eight years, Florida Atlantic University's work-study program has provided me with research assistants. I thank Stanley Tang, Connie Tang, Eiji Murai, and James McCluskie for being such expert trackers, hunters, and gatherers. Dr. Paul Cantrell prepared the index for this book in his usual masterful fashion. Joan Schilling deserves more credit than she gets for typing the manuscript, keeping the records and correspondence related to it, and always being ready with hot coffee and a cheerful word when the author was tired or discouraged. Dick Martin invited me to contribute to the excellent list of publications put out by the University of Illinois Press and has proved to be the excellent editor that this press deserves to have. For errors of fact, commission, and omission, I take full responsibility.

Introduction

For almost a century, the discourse on ethnoracial minorities in the United States has turned on the dichotomy of assimilation versus pluralism. The issues entailed in this debate embrace the questions of color, culture, and civilization and often conflate them. Conventional approaches to this topic have sought to add further distinctions to each element in the polarity. Hence, assimilation was to be distinguished from possibly concomitant processes of acculturation and amalgamation and analyzed into no less than seven discrete cultural components;[1] pluralism was distinguished according to its pre-colonial,[2] colonial,[3] post-colonial,[4] and civil society models[5] and queried about its Eurocentric base.[6] As desiderata of a modern society, both assimilation and pluralism have their advocates, and each has been a situs for empirical investigation and normative dialogue.[7]

Both assimilation and pluralism are affected by and affect the related discourses on race prejudice, xenophobia, and the "other"—on the marginalizing of discrete peoples and of the ethnoracial self.[8] Moreover, the casuistries of each have been subjected to critical analysis. The rhetoric of assimilation is accused of being all too often suffused by a bland endorsement of the moral qualities attributed to the middle class Anglo-Saxon group in the society; of encouraging a filiopietistic worship of the society's national statemakers as founding fathers; and of legitimating a denigration of the color, customs, and cultures of racially or ethnically different peoples. The casuistries of pluralism, on the other hand, have been alleged to encourage a non-normative approach to all cultural practices; to idealize the values associated with folk societies; and to be less than forthcoming about the various forms of oppression that emanate from nondemocratic forms of ethnic community leadership. In response,

each discourse has presented its own idealized praxis as the best solution, or as the prerequisite to the only solution, to the race problem
in America; each has claimed to be the true champion of racial justice; and, each has had an ambivalent attitude about the relation of
state power to its own processes and programs.

Roscoe Pound, the father of sociological jurisprudence, once observed that, "Historically war and the administration of justice are
the two great functions of the state."[9] When, years later, Herbert
Blumer envisioned America's hierarchicalized color line as a
fortress-like barrier against racial justice, he, in effect, brought these
two functions of the state into complementarity.[10] The law, thence,
would appear to be the principal weapon with which to batter down
what Blumer once called America's "Maginot Line" of color; while
the Thirteenth, Fourteenth, and Fifteenth Amendments to the
United States Constitution become the nation's arsenal of true democracy. However, as Pound was quick to warn, "We must remember that law, as a practical matter, must deal largely with the outside
and not the inside of men and things, and must keep in mind that
the legal system is obliged to rely upon external agencies to put its
machinery in motion. Even the best of laws do not enforce
themselves."[11] Pound, in this and other passages in his writings, did
not seek to reinforce William Graham Sumner's skepticism about the
law's ability to supplant America's ethical failure to establish racial
justice after Emancipation, or its inability to overcome the nation's
ethnocentric mores; rather, he conceived the efficacy of law to be
proportionally related to the strength of the interests that it either
promoted or opposed. "A rule may run counter to the individual interests of a majority or of a militant minority or of a powerful class,"
he wrote, "or it may run counter to the moral ideas of individuals, as
in the case of the Fugitive Slave law; or it may be that no immediate
interests of individuals are involved and hence they are indifferent."
To work in the interests of justice, thus, requires one to ascertain just
what those interests are and what kinds of morals, customs, and culture inform them.

The diverging emphases in the perspectives of Sumner and
Pound find their current counterpart in what Cornel West, director
of Princeton University's Afro-American Studies Program, has recently called "the narrow framework of the dominant liberal and
conservative views of race in America."[12] That framework pits liberal advocates of an ethnoracially conscious and class-concerned
public policy against conservative ideologues who insist that only a
self-imposed and religiously reinvigorated metamorphosis in the

inner-worldly ethics of inner-city blacks will provide the basis for the latter's societal amelioration. With "its worn-out vocabulary," West asserts, this apparently hopelessly divided outlook "leaves us intellectually debilitated, morally disempowered, and personally depressed." Moreover, he concludes, it "reinforces intellectual parochialism and political paralysis." Such creedal interests not only inform but confound the quest for racial justice in America.

Divisions in the Interests of Racial Justice

Broadly speaking, the camps of those fighting for racial justice have long been divided over whether America will have fulfilled its promise as the "first new nation"[13] of the Enlightenment by establishing an unalloyed, universal, and personal achievement-oriented society, or by institutionalizing a pluralistic social order rooted in peaceful particularism and a noninvidious but culturally preservationist ascription. The former seeks the emancipation of the individual from all forms of hereditary claim;[14] its validation of acculturation will have occurred when an individual can honestly credit and be credited with his or her successes or failures in accordance with that which he or she has been able or unable to do rather than be.[15] The latter seeks collective emancipation and social as well as personal well-being in accordance with the sense of necessary self-esteem and rightful entitlement that derive from ethnocultural perpetuation, recognition, and response; its validation of acculturation will have occurred when each and every one of the peoples of America are corporately constituted as a heritage group with an equal right to persevere and to seek after all of the material and moral benefits that the society has promised to each individual. The former finds its ideal typification and root metaphor in the "melting pot"; the latter in the "mosaic," or, more prosaically, the "salad bowl."[16] The former emphasizes the benefits that will accrue from assimilation, acculturation, and amalgamation; the latter encourages multiculturalism, multiracial accommodation, and ethnoracial endogamy. Each regards its table of desiderata as the exemplification of racial justice. Each has its eminent scholar antecedents—J. Hector St. John de Crèvecoeur (1735–1813)[17] and Israel Zangwill (1864–1926)[18] for the assimilationists; Horace Kallen (1882–1974)[19] and Randolph Bourne (1886–1918)[20] for the pluralists.

It is not irrelevant to our discussion to observe that both positions owe their philosophical development in twentieth-century America to intellectual responses to the "Jewish Question." Although the matter had arisen in policy considerations in Eastern Europe in the late eighteenth century,[21] the question of whether and how diasporic Jews could be accommodated in industrializing nineteenth-century nation states came to haunt the sociocultural theories of such classical European social thinkers as Karl Marx, Max Weber, and Theodor Mommsen, and the resolution of that issue would become a point of departure for the American sociologists' approach to their own country's response to its rapidly enlarging ethnoracial mix. Karl Marx (1818–83) had treated the question in his pithy, scathing, but endlessly ambiguous statement: "The social emancipation of the Jew implies the emancipation of society from Judaism."[22] In this and other statements on the issue, Marx, according to one of his most astute critics, was asserting "that Jews had a right to emancipation in spite of their 'anti-social' role in society, because the whole of society was adopting their 'anti-social,' i.e., commercial, practices."[23]

However, even if one were to accept Marx's extraordinarily tendentious equation of the socioreligious tenets of Judaism with the spirit and practice of capitalism, one would still want to know whether he envisioned Jewish emancipation as utterly de-Judaizing; as dependent on the rise of a new yet-to-be realized noncapitalist societal form into which both Jews and Christians would be equally secularized and assimilated; or whether he somehow envisioned the survival of an "ethnic" Jewishness that would become attenuated from its religious origin but associated with one or another of the disparate conceptions of Jews as a people either united by a commonality of beliefs, culture, or traditions; sharing a community of interests; forming a nation; comprising a race; or existing merely as an aggregate, that is, as an economic category.[24]

Marx, baptized at the age of six (August 24, 1824), had been born into a family whose paternal ancestry included several generations of rabbis. His father had undergone baptism a year or more before Karl's birth. He had accepted a nominal Christianity in order to enter into the legal profession, wherein he defended the rights of Jews. Karl Marx did not maintain either a Protestant or Jewish identification during the course of his life.[25] Rudolf Bienenfeld has described a philosophy of Jewishness that is sometimes ascribed to Marx; its precepts derived neither from nationality, race, nor religion, but rather from a commitment to four Jewish tenets: *equality* as a matter of right rather than grace; *justice* as a matter of principle and not convenience; *reason* as a duty associated with continuous learning; and an *inner-worldliness* that requires the establishment of human and institutional perfection in the here-and-now rather than in the afterlife.[26] Whether Marx subscribed to these principles is, however, less important than the fact that they refer to a belief in the good society as one grounded in a civil association of law rather than in one dependent upon a communion of faith, that is, that they form the basis for a fundamental division between Jewish and Protestant social thought and give one pause when a "Judaeo-Christian" tradition is invoked.

Most of the early American sociologists who came to espouse an assimilationist orientation received their higher education in Wilhelmine, Germany.[27] There they came in contact with the *Methodenstreit* scholars' orientation toward Bismarck's "blood-and-iron" approach to imperial, cultural, and national hegemony. But upon returning to the United States, and in the spirit of Sarah E. Simons's careful distinctions among the several forms of assimilation,[28] they tended to transpose the phenomenon of social adjustment in a multiethnic society from a coercive Prussian public policy into either a gradual karyokinetic process or a merely acculturative American telos. However, the Jewish Question had challenged both program and process in Germany—and would do so again in America. For Max Weber (1864–1920) the Jews were a "pariah people" because of their religion.[29] In contrast to both Marx's and Sombart's (1863–1941) claims[30] about their originating role in the construction of modern capitalism, although they had had a definite role in premodern capitalistic economic formations, Weber insisted that Jews had done very little with respect to establishing two of the major institutions of production of modern capitalism, namely, domestic industry and the factory.[31] Weber's position on the Jewish Question ultimately was in keeping with that of other fin-de-siècle German scholars, that is, the position of progressive Gentiles whose political-economic ideology was national liberalism. To these, As Gary A. Abraham has summed up the matter, "emancipation was . . . seen . . . as a means to the end of normalizing minority-majority relations under the new conditions of open and 'civil' societies." In return for their admission into civil society, Jews were expected to acculturate, that is, to "cease to organize their attentions around an ancient subculture and social group and [to] turn toward the center along with all other citizens."[32] In fine, Weber's solution to *die Judenfrage* in Germany was not too dissimilar from that enunciated by the Chicago sociologist Ellsworth Faris for America in 1937[33]—a group commitment to radical assimilation that would ultimately extinguish altogether their existence in and as a religious or cultural peoplehood.

The society to which Jews (and, later, all other ethnoracially distinctive peoples) were advised to assimilate was modern, industrial, civilized—and *Christian*. Indeed, such a society was said to be not exclusive to a particular European or American nation-state but to modern civilization itself. This is the civilization that lauds the Protestant ethic as the spirit of capitalism, the civilization whose mainline Protestant denominations illuminate "a picture of what it might mean to live a biblical life in America,"[34] a civilization whose most eminent theologians "held America under the judgment of God."[35] Theodor Mommsen (1817–1903), a scholar who had considerable influence on Max Weber, treated the Jewish Question in such civilizational terms and observed in 1880, "the word *Christianity* in our day no longer means what it used to mean; nevertheless it is the only word which still defines the entire international civilization of our day and which numerous millions of people of our highly populated globe accept as their intrinsic link."[36] For neither Weber nor Mommsen could the Jews escape from their destiny: absorption into this expanding world civilization. Weber warned Jews against tarrying in unacculturated exile, in the hope of deliverance by a messiah.[37] Mommsen agreed, prophesying in relation to the new Zionist movement that had startled the Gentile peoples of Europe and America,[38] "the Jews . . . will not be led by another Moses into the Promised Land"; and admonishing them in what should be recognized as lingering vestiges of his generalized anti-Jewish attitude, "whether they sell trousers or write books, it is their duty to do away with their particularities wherever they can do so without offending their conscience."[39] But even offenses to their Jewish conscience did not seem to matter ultimately to Mommsen. He concluded his essay on the subject with a command: Jews "must make up their minds and tear down all barriers between themselves and their German compatriots."[40]

The German discourse on assimilation became one basis for America's second great *Kulturkampf*. It entered the fray in the form of a multifaceted debate over whether not only the Jew, but also the immigrant, the Asiatic, the Indian, and the Negro could be made full-fledged members of the rapidly industrializing, urbanizing nation. In its earlier version—that of the letters from the eighteenth-century "American farmer," Crèvecoeur—the Jewish question had not arisen. Rather, Crèvecoeur had focused on the role that intermarriage and an emergent Christian ecumenism would have on Americanizing the denizens of the newly decolonized nation in embryo. The "American farmer" had supposed that international matrimony and its socioculturally melding effects on the ways of life of subsequent generations would not only dissolve the bonds of nationality and culture that isolated the peoples of Europe from one another, but also would fuse the European settlers with America's red aborigines. However, Crèvecoeur, who opposed slavery, did not include the African American in his delineation of the "American . . . [a] new man, who acts upon new principles." Black-white relations did not loom large in Crèvecoeur's sociological imagination. For this first proponent of amalgamative assimilationism, however, the religious divisions that had led to so much conflict in Europe would be ended in America: "The various Christian sects," he prophesied, "[will] wear out, and . . . this mixed [American] neighborhood will exhibit a strange religious medley, that will be neither pure Catholicism nor pure Calvinism."[41]

The second debate over how America might construct its cultural configuration began in the latter part of the nineteenth century. It compounded Crèvecoeur's imagery by adding to its beneficent message a number of agonizing questions about the place of color, race, ethnicity, and non-Christian religions in a modernizing democratic republic—and by posing a pluralist alternative to assimilation.

The Jewish Question figured significantly in this reopening of the cultural debate about America. Israel Zangwill led off with his melodramatic promise that Christian-Jewish intermarriage would be but one forerunner of America's "great Melting Pot." Interethnic intimacies would make for a bubbling cauldron that would fuse the bloodlines and combine the cultural heritages of "Celt and Latin, Slav and Teuton, Greek and Syrian—black and yellow—Jew and Gentile."[42] Zangwill was motivated in great part by his concern over the revival of the Jewish Question in Europe and America. He had served as president of the Emigration Regulation Department of the Jewish Territorial Organization, a body that undertook to settle thousands of victims of Russia's anti-Semitic pogroms in the United States.[43] However, widely publicized apprehensions about Jewish "anarchists,"[44] fears about the type, number, and spread of crimes that New York City's Jewish gangs might commit,[45] a concern over the ambiguous American response to the Dreyfus affair,[46] and worry over the effect the revival of the notorious "blood libel" might have on American-Jewish relations,[47] led some Jewish intellectuals, including Zangwill, to espouse Zionism for Europe's Jews and to issue a promissory note of Jewish disappearance in America, a virtual dissolution of one people's ethnocultural identity that would in the process also help to relieve the United States of all of its non-WASP ethnic groups.[48]

Horace Kallen's and Randolph Bourne's versions of pluralism were developed in part to oppose Zangwill's advocacy of Jewish ethnocultural extinction. Kallen, as John Higham observes, "argued for the indestructibility of ethnic cultures in an effort to resist the disintegration of his own."[49] An active cultural Zionist who had been brought to Boston from his birthplace, Silesia, when he was five years old, Kallen had founded the Harvard Menorah Society in 1906 while serving simultaneously as William James's protégé at that university and discovering through the teachings of Barrett Wendell that the assimilationists' model of the ideal culture for America, that of genteel, Puritan, New England, owed its origins to the values and credos enunciated by the ancient Hebrew prophets.[50] Applying James's idea that the universe is "more like a federal republic than like an empire or a kingdom"[51] to the ethnocultural structure of the United States, Kallen began to formulate a thesis that found its most powerful statement in the claim that a true democracy would oppose a melting pot.[52] Granting a sphere of public policy and economic life to the modern equivalent of an assimilationist-oriented and democratically elected Caesar, Kallen nevertheless hoped to preserve an inner, private, but unghettoized sphere of Jewish communal existence against the siren song of Protestant, Anglo-Saxon, cultural conformity.[53] In formulating his thesis as a general proposition, however, Kallen perceived that Jewish ways of life could not be preserved and protected unless those of every other ethnic group could be made equally secure. Hence, he abjured adherence to Zangwill's melting pot of merely once-proud nations, envisioning in its stead a democratic republic of English-speaking but culturally distinctive nationalities and dialects—"a multiplicity in a unity, an orchestration of mankind."[54]

Bourne, destined by the accidents attending his birth to go through his short life a hunchback and a dwarf, and by his uncompromising individuality and shrewd intelligence, as well as the example of his father's own business failures, to revolt against his aristocratic, Presbyterian, and Puritan New England heritage, adapted Kallen's ideas to his own formulation of an emergent United States that he called "trans-national America."[55] Convinced that the "allure of fresh and true ideas, of free speculation, of artistic vigor, of cultural styles, of intelligence fused with feeling, and feeling given fibre and outline by intelligence"[56] could never arise from the reigning American philosophy of technocentric instrumentalism, and that the Anglo-conformity that characterized the official program of Americanization had been both a failure and a mistake,

Bourne pointed out that, in fact, the actual processes of "Assimilation . . . instead of washing out the memories of Europe, [had] made them more and more intensely real,"[57] and, he insisted, this counter-Zangwillian process had been truly beneficial for the nation.

For the gentile Bourne, as for the Jewish Kallen, American Zionism provided the ideational model for what he believed was a burgeoning American cultural pluralism. Bourne understood the American variant of Zionism to have proclaimed that a nonmilitarized and antichauvinist "Palestine is to be built as a Jewish centre on purely religious and cultural foundations . . . [and] is not to be the home of all the Jewish people."[58] Hence, for Bourne, Zionism instantiated the best example of his own proposal for a fundamental separation of state citizenship from group ethnonational identity. Zionist Jews in America might send their cultural and even financial support to a reconstituted religious and cultural center in Israel, but they would remain loyal citizens of the United States. "Cultural allegiance," he prophesied, "will not necessarily coincide with political allegiance."[59] Under such a political and cultural praxis, true internationalism would flower *within* America, itself to become a culturally conscious state-societal mosaic of nationalities. Bourne believed that his philosophy of diversity might be institutionalized, finding its best expression in a cosmopolitan celebration of ethnic distinctiveness that had even broader implications for global unity: "America is already the world federation in miniature," he observed, "the continent where for the first time in history has been achieved that miracle of hope, the peaceful living side by side, with character substantially preserved, of the most heterogeneous peoples under the sun."[60]

In addition to their common foundation in alternative responses to the Jewish Question, the advocates of assimilation and pluralism each developed different orientations toward the white Anglo-Saxon peoples dominating the culture of America. Central to the assimilationist position is a public denial—coupled all too often with a private assurance to the contrary—that the several races and cultures of America are permanently arrayed along a more or less fixed, vertical, and invidious line of rights, opportunities, privileges, and status. The proclamation of that line speaks to what Herbert Blumer reminds us is the basic characteristic of race prejudice—a hierarchicalized sense of group position;[61] the denial of its fixity, to the Jeffersonian ideal of the eighteenth century American Enlightenment—that all men are created equal. Taken together, this fundamental contradiction constitutes what Gunnar Myrdal in 1944 called the "American dilemma."[62] Treated analytically, however, the easily demonstrated thesis that the vertical ethnic order continues to exist undermines both the assurances of equalitarian ethnoracial assimilation and the promises of egalitarian ethnocultural pluralism.

In their critiques of assimilation, Bourne and Kallen exposed the privileged place of the white Anglo-Saxon and Protestant elite in America, but neither quite perceived how the latter group's securely entrenched position in society—which they harshly criticized—might not only subvert their respective programmatic philosophies of a federated multicultural America, but also cool the fires of Crevecoeur's and Zangwill's melting pot. Two issues contributed to this potentiality for a double-sided subversion—intermarriage and the conflation of the color-culture question.

Marriage across religious and Old World national lines was central to Zangwill's theatricalized picture of the melting pot, and crossing the color as well as the culture line was certainly indicated in the rhetoric of his play's denouement. Yet, by 1922, when he published a "new and revised edition" of his drama, Zangwill provided an "Afterword" that reveals an extraordinary confusion of biosocial ideas as well as an increased ambivalence about Negro-white marriages. Insisting that "it is as much social prejudice as racial antipathy that today divides black and white in the New World,"[63] he nevertheless tells his readers that "no doubt there is an instinctive antipathy which tends to keep the white man free from black blood";[64] that "the [African's] prognathous face is an ugly and undesirable type of countenance . . . that . . . connotes a lower average of intellect and ethics";[65] that "Melanophobia, or fear of the black, may be pragmatically as valuable a racial defence for the white as the counter-instinct of philoleucosis, or love of the white, is a force of racial uplifting for the black";[66] and that "white and black are as yet too far apart for profitable fusion."[67] Holding that such African American painters as the expatriate Henry Ossawa Tanner or such black poets as Paul Lawrence Dunbar "show the potentialities of the race even without white admixture," Zangwill preferred that persons of this class and status intermarry rather than having miscegenation occur among "the dregs of both races."[68] Yet, even in these cases, he hesitated. "Blacks of this temper," he suggested, referring to those "heroic souls . . . [who] dare the adventure of intermarriage," "would serve their race better by making Liberia a success or building up an American negro State . . . or at least asserting their rights as American citizens in that sub-tropical South which without their labour could never have been opened up."[69]

Although he allowed that the "African negro has . . . not a few valuable ethnic elements—joy of life, love of colour, keen senses, beautiful voice, and [an] ear for music," and that these might come to fruition through intermarriage as "contributions that might somewhat compensate for the dragging-down of the white and, in small doses at least, might one day prove [to be] a tonic to an anaemic and art-less America,"[70] Zangwill now put the full force of his assimilationist faith behind "the spiritual [rather than physical] miscegenation which, while clothing, commercialising, and Christianising the ex-African, has given 'rag-time' and the sex-dances that go to it, first to white America and thence to the whole white world." Ultimately, Zangwill perceived his cautiousness about black-white marriages as also providing a way for Jewish endogamy to continue in melting-pot America: "The Jew may be Americanised and the American Judaised without any gamic interaction."[71] In effect, he seemed to disavow the necessity and advantage of intermarriage that had been the core argument of his melodrama, The Melting Pot. Assimilation could occur without amalgamation.

Intermarriage was neither an issue nor a desideratum in Kallen's or Bourne's conception of cultural pluralism. Their outlook (especially that of Kallen) took equality to be centered in the right to be racially, ethnically, and culturally different: "The men who wrote and signed the Declaration [of Independence] and the men and women who fought and suffered and died for it," he wrote in 1948, "did not intend by that proposition either to abolish or to penalize differences. They intended to vindicate differences, to acknowledge, and to defend their equal right to life, liberty, and the pursuit of happiness."[72] Among the differences to be kept both free and equal were those of race, ethnicity, and nationality. For Kallen, the invidious distinctions among races, nations, and ethnic groups in the various "Americanization" programs of his day exemplified a fundamental misunderstanding of the Jeffersonian ideal of democracy. To Kallen, the "full practical meaning of the democratic faith as a program of conduct is exemplified by nothing so much as its repudiation of slavery."[73] And, as the central theme of his philosophy implied, this repudiation did not entail the genocidal, cultural, or social extermination of blacks. Rather, as one people of the American ethnoracial multiverse, their color as well as their cultural and ethnic integrity were to be protected and cherished. Endogamy certainly seemed to be implied—but not required—in Kallen's conception of pluralism. Intermarriage seems not to be ruled out altogether; for the whole of his philosophy emphasized the freedom of the individual to realize him- or herself through making courageous, if risky, choices.[74]

However, pluralism has often foundered on the question of color and its relation to culture. Bourne's and Kallen's perspectives on pluralism emphasized the equality of cultures and envisioned American society as providing, in Bourne's words, for "a cosmopolitan federation of national colonies, of foreign cultures, from whom the sting of devastating competition has been removed,"[75] or, in Kallen's words, for "orchestration . . . modes of the free association of the different"[76] Much of their efforts were expended in extolling the benefits that would accrue to America from the energizing of the transplanted cultures of the peoples from Europe. But a burning question in their own day as well as the present era is whether and to what extent the cultures of the enslaved peoples from Africa had survived the Middle Passage, the "seasoning" in the West Indies, and the 225 years of bondage in America, and, if they had, what place they deserved in an American cultural mosaic.

Bourne insisted that all races and nations could contribute to the "cultural progress" of America and observed that "the Southern white man's policy of keeping down a race . . . is the least defensible thing in the world."[77] Later, he went on to denigrate life in the states of the white South as "culturally sterile because it has had no advantage of cross-fertilization like . . . Wisconsin and Minnesota . . . [where] strong foreign cultures have struck root . . . [and where] German and Scandinavian political ideas and social energies have expanded to a new potency."[78] But he made no mention of any African political ideas and social energies that might be liberated to work their wonders on the states of the former slavocracy. Kallen was even more cautious, postponing analysis of African cultures in America and the designation of their value to a special investigation that in fact he never carried out: "I do not discuss the influence of the negro upon the esthetic material and cultural character of the South and the rest of the United States," he wrote in 1924. "This is at once too considerable and too recondite in its processes for casual mention. It requires a separate analysis."[79]

The perspectives of Zangwill on the one side and Bourne and Kallen on the other were largely philosophical and broadly programmatic in character.[80] None of these men had carried out detailed sociological analyses of the actual situations of the several racial and ethnic groups then contending for recognition and response in the United States. The social and cultural adjustment—as well as the civic status and economic opportunity—of the European and Asian immigrants and the freedmen-and-women and their offspring had from 1880 to 1920 been left largely to the ministrations of the newly aroused Social Gospel movement and its urban settlement house missionaries. In these newly established settlement houses, the "race question"[81] came together with the "Jewish question"[82] each having to contend in its own way with the "immigrant" and "urban" questions of which it had become an unresolved part.[83] By 1913 Robert Park—who had formulated a thesis relating racial oppression to European expansion while serving as an investigative reporter for and international secretary of the Congo Reform Association, who had studied the situation affecting African American life chances in the rural and urban South during an eight year stint as private secretary, ghost writer, and amanuensis to Booker T. Washington,[84] who had journeyed together with the Tuskegeean leader through Europe to find "the man farthest down,"[85] and had taken an interest in the emerging "Japanese problem"[86] that had arisen on the Pacific coast—put forward a pessimistic thesis on the resolution of the race issue: "the chief obstacle to the assimilation of the Negro and the Oriental are [sic] not mental but physical traits. . . . The Japanese, like the Negro is condemned to remain among us an abstraction, a symbol not merely of his own race, but of the Orient and of that vague, ill-defined menace we sometimes refer to as the 'yellow peril.'"[87]

During the 1920s and 1930s, as the living conditions and economic opportunities for blacks, Asians, Amerindians, and Hispanics seemed not to improve appreciably, Park, who had become a leading theorist of assimilation, grew less and less sanguine about the likelihood that America would accomplish its officially proclaimed mission of becoming the modern world's first fully integrated melting pot democracy.[88] The assimilation-oriented Social Gospel movement began to wane after the First World War. Its surviving settlement houses "did not recognize race relations as a major problem during the 1930s."[89] For the most part the movement's leaders continued to segregate blacks in separate settlement houses and accommodated their philanthropic programs at the state and local levels to prevailing Jim Crow sentiments. As Trolander observes, "They still thought of their movement primarily in terms of white middle class workers living in poor white neighborhoods."[90] "Their greatest successes," she concludes, "had been in helping immigrants to assimilate, and by the 1930s they had not totally adjusted to the decline in immigration."[91]

Nor did the Social Gospel-inspired aid to European immigrants to America do much to resolve the Jewish Question. Many of the settlements were strictly religious in character and aimed their "Americanization" programs toward the fulfillment of a proselytizing mission—to make the society into a Christian republic.[92] Yet, for "world Jewry," as Aaron Berman has pointed out, "the decade and a half between 1933 and 1948 was traumatic and cataclysmic."[93] Even after Hitler had been defeated and the Holocaust brought to a halt, there remained the unresolved status of the thousands of homeless and stateless Jewish survivors, a people whose horrifying experiences challenged theodicy itself[94] and whose immediate needs accelerated the pressure to establish a Jewish homeland. This situation, in turn, reopened the debate over whether the meaning given to Zionism by Kallen and Bourne would in fact prevail against the tide of events[95] and the undercurrent of suspicion[96] and ambivalence that had shadowed it—from within and without[97]—from the beginning.

The Jewish ambivalence over whether to opt for assimilation or pluralism is no better personified than in the life choices made by Israel Zangwill. Zangwill had explained the larger message of his play, The Melting Pot, to an enthusiastic Theodore Roosevelt, then President of the United States: the play "dramatises your own idea of America as a crucible in which the races are fusing into a future America . . . combining as it does, the American and the American-Jewish problem."[98] Despite this apparent capitulation to assimilationism, Zangwill, who had married a gentile in 1903, announced his unswerving support for Zionism, that is, he became a Jewish nationalist, thereby opposing the very fusion his melodrama had celebrated. As his most recent biographer observes, "Precisely at the time he decided to cast his lot in with the apparent historical destiny of Western Jewry to have its identity absorbed ineluctably into the majority population, he joined actively with those determined to rescue and preserve the Jewish people from just such absorption."[99] The paradox is resolved, perhaps, by imputing to Zangwill and other ethnoculturally concerned Jews a belief in America's exceptional promise with respect to the race issue in general and the Jewish question in particular. After 1919 some American Jewish leaders hoped that such promulgations as the Bolshevik Declaration of the Rights of Peoples and the several minority treaties agreed to by the postwar conferences would protect their coreligionists from the worst features of prewar anti-Semitism,[100] while Britain's Balfour Declaration held out the promise of a future Jewish homeland in Palestine.[101] America, they hoped, would solve its Jewish problem either by assimilation or by a muted Kallen-Bourne style of ethnoracial pluralism, separating the cultural elements of Jewishness from the political sphere of an increasingly civil society.

Despite his own paradoxical response to it, Zangwill's philosophy persisted for five decades as a societal desideratum for America's ethnocultural minorities. At the level of social action and institutional change the years following World War II witnessed the dismantling of judicially and legislatively supported racial segregation, the virtual elimination of avowedly "Jim Crow" practices, and, at the national, state, and local levels, the passage of laws aiming to ensure the civil rights of racial as well as some other minorities. In effect, what Blumer had designated as the outer bastion of America's color line fortress had been breached, but its inner walls remained more or less intact. Whereas Myrdal's vision of the "American dilemma," namely, the contradiction between the "higher" values of freedom and equality on the one side and the sense of racial invidiousness on the other, was that of a problem that could be resolved by the reaffirmation of the former at the levels of law, politics, and, to a lesser extent, economic opportunity, the assimilation/pluralism debate, that is, the questions of the place of racially based color consciousness and of ethnic culture, as well as of their relation to each other and to the emerging national and world orders, remain unanswered to the present day.[102]

Color, Culture, Civilization explores the dynamics of the still unresolved debate over pluralism and assimilation. At the present time, the concept of assimilation is all but rejected in academic circles,[103] but its promise and ideal still energize new immigrants and the makers of much of public policy, while the ideology of pluralism is in its ascendancy.[104] But the ethnoracial compact that is necessary to secure the basis for a peaceful ordering of racial and cultural diversity has not yet been clearly enunciated nor has it been "signed" and "ratified" by the parties who would have to live according to its tenets. In May 1992 Americans across the country could see that neither the once bright promise of assimilation nor the heady prospect of an egalitarian pluralism seemed assured. Their television screens pictured significant numbers of enraged blacks, Latinos, and Asians, as well as a few whites, engaging in violent protest over a suburban jury's exoneration of four white Los Angeles policemen who, allegedly "in the line of duty," had beaten a black man so severely as to inflict brain damage.[105] The 1992 "riots," as the media labeled them, occurred twenty-four years after the Kerner Commission had issued its report on the "civil disorders" that had broken out during the 1960s.[106] That report appended to its conclusion a statement by Dr. Kenneth B. Clark, the psychologist whose studies of the effects of racial segregation on school children had contributed to the Supreme Court's landmark decision in *Brown v. Board of Education of Topeka*.[107] Dr. Clark set the matter in terms of a history of neglect and a future that seemed only too likely to be characterized by the unrest that had occurred in the past:

> I read that report . . . of the 1919 riot in Chicago, and it is as if I were reading the report of the investigating committee on the Harlem riot of '35, the report of the investigating committee on the Harlem riot of '43, the report of the McCone Commission on the Watts riot.

> I must again in candor say to you members of this Commission—it is a kind of Alice in Wonderland—with the same moving picture re-shown over and over again, the same analysis, the same recommendations, and the same inaction.[108]

A few weeks before the 1992 outbreaks of violence in Los Angeles, San Francisco, Berkeley, and a few other cities, Andrew Hacker had published his analysis of the current state of the race question in the United States. Entitled *Two Nations: Black and White, Separate, Hostile, Unequal,* Hacker's study in fact describes a far more complex situation than his title suggests.[109] The still unresolved race question depicted in Hacker's book embraces not only the economic, political, social, and cultural rifts among African Americans and whites, but also a host of concomitant ethnoracial divisions and their attendant conflicts that prevent not only blacks and whites from developing harmonious relations with each other, but also separate them from first, second, and third generation Chinese, Japanese, and Korean Americans as well as from Vietnamese, Cambodian, Hmong, and other Southeast Asian newcomers, and Mexican, Puerto Rican, and the many other Latino denizens of America's diversely populated ghettos, barrios, and urban enclaves. America is not merely a biracial republic—as was much of the antebellum South—but, rather, a loose and unintegrated congeries of peoples. These peoples include a great many descendants of earlier immigrants from Europe, Asia, and the various Hispanic areas; about thirty million persons of African descent; a growing population of Indians, many of whom no longer reside on reservations, and the various peoples of Asian, Oceanic, Latino, and European heritages who have come to the United States since 1945.[110] It is a potentially rich, culturally diverse, but deeply troubled mix that holds out as much (or as little) possibility for Crevecoeur's vision of an amalgamated "new America" as it does for Kallen's well-tempered chorus of ethnoculturally diverse voices.

When Wilson Jeremiah Moses, a contemporary (b. 1942) African American scholar,[111] who combines in his quite original perspective on the race question the outlooks of his adopted Roman Catholicism, his background in Afro-Baptist Protestantism, and his sympathetic if anomalous respect for an American variant of black nationalism, observed that "the pattern of Afro-American life in the United States has been one of gradually increasing acculturation, despite persistent segregation and despite the fact that separate institutions within black communities continue to spring up and to thrive,"[112] he, in effect, had presented a thesis not too intellectually distant from that of the much-honored but also much-misunderstood Robert E. Park (1864–1944). Although Park was at one time regarded as sociology's foremost investigator of the theory and practice of American race and minority relations, a comprehensive understanding of his cosmology has been prevented by a virtually systematic disregard of his early writings.[113]

A critical exposition and appreciation of these writings forms the basis for the first three chapters of this book. Park, it is asserted there, is best understood as a theorist of assimilation as both the cause and the effect of civilizational advance. Modern civilization, for Park, acted as an almost inexorable social force as well as a transnational process. As such, it operated so as to draw the folk cultures of non-industrial, peasant, and handicraft peoples into a global commercial vortex from which there was little likelihood of escape. Nonindustrial peoples—especially those whose skin color was black, brown, red, or yellow—were being marginalized within modern societies at the very same time they were being absorbed by the civilizational process. Their new status arose as they migrated, or were invaded, subjugated, and brought as captives, servants, or slaves into the urban metropoles of the several European imperial powers and of the United States.[114]

Without saying so directly, Park's outlook on civilization elaborated on and depicted the double-sided character of the Protestant ethic. That ethic, as well as its Catholic variant,[115] and its increasingly secularized capitalist spirit,[116] found one side of its expression in the program of uplift, sobriety, moral steadfastness, and hard work that had been urged on the African-American freedmen-and-women by Booker T. Washington's Tuskegee experiment.[117] However, its darker side—what I have called its "Gothic" aspect—was revealed in the depredations and atrocities committed by the agents of King Leopold II—a "king in business," as Park called him[118]—as part of their errand of mercy and commerce into the so-called Congo Free State.

Wilson Jeremiah Moses once criticized Park's disciple, E. Franklin Frazier (1894–1962), for the latter's conception of assimilation as "the cultural absorption of blacks into an America known for its crassness, vulgarity, and venality."[119] Moses asserted that, in assaulting the black bourgeoisie's ways of life,[120] Frazier had exposed a glaring contradiction in his own position; for, Moses pointed out, Frazier was an avid supporter of integration. Segregation, Moses riposted, regardless of its isolating and provincializing effects, ought, from Frazier's point of view, to have been defended as "a bulwark against the absorption of blacks into a society that is noted for its sanctimonious ethnocentrism, swaggering anti-intellectualism, and hypocritical self-righteousness."[121] Moses's critique, however valuable its insight in the matter, overlooks how much of the fatalistic perspective on civilization and its effects Frazier had absorbed from his mentor, Park, as well as how much of that outlook had been derived from his own experiences as a much put-upon black scholar.[122] Park's characterization of modern Euro-American civilization—motored by militarization, as was fin de siècle Germany,[123] and, later, the United States;[124] impelled to extend its moralistic and commercial hegemony over the entire globe, as evidenced by Leopold of Belgium's machinations in Asia and Africa;[125] and assured of its duty, as well as its capacity, to subjugate the peoples and cultures residing within its expanding imperium, and then to assimilate them[126]—could only lead one who revelled in the ethnoracial diversity of the world to despair over what appeared to be an inevitable trend. Blacks would not be an exception. If, their African cultures having been eroded by the totalizing effects of slavery and,[127] after Emancipation, their identities having been degraded by a forced descent into what arguably became a color caste,[128] their more successful members rose to a modest place in a biracial but enervated middle class, a Park-inspired sociologist such as Frazier might well say that the hypothesized historical cycle—that is, Park's race relations cycle, which, after three consecutive stages, ends in assimilation—had been completed—with results inherent in and appropriate to its fundamental character.[129]

There are, however, many ways for seemingly subordinated people to resist the inevitable.[130] In fact, assimilation—either of the crass kind later envisioned by Frazier or of the more benevolent form proposed in the 1920s by Emory Bogardus[131]—was ultimately relegated to the limiting status of being but one possible outcome of the race relations cycle by Park himself. In 1937 he came to see that the global contact and confrontation of races that had been taking place for at least the last three centuries of the modern era would finally result in either a caste system like that of India, subjection to permanent minority status as was being visited upon the Jews of Europe at that time, or complete assimilation as he supposed took place in China.[132] Silent about the outcome in America, Park's final essay on the matter, presented as a lecture in 1943, spoke not about every nonwhite, non-Anglo minority's destiny to be dissolved in the flux of a deracinated worldwide commercial cosmopolitanism, but rather about the American polity's unfulfilled obligation to grant and ensure the full panoply of civil rights to the blacks, Asians, Hispanics, and Native Americans in its midst.[133]

The histories of interracial contacts are filled with examples of various adaptations to or modes of resistance against cultural and more brutal forms of domination by the more powerful elements in the encounters.[134] Among the tools of assimilation, as well as among the weaponry available in the arsenal of group preservation, are the mutual, or, often enough, the nonmutual images that each ethnoracial group builds up about itself and about the other. Chapters 4 through 6 of the present work explore several of the dimensions of these imageries, critically examining their effectiveness, their basis in history and myth, their effects on law and public policy, and their phenomenological grounding in modernist or postmodernist epistemologies. Central to the argument of the entire body of materials discussed therein is the irregular dynamic that pervades the construction, adoption, legitimation, and downfall of the historiographies, as well as the sociological ideal typifications of the several peoples, that make up the United States of America.

In chapter 4 I explore "Hansen's Law of Third Generation Return" for the unexamined implications for the race question that its thesis contains.[135] Marcus Lee Hansen (1892–1938) not only asserted that the third generation descendants of America's immigrants would assume the task of discovering and refurbishing their grandparents' life stories and histories, but also extended his argument to cover the resurgence of interest in the history of the antebellum and Reconstruction eras in the American South.[136] He congratulated the American Historical Association for its declaration in behalf of the authenticity of Margaret Mitchell's novel *Gone With the Wind*, and

he designated it as an illuminating example of third generational return of the white southern planter class. Remarkably, Hansen chose
not to examine or even take notice of any third generation return
among the grandchildren of America's slave population, thus not
only missing an opportunity to analyze the writings of the postbellum African American historians[137] or of those by Carter G.
Woodson and his fellow African Americans, who as early as 1915
had founded the *Association for the Study of Negro Life and
History*,[138] but also continuing the long and less than benign neglect
of the annals of African American history.[139] Because Hansen chose
to cite the rise of historical fiction, together with the establishment of
ethnic historical and antiquarian societies, as exemplary of his
"law," I examine *Clotel or, the President's Daughter*,[140] a novel published in 1853 by the ex-slave and abolitionist pamphleteer William
Wells Brown (1815–84),[141] showing that it too could be treated as a
work of third generation return. For *Clotel* irrevocably links the African American slave population to the white heritage group that
founded the United States. In the closing chapter of the novel,
Thomas Jefferson, the author of the Declaration of Independence and
the third president of the United States, is being inaugurated as slave
catchers close in on the eponymous heroine of the story, Jefferson's
unacknowledged daughter by one of his slave mistresses.

The fictionalized slave narrative by William Wells Brown,[142] as
well as the many autobiographical slave narratives presented in the
years preceding and following Emancipation,[143] despite their value
as works of protest, had the unanticipated effect of giving occasional
credence to the pro-slavery imagery of blacks as being given over to
a more than circumstantial condition of slothfulness.[144] The dilemmas and contradictions that such a stigma imposes on African Americans are explored in chapter 5 of the present work. There it is
argued that the sin of sloth—for it is one of the seven deadly
sins[145]—has been granted virtual neo-Lamarckian status—that is, it
appears as the occasionally biological, but, more often in this age
wherein there has been a natural scientific retreat from racism,[146] the
sociocultural inheritance of an acquired characteristic—in the writings of such contemporary commentators on the African American
scene as Thomas Sowell and Lawrence M. Mead. Sowell has written, "The slaves were kept dependent on the slave owners for rations
of food or clothing and for the organization of their daily lives and
living conditions. . . . With many generations of discouragement of
initiative and with little incentive to work any more than to escape
punishment, the slaves developed foot-dragging, work-evading pat-

terns that were to remain as a cultural legacy long after slavery itself disappeared."[147] It is Sowell's thesis that the virtually inherent patterns of slothful conduct are given even more impetus by present-day practices of "job quotas, charity, subsidies, [and] preferential treatment," while they, like slavery before them, tend to undermine "those methods [of raising income among blacks and other disadvantaged minorities] which have historically proved successful— self-reliance, work skills, education, [and] business experience."[148]

Lawrence M. Mead goes a step further, treating the conduct of today's unemployed urban black youth as exemplary of the condition of "masterless men"[149] and attributing their problematic status "to social structure . . . further back in history."[150] As Mead perceives the matter, "today's black poor function poorly because their parents did, and their parents did, a pattern that ultimately goes back to the black experience as a subordinate caste in America."[151] Nevertheless, he believes that "the effect of racial bias is mainly to limit the quality of jobs blacks can get, not to deny them all employment."[152] Hence, Mead opposes any enlargement of the welfare state, expansion of government-sponsored jobs, programs, or any furtherance of racially conscious affirmative action. "The best single cure," he observed a few days after the uprising in Los Angeles, "would be to enforce the work requirement more fully. A less idle poor would not feel so powerless."[153] Mead undercuts the force as well as the general applicability of his neo-Lamarckian thesis by attributing the success of today's modestly sized black middle class to those whose parents believed in "working hard and going to church."[154] The offspring of these parents, according to Mead, overcame the stigma of sloth by "conforming to common civilities and satisfying authority figures such as teachers and employers . . . [while] competing for success in legitimate ways."[155] This contemporary political economist believes that the Protestant ethic that served blacks so well as a deterrent to sloth in Booker T. Washington's days is no longer recognized as a positive norm by today's inner-city African American youth. "Today," he writes, "tragically, [black culture] is more likely to mean rock music or the rapping of drug dealers on ghetto street corners."[156]

To the contrary of the theses put forward by Sowell and Mead, I hold that, at least since the slavery period, African Americans have been stigmatized by a multifaceted attributional argument that consigns all but a morally exceptional few of them to irrevocable membership in a caste of permanently and inescapably slothful persons. Until and unless they are relieved of the policy implications of this thesis, I believe blacks will continue to be treated as blameworthy victims of a putatively self-precipitated condition, advised to refurbish the content of their perhaps temperamental character,[157] or invited to subjugate themselves to a modern variant of what used to be called "warranteeism," that is, an obligation to serve faithfully a master class of morally superior whites.[158] The stigma of sloth, like race prejudice, is one of the badges of bondage still pinned onto the breastplates and the escutcheon of the descendants of those who labored in America's "peculiar institution."[159]

The attribution of sloth to blacks is part of a larger complex of stereotypy and myth that has been given added stimulation by the movie industry in Hollywood and the filmic scenarios it produces.[160] The extent to which these cinematic images have retarded the social acceptance of African Americans and at the same time lent support to a less than egalitarian relationship among the races is detailed in chapter 6. Hollywood's version of African history and anthropology took its point of departure from a variant of the Comtean method of comparative study.[161] Such a filmic sociological imagination placed blacks on the lowest rung of human development and depicted them as lust-driven savages intent on making an assault on white civilization. Whether presented as brutish males attempting the rape of white women or as seductive sirens of brown-skinned pulchritude seeking to subvert the norms of Occidental familism, African American men and women were revealed as dangerous unless kept in docile servitude or confined to occasional and always punishable illicit sexual liaisons across the color line. Although in recent years the civil rights movement has had an enlightening effect on America's moviemakers so that the presentation of blacks as "toms," "coons," "bucks," "mammies,"[162] and "luscious brown sugar"[163] is no longer acceptable film fare,[164] I argue that elements of the underlying thematic still remain. I suggest that the vestiges of "primitivism" originally adapted from what are now recognized as invalid ethnological theories have not yet been dishabituated from the outlook of those who create or attend perhaps the most important product of America's mass culture.

The ethnohistorical theses about civilization and its development in the Americas have long been buttressed by a widely accepted temporal and cultural periodization separating the pre-Columbian from the post-Conquest eras. A little-known challenge to this perspective—and its implications for the civil rights of Asian Americans and Amerindians as well as for a new vision of the prehistoric connections between paleolithic Asians and America's aborigines[165]—

is presented in chapter 7, opening a five-chapter section of the present volume that seeks to "bring Asians and Amerindians back into" sociological discussions of the race question in America. Not only is the conventional anthropological wisdom about the Asiatic origins of Amerindian civilization subjected to a searching if ultimately inconclusive query—one that opens up the possibility that America was the "old world" and Asia the "new" one—but also the demographic history of Chinese migration to America is, in chapter 8, shown to be part of a global diaspora of the peoples from that land. That diaspora compares with that of the Jews[166] and may exceed in scope of diverse settlement areas that of Africans.[167] The diasporic character of the largely Cantonese immigration, as well as the effects of the collision of the norms of local Sinic cultures with the limitations on family formation imposed by the anti-Chinese laws of the United States, made for a fundamental difference with respect to the situations affecting the respective community organization of Chinese and Japanese immigrants in America.[168] Chapter 9 details these differences and offers a sociocultural explanation for the longevity of urban "Chinatowns" and the relatively shorter life of traditional "Little Tokyos." An extension of the latter thesis is presented in chapter 10 wherein I report the results of my two-decade field study of Japanese-Americans in San Francisco. Nisei, the American-born offspring of immigrants from Japan, are extraordinarily conscious of their geogenerational status and the different sense of the proprieties that it imposes on each generation's daily deportment. Their quotidian adaptation of a culturally derived Meiji-Taisho characterology, while it has served them quite effectively in the often turbulent trials of their lives in a less than hospitable America, also—because of its irrecusable connection to its place on the Nikkei geogenerational time clock—serves as a calendrical reminder that, like its predecessors' character before it, the Nisei style of self-presentation will soon pass into memory.[169]

In chapter 11 I discuss those features of anti-Asian, anti-Hispanic, and Anti-Amerindian sentiment and action that emanated out from the stigmatizing badge of black slavery and engulfed virtually all persons of color in America. William Wells Brown noted as early as 1874: "The fact is, slavery has been the cause of all the prejudice against the negro. Wherever the blacks are ill-treated on account of their color, it is because of their identity with a race that has long worn the chain of slavery."[170] The ignominious badge of slavery led to both prejudice and caste feeling being directed toward the freedmen-and-women—and toward all those other persons of color who might be similarly degraded. The point was well made by the abolitionist writer William Goodell in 1853 when he inquired: "By what authority, by what rule, on what principle, with what consistency, and with what ultimate success, will the law, or the administrators and expounders of law, attempt to maintain, by the sanctions of penal infliction, the rights of WHITE men, while they refuse thus to maintain the rights of BLACK, or YELLOW, or SWARTHY, or BROWN men?"[171] Goodell's question calls attention to the often overlooked thesis that the opprobrious treatment of America's non-white, non-Anglo minorities is related to their subordinate position in the social structure, to their being forced to wear the "badge of slavery" despite the fact that, with only rare and occasional exception, only blacks were enslaved. When Congress enacted and the states ratified the Thirteenth Amendment to the United States Constitution, its leading proponents insisted that they intended to abolish not only the institution of slavery, but also to eradicate its "badges," "indicia," and "incidents."[172] Soon after, Justice Harlan defined the "badge" of slavery as that form of "race prejudice" that not only acted as both a cause and effect of the Africans' enslavement, but also had had a proactive life beyond that of the peculiar institution's. It too, he asserted in an eloquent dissent, is outlawed by the Thirteenth Amendment.[173]

Even before Emancipation, the slavery-induced race prejudice that Harlan's plea had failed to eliminate from the body politic had spread beyond its original ethnoracial limit to encompass and taint Asian, Mexican, and Amerindian peoples. In contrast to the arguments put forward by Sowell and Mead, I believe that this prejudice became institutionalized and served to restrict the opportunities, reduce the life chances, and in general retard the social, economic, political, and personal advancement of each of these peoples. I propose the following conclusions from my investigation of this matter: that unpinning the badge of slavery remains a legislative and judicial obligation arising from the as yet uncompleted mandate of the Thirteenth Amendment; that, properly understood, that amendment provides a unique civic machicolation down from which could descend congressional enactments and court decisions in support of programs of affirmative action; that these programs, in turn, could reduce if not obliterate altogether the cumulative effects of slavery-originated race prejudice; and, that once such programs are placed under the protective penumbra of the Thirteenth Amendment, once that amendment is revived in service to Justice Harlan's statement of its original intent, and once that intent is recognized as applying to

all those peoples whose lives have been tarred with the brush of slavery's legacy, race prejudice, the charge of "reverse discrimination"
that is so often leveled against these efforts will be understood to
have been made in error.

In chapter 12 I return to the issue with which this book began,
namely, the debate over assimilation and pluralism. Here, however,
I take a new approach, crossing the postmodern divide[174] and entering into the intellectual mindscape currently being disturbed by
the new ethnoracial culture wars.[175] Richard Harvey Brown has recently observed that, "at the epistemological level, having begun
by disenchanting the world, sociologists have come to disenchant
their own absolutist mystique, forcing upon themselves a new
methodological self-consciousness as a prerequisite to any future
inquiry."[176] Sociologists, however, are not alone in this agonizingly
reflexive project.[177] Not only are the several academic disciplines
associated with the social sciences, the natural sciences, and the humanities attempting, each in its own way, to come to grips with the
"decentering" of its particular object of inquiry, the disprizing of its
fundamental conceptual outlook, and the dethronement of its heretofore privileged statement,[178] but also the intellectual leaders of
such social movements as environmentalism, feminism, and the revival of race consciousness are forging innovative ways of speaking,
writing, and enacting the social, economic, political, and naturalis-
tic "texts" of their respective "worlds."[179] The works of these
spokespersons for major civic issues are simultaneously providing
trenchant critiques of the received wisdom and hoary traditions of
the relevant academic disciplines and presenting innovative perspectives on the topics that concern them. Among these are the adaptations of French postmodernist thought by the proponents of
multiculturalism[180]—and, more specifically of a black epistemological consciousness about literature and society.[181] The impact of
these perspectives on the assimilation-pluralism debate is potentially instaurative, promising to decide the issue in behalf of a
seemingly essentialist reconstitution of ethnoracial literary and sociological knowledge.

My own contribution to this debate consists in a suggested resolution of its basic polarity. This, I contend, is accomplishable by in-
voking the temporal dimension of Derrida's key concept, *differance*,
and applying it to a deconstruction of a strategically significant text
of the problem. The result, I argue, is an "allusion"—a concept I
have borrowed from the Italian classical philologist Gian Biagio
Conte.[182] The move to "allusion" requires an elaboration of the

ideas of some of the major African American literary and social critics.[183] The startlingly postmodern discourse of Henry Louis Gates, Jr.,[184] for example, attempts to present a new ethnoracial text for the American black community. As such, it bids fair to become an "epic code" of the kind that Virgil provided for the Romans of antiquity. "Such a code," writes Conte, "is a source and a storehouse of interconnected values, vividly displayed in the actions of heroes, on which the community can draw as an organic arrangement of its own cultural foundations."[185] For Gates, however, reconstruction begins with the observation that the heroes are all too often unknown and anonymous—their names lost and their deeds unreported in the Occidental canons of historical and literary knowledge that claim universality but in fact privilege the words delimiting and the actions defining Eurocentric praxes.[186] In brief, the conventional Occidental canon is said to privilege the discourse of white males, past and present. The newly projected code, hence, serves the mission of reviving the thymotic spirit of an ethnoracially conscious African American community. In that sense, it takes its place on the side of pluralism in the pre-postmodern debate. In the words of Conte (who is, of course, writing about the epic poetry of antiquity), it promises to "change the nature of things and facts; the epic code is the medium through which society takes possession of its own past and gives that past the matrix value of a model."[187]

Gates appears to have adapted his deconstructive analysis to complex variants of an Afrocentric essentialism, thus departing from the fundamental first principle of Derridean deconstructionism. "Deconstruction," observes Vincent Pecora, "is a critique of essentialism."[188] For Gates, who recognizes the issue, "it is a question of perspective, a question of emphasis."[189] It is precisely this perspective and emphasis, however, that leads Afrocentric theorists to put deconstructive analysis to work in uncovering the "blackness" of such assimilation-oriented literary figures as the part-Negro writer Jean Toomer. My own approach, to the contrary, entails dissolving the polarity of assimilation/pluralism through deconstructing Gates's deconstruction of Toomer. This leads to "deferring"[190] the presentist rhetoric of assimilationists like Toomer and other similarly minded intellectuals, maintaining its integrity, but putting off its ultimate outcome to a temporally spaced future. This, in turn, permits a reconciliation of the debate as an "allusion," that is, "the simultaneous presence of two different realities that try to indicate a single reality."[191]

The simultaneity of this complex and multifaceted single reality sensitizes us to what might be called the African American dilemma.

That dilemma arises from the felt necessity for highly acculturated black Americans to discover the roots of their lost ethnoracial background as part of a strategy for fostering an independent psychic self-sufficiency; but that intracommunal psychic strength is to energize their five hundred years quest for equal rights of participation in the political, legal, social, and cultural construction of a truly *civil* society, that is, a society where color is neither a stigma nor a source of hegemonic sovereignty.

It is to the fulfillment of that quest that this book is dedicated and hopes to make a contribution.

NOTES

1. Milton M. Gordon, *Assimilation in American Life: The Role of Race, Religion, and National Origin* (New York: Oxford University Press, 1964), pp. 60–83.

2. See Cheikh Anta Diop, *Precolonial Black Africa: A Comparative Study of the Political and Social Systems of Europe and Black Africa, from Antiquity to the Formation of Modern States*, trans. Harold J. Salemson (Trenton, N.J.: Africa World Press, 1987), esp. pp. 43–158, 212–34.

3. Lord Lugard, *The Dual Mandate in British Tropical Africa* (Hamden, Conn.: Archon Books, 1965 [1922]), esp. pp. 193–229; and J. S. Furnivall, *Colonial Policy and Practice: A Comparative Study of Burma and Netherlands India* (New York: New York University Press, 1948, pp. 1–22, 276–318, 513–50.

4. See two works by Robert Blauner, *Racial Oppression in America* (New York: Harper and Row, 1972), pp. 51–182; and *Black Lives, White Lives: Three Decades of Race Relations in America* (Berkeley: University of California Press, 1989).

5. William M. Newman, *American Pluralism: A Study of Minority Groups and Social Theory* (New York: Harper and Row, 1973), pp. 47–96, 286–94.

6. Richard D. Alba, *Ethnic Identity: The Transformation of White America* (New Haven: Yale University Press, 1990); and Mary C. Waters, *Ethnic Options: Choosing Identities in America* (Berkeley: University of California Press, 1990), pp. 16–89, 147–68.

7. See Lawrence H. Fuchs, *The American Kaleidoscope: Race, Ethnicity, and the Civic Culture* (Hanover, N.H.: Wesleyan–New England University Press, 1990).

8. See Janice E. Perlman, *The Myth of Marginality: Urban Poverty and Politics in Rio de Janeiro* (Berkeley: University of California Press, 1976), pp. 91–194, 242–62.

9. Roscoe Pound, "Juristic Problems of National Progress," *American Journal of Sociology*, 22:6 (May 1917), p. 733.

10. Herbert Blumer, "The Future of the Color Line," in *The South in Continuity and Change*, ed. John C. McKinney and Edgar T. Thompson (Durham, N.C.: Duke University Press, 1965), pp. 322–36.

11. Here and below I draw on Roscoe Pound, "Legislation as a Social Function," *American Journal of Sociology*, 18:4 (May 1913), p. 766.

12. The following draws on Cornel West, "Learning to Talk of Race," *New York Times Magazine*, sec. 6 (Aug. 2, 1992), pp. 24, 26. Quotations from p. 24.

13. Seymour Martin Lipset, *The First New Nation: The United States in Historical and Comparative Perspective* (New York: W. W. Norton, 1979), esp. pp. v–xl, 207–348.

14. See, e.g., Kingsley Davis, "American Society: Its Groups Structure," *Contemporary Civilization 2* (Chicago: Scott Foresman and Co., 1961), pp. 171–86.

15. See Leonard Broom and John Kitsuse, "The Validation of Acculturation: A Condition of Ethnic Assimilation," *American Anthropologist*, 57 (Feb. 1955), pp. 44–48.

16. See Harold J. Abramson, "Assimilation and Pluralism," *Harvard Encyclopedia of American Ethnic Groups*, ed. Stephan Thernstrom (Cambridge: Belknap Press of Harvard University Press, 1980), pp. 150–60.

17. J. Hector St. John de Crèvecoeur, *Letters from an American Farmer* (New York: E. P. Dutton, 1957 [1782]), pp. 35–82.

18. Israel Zangwill, *The Melting-Pot: Drama in Four Acts*, new and rev. ed. (New York: Macmillan, 1922 [1909]), esp. pp. 184–85.

19. Horace Kallen, *Culture and Democracy in the United States: Studies in the Group Psychology of the American Peoples* (New York: Boni and Liveright, 1924; reprint, New York: Arno Press and the New York Times, 1970), pp. 67–232.

20. Randolph S. Bourne, *War and the Intellectuals: Collected Essays, 1915–1919*, ed. Carl Resek (New York: Harper Torchbooks, 1964), pp. 107–33.

21. See John Doyle Klier, *Russia Gathers Her Jews: The Origins of the "Jewish Questions" in Russia, 1772–1825* (DeKalb: Northern Illinois University Press, 1986); and M. J. Rosman, *The Lords' Jews: Magnate-Jewish Relations in the Polish-Lithuanian Commonwealth during the Eighteenth Century* (Cambridge: Harvard University Press, 1990).

22. Karl Marx, "On the Jewish Question," in *Early Texts*, trans. and ed David McLellan (Oxford, U.K.: Basil Blackwell, 1972), p. 114.

23. Julius Carlebach, *Karl Marx and the Radical Critique of Judaism* (London: Routledge and Kegan Paul, 1978), p. 163.

24. Ibid., p. 313. See also two works by David McLellan, *The Young Hegelians and Karl Marx* (London: Macmillan, 1969), pp. 75–81; and *Marxism and Religion: A Description and Assessment of the Marxist Critique of Christianity* (New York: Harper and Row, 1987), pp. 8, 10–13, 67–69; and Dennis Fischmann, *Political Discourse in Exile: Karl Marx and the Jewish Question* (Amherst: University of Massachusetts Press, 1991), pp. 3–120.

25. Saul K. Padover, *Karl Marx: An Intimate Biography* (New York: McGraw-Hill, 1978), pp. 1–30. For a thoughtful discussion of Marxism as a religion in its own right, as well as its relation to Judaism and Christianity, see Robert John Ackerman, *Religion as Critique* (Amherst: University of Massachusetts Press, 1985), pp. 31–35, 43–48, 65–76, 142–52.

26. Carlebach, *Karl Marx*, p. 314. Judaism itself underwent a divisive sectarian turn toward mystical fundamentalism in the eleventh, twelfth, and thirteenth centuries. Jose Faur, *In the Shadow of History: Jews and "Conversos" at the Dawn of Modernity* (Albany: State University of New York Press, 1992), proposes that mystical and fundamentalist Judaism undermined the Maimonidean legalist tradition of Andalusian Jewry and inadvertently contributed to the vulnerability of Spain's Jews to the horrors of the Inquisition. The appearance of *conversos*, some of whom were secret Jews, fostered a debate over whether assimilation or pluralism would be the best way to preserve Jewish life, liberty, and property. Spinoza's heresy and its effects are regarded as a wrong and harmful move by Faur, who credits R. Solomon ibn Verga (?–c. 1520), a philosopher who abjured categories, favored historical rationality, proposed a veritable forerunner of symbolic interaction, subjectivity, and cultural and religious pluralism, as being the harbinger of postmodern society. Faur's remarkable thesis should be read in relation to such earlier commentators on the role of Spinoza's heresy for modernity, the Enlightenment, and Occidental social, cultural, and political formations as Leo Strauss, *Spinoza's Critique of Religion* (New York: Schocken Books, 1965); two works by Lewis Samuel Feuer, *Spinoza and the Rise of Liberalism* (New Brunswick, N.J.: Transaction Books, 1987) and *The Scientific Intellectual: The Psychological and Sociological Origin of Modern Science* (New Brunswick, N.J.: Transaction Books, 1992), pp. 297–318; and Yirmiyahu Yovel, *Spinoza and Other Heretics, Vol. 1: The Marrano of Reason, Vol. 2: The Adventures of Immanence* (Princeton: Princeton University Press, 1989).

27. See Jurgen Herbst, *The German Historical School in American Scholarship: A Study in the Transfer of Culture* (Port Washington, N.Y.: Kennikat Press, 1972), pp. 129–230; and Albion W. Small, "Fifty Years of Sociology in the United States (1865–1915)," *American Journal of Sociology*, 21:6 (May 1916), pp. 721–864.

28. Sarah E. Simons, "Social Assimilation," *American Journal of Sociology*, 6:6 (May 1901), pp. 808–15; 7:1 (July 1901), pp. 53–79; 7:2 (Sept. 1901), pp. 234–48; 7:3 (Nov. 1901), pp. 386–404; 7:4 (Jan. 1902), pp. 539–56.

29. Gary A. Abraham, *Max Weber and the Jewish Question: A Study in the Social Outlook of his Sociology* (Urbana: University of Illinois Press, 1992), p. 8.

30. See Werner Sombart, *The Jews and Modern Capitalism*, trans. M. Epstein (New Brunswick, N.J.: Transaction Books, 1982).

31. Abraham, *Max Weber*, p. 231.

32. Ibid., p. 269.

33. See Ellsworth Faris, "If I Were a Jew," in *The Nature of Human Nature and Other Essays in Social Psychology* (New York: McGraw-Hill, 1937; reprint, Dubuque, Iowa: Brown Reprints, 1971), pp. 350–53.

34. Robert N. Bellah, Richard Madsen, William M. Sullivan, Ann Swidler, and Steven M. Tipton, *Habits of the Heart: Individualism and Commitment in American Life* (Berkeley: University of California Press, 1985), p. 237.

35. Robert N. Bellah, Richard Madsen, William M. Sullivan, Ann Swidler, and Steven M. Tipton, *The Good Society* (New York: Alfred A. Knopf, 1991), p. 306.

36. Theodor Mommsen, *Auch ein Wort ueber unser Judentum* (Berlin: Weidmannische Buchhandlung, 1880), pp. 1–16. Translated as "Another Word about Our Jewry," by J. Hessing and published in *The Jew in the Modern World: A Documentary History*, ed. Paul R. Mendes-Flohr and Jehuda Reinharz (New York: Oxford University Press, 1980), pp. 284–87. Quotation from p. 286.

37. Max Weber, "Science as a Vocation," in *From Max Weber: Essays in Sociology*, trans and ed. Hans H. Gerth and C. Wright Mills (New York: Oxford University Press, 1946), p. 156.

38. See Theodor Herzl, *The Jewish State* (New York: Dover Publications, Inc., 1988), pp. 67–157. See also Ernest Pawel, *The Labyrinth of Exile: A Life of Theodor Herzl* (New York: Farrar, Straus and Giroux, 1989); and Steven Beller, *Herzl* (New York: Grove Weidenfeld, 1991), esp. pp. 35–61, 107–26. For the debate over which values—those of the "old Yishuv" in pre-Zionist Palestine, or those of the "enlightened" Zionist from fin de siècle Europe—should prevail in the Jewish homeland, see Jeff Halper, *Between Redemption and Revival: The Jewish Yishuv of Jerusalem in the Nineteenth Century* (Boulder: Westview Press, 1991).

39. Mommsen, *Auch ein Wort*, p. 287.

40. Ibid.

41. Crèvecoeur, *Letters*, pp. 40, 44, 46.

42. Zangwill, *Melting Pot*, p. 184.

43. Ibid., p. 199.

44. See Gerald Sorin, *The Prophetic Minority: American Jewish Immigrant Radicals, 1880–1920* (Bloomington: Indiana University Press, 1985).

45. See Jessa Weissman Joselit, *Our Gang: Jewish Crime and the New York Jewish Community, 1900–1940* (Bloomington: Indiana University Press, 1983); Arthur A. Goren, *New York Jews and the Quest for Community: The Kehillah Experiment, 1908–1922* (New York: Columbia University Press, 1970); Albert Fried, *The Rise and Fall of the Jewish Gangster in America* (New York: Holt, Rinehart, and Winston, 1980).

46. See Egal Feldman, *The Dreyfus Affair and the American Conscience, 1895–1906* (Detroit: Wayne State University Press, 1981).

47. See Albert S. Lindemann, *The Jew Accused: Three Anti-Semitic Affairs (Dreyfus, Beilis, Frank), 1894–1915* (Cambridge: Cambridge University Press, 1991); and Abraham G. Duker, "Twentieth-Century Blood Libels in

the United States," in *The Blood Libel Legend: A Casebook in Anti-Semitic Folklore*, ed. Alan Dundes (Madison: University of Wisconsin Press, 1991), pp. 233–60.

48. See John Higham, *Send These to Me: Jews and Other Immigrants in Urban America* (New York: Atheneum, 1975), pp. 138–220.

49. Ibid., p. 203

50. Ibid., p. 205. See also Howard M. Sachar, *A History of the Jews in America* (New York: Alfred A. Knopf, 1992), pp. 418–27.

51. Quoted from pp. 321–22 of William James's book of 1909, *A Pluralistic Universe*, in Higham, *Send These to Me*, p. 206.

52. Horace Kallen, "Democracy versus the Melting Pot," *The Nation*, 100 (Feb. 18 and 25, 1915) is reprinted in Kallen, *Culture and Democracy*, pp. 67–125.

53. Higham, *Send These to Me*, pp. 206–8.

54. Kallen, *Culture and Democracy*, p. 124.

55. Bourne, *War and the Intellectuals*, pp. 107–23.

56. Ibid., p. 63.

57. Ibid., p. 108

58. Ibid., p. 129.

59. Ibid.

60. Ibid., p. 117.

61. Herbert Blumer, "Race Prejudice as a Sense of Group Position," *Pacific Sociological Review*, 1 (Spring 1958), pp. 3–7.

62. Gunnar Myrdal, with the assistance of Richard Sterner and Arnold Rose, *An American Dilemma* (New York: Harper and Brothers, 1944).

63. Zangwill, *Melting Pot*, p. 205.

64. Ibid., pp. 204–5.

65. Ibid., p. 206.

66. Ibid.

67. Ibid.

68. Ibid., pp. 206–7.

69. Ibid., p. 207.

70. Ibid., p. 206.

71. Ibid., p. 207.

72. Horace M. Kallen, "Humanistic Sources of Democracy," in *The Liberal Spirit: Essays on Problems of Freedom in the Modern World* (Ithaca: Cornell University Press, 1948), pp. 169–70.

73. Ibid., p. 178.

74. See Horace M. Kallen, *William James and Henri Bergson: A Study in Contrasting Theories of Life* (Chicago: University of Chicago Press, 1914), pp. 206–42.

75. Bourne, *War and the Intellectuals*, p. 117.

76. Kallen, "Humanistic Sources of Democracy," p. 190.

77. Quoted in Edward Abrahams, *The Lyrical Left: Randolph Bourne, Alfred Stieglitz, and the Origins of Cultural Radicalism in America* (Charlottesville: University Press of Virginia, 1986), p. 68.

78. Bourne, *War and the Intellectuals*, pp. 112–13.

79. Kallen, "Culture and Democracy in the United States," in *Liberal Spirit*, p. 226 n. 1.

80. Peter Kivisto, "The Transplanted Then and Now: The Reorientation of Immigration Studies from the Chicago School to the New Social History," *Ethnic and Racial Studies*, 13:4 (Oct. 1990), pp. 455–81, esp. pp. 463–68.

81. For the details of this encounter, see Ralph E. Luker, *The Social Gospel in Black and White: American Racial Reform, 1885–1912* (Chapel Hill: University of North Carolina Press, 1991).

82. See Lillian D. Wald, *The House on Henry Street* (New York: Henry Holt, 1915; reprint, New Brunswick, N.J.: Transaction Publishers, 1991), pp. 97–100, 216–19, 252–54, 263–66, 270–72, 302–3, 308.

83. Residents of Hull House, *Hull House Maps and Papers: A Presentation of Nationalities and Wages in a Congested District of Chicago, Together with Comments and Essays on Problems Growing Out of the Social Conditions* (New York: Thomas Y. Crowell, 1895; reprint, New York: Arno Press, and the New York Times, 1970), esp. pp. 91–114, 115–30, 131–42, 207–30; Arthur C. Holden, *The Settlement Idea* (New York: Macmillan, 1922; reprint, New York: Arno Press and the New York Times, 1970); Robert A. Woods and Albert J. Kennedy, *The Settlement Horizon* (New York: Russell Sage, 1922; reprint, New Brunswick, N.J.: Transaction Publishers, 1990), pp. 326–40.

84. See Stanford M. Lyman, *Militarism, Imperialism, and Racial Accommodation: An Analysis and Interpretation of the Early Writings of Robert E. Park* (Fayetteville: University of Arkansas Press, 1992), pp. 41–135, 205–305.

85. Booker T. Washington, with the collaboration of Robert E. Park, *The Man Farthest Down: A Record of Observation and Study in Europe* (Garden City, N.Y.: Doubleday, Page, 1912; reprint, New Brunswick, N.J.: Transaction Publishers, 1984).

86. See, e.g., H.A. Millis, *The Japanese Problem in the United States* (New York: Macmillan, 1915); and James A. B. Scherer, *The Japanese Crisis* (New York: Frederick A. Stokes Co., 1916).

87. Robert E. Park, "Racial Assimilation in Secondary Groups with Particular Reference to the Negro," in *Race and Culture: The Collected Papers of Robert Ezra Park*, vol. 1, ed. Everett Cherrington Hughes, Charles S. Johnson, Jitsuichi Masuoka, Robert Redfield, and Louis Wirth (Glencoe, Ill.: The Free Press, 1950), pp. 208–9.

88. See Stow Persons, *Ethnic Studies at Chicago, 1905–1945* (Urbana: University of Illinois Press, 1987), pp. 77–97.

89. Judith Ann Trolander, *Settlement Houses and the Great Depression* (Detroit: Wayne State University Press, 1975), p. 134.

90. Ibid., p. 146.

91. Ibid.

92. Ibid., pp. 27–28.

93. Aaron Berman, *Nazism, the Jews and American Zionism, 1933–1948* (Detroit: Wayne State University Press, 1990), p. 181.

94. See Robert G. Goldy, *The Emergence of Jewish Theology in America* (Bloomington: Indiana University Press, 1990); and Abraham J. Peck, ed., *Jews and Christians after the Holocaust* (Philadelphia: Fortress Press, 1982).

95. See Peter Grose, *Israel in the Mind of America* (New York: Alfred A. Knopf, 1983), pp. 46–318; and Robert W. Ross, *So It Was True: The American Protestant Press and the Persecution of the Jews* (Minneapolis: University of Minnesota Press, 1980).

96. See Edward Alexander, *The Jewish Idea and Its Enemies: Personalities, Issues, Events* (New Brunswick, N.J.: Transaction Publishers, 1991), pp. 77–96, 143–64. Alexander's work is polemical and should be read in relation to the writings of *Tikkun* editor Michael Lerner (see n. 102).

97. See Howard M. Sachar, *History of the Jews*, pp. 563–94; Milton Plesur, *Jewish Life in Twentieth-Century America: Challenge and Accommodation* (Chicago: Nelson-Hall, 1982), pp. 131–205; Nathan C. Belth, *A Promise to Keep: A Narrative of the American Encounter with Anti-Semitism* (New York: Schocken Books, 1981), pp. 146–294; and Thomas A. Kolsky, *Jews against Zionism: The American Council for Judaism, 1942–1948* (Philadelphia: Temple University Press, 1990).

98. Quoted in Joseph H. Udelson, *Dreamer of the Ghetto: The Life and Works of Israel Zangwill* (Tuscaloosa: University of Alabama Press, 1990), p. 194.

99. Ibid., p. 152.

100. See Gary Dean Best, *To Free a People: American Jewish Leaders and the Jewish Problem in Eastern Europe, 1890–1914* (Westport, Conn.: Greenwood Press, 1982), pp. 218–23.

101. Ronald Sanders, *The High Walls of Jerusalem: A History of the Balfour Declaration and the Birth of the British Mandate for Palestine* (New York: Holt, Rinehart and Winston, 1983).

102. For the current version of the debates among and between blacks and Jews over assimilation, culture, and pluralism, see Jack Salzman et al., eds., *Bridges and Boundaries: African Americans and American Jews* (New York: George Braziller in association with the Jewish Museum, 1992); and the essays by Jesse Jackson, James McPherson, Cornel West, Marshall Berman, Arnold Eisen, Roger Perry and Patricia Williams, Rachel Adler, Arthur Waskow, and Jacob Neusner, in *Tikkun: A Jewish Critique of Politics, Culture and Society*, ed. Michael Lerner (Oakland, Calif.: Tikkun Books, 1992).

103. Abramson, "Assimilation and Pluralism," pp. 150–60.

104. See Ewa Morawska, "The Sociology and Historiography of Immigration," in *Immigration Reconsidered: History, Sociology, and Politics*, ed. Virginia Yans-McLaughlin (New York: Oxford University Press, 1990), pp. 187–238.

105. See Ellen K. Coughlin, "Following Los Angeles Riots, Social Scientists See Need to Develop Fuller Understanding of Race Relations," *Chronicle of Higher Education*, 38:36 (May 13, 1992), pp. A10–A11; and Peter

Marris, "How Social Research Could Inform Debate over Urban Problems," *Chronical of Higher Education*, 38:37 (May 20, 1992), p. A40.

106. See Fred R. Harris and Roger W. Wilkins, eds., *Quiet Riots: Race and Poverty in the United States—the Kerner Report Twenty Years Later* (New York: Pantheon Books, 1988).

107. See Kenneth B. Clark, *Prejudice and Your Child* (Middletown, Conn.: Wesleyan University Press, 1988), pp. 143–272.

108. *The Kerner Report: The 1968 Report of the National Advisory Commission on Civil Disorders*, with a preface by Fred R. Harris and a new introduction by Tom Wicker (New York: Pantheon Books, 1988), p. 483.

109. Andrew Hacker, *Two Nations: Black and White, Separate, Hostile, and Unequal* (New York: Charles Scribner's Sons, 1992).

110. "Although the proportion of blacks, Asians and Hispanic people in the country climbed over the past decade, all three were outnumbered by whites claiming English ancestry (32.6 million), German (57.9 million), and Irish (38.7 million). Other European ancestries most frequently claimed were Italian and Polish.

"About 30 million black residents were counted in the 1990 census, along with 7.3 million Asians or Pacific Islanders, and 1.9 million American Indians, Eskimos or Aleuts. There were also 22.3 million Hispanic people, who can be of any race, among the total resident population of 248.7 million people." Felicity Barringer, "Census Data Show More U.S. Children Living in Poverty," *New York Times*, 141:48,981 (May 29, 1992), pp. A1, A12. Quotation from p. A12.

111. See three works by Wilson Jeremiah Moses, *Black Messiahs and Uncle Toms: Social and Literary Manipulations of a Religious Myth* (University Park: Pennsylvania State University Press, 1982); *The Golden Age of Black Nationalism, 1850–1925* (New York: Oxford University Press, 1988); and *Alexander Crummell: A Study of Civilization and Discontent* (New York: Oxford University Press 1989).

112. Wilson Jeremiah Moses, *The Wings of Ethiopia: Studies in African-American Life and Letters* (Ames: Iowa State University Press, 1990), p. 27.

113. For a critique of the conventional interpretations of Park's ideas on the race question and a revisionist approach, see Lyman, *Militarism, Imperialism*, pp. xv–xxi, 1–135.

114. Robert E. Park, "Human Migration and the Marginal Man," in *Personality and the Social Group*, ed Ernest W. Burgess (Chicago: University of Chicago Press, 1929; reprint, Freeport, N.Y.: Books for Libraries Press, 1969), pp. 64–77.

115. See Bernard Groethuysen, *The Bourgeois: Catholicism vs. Capitalism in Eighteenth-Century France*, trans. Mary Ilford (New York: Holt, Rinehart and Winston, 1968), esp. pp. 191–240.

116. Max Weber, *The Protestant Ethic and the Spirit of Capitalism*, trans. Talcott Parsons (New York: Charles Scribner's Sons, 1930).

117. Robert E. Park, "Agricultural Extension among the Negroes," *The World To-Day*, 15 (Aug. 1908), pp. 820–26.

118. Robert E. Park, "A King in Business: Leopold II of Belgium, Autocrat of the Congo and International Broker," *Everybody's Magazine*, 15 (Nov. 1906), pp. 624–33.

119. Moses, *Wings of Ethiopia*, p. 110.

120. E. Franklin Frazier, *Black Bourgeoisie: The Rise of a New Middle-Class in the United States* (Glencoe, Ill.: The Free Press and Falcon's Wing Press, 1957).

121. Moses, *Wings of Ethiopia*, p. 110.

122. See, e.g., Anthony M. Platt, *E. Franklin Frazier Reconsidered* (New Brunswick, N.J.: Rutgers University Press, 1991).

123. Robert E. Park, "The German Army: The Most Perfect Military Organization in the World," *Munsey's Magazine*, 24:3 (Dec. 1900), pp. 376–95.

124. See Winifred Raushenbush, *Robert E. Park: Biography of a Sociologist* (Durham, N.C.: Duke University Press, 1979), p. 168.

125. See four essays by Robert E. Park, "Recent Atrocities in the Congo State," *The World To-Day*, 8 (Oct. 1904), pp. 1328–31; "A King in Business," "The Terrible Story of the Congo," *Everybody's Magazine*, 15 (Dec. 1906), pp. 763–72; "The Blood-Money of the Congo," *Everybody's Magazine*, 16 (Jan. 1907), pp. 60–70. See also the essay Park wrote for Booker T. Washington, "Cruelty in the Congo Country," *Outlook*, 78 (Oct. 1904), pp. 375–77.

126. See Robert E. Park, "Our Racial Frontier on the Pacific," *Survey Graphic*, 56:3 (May 1, 1926), pp. 192–96.

127. See Stanley M. Elkins *Slavery: A Problem in American Institutional and Intellectual Life* (Chicago: University of Chicago Press, 1959), pp. 86–139.

128. See, e.g., Oliver Cromwell Cox, *Caste, Class, and Race: A Study in Social Dynamics* (New York: Monthly Review Press, 1959), pp. 3–120, 317–488, 539–44.

129. See Stanford M. Lyman, *The Black American in Sociological Thought: A Failure of Perspective* (New York: G. P. Putnam's Sons, 1972), pp. 27–70.

130. See James C. Scott, *Domination and the Arts of Resistance: Hidden Transcripts* (New Haven: Yale University Press, 1990), esp. pp. 108–201.

131. See Emory Bogardus, *Essentials of Americanization* (Los Angeles: University of Southern California Press, 1920), pp. 223–98.

132. Robert E. Park, "Introduction" to Romanzo Adams, *Interracial Marriage in Hawaii: A Study of the Mutually Conditioned Processes of Acculturation and Amalgamation* (New York: Macmillan, 1937; reprint, Montclair, N.J.: Patterson Smith, 1969), pp. xiii–xiv.

133. Robert E. Park, "Racial Ideologies," in *American Society in Wartime*, ed. William Fielding Ogburn (Chicago: University of Chicago Press, 1943; reprint, New York: Da Capo Press, 1972), pp. 165–84.

134. See e.g., Gilbert Osofsky, ed., *Puttin' On Ole Massa: The Slave Narratives of Henry Bibb, William Wells Brown, and Solomon Northrup* (New York: Harper and Row, 1969), pp. 9–44; Roy Simon Bryce-Laporte, "Slaves as Inmates, Slaves as Men: A Sociological Discussion of Elkins' Thesis," in

The *Debate Over Slavery: Stanley Elkins and His Critics*, ed. Ann J. Lane (Urbana: University of Illinois Press, 1971), pp. 269–92.

135. Marcus Lee Hansen "The Third Generation in America" [Originally entitled "The Problem of the Third Generation Immigrant," 1938], *Commentary*, 14 (Nov. 1952), pp. 492–500.

136. For various critiques of Hansen's thesis, see Werner Sollors, *Beyond Ethnicity: Consent and Descent in American Culture* (New York: Oxford University Press, 1986), pp. 208–36; and Peter Kivisto and Dag Blanck, eds., *American Immigrants and Their Generations: Studies and Commentaries on the Hansen Thesis after Fifty Years* (Urbana: University of Illinois Press, 1990).

137. See Earl E. Thorpe, *Black Historians: A Critique* (New York: William Morrow, 1971), pp. 27–153.

138. See three works by Carter G. Woodson, *The Education of the Negro Prior to 1861: A History of the Education of the Colored People of the United States from the Beginning of Slavery to the Civil War* (Washington, D.C.: Associated Publishers, Inc., 1919; reprint, New York: Arno Press and the New York Times, 1968); ed., *Negro Orators and Their Orations* (New York: Russell and Russell, 1969 [1925]); and *Mis-education of the Negro*, ed. Charles H. Wesley and Thelma D. Perry (Washington, D.C.: Associated Publishers, 1933, 1969). See also Lorenzo J. Greene, *Working with Carter G. Woodson, the Father of Black History: A Diary, 1928–1930*, ed. Arvah E. Strickland (Baton Rouge: Louisiana State University Press, 1989).

139. In addition to Thorpe, *Black Historians*, pp. 169–240, see also Benjamin Quarles, *Black Mosaic: Essays in Afro-American History and Historiography* (Amherst: University of Massachusetts Press, 1988) pp. 181–213; Darlene Clark Hine, ed., *The State of Afro-American History: Past, Present, and Future* (Baton Rouge: Louisiana State University Press, 1986); and August Meier and Elliott Rudwick, *Black History and the Historical Profession, 1915–1980* (Urbana: University of Illinois Press, 1986).

140. William Wells Brown, *Clotel or, The President's Daughter: A Narrative of Slave Life in the United States* (New York: Citadel Press, 1969 [1853]).

141. See William Edward Farrison, *William Wells Brown: Author and Reformer* (Chicago: University of Chicago Press, 1969).

142. For other writings by William Wells Brown, see *The Blackman, His Antecedents, His Genius, and His Achievements* (Miami: Mnemosyne, 1969 [1865]); *The Negro in the American Rebellion: His Heroism and His Fidelity* (New York: Citadel Press, 1971 [1867]); *The Rising Son; or, The Antecedents and Advancement of the Colored Race* (New York: Negro Universities Press, 1970 [1874]); *The Travels of William Wells Brown, including Narrative of William Wells Brown, a Fugitive Slave, and the American Fugitive in Europe. Sketches of Places and People Abroad*, ed. Paul Jefferson (New York: Markus Wiener, 1991).

143. See B. A. Botkin, *Lay My Burden Down: A Folk History of Slavery* (Chicago: University of Chicago Press–Phoenix Books, 1958 [1945]); Stanley Feldstein, *Once a Slave: The Slaves' View of Slavery* (New York: William

Morrow, 1971), pp. 125–58; John W. Blassingame, ed., *Slave Testimony: Two Centuries of Letters, Speeches, Interviews, and Autobiographies* (Baton Rouge: Louisiana State University Press, 1977); Paul D. Escott, *Slavery Remembered: A Record of Twentieth-Century Slave Narratives* (Chapel Hill: University of North Carolina Press, 1979); Belinda Hurmece, ed., *Before Freedom: 48 Oral Histories of Former North and South Carolina Slaves* (New York: Mentor, 1990); Henry Louis Gates, Jr., ed., *The Classic Slave Narratives* (New York: Mentor, 1987); and Charles T. Davis and Henry Louis Gates, Jr., eds., *The Slaves' Narrative* (New York: Oxford University Press, 1985).

144. See Eric L. McKitrick, ed., *Slavery Defended: The Views of the Old South* (Englewood Cliffs, N.J.: Prentice-Hall, 1963); Larry E. Tise, *Proslavery: A History of the Defense of Slavery in America, 1701–1840* (Athens: University of Georgia Press, 1987); Eugene D. Genovese, *The World the Slaveholders Made: Two Essays in Interpretation* (New York: Pantheon Books, 1969), pp. 195–234.

145. See Stanford M. Lyman, *The Seven Deadly Sins: Society and Evil*, rev. ed. (Dix Hills, N.Y.: General Hall, Inc., 1989), pp. 5–52.

146. Elzar Barkan, *The Retreat of Scientific Racism: Changing Concepts of Race in Britain and the United States between the World Wars* (Cambridge: Cambridge University Press, 1992), pp. 66–134, 279–340.

147. Thomas Sowell, *Ethnic America—A History* (New York: Basic Books, Inc., 1981), p. 187.

148. Thomas Sowell, *Race and Economics* (New York: David McKay Co., Inc., 1975), p. 238.

149. Lawrence M. Mead, *Beyond Entitlement: The Social Obligations of Citizenship* (New York: The Free Press, 1986), pp. 87–88.

150. Lawrence M. Mead, *The New Politics of Poverty: The Nonworking Poor in America* (New York: Basic Books, 1992), p. 149.

151. Ibid.

152. Lawrence M. Mead, "Jobs, Programs and Other Bromides," *New York Times*, May 19, 1992, p. A15.

153. Ibid. For an effective reply to Mead's type of reasoning on the relation of race to employment, the reader should examine the researchers of Herbert Hill, among which are *Black Labor and the American Legal System* (Madison: University of Wisconsin Press, 1985); and "Myth-Making as Labor History: Herbert Gutman and the United Mine Workers of America," *International Journal of Politics, Culture, and Society*, 2:2 (Winter 1988), pp. 132–200.

154. Mead, *New Politics of Poverty*, p. 151.

155. Ibid., p. 150.

156. Ibid., p. 151.

157. See Shelby Steele, *The Content of Our Character: A New Vision of Race in America* (New York: St. Martin's Press, 1990).

158. For warranteeism, see Henry Hughes, *A Treatise on Sociology, Theoretical and Practical* (Philadelphia: Lippincott and Grambo, 1854; reprint,

New York: Negro Universities Press, 1968), pp. 79–292. See also two essays by Stanford M. Lyman, "Henry Hughes and the Southern Foundations of American Sociology," in *Selected Writings of Henry Hughes: Antebellum Southerner, Slavocrat, Sociologist*, ed. Stanford M. Lyman (Jackson: University Press of Mississippi, 1985), pp. 1–72; and "System and Function in Ante-Bellum Southern Sociology," *International Journal of Politics, Culture and Society*, 2:1 (Fall 1988), pp. 95–108; reprinted in Lyman, *Civilization: Contents, Discontents, Malcontents, and Other Essays in Social Theory* (Fayetteville: University of Arkansas Press, 1990), pp. 191–201.

159. See also Kenneth M. Stampp, *The Peculiar Institution: Slavery in the Ante-Bellum South* (New York: Alfred A. Knopf, l956).

160. See Thomas Cripps, "The Dark Spot in The Kaleidoscope: Black Images in American Film," in *The Kaleidoscopes Lens: How Hollywood Views Ethnic Groups*, ed. Randall M. Miller (Englewood Cliffs, N.J.: Jerome S. Ozer, 1980), pp. 15–35.

161. For a critical evaluation of Comte's approach, see Kenneth E. Bock, *The Comparative Method* (Ph.D. diss., University of California at Berkeley, 1948), pp. 11–36.

162. Donald Bogle, *Toms, Coons, Mulattoes, Mammies, and Bucks: An Interpretive History of Blacks in American Films*, expanded ed. (New York: Continuum, 1989).

163. See Edward Mapp,"Black Women in Films: A Mixed Bag of Tricks," in *Black Films and Film-makers: A Comprehensive Anthology from Stereotype to Superhero*, ed. Lindsay Patterson (New York: Dodd, Mead and Co., 1975), pp. 196–205; and James R. Nesteby, *Black Images in American Films, 1896–1954: The Interplay between Civil Rights and Film Culture* (Washington, D.C.: University Press of America, 1982), pp. 195–205.

164. See Donald Bogle, *Blacks in American Films and Television: An Encyclopedia* (New York: Simon and Schuster, 1988).

165. On this issue the interested reader might wish to consult three essays by Stanford M. Lyman, "Stewart Culin and the Debate over Trans-Pacific Migration,"*Journal for the Theory of Social Behavior*, 9 (Mar. 1979), pp. 91–115; "Two Neglected Pioneers of Civilizational Analysis: The Cultural Perspectives of R. Stewart Culin and Frank Hamilton Cushing," *Social Research*, 49:3 (Autumn 1982), pp. 690–729; and "Asian American Contacts before Columbus: Alternate Understandings for Civilization, Acculturation, and Ethnic Minority Status in the United States," in *Japanese Americans: Iju Kara Jiritsu Eno Ayumi*, ed. Togami Sohken (Kyoto: Mineruva Shobo, 1985), pp. 341–92. The latter two essays are reprinted on pp. 22–45 and 46–75, respectively, in Lyman, *Civilization: Contents, Discontents, Malcontents*.

166. Werner Keller, *Diaspora: The Post-Biblical History of the Jews* (New York: Harcourt, Brace and World, Inc., 1969); and Howard M. Sachar, *Diaspora: An Inquiry into the Contemporary Jewish World* (New York: Harper and Row, 1985).

167. Joseph E. Harris, ed., *Global Dimensions of the African Diaspora* (Washington, D.C.: Howard University Press, 1982).

168. See Stanford M. Lyman, *Chinatown and Little Tokyo: Power, Conflict, and Community among Chinese and Japanese Immigrants to America* (Port Washington, N.Y.: Associated Faculty Press, 1986).

169. This essay has recently been the subject of an exchange between the author and sociologist S. Frank Miyamoto. See S. Frank Miyamoto, "Problems of Interpersonal Style among the Nisei," *Amerasia Journal*, 13:2 (1986–67), pp. 29–45; Ken Mochizuki, "The Ideal Nisei has 'Mastered the Art of Personal Control,' " *The International Examiner*, 14:22 (Nov. 18, 1987), p. 4; reprinted as "The Interpersonal Style of the Nisei has been Inherited by the Sansei," *Hokubei Mainichi*, no. 11709 (Dec. 11, 1987), p. 2; Stanford M. Lyman, "On Nisei Interpersonal Style: A Reply to S. Frank Miyamoto," *Amerasia Journal*, 14:2 (1988), pp. 105–8; "Miyamoto Reply to Stanford Lyman," Ibid., pp. 109–13; Stanford M. Lyman, " 'American' Interpersonal Style and Nikkei Realities: A Rejoinder to S. Frank Miyamoto," Ibid., pp. 115–23. One of the issues addressed in this exchange—that known as the "insider-outsider debate" (See Peter Rose, *Mainstream and Margins: Jews, Blacks and Other Americans* [New Brunswick, N.J.: Transaction Books, 1983], pp. 205–24)—has also been addressed, inadequately in my opinion, by Stephen O. Murray, "Ethnic Differences in Interpretive Conventions and the Reproduction of Inequality in Everyday Life," *Symbolic Interaction*, 14:2 (Summer 1991), pp. 187–204. For further discussion of how this issue impacts on my investigations of the Asian American situation, see two works by Stanford M. Lyman, *Chinatown and Little Tokyo*, pp. 9–12, 21–24; and "Background to Internment: Bishop Yoshiaki Fukuda's Mission of Justice in America," in Rev. Yoshiaki Fukuda, *My Six Years of Internment: An Issei's Struggle for Justice* (San Francisco: Konko Church of San Francisco, 1990), pp. 85–99.

170. William Wells Brown, *Rising Son*, p. 387.

171. William Goodell, *The American Slave Code in Theory and Practice: Its Distinctive Features Shown by Its Statutes, Judicial Decisions, and Illustrative Facts* (New York: American and Foreign Anti-Slavery Society, 1853; reprint, New York: Johnson Reprint Corp., 1968), p. 400.

172. See two studies by Jacobus ten Broek, "Thirteenth Amendment to the Constitution of the United States: Consummation to Abolition and Key to the Fourteenth Amendment," *California Law Review*, 39:2 (June 1951), pp. 171–203; and *The Antislavery Origins of the Fourteenth Amendment* (Berkeley: University of California Press, 1951), pp. 137–224.

173. See Justice Harlan's dissent in *Civil Rights Cases*, 109 U.S. 3 (1883).

174. Cf. Albert Borgmann, *Crossing the Postmodern Divide* (Chicago: University of Chicago Press, 1992).

175. See Henry Louis Gates, Jr., ed., *"Race," Writing, and Difference* (Chicago: University of Chicago Press, 1985).

176. Richard Harvey Brown, "Social Science and Society as Discourse: Toward a Sociology of Civic Competence," in *Postmodernism and Social*

Theory: The Debate over General Theory, ed. Steven Seidman and David G. Wagner (Cambridge: Blackwell, 1992), p. 224.

177. Richard Harvey Brown, *Society as Text: Essays on Rhetoric, Reason, and Reality* (Chicago: University of Chicago Press, 1987).

178. For an interesting example of this daring reconstructive thinking by a biologist, see Lawrence B. Slobodkin, *Simplicity and Complexity in Games of the Intellect* (Cambridge: Harvard University Press, 1992).

179. Cf. Richard Harvey Brown, ed., *Writing the Social Text: Poetics and Politics in Social Science Discourse* (New York: Aldine de Gruyter, 1992).

180. See, e.g., Todd Gitlin, "On the Virtues of a Loose Canon," in *Beyond PC: Toward a Politics of Understanding*, ed. Patricia Aufderheide (St. Paul, Minn.: Graywolf Press, 1992), pp. 185–90.

181. See Donald A. Petesch, *A Spy in the Enemy Country: The Emergence of Modern Black Literature* (Iowa City: University of Iowa Press, 1989), pp. 3–76.

182. Gian Biagio Conte, *The Rhetoric of Imitation: Genre and Poetic Memory in Virgil and Other Latin Poets*, trans. and ed. Charles Segal (Ithaca: Cornell University Press, 1986).

183. I do not discuss the three works by Molefi Kete Asante, *The Afrocentric Idea* (Philadelphia: Temple University Press, 1987); *Kemet, Afrocentricity and Knowledge* (Trenton, N.J.: African World Press, Inc., 1990); and *Afrocentricity* (Trenton, N.J.: African World Press, Inc., 1988). Asante's work is of a different order than that of Henry Louis Gates, Jr., or Toni Morrison, in that Asante feels no compunction about introducing a conjectural history to bolster his argument and fails to recognize that the true thrust of Derridean deconstruction is to obviate and disprivilege all "centrisms."

184. See three works by Henry Louis Gates, Jr., *Figures in Black: Words, Signs, and the 'Racial' Self* (New York: Oxford University Press, 1987); *The Signifying Monkey: A Theory of Afro-American Literary Criticism* (New York: Oxford University Press, 1988); *Loose Canons: Notes on the Culture Wars* (New York: Oxford University Press, 1992).

185. Conte, *Rhetoric of Imitation*, p. 142.

186. See, e.g., George G. M. James, *Stolen Legacy: The Greeks were not the authors of Green Philosophy, but the people of North Africa, commonly called the Egyptians* (San Francisco: Julian Richardson Associates, 1988). For the beginnings of the modern era, see John Thornton, *Africa and Africans in the Making of the Atlantic World, 1400–1680* (Cambridge: Cambridge University Press, 1992).

187. Conte, *Rhetoric of Imitation*, p. 142.

188. Vincent P. Pecora, "What Was Deconstruction?" *Contention: Debates in Society, Culture, and Science*, 1:3 (Spring 1992), p. 63.

189. Gates, *Loose Canons*, p. 39.

190. Jacques Derrida, *Speech and Phenomena and Other Essays on Husserl's Theory of Signs*, trans. David B. Allison (Evanston: Northwestern University Press, 1973), pp. 82 n. 8, 129 n. 1.

191. Conte, *Rhetoric of Imitation*, p. 38.

PART 1

Robert E. Park, American Civil Society, and the Race Question

The end of the war will be the end of slavery, and
then our land will be the "Land of the free."
—Elisha Hunt Rhodes
March 30, 1865

1

Civilization, Culture, and Color:
Changing Foundations of Robert E. Park's
Sociology of Race Relations

Park's Race Relations Cycle and the
Civil Ordering of Conflicts

In an autobiographical note that was found after his death, Park stated that he had, finally, become convinced that in his researches on blacks in the South, he had in fact been "observing the historical process by which civilization, not merely here but elsewhere, has evolved, drawing into . . . its influence an ever widening circle of races and peoples."[1] In its broadest sense, Park's sociology of race and ethnic relations takes the civilization process as its central concern. His well-known formulation of the four stages through which a race relations cycle would pass—namely, contacts, competition, accommodation, assimilation[2]—though not without considerable difficulties as a theory describing the order and direction taken by the several races' actual experiences[3]—postulates the ultimate victory of modern market civilization over all traditional modes of social organization. As Park conceived of the matter, modern societies—with their centers in multiracial and multiethnic cities—are characterized by "changes of fortune [that] are likely to be sudden and dramatic," by an "atomization" in which "every individual is more or less on his own," by "social forms [that] are flexible and in no sense fixed," and by a *polis* in which "fashion and public opinion take the place of custom as a means and method of social control."[4]

These modern "mobile societies," as Park called them, have an inexorable tendency to attract to themselves the still tradition-oriented peoples and, in the event, to convert them from their custom-bound ways of life into civic-minded citizens of a new Occidental socioeconomic order. That order, in turn, would shift them away from their membership in collective, family-based primary groups and move them into individuated, impersonal, and secondary associations of persons who must struggle for necessarily scarce material and spiritual rewards in a society built around commerce and competition. "Occidental, and particularly modern and American, culture," Park told delegates to an Institute of Pacific Relations conference at Hangchow, China, in 1931, "may be said to have had their origin and to have found their controlling ideas in the market place, where men come together to barter and trade, and by the exchange of commodities and services . . . to improve—each for himself, and according to his own individual conception of values—his condition of life."[5]

How America's blacks fitted into this universal process became a matter of special significance to Park, and proved to be the most difficult and ambiguous instance of the operation of his postulated race relations cycle. As Park saw the matter, much but not all of the assimilation process for African Americans had already taken place during their 225 years of enslavement.[6] However, the incorporation of the Negro into the lifeways, economy, culture, and polity of both slave and postslavery America had proceeded unevenly and selectively. A household slave, for example, "very soon possessed himself of so much of the language, religion, and the technique of the civilization of his master as, in his station, he was fitted or permitted to acquire," but the "assimilation of the Negro field hand, where the contact of the slave with his master and his master's family was less intimate, was naturally less complete."[7] Moreover, in such regions of the South as "the Sea Island plantations off the coast of South Carolina," regions, that is, that had been "less touched . . . by the white man's influence and civilization," or on those large plantations where class distinctions within the enslaved group had reduced master-slave contacts to a minimum, "the assimilation of the masses of the Negro people took place more slowly and less completely."[8] Nevertheless, Park pointed out, by 1860, although only one out of eight blacks were free while the great majority, numbering nearly four million were still in bondage, "it is safe to say [that] the great mass of . . . Negroes were no longer, in any true sense, an alien people."[9] But, Park was quick to add, "they were, of course, not citizens. . . . It might, perhaps, be more correct to say that they were less assimilated than domesticated."[10]

For the emancipation of the slaves to proceed beyond domestication and toward the kind of assimilation appropriate to a modern, industrial society, Park perceived, the black Americans would have to be incorporated into what was veritably a new social order, a society undergoing a fundamental and rapid reorganization, a society that was more and more coming to be characterized by impersonal relations, the drive for individual achievement, and the sequestration of affective feelings and familism to the arena of private life. During the period of slavery, as Park conceived of the matter, assimilation had occurred in great measure as a by-product of the intimate and personal relations among masters and (house) slaves. While aspects of these patronizing but primary relations continued in force after the Civil War, especially for those ex-slaves who continued to live near or work for their former masters, emancipation had opened the hitherto rural-bound blacks to the opportunities of moving around, of migrating north or west, of going to the cities, or, in a few cases, of becoming pioneers of a liberated Africa. Their mobility, in turn, had fostered individualizing tendencies. Except for the supervening fact that the Southern Redemptionist forces had imposed on the newly freed blacks a caste structure to replace the old and discredited slave system, these individualizing tendencies might have encouraged freedmen-and-women to develop their aptitudes and talents and, hence, to participate directly and fully in the incorporating process.[11] But such had not been the case. The return of "home rule" to the former Confederate states, the abrogation of Emancipation's promise in the form of black codes, Negro disfranchisement, and a host of new segregation practices had in effect erected a formidable barrier to the assimilation of the Negroes. During the period of his secretaryship to Booker T. Washington (1905–13), Park subscribed to a strategy that shielded the blacks from the worst features of southern racism, but kept the African Americans away from cities and civilization.

In the face of these developments, Park's vision of their complete assimilation required that some agency of progress, individuation, and initiative become activated within the ranks of the rural Afro-Americans. It is not the case that Park discounted the effects that a dedicated implementation of the provisions of the Thirteenth, Fourteenth, and Fifteenth Amendments or a vigorous enforcement of the Civil Rights Acts of 1866 and subsequent years would have had on black assimilation; rather, he developed his strategic outlook on the matter after 1876 when that option had been foreclosed by the return of "home rule" to the retrogressive white supremacist forces in the South. "As it turned out," he would recall in 1935, "the interests of race and caste triumphed over the interests of class and party." Prescient as he so often was, Park looked to the courts of the twentieth century to carry out the mandate of the Radical Republican Congress of 1866. In effect, to build on and to paraphrase Sumner, although Park at first supported Booker T. Washington's program of segregated

Protestant ethicism, he eventually came to encourage the use of what might be called "courtways" to bring "mores" into alignment with "stateways": "The courts must complete the work of the legislature," he observed almost twenty years before de jure segregation of public schools would be declared unconstitutional, "and until the law, as interpreted and enforced, has brought about what the psychologists might describe as a 'reconditioning' of the people for whom it was enacted, one cannot say the political process is complete."[12]

Color, Culture, and Civilization
in Park's Sociology, 1914–44

Although its basic assumptions remained the same, Park's outlook on the race question underwent considerable modification after he left the service of Booker T. Washington. Most significantly, he enlarged his perspective to embrace more than the black-white question. Park came more and more to regard the issues entailed in the debates over the southern race-caste system, the prohibitions on Asian entry into the United States, the quota restrictions on non–Anglo-Protestant immigration embodied in the Omnibus Immigration Act of 1924, and the rise of black, Chinese, and Japanese ghettos in America's major cities, together with the growth of race consciousness, not only as qualifying events in the race relations cycle, but also as incidents that "socialized" the "natural history" of a worldwide civilizational process. Modernity would usher in the discontents associated with progress: some races and many cultures would die, dissolve, or become deformed; economic development would complicate, modify, but not altogether obliterate the several racial caste structures; and America's response to its internal race problem would become a part of, as well as a contribution to, a new civilized global order. Qualifying all of these matters was Park's growing apprehension about the rise of fascism and Nazism and the retrogressive effects these ideologies and their attendant programs and policies would have on the evolution of race relations.

Park's earlier emphasis on the ameliorative role played by such "mission stations" as the one established at Tuskegee became less important to his theorizing as he took notice of the decline of the Social Gospel movement, the migration of southern blacks to the cities of the North and West, the sociocultural and economic features common to the situation of blacks, Asians, and Jews in America and elsewhere, and the growing importance of a newfound racial identity to a rising generation of Afro-Americans. With Booker T.

Washington's death in 1915, the new leaders and researchers at Tuskegee took notice—and tried, albeit unsuccessfully—to halt the migration of southern blacks to the cities of the North by reinvigorating the school's agricultural extension service to black farmers,[13] and, at the same time, by publicizing in the white media how the region's humiliating racialist practices were costing it a valuable human resource.[14]

In the same period, the settlement house phase of the Social Gospel mission to immigrants and blacks in the cities began to wind down.[15] As black city-dwellers—including such erstwhile followers of Washington's philosophy as William Pickens (1881-1954), who became a field secretary for the NAACP, the organization whose civil rights philosophy the Tuskegean had assiduously opposed[16]—shifted their attention from abject accommodationism toward political activism and social protest, the white Protestant churches and social settlements continued to preach the gospel of self-help, to teach Victorian urban folkways to Negro newcomers, and to practice racial separation in their parishes and conferences.[17] As a result of these changes in the status, station, and situation of the African Americans, Park increasingly turned his critical attention onto the "New Negro," and onto the rapidly increasing black urban proletariat and its fate in America's cities and the world's civilization.

Central to his new conception of the changing black experience in America was Park's recognition that a secular race-consciousness and the development of a people's collective identity as a national minority are necessary developments in the march toward assimilation in a modern cosmopolitan society.[18] The old-time religion receded in its effects on conduct in the face of these modern developments. Hence, Park pointed to the cultural discontinuity that he thought he perceived emerging out of the literary, artistic, and musical productions of the younger, urban, black generation of the 1920s. "The modern Negro folk songs, 'the Blues,'" he observed in 1928, "are secular and mundane rather than sacred."[19] Moreover, the facts of the black experience in America showed that the diachronic linearity of progress supposed to operate for all peoples in the process of cultural development had been replaced by a nomothetic juxtapositioning of stages.

Rather than participating in a chronological movement from a stage of primitive to one of modern culture, Park now asserted, America's blacks had been unique. "No other people, in the United States at least, have compressed into a career so brief so many transfigurations of their racial life." This remarkable fact, in turn, had led to the present peculiar cultural situation of the Negro, namely, that "no other racial group . . . [could] count among its living members representatives of so many grades of culture, ranging from the primitive peasant of southern plantations to the sophisticated singers of the Harlem cabarets and the radical poetry of the so-called 'Negro Renaissance.' "[20] And the temporal co-presence among America's blacks of all these otherwise sequential stages of culture meant, as Park came to see, that, for the emerging future at any rate, the African American's own consciously directed efforts would contribute to and alter that people's "natural history." "In a sense," Park observed in 1923, "it may be said that Negroes did not begin to have a history until Emancipation. . . . It was only after Emancipation, finding themselves in the middle of an intolerant and hostile society in which they were forced to fight for recognition and status, that black folk began to have a tradition and a history quite their own." When members of a living people, such as the Afro-Americans, regard themselves and are regarded by others "merely as representatives of a race, i.e., a species or variety of mankind, it is hard to understand how there could be any history of the[m] . . . except a natural history."[21] Race consciousness, as Park saw it, would operate on a race with something like the effect that class consciousness, in Marx's vision of that phenomenon, would have on aggregates of workers, that is, it would turn them into conscious members and active participants in their own lives and futures.

However, Park became ever more pessimistic as less than ameliorative racial relations unfolded in the three decades that followed his departure from Tuskegee. As he pointed out in 1928, "the modern Negro folk songs . . . record, on the whole . . . the Negro's disillusionment." The "Blues seem to be . . . the reflection of a life that is ineffectual and unsatisfying, 'flowering into song.' "[22] In 1925, Park had applied Ray Stannard Baker's phrase—the very same phrase that he and Booker T. Washington had previously used to entitle their 1913 study of impoverished Europeans[23]—to the situation of the contemporary black American: "The black man in America . . . 'the man farthest down,' the man most removed from the understanding and sympathy of the larger world in which he lives . . . is now engaged in a mortal struggle to attain actually, within the American community, the status which he has legally."[24] And in that same year he hinted at the reformulation of his race relations cycle that so many recent events—the comparable situations of the Jew and Negro, the unusually well documented racially separatist thesis of W. D. Weatherford,[25] the brilliant cultural pluralist argument advanced by William James's disciple, Horace Kallen,[26] and, most ominously, Park's own comparison of the preachings of the Ku Klux Klan with the propaganda of the Nordic supremacists— seemed to suggest:

> The Negro race, as Booker Washington used to say, is a nation within a nation. For somewhat different reasons the Jews in this country are in a similar situation. The Jews are seeking to preserve their culture while accommodating themselves in other respects to the conditions of American life. Different as they are in other respects, the Negro and the Jew are alike in this. . . . The Jew and the Negro are . . . the two outstanding illustrations of the impending cultural pluralism so interestingly advocated by Horace Kallen. What Mr. Weatherford proposes for the Negro, Mr. Kallen proposes for all the races and language groups in America. He would add to the federation of states the federation of races. The American people have not fairly faced this issue. But the Ku Klux Klan and the Nordic propaganda are unquestionably preparing the way for such a new constellation of the forces in the cultural life of America.[27]

As Park was to warn in 1927 (in a critical discussion of fellow-sociologist Jerome Dowd's book-length meditation on thirty years of social scientific literature about the race question), "In view of recent developments—the movement of the Negro to the industrial societies of the North, the new race consciousness of the Negro as reflected in the new Negro literature [and, he might have added, the revival and spread of the Ku Klux Klan into parts of America outside the South and the rumblings of racist fascism in Europe]—the benevolent mood in which [Professor Dowd's encyclopedic volume] is written, strike[s] one as rather antiquated and out of date."[28]

"Civilization," Park once observed in a paper not published until after his death, "is built up by the absorption of foreign ethnic groups, by undermining them, and by secularizing their cult and sacred order."[29] Although Park held to the thesis that "civilization is always a territorial affair,"[30] he did not hold to the view that the boundaries of national states, or any other kind of politically organized unit, would necessarily be coextensive with those of civilization. In this sense, Park's conception of civilization bears a certain resemblance to that of Emile Durkheim and Marcel Mauss, who sought to establish a new science of social morphology that would take as its central concern those cultural phenomena that could not be contained within geopolitical state formations.[31] In Park's case, however, the modern civilizational process is associated with the growth of cities and the fact that such growth is concomitant with the rise of a money economy, the rationalization of life activities, and the coming together of racially and culturally distinctive peoples. Thus, to Park, the contact, conflict, accommodation, and assimilation of races is both incidental and integral to the civilizational process.

However, the fact that the process had moved out from its once central focus in the United States, out even from the Occident, and had proceeded to envelop the entire world introduced a new era in race relations. "The race problem as it exists today," Park observed in 1925, "is primarily a product of the expansion of international trade and the improvement of transportation and communication."[32] As such, the problem could be resolved if the race relations cycle were to be completed in a general assimilation that would dissolve all racial groups in the solvent of market interests and within a world market-society. However, as Park was at pains to assert, the civilizational character of this modern form of assimilation would have to overcome both the aspiring nationalisms of racial and ethnic minorities as well as the racially biased ethnocentrism of such already established state societies as the United States. As he put it in 1926, "If America was once in any exclusive sense the melting pot of races, it is so no longer. The melting pot is the world."[33] But, as Park was quick to see—he pointed to the erection of immigration restrictions and other new barriers to immigration set up at "our racial frontier on the Pacific"[34]—few had recognized this fact or its implications.

Historical Blacks in an Ahistorical America.

Park claimed that black Americans had passed beyond the stage wherein their situation as members of a race could be depicted only in a "natural history" and in fact had entered a new one in which their experience as participants in a peoplehood could be investigated in a social history. Whatever the historical attitude, however, Park insisted that the direction of history—including the history of Africa and overseas peoples of African descent—was toward the ultimate incorporation of all peoples, nations, and classes in a global system governed by the interests of commerce and industry. Such a system was the essence of modern civilization.

Although Park seemed to accept the rise of racial and ethnic nationalisms in America and elsewhere as both incidents in a more group-determined march from a natural to a social history and as evidence of the progressive advance of universal assimilation—as early as 1914, he had asserted, "The fact is that nationalist sentiment among the Slavs, like racial sentiment among the Negroes, has sprung up as the result of a struggle against privilege and discrimination based upon racial distinctions. . . . Under conditions of secondary contact, that is to say, conditions of individual liberty and individual competition characteristic of modern civilization, depressed racial groups tend to assume the form of nationalities"[35]—he insisted that Africanisms, insofar as they were claimed as a vital part of the Afro-American minority's quest for a usable past, are both misconstrued and debilitating. Assuming as he did that both on the continent of their origin and among their present-day representatives overseas, "Africans are the only contemporaneous primitive people who have anywhere achieved race consciousness and civilization without losing their identity," Park had concluded that, as "a consequence almost every fundamental process and stage of civilization, from the most primitive to the most cosmopolitan . . . is somewhere represented in the contemporary life of the Negro in Africa and America."[36]

Despite this claim—or, more accurately, to explain its foundations—Park insisted that it was their inherited tropical temperament rather than the few survivals of their African culture that had made it possible for African Americans to still exhibit exoticisms in their conduct. As for the eruption of nationalistic fervor among blacks in the United States and the Caribbean, Park asserted that this was nothing less than "another spontaneous manifestation of that unrest . . . which has found [its latest] expression in pan-Africanism and in the movement in this country headed by Marcus Garvey, whose program is Africa for the Africans."[37] When, in 1937, Melville Herskovitz suggested that his culture-conflict approach to understanding voodoo cults among Haitian villagers might also throw new light on the dilemmas and contradictions attending black life in the United States, Park dismissed the idea out of hand, asserting that "the amount of . . . [the American Negro's] African heritage must be very small, indeed," and went on to insist "that the African in the United States has, for reasons that are obvious to those familiar with his history, retained less of his African heritage than is true of the Negro in any other part of the new world."[38]

Instead of concentrating their attention on the personal and social conflicts engendered by the alleged presence of African survivals in black Americans' daily life, social analysts of the Negro question might, in Park's estimation, become better informed on the matter if they would examine the new cultural expressions emanating from "the centers of Negro urban life in the North." These included "a new, surprisingly vigorous, and radically independent literature, in which a new generation of Negro intellectuals have sought to describe and interpret Negro life as they see and feel it, and to give, at the same time, a new orientation and a more positive expression of the Negro's rising race consciousness."[39] Park no doubt had in mind the race consciousness represented by such "New Negro"[40] and "Harlem Renaissance"[41] expressions as jazz music,[42] or such genre-defying novels as Jean Toomer's *Cane*,[43] Countee Cullen's plaintive ode to a lost African culture, "Heritage,"[44] and the modernist depiction of black American city-dwellers, scenes, and situations in the paintings of Aaron Douglas, Meta Warrick Fuller, Palmer Hayden, and William H. Johnson.[45] But that race consciousness did not arise out of any cultural legacy brought from Africa to America. "My own conclusion," Park wrote in 1937, "is that all that the Negro in the United States has retained is his temperament."[46]

Segregation, Racism, and the World Racial Order

The modern race problem, Park would assert in 1943, had arisen as a most significant incident in, as well as an effect of, the 450 year history of European civilizational expansion, a history that had first begun with Columbus's voyages in 1492. However, the quintessentially significant moment in that history has occurred only recently and could be understood through recognition of "the fact that within the last seventy-one years European expansion has finally reached the limits of the habitable world."[47] There had been, in effect, an enclosure of the racial frontiers of the world, and with it an evocation of new conflicts of consciousness and action that were bound to alter the shape of civilizational things to come. Whereas some had supposed that the four stages of his race relations cycle would always occur consecutively, in a chronological sequence, each succeeding the other and overturning its institutional arrangements and undermining its attendant attitudes, now it would likely be the case that the situations and sentiments appropriate to each stage would coexist in time and space with one another.

In 1937 Park had succumbed before the thrust of events in Europe, Asia, the Pacific, and the United States and begun to reformulate his estimate of what form the final stage of the race relations cycle would assume. At that time the Asian rather than the Afro-American issue seemed foremost in his mind. In 1931, Park had called attention to the cultural contradictions that were likely to engender conflict between the Occident and the Orient. "American civilization is founded typically upon the market place, where people come together for trade and barter; Chinese civilization, on the contrary, is founded on the family, where people come together for comfort, for security, and for moral support."[48] What forms would emerge, Park seemed to be asking, when a society whose most telling symbol was the ringing of the stock exchange bell came into contact, conflict, and an as yet undeveloped mode of accommodation with a civilization whose symbol of moral authority was a Confucian patriarch? "Chinese morality," Park had noted in 1927, the year that the Kuomintang split into nationalist and communist factions and began a civil war that would not end until 1949, "has not yet adapted itself to corporate management"; moreover, he went on to observe, "China . . . has had neither the experience nor the means for making the adjustments which the commercial and industrial invasion of Europe and America demands."[49] Moreover, the very principle upon which the Chinese polity had been founded stood in sharp contradiction to that which had engendered the Occidental state. In China, "it is demanded of servants of the government not merely that they obey the commands of their superiors but that they be successful in carrying these commands into effect," Park pointed out.[50] And, he asserted, "it is only in respect to the principle of personal responsibility that the difference between Chinese and European legal conceptions finds its most obvious expression."[51] But these legal conceptions illustrated an age-old civilizational dichotomy: "There has always been, apparently, one law of the family and of the tribe, and another law of the market place."[52] The problem of the Pacific rim was, in effect, being exacerbated because, currently, there was occurring a collision of these two laws under conditions that gave little promise for the Chinese one to remain efficacious.

South Asia, and more especially, India, on the other hand, was being inducted into modernity and its civilizational complex more rapidly than China. "The 'passionate confusion' of present-day India," Park pointed out in 1926, "is part of the general unrest of Asia, and this pullulation of new life in these ancient civilizations is one of the significant facts of the modern world."[53] However, less like China, India had already undergone a considerable amount of industrialization. Indeed, Park, noted, "India is not only the chief industrial country in the tropics, but the eighth greatest industrial country in the world."[54] As Park saw the matter, "the cycle of change which began with the extension of European trade to the Orient has, in the case of India at least, been completed."[55] Even though "its population of 320,000,000 [was still] mostly agricultural," Park pointed to the fact "that the cotton spinners in India are now in active competition with Lancashire, England, and the steel mills of Bengal are manufacturing steel plates and sheets in competition with the mills of Germany, England, and the United States."[56] Industrial development, Park concluded, "measures more accurately than anything else the extent and the character of changes in the life of India. . . . These changes touch every aspect of Indian life . . . [and] are . . . undermining the most characteristic feature of Indian civilization, mainly her caste system . . . not to mention other and less obvious consequences they have created in a people speaking 222 distinct languages."[57] What was emerging in India was, "if not a nation, at least a nationality."[58]

However, for Park, the strategic site for following the pace and direction of the race relations cycle was Hawaii. "The Hawaiian Islands," he had claimed in 1926, "at the present moment have become a laboratory for the study of the race problem. In these islands all the races of the Pacific have come together in numbers and under conditions more favorable to the successful working of the melting-pot than are likely to be found elsewhere on the planet."[59] Eleven years later, the researches of his student Romanzo Adams on the extent and effects of interracial marriage in this territory of the United States, as well as the militarization of these islands in the face of the threat posed by Japan to American interests in the Pacific, led Park to reconsider the matter.[60] Race relations, he now proposed, occur in three dimensions—as adjustments, in long-term cycles, and fortuitously—that interpenetrate and complicate their pattern and movement. Yet, "what are popularly referred to as race relations ordinarily involve some sort of race conflict . . . [but] can best be interpreted if what they seem to be at any time and place is regarded merely as a phase in a cycle of change which, once initiated, inevitably continues until it terminates in some predestined racial configuration, and one consistent with an established social order of which it is a part."[61] Because of the varying character of the social orders extant in the world—because, in effect, Occidental civilization had not yet remade every society and culture into an analogue of itself—the final stage of the race relations cycle would also vary. "When stabilization is finally achieved," Park pointed out, "race relations will assume one of three . . . configurations. They will take the form of a caste system, as in India; they will terminate in complete assimilation as in China; or the unassimilated race will constitute a permanent racial minority within the limits of a national state, as is the case of the Jews in Europe."[62] It is noteworthy that in restating the character and terminal phase of the race relations cycle, Park made no prediction about the future status of blacks or any other of the nonwhite peoples in the American variant of that cycle.

War, Race Conflict, and the Race Relations Cycle in America

With the advent of the Second World War, Park, in one of his final papers, once again sought to reframe the issues entailed in American and global race frictions. "What the war has done thus far," he opined in 1943, "has been to make race relations an international rather than a local and national problem."[63] Nevertheless, there remained the deeply engrained attitudes, the apparently inflexible institutions, and the seemingly fixed opinions that in fact expressed racist ideologies. These ideologies had become embedded in the national culture and psyche and had had their own origin in the era of slavery. Although Park regarded the war to be, potentially at least, also a revolution in the ordering of humankind, he felt it necessary to point out that "revolutions are the product not of changes in opinion but of changes in ideology." And he noted that, "in the prosecution of the war and in the organization of the peace, [the] racial diversities of the American population will be either a national handicap or a national asset, depending on our ability to make our racial policies and our racial ideology conform to our national interests."[64] Park asserted that "a revolution in race relations in the United States may be impending, but it has not yet arrived,"[65] a thesis that the researches of his former student, E. Franklin Frazier, had already documented.[66]

Park ultimately came to apply his thesis about the ubiquity of conflict to the manner in which blacks would have to proceed as they moved along their own path to assimilation in America's market-oriented, class-based social order. Biracial social and economic organization had already proposed parallel hierarchies of black and white professional, middle, and working classes, but the blacks' change in status from that of a caste to a minority group had been accompanied by a shift from their condition as a race buffeted about by an externally determined destiny to one in which they had assumed self-directed autonomy over the formulation of their own identity, interests, future, and leadership. Their rising status would encounter resistance from those whites determined to maintain the caste position under attack, but as Park put in a letter to his former student Horace Cayton, "If conflicts arise as a result of the efforts [of blacks] to get their place it will be because the white people started them." And, as he concluded, in that epistolary statement, "these conflicts will probably occur and are more or less inevitable but conditions will be better after they are over."[67] The struggle for emancipation would continue, Park supposed, until that moment when race conflicts had disappeared altogether—only to be replaced by those of classes.[68] "One thing, however, seems certain," he wrote in 1943: "the races and peoples which fate has brought together in America and within the limits of the larger world economy will continue, in the emerging world society, their struggle for a political and a racial equality that was denied them in the world that is passing."[69]

NOTES

This essay originally appeared in The International Journal of Politics, Culture, and Society, 4:3 (Spring 1991), pp. 285–300.

1. Robert E. Park, "An Autobiographical Note," in Race and Culture: The Collected Papers of Robert Ezra Park, vol. 1, ed. Everett Cherrington Hughes, Charles S. Johnson, Jitsuichi Masuoka, Robert Redfield, and Louis Wirth (Glencoe, Ill.: The Free Press, 1950), p. viii.

2. Robert E. Park, "Our Racial Frontier on the Pacific," Survey Graphic, 56:3 (May 1, 1926), pp. 192–96.

3. See Stanford M. Lyman, "The Race Relations Cycle of Robert E. Park," Pacific Sociological Review, 11:1 (Spring 1968), pp. 16–22. This essay has been reprinted in Lyman, Civilization: Contents, Discontents, Malcontents, and Other Essays in Social Theory (Fayetteville: University of Arkansas Press, 1990), pp. 127–35.

4. Robert E. Park, "The Problem of Cultural Differences," in Race and Culture, p. 12.

5. Ibid., p. 14.

6. The following draws on Robert E. Park, "Racial Assimilation in Secondary Groups with Particular Reference to the Negro," American Journal of Sociology, 13:5 (Mar. 1914), pp. 606–19.

7. Ibid., p. 612.

8. Ibid., p. 613.

9. Ibid.

10. Ibid.

11. Ibid., pp. 615–17.

12. Robert E. Park, "Politics and 'The Man Farthest Down,' " in Park, Race and Culture, p. 172.

13. See Emmett J. Scott, Negro Migration during the War. Preliminary Economic Studies of the War, no. 16. Carnegie Endowment for International Peace (New York: Oxford University Press, 1920; reprint, New York: Arno Press and the New York Times, 1969), pp. 81–82.

14. See Linda O. McMurry, *Recorder of the Black Experience: A Biography of Monroe Nathan Work* (Baton Rouge: Louisiana State University Press, 1985), pp. 81–82.

15. See Judith Ann Trolander, "Introduction to the Transaction Edition," of Robert A. Woods and Albert J. Kennedy, *The Settlement Horizon* (New Brunswick, N.J.: Transaction Publishers, 1990 [1922]), pp. xvii–xix.

16. Sheldon Avery, *Up from Washington: William Pickens and the Negro Struggle for Equality, 1900–1954* (Newark, Del.: University of Delaware Press, 1989), pp. 15–111.

17. Paul A. Carter, *The Decline and Revival of the Social Gospel: Social and Political Liberalism in American Protestant Churches, 1920–1940* (Hamden, Conn.: Archon Books, 1971), pp. 130–33.

18. See Robert E. Park, "Negro Race Consciousness as Reflected in Race Literature," *American Review*, 1 (Sept.–Oct. 1923), pp. 505–16.

19. Robert E. Park, review essay of ten books on black American songs, folklore, drama, and poetry in *American Journal of Sociology*, 33:6 (May 1928), p. 990.

20. Robert E. Park, in an untitled review essay of six literary, musical, and cultural books in *American Journal of Sociology*, 31 (May 1926), p. 822.

21. Robert E. Park, review of *The Negro in our History*, by Carter G. Woodson, and *Social History of the American Negro*, by Benjamin Brawley, *American Journal of Sociology*, 28:5 (March 1923), p. 614.

22. Park, review essay on ten books on black American songs, folklore, drama, and poetry, p. 990.

23. Booker T. Washington, with the collaboration of Robert E. Park, *The Man Farthest Down: A Record of Observation and Study in Europe* (Garden City, N.Y.: Doubleday, Page and Co., 1913).

24. Robert E. Park, review of *The Negro from Africa to America*, by W. D. Weatherford, *American Journal of Sociology*, 31:2 (Sept. 1925), p. 259.

25. W. D. Weatherford, *The Negro from Africa to America* (New York: George H. Doran and Co., 1924).

26. Horace Kallen, *Culture and Democracy in the United States: Studies in the Group Psychology of the American Peoples* (New York: Boni and Liveright, 1924; reprint, New York: Arno Press and the New York Times, 1970).

27. Park, review of *The Negro from Africa to America*, p. 260.

28. Robert E. Park, untitled review of seven books on slavery and race relations in the United States, in *American Journal of Sociology*, 32:4 (Jan. 1927), p. 642.

29. Robert E. Park, "Culture and Civilization," in Park, *Race and Culture*, p. 16.

30. Ibid.

31. See Marcel Mauss, "A Category of the Human Mind: The Notion of Person, the Notion of 'Self,'" *Sociology and Psychology: Essays*, trans. Ben Brewster (London: Routledge and Kegan Paul, 1979), pp. 57–94; Emile Durkheim and Marcel Mauss, *Primitive Classification*, trans. and ed. Rodney Needham (Chicago: University of Chicago Press–Phoenix Books, 1967 [1903]); Emile Durkheim, "Note on Social Morphology," *On Institutional*

Analysis, trans. and ed. Mark Traugott (Chicago: University of Chicago Press, 1978), pp. 88–92.

32. Robert E. Park, review of The Menace of Colour . . . , by J. W. Gregory, in American Journal of Sociology, 31:3 (Nov. 1925), p. 403.

33. Robert E. Park, "Our Racial Frontier on the Pacific," Survey Graphic, 9 (May 1926), p. 196.

34. Ibid., pp. 192–95.

35. Park, "Racial Assimilation in Secondary Groups," p. 622.

36. Robert E. Park, review of Harvard Studies. 1. Varia Africana, ed. Oric Bates, in Journal of Negro History, 3:2 (April 1918), p. 199.

37. Robert E. Park, review of Les Daimons du Culte Voudo, by Arthur Holly in Journal of Negro History, 7:2 (April 1922), p. 226.

38. Robert E. Park, review of Life in a Haitian Valley, by Melville J. Herskovitz in American Journal of Sociology, 43:2 (Sept. 1937), pp. 346–48.

39. Robert E. Park, review essay of ten books on black American songs, folklore, drama, and poetry, p. 989. See also two reviews by Park, review of six books on black American songs, spirituals, poetry and the New Negro, in American Journal of Sociology, 31:6 (May 1926), pp. 821–24; and review of Negro Americans, What Now? and Along This Way, both by James Weldon Johnson, in American Journal of Sociology, 40 (May 1935), pp. 837–40.

40. Alain Locke, ed., The New Negro (New York: Atheneum, 1968 [1925]).

41. Nathan Irvin Huggins, ed., Voices from the Harlem Renaissance (New York: Oxford University Press, 1976).

42. Alain Locke, "The Negro and His Music" in Locke, The Negro and His Music and Negro Art: Past and Present (New York: Arno Press and the New York Times, 1969 [1936]), pp. 70–117.

43. Jean Toomer, Cane (New York: Harper and Row, 1969 [1923]).

44. Countee Cullen, "Heritage," in The Poetry of the Negro, 1746–1949, ed. Langston Hughes and Arna Bontemps (Garden City, N.Y.: Doubleday and Co., 1949), pp. 121–25.

45. Harlem Renaissance: Art of Black America, introduction by Mary Schmidt Campbell (New York: Harry N. Abrams, Inc., 1987), pp. 105–54.

46. Park, review of Life in a Haitian Valley, p. 348.

47. Robert E. Park, review of European Colonial Expansion since 1871, by Mary Evelyn Townsend, American Journal of Sociology, 48:4 (Jan. 1943), p. 516.

48. Robert E. Park, review of Mobilität der Bevölkerung in den Vereinigten Staaten, by Rudolph Heberle, in American Journal of Sociology, 36:4 (Jan. 1931), p. 658.

49. Robert E. Park, review of six books on China, American Journal of Sociology, 33:3 (Nov. 1927), p. 474.

50. Robert E. Park, review of The Development of Extraterritoriality in China, by G. W. Keeton, American Journal of Sociology, 37:5 (Mar. 1932), p. 809.

51. Ibid.

52. Ibid., p. 807.

53. Robert E. Park, review of four books on India, *American Journal of Sociology*, 32:2 (Sept. 1926), p. 303.

54. Ibid., p. 304.

55. Ibid.

56. Ibid.

57. Ibid.

58. Ibid.

59. Robert E. Park, review of five books on immigration, race, and intelligence, *American Journal of Sociology*, 32:2 (Sept. 1926), p. 303.

60. Robert E. Park, "Introduction" to *Interracial Marriage in Hawaii: A Study of the Mutually Conditioned Processes of Acculturation and Amalgamation*, by Romanzo Adams (New York: Macmillan, 1937; reprint, Montclair, N.J.: Patterson Smith, 1969), pp. vii–xiv.

61. Ibid., pp. xiii–xiv.

62. Ibid., p. xiii.

63. Robert E. Park, "Racial Ideologies," in *American Society in Wartime*, ed. William Fielding Ogburn (Chicago: University of Chicago Press, 1943; reprint, New York: Da Capo Press, 1972), p. 183.

64. Ibid.

65. Ibid.

66. E. Franklin Frazier, "Ethnic and Minority Groups in Wartime, with Special Reference to the Negro," *American Journal of Sociology*, 48 (Nov. 1942), pp. 369–77.

67. Robert Park to Horace Cayton. Quoted in Horace R. Cayton, "Robert Park: A Great Man Died but Leaves Keen Observation on Our Democracy," *Pittsburgh Courier*, February 26, 1944. The late Mr. Cayton kindly presented me with a typed copy of his obituary to Park.

68. Robert E. Park, "The Nature of Race Relations," in *Race Relations and the Race Problem: A Symposium on a Growing National and International Problem with Special Reference to the South*, ed. Edgar T. Thompson (Durham, N.C.: Duke University Press, 1939), p. 45.

69. Park, "Racial Ideologies," p. 183.

2

Park and Realpolitik:
Race, Culture, and Modern Warfare

In December 1900, Munsey's Magazine published Robert E. Park's first and only essay on the character and organization of the German army.[1] Subtitled "The Most Perfect Military Organization in the World," Park's essay seemed to celebrate the tactical effectiveness, strategic philosophy, and national chauvinism of the new Reich's armed forces. On the surface the essay appeared to be an English-language expression of the more militant ideas of Heinrich von Treitschke and, more generally, to have arisen out of the world-influencing German school of national-historical thought associated with such figures as Johann Gustav Droysen and Leopold von Ranke. However, Park's essay is a macrosociological study and can neither be relegated to the historical dustbin, nor treated as merely an American scholar's representation of the imperial German Zeitgeist. It contains the latter, but also transcends it. Not only does Park carefully analyze the process whereby the once feudal officer corps was democratized, he also pinpoints the social psychology that animates the *Reichswehr*. In so doing, Park forewarns us about the dilemmas and contradictions that would plague all forms of militant and militarized ethnonationalism and anticipates the fundamental political reorganization that would come to haunt and horrify the twentieth century—the rise of the garrison state and the extension of international conflicts to total war.

Park's essay on the German army may be read today in a double context: as an early attempt at preparing Americans for living in a multinational, multicultural world that, he foresaw, would be inescapably fraught with perils; and, as an instance of Simmel's ideas about the conflict and tragedy of culture. The larger context of Park's essay was the emerging militarization that was attending the rise of ethnonational states, the technological advancements in transportation and communication, the bureaucratic reorganization of political, economic, and sociocultural life, and the conflicts over the extension of citizenship and the spread of democracy. The historicism of Treitschke, Droysen, and Ranke was an intellectual strand of these developments and became, in effect, an implicit topic of, as well as an explicit resource for, Park's observations. Ultimately, Park seems to have glimpsed the darker implications of war's emergence out from the limitations of cultural and moral constraints—of war's "liberation" to complete its ultimate mission, annihilation.

Treitschke and Prussian Ethnonationalism

Friedrich Meinecke, a student of Treitschke's thought, points out that the German variant of Europe's "classical liberalism" arose from a proposed synthesis of instrumental reason and military force. Among Germany's classical liberals, Meinecke regarded "Heinrich von Treitschke [as] . . . perhaps their greatest, at any rate their most influential, representative."[2] It was von Treitschke (1834–96) who gave substance and support to a conception of reason that emphasized the Teutonic national will. That will not only superseded the will of the ordinary citizen, but also exerted absolute authority over the latter.

Six years after Park published his essay, Meinecke—who had been born two years before Park and who would live ten years longer than the latter—had voiced a cautious optimism about the reforms made in Germany before the rise of the classical liberals, during the first decades of the nineteenth century. "If in the first decade of the twentieth century men can regard the state as more than a cold and oppressive force, and the nation as more than a primitive racial concept, if both seem to offer spiritual clarity and warmth, an atmosphere in which the free individual can breathe, then in Germany it is due largely to the Prussian reformers" who, he insisted, had responded to the exigencies of the Napoleonic era.[3] This sanguine assessment overlooked the arrogantly nationalistic and virulently anti-Semitic interpretation of these reforms that would be made by Treitschke; it was a failure of judgment that Meinecke, who had succeeded Treitschke as editor of the *Historische Zeitschrift* and who regarded the latter as "the man who surpassed all of us, young as well as old,"[4] would—all too late—deplore.[5] "Out of the anti-Semitic feeling [that Treitschke and his followers had begun in the 1880s]," Meinecke lamented in 1946, "it was possible for an anti-liberal and an anti-humanitarian feeling to develop easily—the first steps toward National Socialism."[6]

Treitschke had elaborated on his peculiar brand of ethnocentrism, in the process of denigrating both Jews and African Americans. He regarded Jews as not only a deservedly stateless people, but also as a threat to the burgeoning Prussian hegemonism that he and his fellow historians were championing. "In plain words," he exhorted his readers, "the Jews have always been an 'element of national decomposition'; they have always helped in the disintegration of nations."[7] Although Treitschke allowed that a "certain number of European Jews have, as a matter of fact, succeeded in really adopting the nationality of the people among whom they live . . . it is equally certain that in Berlin, and eastwards from that city, there are many Jews who are inwardly real Orientals, in spite of the language they speak."[8] Holding that in antiquity Jews had played "an essential role" in the Alexandrian and Roman Empires, and that later, in "the early Middle Ages . . . Jews [had] controlled the trade of the world," Treitschke believed that "the Jews [had] ceased to be indispensable" with the onset of the age of national state-building.[9] Once having lost their indispensability, he hinted, they had become expendable.

Not content to encourage an anti-Jewish, inhumane, and generally ethnocentric national struggle in behalf of Prussian domination of German culture, Treitschke turned his vitriolic pen onto the situation affecting freedom in the United States of America in the aftermath of that nation's Civil War. Holding to his premise that "when several nations are united under one State, the simplest relationship is that the one which wields the authority should be the superior in civilization,"[10] Treitschke pointed to what he regarded as the absence of civilization altogether among black Africans and Afro-Americans: "The black races have always been servants, and looked down upon by all the others, nor has any Negro State ever raised itself to a level of real civilization."[11] Treitschke's version of Aryan supremacist history led him to ignore altogether the once-flourishing African kingdoms of Songhay and Mali. Instead, Treitschke's racial and national views led him to connect genetic peoplehood to nationality, nationality to state, state to patriotism, and patriotism to war. In all of this, as we shall see, Park did not only not follow him, but hotly opposed Treitschke's tendentious reasoning.

Park and Realpolitik

Nowhere in Park's essay on the German army does he mention the name or present the perspective of Treitschke; rather, the latter's racialist and bellicose historicism haunts the thematic of Park's study.

Park's depiction of the collective conscience that gives German militarism its patriotic esprit de corps is that developed by Helmuth von Moltke the Elder (1800–1891), chief of the German army's general staff from 1857 to 1887.[12]

Moltke, as Park described him, personified not only the German nation at war preparedness, but also the modern type of authoritarian technocrat that national states of the twentieth century would demand as their own military leaders. "Every organization," Park observed, "—and the German army is a striking illustration of the principle—presents a double aspect. On the one side, it is a machine, a tool, and on the other it is what I may call an organized experience, a will."[13] As a machine and tool, Moltke had understood, the soldiers in the ranks had to be completely obedient to the orders that were formulated by the general staff and the officer corps and embodied in the will of their commander. Hence, while the national army, after its reorganization on the basis of universal military conscription, might offer the hitherto stratumbound son of a *bauer* a path to social and economic advancement, it could not be governed according to the principles of democracy. The "machine-like automation that one finds in a well drilled army," Park pointed out, depends on a "centering of control" in the "leadership element."[14]

Park's interest in Germany's new militarism arose out of his conviction—derived, intellectually, from his studies with Simmel and, personally, from his many and varied experiences in the knockabout world—that conflict was a general process of social life while violent altercations were merely one of its forms. "War," on the other hand, he regarded as "a crude form of social competition" that had "as its goal . . . the suppression of the opponent."[15] In 1916, two years after Europe had become embroiled in what was to be designated as the First World War, Park noted in a letter to his daughter how "the simplest problems . . . are world problems, the problems of the contacts and the frictions and the interactions of nations and races." Park reported that he hoped to do a study of war posing the following questions: "Why do we, irrespective of specific causes, have wars? Why do men fight? What is the function of war? Is war one way, one necessary way, of getting on in the world? Is it part of the cosmic process of evolution, part of the struggle for existence? Are human beings so made that the world would be worse off if these tremendous struggles did not exist? In short, is war founded in the nature of human beings?"[16] Although Park's other studies diverted his attention from these questions, he never ceased his interest in the study of war in particular and more generally in ferreting out the bases and consequences of bellicose conflicts.

The German Army, the Garrison State, and Total War

State Militarization

When, in 1922, Park prophesied that "when the final history of the World War comes to be written, one of its most interesting chapters will be a description of the methods and devices which were used by the armies of both sides to destroy the will to war in the enemy's troops and among the peoples behind the lines,"[17] he was not only echoing an observation he had made two decades earlier in his study of the German army, but also elaborating upon the Treitschkean model of a German national will to war. In 1900, Park had taken cognizance of a development in Germany that would usher in a new era: the century of total war. It was General von Moltke, Park pointed out, who had come to the conclusion that future wars would "be waged with the railway and telegraph," that is, that "modern science had given to a capable leader the means of concentrating and putting in action an army larger than had ever before been dreamed of, an army that was nothing less than a nation in arms."[18] Park had delineated the policies and programs whereby imperial Germany had accomplished the institutional reconstruction requisite for converting itself into a militarily prepared and fully garrisoned national state, a Treitschkean war-state.

However, Park had been misled about the much vaunted upward mobility said to have "democratized" the German officer corps. Despite his citation of Bismarck's good-natured complaint—that his own son had not been promoted from the ranks as rapidly as other conscripts from less-favored lineages—as a telling piece of evidence of the elimination of aristocratic privilege in the new German army,[19] we have no less than the authority of Friedrich Meinecke that, despite the liberal reforms, "the tradition of the officer corps as a corporation held together by unique attitudes and qualities was not abandoned." Meinecke observed that, "in the course of time this development carried the officer corps back to its aristocratic, old-Prussian roots, and former qualities reasserted themselves more than the reformers has wished."[20] Hans Kohn has been even more emphatic, locating the source of Prussian aristocratic predominance in the very workings of the system of universal conscription that Park had described: "Whereas in Germany the 'common man' served three years," Kohn pointed to the fact that, "the high-school graduate, then always a member of the upper classes, had to serve only one year, and at the end of the year if he chose to stay in the reserves as an officer was generally commissioned as a second lieutenant." Such a system, Kohn concluded, "helped to preserve the strict class character of the German army."[21]

Although Park was sure that the "rule which treated all alike had an inspiring effect upon the rank and file of the soldiers,"[22] he had failed to notice another proactive feature of the universal military conception program that would make his claim about all of Germany being a "nation in arms"[23] a far more formidable prophecy. That feature would be noticed by Hans Speier in his 1932 study of German white-collar workers—a monograph suppressed by the Nazis. Pointing to the fact that the "veteran of twelve years of army service . . . was especially favored for placement" in the civil service, Speier documented the very high percentage of veterans holding positions in the *Reichsverband der Zivildienstberechtigten* and observed that "the special rights of the veteran . . . guaranteed the militarization of the lower bureaucracy."[24] Moreover, it was Speier who pointed out that Hitler had completed the egalitarianization of the army that had been begun by the National Liberals:

> When Hitler reintroduced universal military service, he abolished the privilege of shorter service in the army which boys with a high school education had enjoyed under the kaiser. In this respect and also with respect to promotion from the ranks the military system of this modern despot is more egalitarian than was that of Imperial Germany. . . . With his resolution to liberate destructive techniques from humanitarian fetters and to sacrifice any tradition to military efficiency, he has brought to a head the martial equalization of society that began in eighteenth century Prussia but required the rise of modern political mass movements to become truly effective.[25]

Although Park had been mistaken about its democratization, he had correctly noted the enlargement of the German general staff, its division into specialized departments, and its adaptation of advances in science and technology to military purposes. "In 1857," he pointed out, "when Moltke became chief [of staff], the personnel of his bureau was composed of sixty-four officers, a number . . . increased [later] to eighty-three. . . . In 1867 his subordinates numbered one hundred and nine. . . . At . . . present . . . there are two hundred and seven officers in the general staff."[26] Moreover, Park saw the relationship of this division of labor to the institutionalization of the

Treitschkean will to war. He likened this steadily enlarging staff to the "brain" of a giant organism that, he said, was the essence of the army; the men in the ranks served that "brain" as a "corresponding automatism."[27]

Park's shrewd observations about the implications of the resurgence of German militarism focused on the fundamental reconceptualization of warfare that Moltke had formulated and introduced to the public. In effect, Park pointed out how Moltke had not only proposed to end those self-imposed restrictions that most modern states had recently adopted, but also ushered in an era of virtually unconditional war. In a speech to the Reichstag that Park quoted, the chief-of-staff had asserted, "I do not agree with the declaration made at St. Petersburg, that the weakening of the enemy's forces constitutes the only proper method of warfare." And, as Park took care to report, Moltke wished to convert warfare into an all-out assault on the enemy's military bases, natural resources, and civilian population. "We should," Moltke insisted, "direct our attack against all the means and resources that the enemy possesses—against his finances, his railways, his food supply, even his prestige."[28] Having adopted Moltke's program, reconstructed its armed forces, fixed their authority in the hierarchy of the general staff, centralized control in the commander-in-chief, and girdled the country with military fortifications, Germany stood poised with its army standing, in Park's words, "upon its own soil, silent, observant, calm, in an attitude of formidable defense."[29] But, as Park hinted in the conclusion of his essay, Moltke's military philosophy was not limited to justifications for wars in *defense* of the realm. " 'Eternal peace,' said he, 'is only a dream, and not even a happy dream. . . . Without war the world would fall into decay, and lose itself in materialism.' "[30]

Park's observation that fin de siècle Germany's social organization had taken on a new form—an entire nation in arms, motored by constantly improved military technology and molded by militaristic indoctrination—portended a frightening future, one wherein wars would become indiscriminate in their infliction of casualties and unrestrained in their assaults on people and property.

The Second World War and the Treitschkean Fulfillment

It would not be until the eve of America's involvement in the Second World War that Park would set down on paper his pessimistic observations about how advances in the means of destruction and the techniques of propaganda had led to the repudiation of the few jurisprudential restraints on the conduct of war that still existed.[31]

Noting in 1941 that neither scholars nor statesmen knew "whether to regard war as a natural phenomenon, like an earthquake or a pestilence, or to classify it as a social phenomenon, like a political contest, or an elementary form of judicial procedure like the ancient trial by battle,"[32] Park pointedly challenged the current applicability of Treitschke's assertion that "between civilized nations . . . war is the form of litigation by which states made their claims valid."[33] Park pointed out that the "so-called 'laws of war' " had been undermined by "the rapid advances in the technology of war [that had] . . . assumed ever vaster proportions and achieved an ever more terrible efficiency"[34] in the decades after Treitschke had written those words. Moreover, Park went on, "international politics . . . [have] become more realistic and more cynical."[35] Ultimately, he concluded, "under these conditions it is difficult to conceive of war as a form of judicial procedure even as elementary as the ancient trial by battle. It is even doubtful whether it can any longer be regarded as it once was, as an 'institution recognized by international law.' "[36] War had burst the bonds of its own self-restraints. "It is an institution—a political institution—in process; an institution whose function has not been defined, whose structure is not yet fixed in custom and in tradition."[37]

Park had earlier proposed that the state, the modern form of geopolitical unity, be conceived as the endpoint of an evolutionary trajectory. That trajectory could be depicted as moving through successive stages of collective group formation, beginning in the crowd and becoming, sequentially, the caste, the sect, the class, and, finally, the state.[38] Although in 1904 Park had supposed that there was "progressive social differentiation and increasing stability from stage to stage," in his later writings he constantly compared the state with the crowd. By 1942 he had come to regard Hitler's Third Reich as, in effect, an atavistic reversal of Hegel's dictum that, as Park had earlier paraphrased the German philosopher, "the general will assumes the self-conscious form of reason only within the State."[39] Two years before his death, Park called attention to the fact that, "most of us have been astounded, and some of us have been terrified, by what Herr Hitler and his associates have accomplished in recreating, in so short a time, the German army and transforming the disorganized German Empire into the most powerful military and political machine the world has ever known."[40] But, more significantly, Park, in an essay written about the same time, called attention to the fact that Hitler and his junto had organized and manipulated a mass psychology of fascism and taken it through all the stages of

political development without ever divesting it of its essentially irrational character. The calamitous spectacle of a modern state society in the throes of a fanatical charismatic atavism, destroying the
gains in rationality supposedly ensured by the Enlightenment gave
Park pause. "It suggests," he wrote, "the relativity of worlds in which
men are actively alive and for whose orderly existence they are in
some way personally responsible."[41] The Nazis had made a sham-
bles out of the relationship of personal responsibility to state action
and democratic values. Energized by its sectarian rites and urged on
by the racialist creed contained in its "bible," *Mein Kampf*, the Nazi
movement had earlier found "in Hitler its prophet, if not its God."[42]
As soon as it captured control of the state it had "attempted to suppress every form of dissent with all the fervor and fanatical vigor of
a newborn religion."[43] Moreover, "Herr Hitler and his associates
seem to have inspired the army, if not the people, with an invincible
faith in their mission and destiny . . . and . . . have sought to support
that faith by ritual, by myth, and above all, by ceremonies that revive . . . the atmosphere and . . . mood of exaltation in which it was
originally conceived."[44]

   Park had once remarked, apropos Sumner's discussion of the mores, that, "it is . . . only in a political society, in which a public exists
that permits discussion, rather than in a society organized on a familial and authoritative basis, that rational principles tend to supersede tradition and custom as a basis of organization and control."[45]
However, the establishment of the Nazi state in Germany and its subsequent war program intending to dominate the entire world, had
ushered in something entirely new, an aggressive state-society that
seemed to have burst both the traditional restraints of custom-bound
orderliness and the deliberative rationality and legal controls of constitutional republics. "World War II," Park observed, "which began
with the assumption that its purpose was to revise the treaties with
which World War I was concluded, is now proclaiming itself a
world-revolution. . . . It is rather an ideological war—a war to establish a new order based upon a new political philosophy and a new
philosophy of life."[46] That new order and philosophy of life would
embrace and intertwine "total war" with "the garrison state."

Total War and Modernity: The Garrison State

There is a foreboding imagery in Park's commentaries on the relation
of war to the perils of modernity. Writers on the history of war have
disagreed with one another on the precise date—or even the precise
era—that marks the onset of truly *modern* warfare. For Park, how-

ever, it was the German General Erich Ludendorff, that "Faustian genius of war," and "military fanatic" as Michael Geyer has called him,[47] who had formulated the societal praxis that was the concomitant of *total* war. In 1936 there had appeared an English translation of Ludendorff's military philosophy. Park quoted the thesis that Ludendorff had enunicated—namely, "A totalitarian policy must put at the disposal of . . . a war the strength of the nation and preserve it. . . . Only a conformity to the fundamental racial and spiritual laws will succeed in welding nation, conduct of war, and politics into that powerful unity which is the basis of national preservation."[48] Park concluded that Ludendorff's philosophy had added validity to George Herbert Mead's assertion that "as a policy for adjudicating national differences, [war] is utterly discredited."[49] The total destruction that Ludendorffian conceptions of modern world wars seemed about to bring forth would, in Mead's words, leave "nothing to be adjudicated, not even the enemy nations themselves."[50]

Park did not develop a comprehensive theory of total war or of the garrison state. The former term he correctly associated with Ludendorff; the latter is a product of the fertile interdisciplinary mind of Harold Lasswell, a social scientist who had spent some time at the University of Chicago. A deeper understanding of the relationship of the garrison state to total war and to the larger dilemmas and contradictions in values that the rise of German militarism had evoked has been presented by Hans Speier, a German emigré scholar.

Were today's political sociologists to study the writings of Robert Park, they might recognize that long before they had sought to "bring the state back in" he had become aware of a specific instance of the structuring of relationships that they think they are the first to have discovered. "A nation," Park had observed, "includes within its wide embrace all ordinary forms of association with which we are familiar, i.e., local, familial, economic, political, religious, and racial."[51] Park had then gone on to note that the problem for any state seeking to weld these potentially disparate elements into an enthusiastic, cooperative, uncritical, and tractable body of civil subordinates had been resolved in Hitler's Germany by adoption of the policy known as *Gleichschaltung*: national morale had "been achieved by coordinating, subordinating, and eventually fusing every local and minor loyalty into a totalitarian loyalty to the national state."[52] Speier's and Lasswell's further analyses of total war and of the garrison state have brought considerable new amplitude to Park's observations. They also have contributed new understandings of the nature and types of state societies and, in effect, had brought the latter "back in" a half-century before Theda Skocpol and her colleagues claimed to be about to do so.

By 1941, Park had reconsidered Moltke's epistolary comment, "Perpetual peace is a dream and not even a happy dream." From this and other statements Park now supposed that the Prussian militarist, whose soldierly skills and organizational genius had brought about the military successes of the Second German Reich, had actually believed that war is "one of the instruments of God's mysterious providence designed not to settle international disputes but (1) to purge society of a political regime and a social order which were decadent and doomed to destruction and (2) to supersede these with forms more vigorous and fit to live."[53] In effect, Park seemed to be saying that Hitler and the Nazis had carried Moltke's vision to its most deadly conclusion, creating and exploiting a mass movement more characteristic of a religious sect than of a secular political party, one that would burst asunder the moral restraints on war.

"Generally speaking," Park once observed, "one may say that war is politics."[54] The garrison state was the product of the amoral and inextricable coalescence of war with the total political reorganization of a society. Four years after he had coined the term, Lasswell conceived of a new and terrifying world order: "Consider the possibility that we are moving toward a world of 'garrison states'—a world in which the specialists on violence are the most powerful group in society."[55] As early as 1941, Lasswell had believed that a transition to garrison statehood was possible, indeed, probable for all of the major world powers, the central question being, merely, "What is the probable order of appearance—Japan, Germany, Russia, United States of America?"[56]

The garrison state heralded the onset of a kind of total war previously unimagined. By 1941, Lasswell had noted how the "growth of aerial warfare . . . has tended to abolish the distinction between civilian and military functions . . . and . . . [pointed out] that . . . in some periods of modern warfare, casualties among civilians may outnumber the casualties of the armed forces."[57] In such a situation, the ethical and juridical limitations that protected violence from becoming "absolute" would lose their force, and the older conception of wars as codified forms of combat would become obsolete.

In the same year, Park observed that what was now being called " 'total warfare' . . . is limited neither to the heavens above nor to the waters under the earth." Moreover, he went on to note, "with the advent of the 'new strategy of treachery and terror,' war has invaded the realm of the spirit."[58]

The Garrison State, Total War, and the Revival of Racism

The rise of garrison states in the modern world shifted the central attention of their political elites toward problems and policies of internal loyalty and national security. Park had taken special notice of this shift during World War I, while conducting his studies of United States governmental agencies' attempts to censor the writings and surveil the activities of immigrant peoples and alien leaders and associations.[59] Despite Germany's supporters' and spokesmen's several attempts to propagandize Americans toward neutrality or toward sympathy with the aims or philosophy animating the Central Powers, as well as such occasional acts of outright sabotage as the Black Tom explosion reportedly carried out by the Kaiser's secret agents in New York City and New Jersey,[60] Park advised against America sacrificing its world status as a democratic republic that stood for ethnic toleration and freedom of speech by succumbing before the fear-mongering advocates of the suppression of dissent. Although he was generally satisfied about Woodrow Wilson's wartime programs for securing the nation against espionage, sabotage, or disunifying propaganda, Park feared that postwar suspicions about Italian anarchists, Japanese invaders, and other alleged subversives of America's national interest would undermine the moral basis of America's enlightenment. Of the several national minorities in the United States of whom Park took special notice, none aroused his concern more than the Japanese.

Park's most general theory about America's modern urban civilization prophesied that the various folk cultures that made up its ghetto enclaves would eventually disappear, the peoples having become fully acculturated to and assimilated within its industrial, civic, and mass society. However, Park had been quick to notice that fears of military invasion by peoples of different color and alien culture were likely to inflame deeply rooted racial prejudices and, thus, retard the otherwise "natural" motion of these sociocultural processes. One people so stigmatized was the Japanese immigrant. In 1913, Park had dolefully predicted that "the Japanese ... is condemned to remain among us an abstraction, a symbol, and a symbol not merely of his own race, but of the Orient and of that vague,

ill-defined menace we sometime refer to as 'the yellow peril.' "[61] The
latter epithet had first been popularized by the German Kaiser in
1900, who may have sought to turn Europe's and America's attention
away from the threat presented by his own country's militarization
and toward the Far East and its "gelbe Gefahr."[62] As America moved
slowly toward its own development of garrison statehood, Park noticed the growth of what he regarded as an atavistic trend toward racialist hostility toward Japanese who had settled on the Pacific coast.

Park first voiced his fears about America's hostile policies and
prejudicial attitudes toward the Japanese in 1926, as he was coming
to comprehend the limits of the national state for encompassing the
concomitant global processes of economic interdependence and intercultural adjustment. Although America's racially restrictive policies—on immigration (the omnibus immigration act of 1924 had
halted virtually all emigration from Asia to America); on naturalization (the 1922 *Ozawa* case had judicially confirmed that United
States citizenship was available only to free white persons and persons of African descent); and on ownership of land and the formation of corporations (California and ten other states had enacted
"alien land laws" prohibiting persons classified as ineligible for citizenship, that is, Japanese and other Asians, to own land or form
corporate enterprises)—had created a situation in the United States
that Park believed was "distinctly racial" in character, he pointed
out that throughout the world "races and peoples are coming out of
their isolation, whether it be geographic, economic or political."[63]
America's racially restrictive legislation, Park went on to assert,
took no notice of these new global processes: "It is as if we had said:
Europe, of which after all America is a mere western projection,
ends here."[64] Such an anachronistic perspective, he suggested, constituted evidence of the American people's failure to realize that
evolution toward the formation of ethnically homogeneous state societies no longer described the trend of civic development. "In a
world in which every event, every significant gesture, reverberates
around the globe, the concept of national independence . . . becomes
a legal fiction."[65] Moreover, Park concluded, even if "America was
once in any exclusive sense the melting pot of races, it is [such] no
longer." "The melting pot," Park proclaimed, "is the world."[66]

Nevertheless, as it became clearer to him that global reformation
was occurring in defiance of economic interdependencies and in behalf of garrisoning the several competitive world powers, Park began
to reconsider what form the final outcome of intercultural associations would take. Until the late 1930s, Park had supposed that a

worldwide cycle of race and ethnic relations would culminate in assimilation, after passing through three consecutive stages of contact, competition, and accommodation.[67] A decade earlier, the situation affecting the Japanese in America had caused him to begin to have second thoughts: "The position of the Japanese in America [has] been completely undermined by the passage of the Alien Land Law. . . . The undertow of public sentiment, [is] carrying the Japanese in the United States, in spite of every effort to conciliate public opinion, into the same sort of social ghetto in which the Chinese before them had found refuge."[68] But it was in 1937, in a commentary on the larger implications of Romanzo Adams's study of interracial marriage in Hawaii—the farthest frontier of America in the Pacific; the place where, in 1926, Park had supposed that "all the races of the Pacific meet and mingle on more liberal terms than they do elsewhere"[69]— that Park gave up his conviction about the ultimate assimilation of everyone. Adams had predicted that the already developed harmony and growing assimilation of the various peoples making up the population of the island territory would continue so long as Hawaii did not become a focal point for international economic competition or aggressive conflict. If, however, "a military government were to be set up in place of the territorial [one]," he wrote, "it is probable that in respect to race relations there would be a reversal of practice. . . . If there should be a war it would modify the character of social relations temporarily and, maybe, for a long time."[70] Park, reflecting on this statement as well as on other global developments, concluded that, with respect to race relations, "it is not possible to predict with any certainty the final outcome, except that when stabilization is finally achieved race relations will assume one of three configurations. They will take the form of a caste system, as in India; they will terminate in complete assimilation, as in China; or the unassimilated race will constitute a permanent racial minority within the limits of a national state, as is the case of the Jews in Europe."[71] Making no prediction about the American outcome suggests that Park had lost confidence in what he had once regarded as the inevitability of the social process. Hawaii's and the rest of America's emerging garrison statehood was begun four years later, when the island territory was placed under military rule.

After the Second World War broke out, America's predominant fears about its own national security took the form of a distrust of the loyalty of certain ethnics among its own citizenry. The nation's sociologists were divided over the extent or even the existence of a problem. Talcott Parsons worried about the depth of patriotic commitment of all those who were not white Calvinists;[72] Herbert Blumer, on the other hand, urged that a ubiquitous desire to get the job over with constituted a sufficient incentive for Americans of all colors and creeds to carry on the war effort effectively.[73] Park's earlier concerns over the treatment of America's racial minorities during a time of great patriotic revival proved well founded. In accordance with President Franklin D. Roosevelt's Executive Order 9066, issued on February 19, 1942, all persons of Japanese descent residing in those portions of the Pacific coast under the command of Lieutenant-General John L. DeWitt were incarcerated in specially constructed places of detention originally called "concentration camps" but soon cosmetically redesignated "relocation centers."[74] Park's son-in-law, the anthropologist Robert Redfield, echoed his father-in-law's worries when he wrote, "The justification for talking about the impact of war on the Japanese-Americans lies rather in consideration of what has happened or may happen to all the rest of us as a result of the evacuation and confinement of the Japanese-Americans and in the larger issues which [this] smaller problem illustrates."[75]

Among the larger issues that Park addressed was the revival and reinforcement of age-old racial prejudices that accompanied America's assumption of garrison statehood but violated American principles of equity and freedom. Although the Japanese Americans were the only group to suffer wholesale arrest, detention, and suspension of their constitutionally guaranteed civil rights,[76] other peoples were also subjected to draconian policies or became victims of a collective paranoia that patriotic and xenophobic fears encouraged. For example, President Roosevelt, in collaboration with FBI Director J. Edgar Hoover, fought an unsuccessful battle throughout the war years to suppress, stifle, or censor the black press in America.[77] In the same period, Mexican Americans, derogated as "pachucos," were made the victims of numerous racist imprecations and were the objects of violent assaults, the worst of which was a mob attack, led by servicemen on leave, that came to be known as the Zoot-Suit Riot of 1943.[78] Some American Indian tribes resisted the government's demand that Amerindians enter military service under terms set in Washington, D.C.: the Iroquois, for example, claiming rights as a nation, declared war separately on the Axis powers;[79] "The Tunica, among other Louisiana Indians, objected to the military draft during World War II, claiming that only the tribe held sovereignty over its manpower and refus[ed] to let Tunica youths be inducted into segregated units, [but] virtually all the young men of that tribe went to war as volunteers."[80] Black American troops in the European theater of operations were segregated into battalions largely used for labor; when employed in combat situations, they were regarded—in the words of a postwar *Time Magazine* article about the all-Negro 92d Division—as having the "handicap of less-than-average literacy and more-than-average superstition";[81] while the efforts of the all black 332d Fighter group—The "Tuskegee Airmen"—went unsung.[82] The all-Nisei 442d Regimental Combat Team—that would emerge from the war with more military decorations than any other unit and with "The Purple Heart Battalion" as its nom de guerre because of its 9,486 dead and wounded members—was attached to the otherwise all-black 92d Division when it began its participation in the invasion of Italy;[83] another unit of Japanese American inductees became so demoralized over their fellow Nisei's treatment by the United States government that they were regarded as unfit for combat and kept on American soil throughout the war;[84] still other Nisei fought under the command of General Stilwell on the China-Burma-India front;[85] and eighty-five Nisei at the Heart Mountain internment camp went to prison as draft resisters, refusing to fight for a society that didn't trust its own citizens enough to allow them to live freely and openly in the places where they had settled.[86] Reviewing the racial situation in the United States in 1943, Park asserted that it could "all be summed up in one, or at least two phrases: 'This is a white man's country' [and] 'The Negro is all right in his place.' "[87] But, taking special note of how the wartime fears had exacerbated racialist sentiments, he went on to note how the antipathies and distrust of the Negro in the South had spread into the North and been extended to apply to other so-called colored peoples. "The difference is," he observed, "that in the South the Negroes have a place, if only they would stay in it; in the North, as far as there is any racial doctrine that could be described as orthodox, the Negro, the Indian, and the Asiatic have no place at all. They are merely more or less tolerated aliens."[88]

The focus of Park's analysis had come full circle. Beginning with a study of the implications of Germany's military modernization for that state's social development and for world peace, he laid the foundation for understanding the ensuing century's total wars and uncovered the character of what would become the garrison state. Germany's *Kulturkampf*—shorn of its enforcement in "blood and iron"—soon became an unacknowledged model for Park's and other American sociologists' theory of how America might absorb and incorporate its several immigrant and minority peoples.[89]

The process of assimilation—what Park once defined as a coordination of sentiments[90]—promised to bring about a national unity that would insure a common front in the face of international crises. However, as militarization and preparation for and participation in international wars came to take precedence over other issues, the trustworthiness that Park supposed should be granted to the peoples not yet fully a part of the much vaunted national consensus was withheld. Persons of alien culture and nonwhite color came to be especially suspect. In the Second World War, the United States entered the conflict reluctantly, ostensibly to preserve and protect the "Four Freedoms" and, in later statements of its war aims, to extend them to all the peoples in the world.[91] But, the aroused fears about disaffection, disunity, and disloyalty led not only to a suspension of those freedoms for select minorities,[92] but also to a climate of distrust that in the postwar years would find outlet in an anguished quest for absolute national security.

While concern for the loyalty of racial minorities diminished in the postwar years, fears about communists, liberals, intellectuals, students, and homosexuals seemed to deny that the idealized ethnonational consensus had taken place. Instead, a seemingly permanent condition of American garrison statehood—one that would not be challenged until the Soviet Union had quite literally disintegrated and Marxist ideology had been discredited—tended to encourage a continuation of surveillance over the thoughts and deeds of whatever portions of the citizenry seemed about to disattend, depart, or dissent from the putatively prevailing national ethos. Ironically, current conflicts, civil wars, and civil uprisings in South Africa, China, the Middle East, Eastern Europe, and the former Soviet Union, as well as in the United States, indicate that an end to the Cold War has not brought an end to ethnonational struggles. Neither America nor the world can reasonably look forward to a near time when there will occur a complete loss of racial or ethnic distinctiveness, or to a future global society in which a melt-down of the individuals of all nations has forged a new race embracing all of humankind.

Park's Sociology of War as a Tragedy of Culture

One reading of Park's sociological observations about war would interpret them as an uncompleted exemplar of Simmel's theses on the conflict and tragedy of culture. To engage this reading we must briefly explore Simmel's ideas about the cultural process. Simmel,

Park's only mentor in the discipline of sociology, had formulated a dialectical theory of culture, a cyclical dynamic that described the never-ending struggle of the effervescent stream of *life* against the *forms* which its spirit creates to enclose its content and encompass itself with order. "We speak of culture," Simmel observed, "whenever life produces certain forms in which it expresses and realizes itself: works of art, religions, sciences, technologies, laws, and innumerable others."[93] However, Simmel went on to point out, "left to itself . . . life streams on without interruption; its restless rhythm opposes the fixed duration of any particular form."[94] Thus it is the case that the true dynamic motoring the history of culture manifests itself as a dialectic of struggle: "Each cultural form, once it is created, is gnawed at varying rates by the forces of life."[95] Ultimately, life strives after release from all forms of itself.

In some respects, Park's sociology of conflict appears to follow Simmel's dialectic of culture. War, in Park's understanding of it, is one of the *forms* of conflict—a crude form, Park notes with bitterness, and one that "has as its goal . . . the drive for domination that causes a nation to test its power in war against other nations."[96] In perfecting that test, the avant-garde among the makers of war—military geniuses such as von Moltke—seek to liberate war from the rules of proprietary and humane conduct that constrain its fullest expression. By endowing war with the elementary characteristics of the sacred—Park pointed out that it was von Moltke who said that in war "the most noble virtues of men find their expression—courage as well as abnegation, fidelity to duty and even love and self-sacrifice"[97]—the new German military radicals had hoped to place it beyond the restraints imposed by the morality that appreciated a common humanity. These restraints had been codified in the international conventions that limited the technics and tactics of combat to those necessary for fighting against the enemy's armed forces. Demanding the right to burst the bonds that thereby held warfare back from realizing its own freedom of destructive action, von Moltke proclaimed the right to extend the field of combat to encompass the enemy's civilian population, culture, morale, and, in effect, every aspect of the enemy's basis for existence. War, the destroyer of life, would, in von Moltke's vision of it, become the agent of a statist *Kulturkampf*, and, in utterly annihilating the forces opposed to it, would realize a new ideal—that of the state conceived as "an individual . . . [with] a destiny which its actual existence serves to realize."[98]

The emancipation of war from the rules of war had led on the one hand to the concept and the reality of total war, and, on the other, to the reconstitution of the state as an instrument devoted to the realization of its own destiny through warfare. In such a state, patriotic self-sacrifice becomes not only the highest duty a citizen can perform, not only the exhibition of the noblest of national virtues, but in fact the veritable epitome of a sacrament. The freeing of war from the limits imposed on it by a commitment to humane morality was in effect signaled by von Moltke's designation of the mundane state as the earthly communion of God and, as such, the proper object of the citizen-soldier's inner-worldly faith—the thing for which he would sacrifice his life. Patristics had given way to patriotics: "War," said von Moltke, "is an institution of God, a principle of order in the world."[99]

Park had completed his doctoral dissertation in 1903. Four years later, Simmel, confronting the philosophies of Schopenhauer and Nietzsche, noted that in the premodern epoch Christianity's vision of the "salvation of the soul and the kingdom of God . . . became an offer of absolute value for the masses, a definitive goal beyond the meaninglessness of an individuated and fragmentary life." But, he went on to point out, "in recent centuries, Christianity [had] lost its appeal to and power over innumerable people." The decline of Christian faith, however, had deprived "life" of its "deep desire for an absolute goal." The unfilled gap of Christianity's heritage is "a need for a definitivum of life's moment, which has continued as an empty urge for a goal which has become inaccessible."[100] Park, who abjured philosophical abstraction, had already seen that the transvaluation of Christianity had, in Germany, taken the form of a sacralization of the militarized state, and that this transmogrification had introduced into the twentieth century a new entity, the warfare state.

Park did not live to see the end of the Second World War nor to record its effects on the changes in state formation that America's victory would entail. That he had a dark premonition of the unhappy shape of things to come was indicated three and one-half months before the attack on Pearl Harbor, when he explained to Louis Wirth about the qualms he had over signing a petition relating to the war: "I am . . . unreservedly in favor of supporting the President and the policy of the government in the crisis. . . . I am in favor of militarism in the United States, not only for the present emergency but for all the other emergencies I see looming up."[101] However, Park worried over the implications of that militarism for America's moral order and its place in what he supposed would be a cockpit of postwar nations at odds with one another. In 1943 he would warn America of the dire necessity to solve the race question in terms of a recognized equality of all peoples and a granting of the full panoply of civil rights to its nonwhite and non-Anglo minorities. Moreover, he warned, America should not presume too much on the benevolence of the world, nor should it seek allies in its restricted world mission. In 1941, he had told Wirth that he did not "favor . . . any permanent or temporary alliance with England or Russia which will impose on us the necessity or the moral obligation of enforcing terms of peace that require us to police the world."[102]

A sociologist with a global vision, Park focused attention on how America's foreign policies related to its domestic programs of social amelioration. In 1939, he observed that "the whole world is living in a kind of symbiosis; but the world community is at present, at least, quite incapable of collective action."[103] Although Park believed that "the web of life which holds within its meshes all living organisms is visibly tightening, and there is in every part of the world . . . a growing interdependence of all living creatures,"[104] he pointed out that "on the political level the freedom and competition of individuals is still further limited by the express recognition of the superior and sovereign interests and rights of the state."[105] For Park, the struggle for a free and interdependent life uniting all the peoples of the world—a struggle that seemed about to complete itself as "the incorporation of all the peoples of the earth in a world-wide economy"—had "laid the foundation for the rising world-wide political and moral order."[106] But this new world society would not—or, in Park's view, ought not—be organized as a victor's spoil of a worldwide war, nor should it be policed by the United States.

NOTES

This essay originally appeared in The International Journal of Politics, Culture and Society, 3:4 (Summer 1990), pp. 565–86.

1. Robert E. Park, "The German Army: The Most Perfect Military Organization in the World," Munsey's Magazine, 24:3 (Dec. 1900), pp. 376–95.

2. Friedrich Meinecke, The German Catastrophe: Reflections and Recollections, trans. Sidney B. Fay (Boston: Beacon Press, 1963. Orig. pub. 1950), pp. 9–10.

3. Friedrich Meinecke, The Age of German Liberation, 1795–1815, ed. Peter Paret, trans. Peter Paret and Helmuth Fischer (Berkeley: University of California Press, 1977), p. 128.

4. Quoted in Hans Kohn, "Introduction to the Harbinger Edition," Heinrich von Treitschke, Politics, abr. and ed. Hans Kohn, trans. Blanche Dugdale and Torbende Bille (New York: Harcourt, Brace and World, Inc., 1963), p. xxi.

5. See Robert A. Pois, *Friedrich Meinecke and German Politics in the Twentieth Century* (Berkeley: University of California Press, 1972), p. 122.

6. Meinecke, *German Catastrophe*, 15. Meinecke's attitude toward the Jews is described by Pois (*Friedrich Meinecke*, p. 123) as that of a "social anti-Semite": "Meinecke might well have been very willing to have Jewish friends and students, presumably as long as each was possessed of a 'German heart'; however, his attitude toward the Jews as a group was decidedly prejudiced, and Nazi persecution of them never seems to have bothered him very much."

7. Treitschke, *Politics*, 132.

8. Ibid., 126–27.

9. Ibid., 133.

10. Ibid., 129.

11. Ibid., 124. Treitschke, like so many others of his day—and, alas, of our own—seems to have been unaware of the imposing civilizations that had flourished in Africa in pre-colonial times. For some representative correctives, see two works of Cheikh Anta Diop, *The African Origin of Civilization: Myth or Reality*, trans. Mercer Cook (New York: Lawrence Hill, 1974); and *Precolonial Black Africa: A Comparative Study of the Political and Social Systems of Europe and Black Africa, from Antiquity to the Formation of Modern States*, trans. Harold Salemson (Westport, Conn.: Lawrence Hill, 1987); J. C. de Graft-Johnson, *African Glory: The Story of Vanished Negro Civilizations* (New York: Walker and Co., 1954); and two works by Basil Davidson, *The Lost Cities of Africa* (Boston: Little-Brown, 1959); and *The African Past: Chronicles from Antiquity* (New York: Grosset and Dunlap, 1964).

12. See Hajo Holborn, "The Prusso-German School: Moltke and the Rise of the General Staff"; and Gunther E. Rothenberg, "Moltke, Schlieffen, and the Doctrine of Strategic Envelopment," both in Peter Paret, with the collaboration of Gordon Craig and Felix Gilbert, eds., *Makers of Modern Strategy: From Machiavelli to the Nuclear Age* (Princeton: Princeton University Press, 1986), pp. 281–95, 296–325.

13. Park, "German Army," p. 385.

14. Ibid., p. 386.

15. Robert E. Park, "The Crowd and the Public," trans. Charlotte Elsner, in Park, *The Crowd and the Public and Other Essays*, ed. Henry Elsner, Jr. (Chicago: University of Chicago Press, 1972), p. 53.

16. Quoted in Winifred Raushenbush, *Robert E. Park: Biography of a Sociologist* (Durham, N.C.: Duke University Press, 1979), p. 80.

17. Robert E. Park, *The Immigrant Press and Its Control* (New York: Harper and Brothers, 1922; reprint, Montclair, N.J.: Patterson Smith, 1971), p. 412.

18. Park, "German Army," p. 393.

19. Ibid., p. 382.

20. Meinecke, *Age of German Liberation*, p. 98.

21. Hans Kohn, "Notes," in Treitschke, *Politics*, p. 321 n. 7.

22. Park, "German Army," p. 382.

23. Ibid., p. 393.

24. Hans Speier, *German White Collar Workers and the Rise of Hitler* (New Haven: Yale University Press, 1986), p. 32.

25. Hans Speier, *Social Order and the Risks of War: Papers in Political Sociology* (New York: George W. Stewart, 1952), p. 293.

26. Park, "German Army," p. 393.

27. Ibid., pp. 385–86.

28. Ibid., p. 393.

29. Ibid., p. 395.

30. Ibid.

31. Robert E. Park, "War and Politics," *American Journal of Sociology*, 46 (Jan. 1941). pp. 551–70. Quotations that follow are paginated according to the reprint of this essay in Robert E. Park, *Society: Collective Behavior, News and Opinion, Sociology and Modern Society*, ed. Everett Cherrington Hughes et al. (Glencoe, Ill.: The Free Press, 1955), pp. 50–68.

32. Ibid., p. 51.

33. Ibid., p. 52.

34. Ibid., pp. 52, 53.

35. Ibid., p. 53.

36. Ibid., p. 54.

37. Ibid., p. 55.

38. Park, "The Crowd and the Public," p. 14 n. 21.

39. Ibid., p. 73.

40. Robert E. Park, "Modern Society," *Biological Symposia* 8 (Lancaster, Penn.: The Jacques Catell Press, 1942), pp. 217–40. The quotations here and below are from the reprint in Park, *Society*, p. 336.

41. Park, "Morale and the News," in Park, *Society*, p. 137.

42. Ibid., p. 136.

43. Ibid.

44. Ibid., p. 138.

45. Park, "Symbiosis and Socialization . . . ," in Robert E. Park, *Human Communities: The City and Human Ecology: The Collected Papers of Robert Ezra Park*, vol. 2, ed. E. C. Hughes et al. (Glencoe, Ill.: The Free Press, 1952), p. 246.

46. Park, "War and Politics," p. 55.

47. Michael Geyer, "German Strategy in the Age of Machine Warfare, 1914–1945," in Paret, *Makers of Modern Strategy*, pp. 537–38.

48. General Erich Ludendorff, *The Nation at War* (London: n.p., 1936), p. 54. Quoted in Park, "War and Politics," p. 55 n. 8.

49. Park, "War and Politics," p. 55.

50. George Herbert Mead, "National-Mindedness and International Mindedness," *International Journal of Ethics*, 39 (July 1929), pp. 400–404. Quoted in Park, "War and Politics," p. 55.

51. Park, "Morale and the News," p. 139.

52. Ibid.

53. Park, "War and Politics," p. 57.

54. Ibid., p. 68.

55. Harold Lasswell, "The Garrison State," *American Journal of Sociology*, 46, (Jan. 1941), pp. 455–68. Quotations here and below are from the reprint in Dwaine Marvick, ed., *Harold D. Lasswell on Political Sociology* (Chicago: University of Chicago Press, 1977), pp. 165–78, at p. 165.

56. Harold Lasswell and Abraham Kaplan, *Power and Society: A Framework for Political Inquiry* (New Haven: Yale University Press, 1950), p. 175.

57. Lasswell, "Garrison State," p. 168.

58. Park, "War and Politics," p. 53.

59. Park, *Immigrant Press and Its Control*, pp. 359–468.

60. See Jules Witcover, *Sabotage at Black Tom: Imperial Germany's Secret War in America, 1914–1917* (Chapel Hill: Algonquin Books, 1989).

61. Robert E. Park, "Racial Assimilation in Secondary Groups with Particular Reference to the Negro," *American Journal of Sociology*, 13 (Mar. 1914), pp. 606–19.

62. Richard Austin Thompson, *The Yellow Peril, 1890–1924* (New York: Arno Press, 1978), pp. 1–6.

63. Robert E. Park, "Our Racial Frontier on the Pacific," *Survey Graphic*, 56 (May 1926), p. 194.

64. Ibid., p. 192.

65. Ibid., p. 195.

66. Ibid., p. 196.

67. Ibid.

68. Robert E. Park, "Behind Our Masks," *Survey Graphic*, 56 (May 1, 1926), p. 135.

69. Park, "Our Racial Frontier on the Pacific," p. 196.

70. Romanzo Adams, *Interracial Marriage in Hawaii: A Study of the Mutually Conditioned Processes of Acculturation and Amalgamation* (New York: Macmillan, 1937; reprint, Montclair, N.J.: Patterson Smith, 1969), p. 326.

71. Park, "Introduction," in Adams, *Interracial Marriage*, p. xiii.

72. See William Buxton, *Talcott Parsons and the Capitalist Nation-State: Political Sociology as a Strategic Vocation* (Toronto: University of Toronto Press, 1985), pp. 97–116.

73. Herbert Blumer, "Morale," in *American Society in Wartime*, ed. William Fielding Ogburn (Chicago: University of Chicago Press, 1943; reprint, New York: Da Capo Press, 1972), pp. 207–32. See also the discussion in Stanford M. Lyman and Arthur J. Vidich, *Social Order and the Public Philosophy: An Analysis and Interpretation of the Work of Herbert Blumer* (Fayetteville: University of Arkansas Press, 1988), pp. 42–55.

74. *Final Report. Japanese Evacuation from the West Coast, 1942* (Washington, D.C.: United States Government Printing Office, 1943). p. 515 et passim; Roger Daniels, *Asian America: Chinese and Japanese in the United States since 1850* (Seattle: University of Washington Press, 1988), pp. 227–28.

75. Robert Redfield, "The Japanese-Americans," in Ogburn, ed., *American Society*, p. 145.

76. See Jacobus ten Broek, Edward N. Barnhart, and Floyd Matson, *Prejudice, War and the Constitution* (Berkeley: University of California Press, 1954), pp. 211–336; and *Personal Justice Denied: Report of the Commission on Wartime Relocation and Internment of Civilians* (Washington, D.C.: United States Government Printing Office, 1982).

77. Patrick S. Washburn, *A Question of Sedition: The Federal Government's Investigation of the Black Press during World War II* (New York: Oxford University Press, 1986).

78. Mauricio Mazon, *The Zoot-Suit Riots: The Psychology of Symbolic Annihilation* (Austin: University of Texas Press, 1984).

79. Michael G. Lacy, "The United States and American Indians: Political Relations," in *American Indian Policy in the Twentieth Century*, ed. Vine Deloria, Jr. (Norman: University of Oklahoma Press, 1985), p. 92.

80. Fred B. Kniffen, Hiram F. Gregory, and George A. Stokes, *The Historic Indian Tribes of Louisiana from 1542 to the Present* (Baton Rouge: Louisiana State University Press, 1987), p. 296.

81. *Time Magazine*, October 23, 1950, p. 29. Quoted in *The Invisible Soldier: The Experience of the Black Soldier, World War II*, comp. and ed. Mary Penick Motley (Detroit: Wayne State University Press, 1975), p. 258.

82. Charles E. Francis, *The Tuskegee Airmen: The Men Who Changed a Nation* (Boston: Branden Publishing Co., 1988).

83. Orville C. Shirey, *Americans: The Story of the 442nd Combat Team* (Washington, D.C.: Infantry Journal Press, 1946), pp. 101–51. Motley, comp. and ed., *Invisible Soldier*, pp. 259–60; John Hersey, " 'A Mistake of Terrifically Horrible Proportions,' " in John Armor and Peter Wright, *Manzanar: Photographs by Ansel Adams* (New York: Random House–Time Books, 1988), p. 35.

84. Tamotsu Shibutani, *The Derelicts of Company K: A Sociological Study of Demoralization* (Berkeley: University of California Press, 1978).

85. United States Department of the Interior, War Agency Liquidation Unit, *People in Motion: The Postwar Adjustment of the Evacuated Japanese Americans* (Washington, D.C.: United States Government Printing Office, n.d.), p. 18; Audrie Girdner and Anne Loftis, *The Great Betrayal: The Evacuation of the Japanese-Americans during World War II* (London: Collier-Macmillan, 1969), pp. 332–35, 379.

86. George Johnston, "Heart Mountain's Fair Play Committee: So. Calif. JACLers Throw Spotlight on Nisei W.W. II Draft Resistance Movement," *Pacific Citizen*, 109 (Sept. 8, 1989), pp. 1, 10, 12.

87. Park, "Racial Ideologies," in Ogburn, ed., *American Society*, p. 176.

88. Ibid.

89. See Arthur J. Vidich and Stanford M. Lyman, *American Sociology: Worldly Rejections of Religion and Their Directions* (New Haven: Yale University Press, 1985), pp. 94, 100 n. 5, 192–93, 205–6, 238–42, 283–84.

90. Park, "Racial Assimilation in Secondary Groups," in *Race and Culture,* pp. 204–9.

91. For a British "realist" analysis of these aims, see Peter Calvocoressi, Guy Wint, and John Pritchard, *Total War: Causes and Courses of the Second World War,* rev. 2d ed. (New York: Pantheon Books, 1989), pp. 298–99. For an ironic treatment of the "Four Freedoms" slogan and other patriotic pronouncements of the period, see Paul Fussell, *Wartime: Understanding and Behavior in the Second World War* (New York: Oxford University Press, 1989), pp. 143–80.

92. See John W. Dower, *War without Mercy: Race and Power in the Pacific War (New York: Pantheon Books, 1986).*

93. Georg Simmel, 'The Conflict in Modern Culture," in Simmel, *The Conflict in Modern Culture and Other Essays,* trans. and ed. K. Peter Etzkorn (New York: Teachers College Press, 1968), p. 11.

94. Ibid.

95. Ibid.

96. Park, *The Crowd and the Public,* p. 53.

97. Park, "German Army," p. 395.

98. Park, *The Crowd and the Public,* pp. 70–71.

99. Park, "German Army," p. 395.

100. Georg Simmel, *Schopenhauer and Nietzsche,* trans. Helmut Loiskandl, Deena Weinstein, and Michael Weinstein, (Amherst: University of Massachusetts Press, 1986), p. 5.

101. Raushenbush, *Robert E. Park,* p. 168.

102. Ibid.

103. Park, "Symbiosis and Socialization: A Frame of Reference for the Study of Society," in Park, *Human Communities,* p. 242.

104. Ibid., p. 253.

105. Ibid.

106. Ibid., p. 260.

3

Robert E. Park's Congo Papers:
A Gothic Perspective on Capitalism
and Imperialism

In a recently published personal reminiscence of Robert E. Park that also contains a subtle critique of his place among the master-thinkers of the sociological discipline, Edward Shils asserts that Park's "work would have had a longer life if he had been able to draw on Max Weber's writings in *Wirtschaft und Gesellschaft* and the *Gesammelte Aufsätze zur Religionssociologie,* and if he had studied and pondered Durkheim's and Mauss's writings."[1] Of course, Park was not unaware of Weber's *verstehende* sociology—he referred to it in one of his writings in the 1930s[2]—nor was he ignorant of the contributions of Durkheim and Mauss to sociological thought—in the index to the famous "Green Bible," that is, the *Introduction to the Science of Sociology* by Park and Ernest W. Burgess, to which Shils finds occasion to refer in another part of his essay,[3] Durkheim is referenced in twenty-five places and Mauss in two.[4] The problem does not arise because of any lacunae in Park's reading; indeed, Shils has mis-stated the issue. Currently, Park's work is in process of devaluation—for example, Lewis Coser has consigned his efforts to those of "a great teacher who managed to inspire his students . . . [but who] wrote relatively little himself . . . [and who] was content . . . to develop a series of general ideas and sensitizing concepts"[5]—and diminution—for example, the fifteen references to Park in Neil Smelser's edition of *The Handbook of Sociology* mention, and then only briefly and usually to criticize, his conception of "emotional contagion"; his ecological and biotic orientation to the study of the city; his sociology of the media; his idea of social control, and his approach to collective behavior and social movements[6]—even though much of it has never been examined for its potential for sociological theory. This is especially the case with respect to the essays, investigations, and research studies that Park wrote between 1900 and 1913, that is, in the more than a dozen productive years before he began his professional academic career at the University of Chicago.[7]

One reason advanced to justify the discipline's division of Park's career into two separate phases—the early years, 1887–1912, during which he alternately worked as a reporter on various newspapers in the midwest and in New York City, studied at Harvard, Berlin, Heidelberg, and Strassburg, and labored anonymously as Booker T. Washington's ghostwriter and amanuensis; and the later period, 1913–44, when he served as a professional academician at the University of Chicago and Fisk University in Nashville, Tennessee—derives from the modern sociologists' desire to legitimate the scientific character of their enterprise and to establish a greater intellectual distance between it and investigative journalism. Scientific ambitions, in turn, have given impetus to various folkways of scientism. In the social sciences in general and sociology in particular, research is all too often associated with the transmogrification of knowledge into numbers and the reification of the latter into the simulacra of theory.[8] Park's career as an academician was confounded by this disciplinary hubris. On the one hand, he sought to dissociate sociology from social reform—which he perceived as a Protestant-based meddling in the private lives of ordinary—and extraordinary—individuals and groups.[9] On the other, he sought to ground the discipline in a diachronically oriented direct empiricism, and in its potential for transposing the data of human experience into a conceptual understanding of the secular social processes at work therein. As Park put it in an autobiographical note found after his death, "According to my earliest conception of a sociologist, he was to be a kind of superreporter, like the men who write for *Fortune*. He was to report a little more accurately, and in a manner a little more detached than the average . . . the 'Big News.' The 'Big News' was the long-time trends which recorded what is actually going on rather than what, on the surface of things, merely seems to be going on."[10] The now commonplace division of his work into early and unsociological journalism and sociological studies in human ecology, urban sociology, race relations, and collective behavior vitiates the very basis of his life and works.

To his credit, Shils does not fall victim to the conventional bifurcation of Park's career at an unnatural joint—"The line of succession of the phases of Park's life," he writes, "was, despite the vagaries of his professional career, as straight as the line of growth of his intellectual interests and accomplishments. It was a line of continuous expansion of experience and knowledge in very diverse situations, all in the service of a coherent, internally consistent and constantly deepening understanding."[11] But, Shils does not recognize the civilizational perspective that Park brought to bear on both the discipline and its topic, human society.[12] Like other critics, he conceives Park's uncompleted project to have been a comprehensive theory of human ecology and of collective behavior. Moreover, Shils contends that Park's concern for the "interestingness of concrete events could not always or even frequently be bound down and articulated," that Park "cared more for the search for answers than for the answer itself," and that these are the reasons "why Park's vision of society—a very profound and true one—could not be passed on easily to succeeding generations of scholars."[13] But Shils neglects to point out how the twin forces of scientism and professionalism—the former in the half-century long hegemonically paired paradigms of positivism and functionalism;[14] the latter in the bureaucratic controls over research attempted successively by the Social Science Research Council and by the discipline's professional cadre[15]—have made Park's kind of sociology at the very least unfashionable and in some quarters even quaint.[16] A case in point is Lewis Coser's attempt to depict the history of American sociology by means of a developmentalist metaphor of organic growth[17] that likens the period of the preeminence of the Chicago School under Park and W. I. Thomas to the discipline's babyhood. Asserting that "the appearance of Talcott Parson's [sic] The Structure of Social Action [in 1937] heralded the emergence of a theoretical orientation considerably at variance with that developed at the University of Chicago," Coser exults in his conclusion that "having passed through a period of incubation during the years of Chicago dominance, sociology could embark on its mature career."[18] Shils doesn't adopt Coser's explanation; instead, he credits the failure of Park's vision to be routinized in the discipline to the doleful Zeitgeist of the 1930s, to the low quality of graduate students attracted to Park, or to the latter's teaching methods: "The authors of the classic monographs [that Park had supervised] wrote very little after they left Chicago," he asserts. "Perhaps the times were too disheartening, perhaps sociology did not attract first-class graduate students, perhaps Park was too powerful, too unrelenting a supervisor. In any case, the 'Chicago School' faded out after his departure."[19]

By locating Park's work at Chicago as constituting the childhood stage of the discipline's history, Coser in effect relegates the pre-Chicago writings of Park to sociology's prehistory, or to continue his biological metaphor, to its fetal stage. Just as today's pro-choice advocates insist on defining the fetus as an entity that exists before the onset of true life, thus permitting its abortion without subjecting the mother to a charge of murder, so the users of the growth and development metaphor for sociology would—if, indeed, they even knew about the early published investigations of Robert E. Park— subject them to an academic equivalent of a disciplinary abortion, pronouncing them "pre-sociological," "subjective," and "journalistic," and thus not fit to be a part of sociology's living canon. Indeed, the virtual exclusion of all of Park's writings before 1913 from the imprimatur of sociology's master reading lists, the nearly universal ignorance of the content of these works, and the insistence on dating Park's career as a sociologist from the time he joined the faculty of the department of sociology at the University of Chicago has legitimated such an "abortion."

Park's sociology, it would seem to any reader of the conventional literature on the subject, emerged de novo, as a newborn infant and went through its "incubation" period, maturation, and death at Chicago in a period of little more than two decades, without any reference to its already dead "siblings," that is, Park's study of the German army, published in 1900; his five essays (one designating Booker T. Washington as the author) detailing the atrocities committed by the agents of Belgium's King Leopold II in the Congo; and his three reports of the economic, social, and community organization of African Americans in Alabama and North Carolina.[20] The projects carried out in the first half of his life—Park was fifty years old when he went to the University of Chicago—have been severed from the rest of his professional career. In the case of Park, sociology has not merely forgotten much of the work of one of its masterbuilders—as Robert K. Merton suggested it do for all of its founders[21]—it never even learned what it was supposed to erase from its disciplinary memory.

Sociology and Evil: Park's Version of a Sociodicy

At the turn of the nineteenth century, as sociology emerged from its immersion in German romantic philosophy,[22] its academicians still clung to its baptism in American Protestant thought, seeking to infuse the latter with the trappings of positive science.[23] In any event, a transvalued and secularizing sociology would have to come to terms with the existence of evil in the world.[24] While such mainstream sociologists as Franklin Henry Giddings would see the need to imperialize an Anglo-American empire in order to spread the blessings of democracy to the more benighted peoples of the world,[25] and less cosmopolitan members of the fledgling science of society, for example, Charles R. Henderson, would conceive what was then called the Social Question in terms of the societal treatment appropriate for its socially dependent, mentally defective, and civilly delinquent members,[26] Robert E. Park would approach the matter from a global and civilizational perspective. While still a graduate student in Germany, he published a study of the German army[27] that not only presented a brief but incisive analysis of the organizational innovations effected by Helmuth von Moltke, the Elder (1800–1891), but also pointed to the emerging militarization that was accompanying the rise of other modern ethnonational states and adumbrated his lifelong concerns about what would come to be called the century of total war.[28] Beginning in 1904 and continuing through 1907, Park published five studies (four under his own name) on the situation in the Congo, elaborating a theme—to be discussed in the balance of this essay—of Gothic horror associated with the spread of religiously and commercially inspired capitalist imperialism. In 1905,[29] 1908,[30] and 1913[31] he published studies of the economic condition and social standards of black life in Winston-Salem, North Carolina, and about the social effects of Booker T. Washington's agricultural extension program in Tuskegee, Alabama. These investigations stand in obverse relation to his Congo papers, revealing in effect the double-sided legacy of the Protestant ethic—on the one side, its spirit of brutal exploitation of dark-skinned, nonindustrial peoples in the name of missionary endeavor; on the other, its spirit of uplift, thrift, frugality, and temperance, applied to America's former slaves and their descendants in the rural South.

Reading Park's Congo papers together with his studies of black life in the South permits one to perceive in the total corpus an as yet unacknowledged extension of the Weber thesis. Park, as is well known, did not study with Weber. However, in light of the possibilities emanating from an interpretation of these early writings, his stature in the discipline should be reconsidered. One aspect of that reconsideration should focus on his Gothic approach to imperialism. Park's contribution to a new sociodicy is made manifest in his remarkable understanding of how evil and good might flow from the same fount.

A Gothic Perspective on Capitalist Imperialism

During the years 1904 to 1907, Park published four signed essays on the Congo situation as well as one additional essay that he ghosted for Booker T. Washington, for whom he worked as a private secretary.[32] Although these essays have never been treated as part of Park's sociological oeuvre—the first one never appears on any bibliography of Park's writings; the ghosted one is often uncredited to him—they constitute an elementary form of what could be developed as an ideational critique of capitalist imperialism. In their original form they present a case study in what I shall call a Gothic sociology of that form of imperialism. Gothic sociology is a critical as well as explanatory perspective that holds that capitalism in both its domestic and imperialist aspects constitutes an institutionalized instance of a metaphysical horror. That horror arises out of the evil underside of the Protestant ethic.

Gothic sociology had an elementary but unspecified formulation in the writings of Marx and Weber, but it has yet to be fully developed as an autonomous perspective. Marx's contribution consists in his recognition of the unique and uncanny power of money, valueless in and of itself, to transform anything into its opposite. A promising insight, derived, as Marx would acknowledge, from Shakespeare's *Timon of Athens*, it is less directly related to Park's subsequent formulations than those of Weber, and, hence need not detain us further.[33] Insisting that the onset of a Protestant-inspired capitalism had brought about a separation of the greedy pursuit of gain from the ascetic pursuit of profit, Weber pointed to the occult creature that Puritanism's dictates against laying up treasures on earth has spawned—the firm, or corporation. A corporation could seek after "profit, and forever renewed profit by means of continuous, rational, capitalistic enterprise."[34] A corporation did not have to fear for its salvation; for although a corporation is recognized as a legal person, it lacks two qualities inextricably associated with human persons: it does not have a soul, and conditional upon its ability to earn profits, it is immortal. In effect, the corporation is, paradoxically, the product of a blasphemous commission of the sin of pride—usurping God's power to create beings—but brought into existence in order to comply with religious mandates. As a "person" who is soulless and immortal, the corporation conducts itself like the fictional vampire it so figuratively resembles. It roams the earth in search of new sources of its élan vital—abject labor power that it can exploit to earn more life-renewing profits.

Park's contribution to Gothic sociology is largely empirical; he took his point of departure directly from the Gothic metaphor and focused critical attention on the macabre and malevolent aspects of monarchical, capitalist imperialism. In 1904–7, when he wrote his four signed (and one ghosted) essays on the Congo, Park hoped to awaken the public conscience so that action would be taken to halt Belgian King Leopold's depredations in the Congo Free State. Park employed a rhetoric that resonated with the popular interest in Gothic occultism and its demonological war against a supposedly benevolent Christianity. For Park, who would later attest to the importance of arousing nonrational beliefs as springs to action,[35] employment of the fantastical imagery of Gothic imagination served a definite purpose: it exposed the dark and unconscionable activities of a real-life human vampire masquerading as a civilized and Christian monarch.

"A new figure looms large on the horizon of Europe! A figure strange, fantastic and ominous—the king who is capitalist, *le roi d'affaires;* the man who unites in himself the political and social prestige of a reigning monarch with the vast material power of a multimillionaire."[36] So opens the second of Park's four signed essays on the Congo. In writing these essays Park had three aims: to remove the mask of Christian piety with which King Leopold cloaked his crimes against Congolese humanity; to expose to the destructive rays of factual light the real-life vampire-king who was literally and figuratively sucking the lifeblood out of the hapless natives of Central Africa; and to show how the devices of modern propaganda and publicity are employed to cover up atrocities. Park's usage of Gothic imagery not only challenged King Leopold's claim to trusteeship over the Congo, but is also proactive. In effect it raises questions about the legitimacy and morality of the entire enterprise of modern capitalist imperialism.

Park's essays follow the scenario of Gothic novels.[37] A serious crime has gone unpunished; a preternatural criminal has become a usurper of the hero-victim's rightful place in the sociopolitical order; the victim of the malefactor's usurpation is in abject circumstances, persecuted still by the as yet unexposed evildoer, and unable to understand or to remedy his or her own situation. But a chain of explanations and circumstances, some of them scientific, others uncanny, works to reveal the true character of the villain, who is eventually overthrown. In the denouement of early Gothic fiction, the victim's stolen patrimony is returned to him, and, by implication, the legitimate hierarchy of power and authority is restored. However, Park's rendition of the real-life-and-death sociological Gothic of the Congo depicts the villain, King Leopold II, more like those of later Gothic fiction in that he, like Count *Dracula* (1897), has evoked a Mephistophelian fascination about himself, while his victims remain in a state of misery that could go on indefinitely.

Like the Gothic mysteries that they so much resemble, Park's four signed Congo essays (as well as the essay he wrote for Booker T. Washington) proceed to unmask the villain. First, he reveals the "crime" committed by Leopold before the latter's Congo venture. Insulated by a carefully cultivated cloak of false Christian piety and the belief that he reigned over a tiny and powerless kingdom, Leopold had converted these weaknesses into international imperial assets. As Park is at pains to show, Leopold's carefully promoted counter-image—as an abstemious old man who rises each day at 5:00 A.M., drinks only water or warm tea, eats sparingly, disposes of his early morning correspondence while taking moderate bodily exercise, goes on three or four solitary walks a day, is punctilious about appointments, has "an extraordinary sense for details," and is "abrupt with his employees, dry with his orderlies, and inflexible with his ministers"[38]—is a mask over his character and intentions. For Park, Leopold personifies the new man of power in the modern world, the predatory but bureaucratic monarch-manager whose actions foreshadow the new modes of evil—modes that Hannah Arendt would more than fifty years later characterize as "banal"[39]—that were beginning to shape and shake the foundations of the twentieth century. As a king in business, the fact that Leopold had "put himself at the head of the Belgian group of financiers and [had] led the crusade for foreign concessions"[40] made him the personification of burgeoning Gothic capitalist imperialism—one who surveys the earth for its potentiality of yielding up new economic life-blood to replenish that of the undead-but-not-soulfully-alive corporate entity that he headed.

Park detailed the intricate manner in which Leopold had succeeded as an inner-worldly vampire-financier-king. Once begun, Leopold's quest to secure markets for Belgium's manufactures moved like that of the vampire bat in Stoker's and others' Gothic fiction. The Belgian monarch had achieved such great world financial power "that there is not [now] a spot on the globe where the weakness or rottenness of local government has cast the scent of concessions on the air that Belgians are not already settled, or hovering about expectantly."[41]

In Park's version of his machinations, Leopold himself acts much like the villainous characters in Gothic fiction. Noble in birth but outwardly seeming to be little more than a powerless potentate among the great powers of Europe, King Leopold II eventually secured for himself and his coterie of venture capitalists a venomous control over many of Europe's colonial possessions, concessions, and foreign investments. Park's analysis of Leopold's nefarious scheme to take over the construction of the Pekin-Hankow railway provides a veritable Gothic case study, involving a weak and decadent Chinese government, the less than honorable British, French, and Russian concession-seekers, Leopold's brokerage service offered to all parties to the struggle, and a conclusion in which the seemingly benevolent evildoers win out not only over their jealous but inept opponents but also over the Occident's innocent (or ignorant) bystanders.

With his foreign venture corporate capitalism always in need of its life-renewing blood supply, abject labor power, Leopold next undertook to take control over the hapless peoples of Central Africa. Like a fictional Gothic figure, he masked his true aims behind a cloak of benevolence—Christian missionary endeavor. True to his task of ripping away the layers of masquerade that covered Leopold's most horrific villainies, Park tears off Leopold's veil of virtue, revealing the monarch's—and by extension, modernity's—true nature. Leopold, Park shows, had put himself at the head of "the most unique government on earth, a commercial monopoly farmed by an autocrat."[42] Hidden behind the persona of a religious and progressive "royal Captain of Industry," Leopold had succeeded in obtaining absolute and cruel sway over the Congolese people. "Leopold," Park notes, "says that the results are civilization. The missionaries say they are hell. *But everybody admits that they are profitable.*"[43]

An unfeeling bureaucratic control over and a callous oppression of dependent peoples for the purpose of garnering ever-greater profits constitute the elementary forms of Gothic capitalist imperialism. Precisely by interposing a soulless corporate being—that is, what Max Weber had recognized as the new form of the firm—between themselves and their objectives, imperialist capitalists had imparted a banality to their evil practices that would both cloak and characterize their atrociousness. In its early years of capitalist development, Belgium, Park points out, had become a country immersed in business. But, he notes, when Leopold insured that the Congo stocks earned enormous dividends on the Antwerp market, took the lead in the formation and aggrandizement of the country's foreign concessions, and opened up Africa and Asia for Belgian manufactures, he virtually converted his role as a pre-capitalist monarch into that of a business corporation's general manager and turned his Continental subjects into his loyal national stockholders. The king had become both the personification and the chief executive officer of the imperial corporation. In so doing, he had manifested in himself the agent of Gothic capitalism—the vampire.

The transformation of king into vampiric corporate manager had inured Leopold against both accusations of moral default and most of the obligations and ethics traditionally associated with monarchy. "We expect personal dignity, intelligent consideration, justice, and the like from a king," Park observed. "We ask only one thing of a General Manager—dividends."[44] The Belgian public had become so conscienceless about and insensitive to the sufferings of Leopold's Congolese victims "because," Park concluded, "they recognize in him the General Manager." He went on, "Those who have not bowed to the prerogative of the king have yielded to the imperious necessities of business."[45] King Leopold was, as Park put it, "the crowned incarnation of the aspirations of a business people and a business age."[46]

The cruel usurpation of the Congo people's land, Park indicated, had been followed by a murderous exploitation of their labor. It was Park's point that it was the supposedly progressive practices of modern civilization, justified by a wedding of commercialism to Christianity—and not Africa's alleged heathenism or the atavistic practices attributed by anthropologists and travelers to the Congolese people—that had brought all this about. Park's refusal to add his voice to the chorus of support for Joseph Conrad's imagery of Africa—for example, Conrad's descriptions of the continent as "the other world," of a voyage up the Congo River as a trip "back to the earliest beginning of the world," of the Congolese male as a "prehistoric man . . . cursing us, praying to us, welcoming us," and of the white man as one who might recognize only a "remote kinship with this wild and passionate uproar"[47]—not only testifies to his unusual departure from the conventions of thought of his age,[48] but also speaks to his perception that the true heart of darkness was to be found in the dominant political and economic institutions of western civilization.

In his third and fourth essays, "The Terrible Story of the Congo" and "The Blood-Money of the Congo," Park employs a full-blown Gothic discourse. The horrors that he details—committed in the name of Leopold's version of civilization—more than match those envisioned by the writers of macabre fiction. Ultimately, Park rips off the final mask—Leopold's claim that his regime of terror in the Congo has, if nothing else, benefited Belgium's economy and enhanced the Congo's development: "The land is being depopulated at the rate of 15,000,000 in twenty years; vast stretches of country are devastated; from these districts the natives who have escaped slaughter have fled into the depths of the forests, miserable, outcast, and hopeless."[49]

In Bram Stoker's *Dracula*, the eponymous arch fiend of the undead is killed by an outraged band of Occidental young people who, guided by a zealous scientist of the occult, administer the ritually appropriate lethal weaponry. According to Park's account of Leopold's atrocities in the Congo, however, the monarch of murder and pillage has aroused only "faint stirrings of conscience . . . resolutions, and discussions, and cries of pity and shame." Against such assaults the predatory Leopold is virtually invulnerable because of the effectiveness of his own "huge machine—his gigantic Press Bureau . . . a machine grinding tirelessly, night and day, that its owner may pose as the Philanthropist, and not be exposed as the Vampire."[50] Unless more is done, unless the mundane equivalent of the nemesis of this real-life *nosferatu* can be found, he and his system will develop even more terrible variations on what Park denotes as "the most highly perfected business methods of the twentieth century."[51] Meanwhile, as Park dolefully concludes, "The Vampire sits sucking the life-blood of the victim that has slowly ceased to struggle."[52] Gothic capitalism had for the moment escaped its just deserts.

The limitations of Gothic discourse as a critique of modernity is suggested by the fate of Park's foray into Gothicist muckraking. Park would later complain that he was used unfairly by the Baptist Mission Society, and assert that through his work with the Congo Reform Association (CRA) he had been inveigled, unwittingly, into taking sides in a jurisdictional dispute between rivalrous Belgian Catholic and English and American Baptist missions to the Congo.

Park's complaint about the missionaries' exploitation of the Congo Question speaks to a fundamental weakness in his own and the CRA's usage of a Gothic perspective. The Gothic is embedded in a subterranean Christian (indeed, largely Catholic) outlook. As Dr. Park reveals the truly evil character of the king of the Belgians, he makes himself into a character not unlike Dr. Van Helsing in Bram Stoker's fictional account of the exposure and death of Count Dracula. The vampire, according to Montague Summers, "is one who has led a life of more than ordinary immorality and unbridled wickedness; a man of foul, gross and selfish passions, of evil ambitions, delighting in cruelty and blood."[53] When Park has shown Leopold II to be just such a being, he has reached the intramundane limits of action of the vampire hunter. His "band of brothers," that is, the members of the international CRA who had joined together to extirpate the evils committed by King Leopold and his minions, the real-life equivalent of Van Helsing's compatriots in the struggle against Dracula, relied on the power of an aroused Christian conscience to put down the veritably preternatural power of the tyrant of the Congo. But, if that source of morality was in its final throes of strangulation, choking on the shards of a commercial civilization that had been fatally lodged in its preachers' and practitioners' throats, a reliance on the Christian homiletic would appear to have been unpromising. Park's essay appeared at a time when Christian ethics were not only under assault from science and other elements of a secularizing modernity, but also from capitalist imperialism's liberation from its originating spirit.

His subsequent disaffection from his efforts at exposing the horrors of Leopold's regime in the Congo and his disparagement of missionaries, seem in retrospect to be instances wherein he himself not only fell victim to the Belgian king's carefully orchestrated disinformation program, but also failed to grasp the full import of his Gothic perspective on capitalist imperialism.

Despite the demise of the Congo Question as a public issue after Leopold's death, the questions it had raised about imperialism, international ethics, and colonial domination remained unanswered. The CRA officially disbanded on June 16, 1913, prematurely claiming that its efforts had brought an end to atrocities, slavery, rubber taxation, restraint of trade, and the corruption of both capitalist commerce and Christian civilization in the Congo.[54] A few years later, the CRA's founder, E. D. Morel, would document the continuation of these heinous practices in the reconstituted Congo colony. How to infuse Europe's and America's capitalist imperialism with a moral conscience remains a problem for the social sciences to the present day precisely because of that system's institutionalized invulnerability to a consistently ethical orientation.[55] The Gothic perspective permits one to see that, by first establishing the corporate firm as a legal and veritable person, and, then, interposing this soulless and profit-devouring zombie between the capitalists and the human sources of their profits, the builders of capitalism had created the conditions for commerce with a cold-blooded face. While "progressive" businessmen of the first two decades of the twentieth century sought either to rest their case for a heartless pursuit of profits on the merits of the new science of Spencerian Social Darwinism,[56] or to insist that the sufferings of workers were inner-worldly versions of a divine dispensation of justice,[57] Christian labor advocates sought to preach a gospel of worthy trade unionism[58] or worried over how they might deter the degradation of work in an industrial society from subverting the Protestant ethic.[59] Meanwhile, unsecularized Gothic sociologists—the last of whom was Albion W. Small (1841–1926)—hoped to obtain victory over the devil-ridden corporate structure of the Occident by implanting the cross in its heart, the board of directors' conference rooms. Small wrote in 1920 that

> a corporation is a deathless superpersonal selfishness vested by the state with superpersonal powers. This monster is commissioned by the state to exercise its superpersonal powers within the society of plain persons. Thus we have unconsciously converted our property system from a protection of similar natural persons against one another, into a licensing system of supernatural persons. . . . The invention is not, and cannot come to, good, unless the society of plain persons can either endow corporations with souls, with souls' liabilities, or create and operate in its own interest an adequate superpersonal enginery of corporations.[60]

Although the casuistries of such a modern theodicy seemed to have reached their apex in Small's final writings on the subject—and, together with much of the left wing of the Social Gospel,[61] to have fallen into desuetude after Small's death—their echoes are occasionally still heard in the writings of ethically concerned economists. A fine example is to be found in an essay by Carl Kaysen. Describing the values underlying the modern American corporation in 1957, this economist simply endows what Small had called a "monster" and a "superpersonal selfishness" with a soul: "There is no display of greed or graspingness; there is no attempt to push off onto workers or the community at large part of the social costs of enterprise. *The modern corporation is a soulful corporation.*"[62] However, only three years later, Kaysen dropped all reference to religious concerns and conceded that business power was likely to be exercised irresponsibly and recognized that while "the process of selection of business leaders may be adaptive with respect to their performance of the economic function of business; there is no reason to expect that it should be with respect to the exercise of power in other realms."[63] Park would seem to have reached a similar conclusion many years earlier.

Park himself would come to regard the more egregious effects of imperialism as an inevitable incident in the history of modern Europe's drive toward world hegemonism. His subsequent writings on Africa, Asia, Europe, and the Pacific did not utilize Gothic imagery. Gothicism, precisely because it was a part of the religious outlook that Europe had inherited from the Middle Ages, seemed no longer serviceable as a discourse for modernist criticism. "The trouble with Europe," Park pointed out in 1935, "is not merely that it is divided economically and politically, but that it has outgrown its traditional and religious faith."[64] In fact, he went on, echoing an earlier observation of Simmel,[65] "with the rise of modern industrial society . . . and the incidental secularization of all the forms of life, the inherited religious beliefs are no longer in accord with the practices of commercial and plutocratic society."[66] It would seem that Gothicism had been liberated from its spiritual origins and had become functionally autonomous, able to work its wicked will with impunity.

NOTES

This essay originally appeared in *The International Journal of Politics, Culture, and Society*, 4:4 (Summer 1991), pp. 501–16.

1. Edward Shils, "Robert E. Park, 1864–1944," *The American Scholar*, 60:1 (Winter 1991), p. 127.

2. Robert E. Park, "Reflections on Communication and Culture," *American Journal of Sociology*, 44 (Sept. 1938), pp. 187–205.

3. Shils, "Robert E. Park," p. 121.

4. Robert E. Park and Earnest W. Burgess, *Introduction to the Science of Sociology* (Chicago: University of Chicago Press, 1921), pp. 1019, 1015.

5. Lewis Coser, "American Trends," in *A History of Sociological Analysis*, ed. Tom Bottomore and Robert Nisbet (New York: Basic Books, Inc., 1978), pp. 316–17.

6. Neil J. Smelser, ed., *Handbook of Sociology* (Newbury Park, Calif.: Sage Publications, 1988), pp. 68, 406, 602, 632, 633, 638, 640, 641, 669, 670, 671, 672, 686, 696, 724.

7. See Stanford M. Lyman, "Robert E. Park Reconsidered: The Early Writings," *The American Sociologist*, 21:4 (Fall 1990), pp. 342–51.

8. See the remarks of Herbert J. Gans, "Sociology in America: The Discipline and the Public," the 1988 Presidential Address to the American Sociological Association, in *Sociology in America*, ed. Herbert J. Gans (Newbury Park, Calif.: Sage Publications, 1990), esp. pp. 324–28.

9. Winifred Raushenbush, *Robert E. Park: Biography of a Sociologist* (Durham, N.C.: Duke University Press, 1979), p. 97.

10. Robert E. Park, "An Autobiographical Note," in *Race and Culture: The Collected Papers of Robert Ezra Park*, vol. 1, ed. Everett C. Hughes et. al., (Glencoe, Ill.: The Free Press, 1950), pp. viii–ix.

11. Shils, "Robert E. Park," p. 125.

12. See Stanford M. Lyman, *Civilization: Contents, Discontents, Malcontents, and Other Essays in Social Theory* (Fayetteville: University of Arkansas Press, 1990).

13. Ibid., p. 127.

14. See Stanford M. Lyman, "The Rise and Decline of the Functionalist-Positivist Paradigm: A Chapter in the History of American Sociology," *Hyoron Shakaikagaku: Doshisha University Social Science Review*, no. 20 (Mar. 1982), pp. 4–19.

15. See Arthur J. Vidich, Stanford M. Lyman, and Jeffrey C. Goldfarb, "Sociology and Society: Disciplinary Tensions and Professional Compromises," *Social Research*, 48:2 (Summer 1981), pp. 322–61; and Arthur J. Vidich and Stanford M. Lyman, *American Sociology: Worldly Rejections of Religion and Their Directions* (New Haven: Yale University Press, 1985), pp. 126–43, 172.

16. Cf. Barbara Ballis Lal, *The Romance of Culture in an Urban Civilization: Robert E. Park on Race and Ethnic Relations in Cities* (London: Routledge, 1990), pp. 90–91.

17. For a critique of this type of metaphorical usage in sociological theorizing, see Robert Nisbet, *The Making of Modern Society* (New York: New York University Press, 1986), pp. 33–69.

18. Coser, "American Trends," p. 318.

19. Shils, 'Robert E. Park," p. 127.

20. These works have been reprinted in Stanford M. Lyman, *Militarism, Imperialism, and Racial Accommodation: An Analysis and Interpretation of the Early Writings of Robert E. Park* (Fayetteville: University of Arkansas Press, 1991).

21. Robert K. Merton, *Social Theory and Social Structure*, rev. and enlarged ed. (Glencoe, Ill.: The Free Press, 1957), p. 3. Park's name does not even appear in the index of this modern classic.

22. See two works by Albion Small, *The Cameralists: The Pioneers of German Social Polity* (New York: Burt Franklin, n.d. [1909]); and *Between Eras: From Capitalism to Democracy* (Kansas City: Inter-Collegiate Press, 1913).

23. Cecil Eugene Greek, *The Religious Roots of American Sociology* (New York: Garland Publishing, Inc., 1992), pp. 21–230.

24. Vidich and Lyman, *American Sociology*, pp. 281–309.

25. Franklin Henry Giddings, *Democracy and Empire, with Studies of Their Psychological, Economic and Moral Foundations* (Freeport, Ill.: Books for Libraries, 1972 [1900]).

26. Charles R. Henderson, *An Introduction to the Study of the Dependent, Defective, and Delinquent Classes* (Boston: D. C. Heath and Co., 1906 [1893]).

27. Robert E. Park, "The German Army: The Most Perfect Military Organization in the World," *Munsey's Magazine*, 24:3 (Dec. 1900), pp. 376–95.

28. See Stanford M. Lyman, "Park and Realpolitik: Race, Culture and Modern Warfare," *International Journal of Politics, Culture, and Society*, 3:4 (Summer 1990), pp. 565–86.

29. Robert E. Park, "A City of Racial Peace," *The World To-Day*, 9 (Aug. 1905), pp. 897–99.

30. Robert E. Park, "Agricultural Extension among the Negroes," *The World To-Day* 15 (Aug. 1908), pp. 820–26.

31. Robert E. Park, "Negro Home Life and Standards of Living," *Annals of the American Academy of Political and Social Science*, 49 (September 1913), pp. 147–63.

32. Robert E. Park, "Recent Atrocities in the Congo State," *The World To-Day*, 8 (Oct. 1904), pp. 1328–31; "A King in Business: Leopold II of Belgium, Autocrat of the Congo and International Broker," *Everybody's Magazine*, 15 (Nov. 1906), pp. 624–33: "The Terrible Story of the Congo," *Everybody's Magazine*, 15 (Dec. 1906), pp. 763–72; "The Blood-Money of the Congo," *Everybody's Magazine*, 16 (Jan. 1907), pp. 60–70; Booker T. Washington, "Cruelty in the Congo Country," *Outlook*, 78 (Oct. 8, 1904), pp. 375–77.

33. For further discussion, see Stanford M. Lyman, *The Seven Deadly Sins: Society and Evil*, rev. ed. (Dix Hills, N.Y.: General Hall, Inc., 1989), pp. 253–59.

34. Max Weber, *The Protestant Ethic and the Spirit of Capitalism*, trans. and ed. Talcott Parsons (New York: Charles Scribner's Sons, 1930), p.17.

35. Robert E. Park and Ernest W. Burgess, *Introduction to the Science of Sociology*, 3d rev. ed. (Chicago: University of Chicago Press, 1969. Orig. pub. 1921), pp. 796–811, 816–46, 970–79.

36. Park, "King in Business," p. 624.

37. See E. F. Bleiler, "Horace Walpole and 'The Castle of Otranto,' " in Bleiler, ed., *Three Gothic Novels* (New York: Dover Publications, 1966), pp. xiv–xv.

38. Park, "King in Business," p. 626.

39. See Hannah Arendt, *Eichmann in Jerusalem: A Report on the Banality of Evil* (New York: Viking Press, 1963), esp. p. 253.

40. Park, "King in Business," pp. 626–27.

41. Ibid., p. 627.

42. Ibid., p. 632.

43. Ibid.

44. Ibid., p. 633.

45. Ibid.

46. Ibid.

47. Joseph Conrad, *Heart of Darkness and The Secret Sharer* (New York: New American Library, 1950), pp. 66, 105–6.

48. See Chinua Achebe, "An Image of Africa: Racism in Conrad's *Heart of Darkness*," in Achebe, *Hopes and Impediments: Selected Essays* (New York: Doubleday, 1989), pp. 1–20.

49. Park, "Terrible Story of the Congo," p. 772.

50. Park, "Blood-Money of the Congo," pp. 60–70.

51. Ibid. p. 61.

52. Park, "Terrible Story of the Congo," p. 772.

53. Montague Summers, *The Vampire: His Kith and Kin* (New Hyde Park, N.Y.: University Books, 1960), p. 77.

54. Paul McStallworth, *The United States and the Congo Question, 1884–1914* (Ph.D. diss., Ohio State University, 1954 [Ann Arbor: University Microfilms, 1988]), p. 335.

55. Cf. Robert Jackall, *Moral Mazes: The World of Corporate Managers* (New York: Oxford University Press, 1988), pp. 3–16. On Germany's particular problems in this regard, see Simon Reich, *The Fruits of Fascism: Postwar Prosperity in Historical Perspective* (Ithaca: Cornell University Press, 1990), esp. pp. 1–73.

56. See Edward Chase Kirkland, *Dream and Thought in the Business Community, 1860–1900* (Ithaca: Cornell University Press, 1956; reprint, Chicago: Quandrangle, 1964), pp. 13–18; and Alfred L. Thimm, *Business Ideologies in the Reform-Progressive Era, 1800–1914* (University: University of Alabama Press, 1976), pp. 40–79, 111–60.

57. See David Matza, "The Disreputable Poor," in *Class, Status, and Power: Social Stratification in Comparative Perspective*, 2d ed., ed. Reinhard Bendix and Seymour Martin Lipset (New York: The Free Press, 1966), pp. 289–302; and Michael B. Katz, *In the Shadow of the Poorhouse: A Social History of Welfare in America* (New York: Basic Books, 1986), pp. 58–84.

58. See Richard T. Ely, *The Labor Movement in America* (New York: Thomas Y. Crowell, 1886; reprint, New York: Arno Press, 1969), pp. v–xiii; and Ken Fones-Wolf, *Trade Union Gospel: Christianity and Labor in Industrial Philadelphia, 1865–1915* (Philadelphia: Temple University Press, 1989). In general see John Rutherford Everett, *Religion in Economics: A Study of John Bates Clark, Richard T. Ely, Simon N. Patten* (New York: King's Crown Press, 1946).

59. See James B. Gilbert, *Work without Salvation: America's Intellectuals and Industrial Alienation, 1880–1910* (Baltimore: John Hopkins University Press, 1977), pp. 3–13, 83–136.

60. Albion W. Small, "Christianity and Industry," *American Journal of Sociology*, 25 (May 1920), p. 693.

61. For a good example of the Social Gospel's "left" position, see Washington Gladden, *Applied Christianity: Moral Aspects of Social Questions* (Boston: Houghton-Mifflin, 1886; reprint, New York: Arno Press, 1976), pp. 38–101, 146–79. For Gladden's denunciation of "tainted money," i.e., the money that corporate leaders donated to charities and to ministers of the Social Gospel, see Jacob H. Dorn, *Washington Gladden: Prophet of the Social Gospel* (Columbus: Ohio State University Press, 1967), pp. 240–66.

62. Carl Kaysen, "The Social Significance of the Modern Corporation," *American Economic Review*, 47 (May 1957), p. 314. Quoted in Arthur J. Vidich, "The Moral, Economic, and Political Status of Labor in American Society," *Social Research*, 49 (Autumn 1982), p. 787 n. 33. Emphasis supplied.

63. Carl Kaysen, "The Corporation: How Much Power? What Scope?" reprinted in Bendix and Lipset, eds., *Class, Status, and Power*, p. 238.

64. Robert E. Park, "review of *Enquiries into Religion and Culture* by Christopher Dawson," *American Journal of Sociology*, 41 (July 1935), p. 110.

65. Georg Simmel, *Schopenhauer and Nietzsche*, trans. Helmut Lois-kandl, Deena Weinstein, and Michael Weinstein (Amherst: University of Massachusetts Press, 1986), pp. 4–5.

66. Park, "review of *Enquiries into Religion and Culture*," p. 110.

PART 2

Interracial Contacts:
History, Sociology, Imagery

Immigration . . . divides the workers into two groups: the native-born and the foreigners, and the latter in turn into (1) the Irish, (2) the Germans, (3) the many small groups, each of which understands only itself: Czechs, Poles, Italians, Scandinavians, etc. And then the Negroes . . .

—Friedrich Engels
Dec. 2, 1893

4

Memory, Forgetfulness; History, Integration: Hansen's Law of "Third Generation Interest" and the Race Question

Thou shalt not abhor an Edomite;
for he is thy brother . . .
—Deuteronomy 23:7

In 1938 the Augustana Historical Society published what, almost a half-century later, Werner Sollors declared to have become the "best known modern formulation of generational succession among immigrants . . . to the United States,"[1] Marcus Lee Hansen's *The Problem of the Third Generation Immigrant*.[2] In that essay Hansen put forward an addition to the laws of history, a generalization that he elevated to a principle: "the principle of third generation interest." Hansen insisted that this principle "is applicable in all fields of historical study," that it "explains the recurrence of movements that seemingly are dead," that "it is a factor that should be kept in mind particularly in literary or cultural history," and that "it makes it possible for the present to know something about the future." Referring to his principle as a theory, Hansen presented it as a virtually universal phenomenon: "what the son wishes to forget the grandson wishes to remember."[3]

Although Hansen exemplified his thesis chiefly in reference to the history-recovering activities carried out by the grandchildren of European immigrants to America, he clearly meant his "law" to apply to third generation legatees of any historically significant event. His citation of *Gone With the Wind* as a third generation product evinces his intention. Moreover, a moment's reflection will reveal that *every* generation (except that of the biblical first couple and their children) is a *third* generation, as well as being one that is first, second, fourth, and so on. Generations are measured in relation to a fateful event.[4] The "second" generation that Hansen criticizes so harshly for aggressively and intentionally "forgetting" its immigrant heritage is also a third generation when counted from the time and space of the immigrant generation's parentage. And the immigrant generation is a third generation in relation to its own grandparentage. The third generation offspring of America's European immigrants is also a second generation, one that has come after that of the first American-born parents in its line; and, it is a first generation as well, one composed of the first American-born children of American-born parents and of foreign-born grandparents. Thus, the actual intention of Hansen's law, and certainly its vital spirit, is embodied in its calling to our attention the temporal dimensions that circumscribe the historicity of significant events: it describes a cycle of *experience-forgetfulness-remembering* that occurs over a period of three generations. It is a statement about a particular kind of time-track.[5]

"Time," Maurice Halbwachs once observed, "is like a blank sheet on which an indefinite number of parallel lines may be drawn."[6] Along one set of these lines, Hansen has singled out certain moments of intense and significant experience and demarcated these as historical. And from these moments he has counted generations and observed the generational period in which the original "historical" moment of experience is erased from the collective mind and, later, in another generational period, remembered. The latter process restores the experience to its eventful place, making it the central part of the heritage of the group as well as a source of its collective identity. Hansen's law describes, thus, a process of pure sociology—a denotation of how it is that groups and group consciousness come to rise, fall, and rise again.

Hansen hoped to show that his principle, law, and theory lent significance to a peculiar development in historiography: it was among the third generation descendants of European immigrants to the United States that there arose a profound interest in recovering and setting down on paper the experiences, understandings, and ways of life of their grandparents. This interest expressed itself in the founding of national or ethnic historical societies, which were in effect the successors of the defunct "pioneer societies" that in their old age the immigrants themselves had established as institutions of nostalgia. What interested Hansen was that the new historical societies were being established by apparently highly acculturated persons who, in stark contradiction to the attitude of their parents, wished to salvage and honor what the latter had self-consciously given up in their own headlong rush to full-fledged Americanization.

Hansen was not the first to prophesy a revival of ancestral consciousness in America; nor was he the first to predict that it would occur long after intergenerational passage, public education, and exposure to America's mass media had worked their supposedly inexorable powers to obliterate and disintegrate the cultures, beliefs, and lifeways of the immigrants. In 1893, the year after Hansen's birth, the Austrian sociologist Gustav Ratzenhofer (1842–1904) had predicted that a time would come in America "when the population will have become dense," when the "struggle for existence will have to be more carefully planned," and when "the people of America will . . . [feel the] need of attaching themselves to the several political groups into which their interests naturally divide them." At that time, Ratzenhofer went on to predict, "the memory of racial extraction may at last be reawakened." Politics would again become ethnical: "The different languages may become the rallying centers for the different interests. Thereupon for the first time will America confront decisively the problems of its national unity."[7] Ratzenhofer did not pinpoint a precise date for the reawakening of ethnocultural identity, nor did he claim that it would be coincident with the emergence of any particular generation. Moreover, he did not perceive this revival's expression as likely to take a historical bent. But, he did believe that its appearance would introduce a fundamental challenge to America's national consensus.

Hansen, too, was worried about the potentially divisive consequences of ethnic revival. He sincerely believed third generation return to be a valuable corrective to the second generation's acceptance of unalloyed Americanization; however, he hoped to ward off the chauvinistic and disuniting effects of an ancestor-oriented historiography by giving advice to its third generation practitioners. He warned them against excessive filiopietism, religious intolerance, a disdain of politics, and any other biases that would lead critics to accuse them of producing works "tainted with partiality." Hansen exhorted the new historians to conceptualize their mission as that of writing "one chapter in the larger volume that is called American history" and to be "men of insight who understand that it is the ultimate fate of any national group to be amalgamated into the composite American race."[8] To this end, Hansen concluded his essay with a plea that the annalists espousing a third generational return tell "a simple story of how troubled men, by courage and action, overcame their difficulties, and how people of different tongues and varied cultures have managed to live together in peace."[9] His earnest entreaty was prefaced by a host of fears: that a prideful history of a particular immigrant group might evoke "prejudice and supernationalism"; that "societies organized with the laudable intention of commemorating the deeds of which any people should be proud may fall into the hands of those who will use them for instruments of propaganda"; or that there might arise "international societies for the promotion of hatred and intolerance." To forestall the appearance of any of these, Hansen asserted that historians had "an obligation to guide the national curiosity to know the past along those lines which will serve the good of all."[10]

Hansen's principle, law, and theory have not been greeted with unanimous enthusiasm or widespread approval. Retitled "The Third Generation in America," the essay was reprinted in the Jewish cultural organ Commentary in November, 1952, bearing the legitimizing imprimatur of Oscar Handlin's introduction; thereby it passed into the canon of authoritative American historical thought.[11] Eight years later, Will Herberg reformulated Hansen's law, moving it out from its locus in historiography, but narrowing its focus to the revival of denominational religious membership among ordinary third generation Americans. Herberg's modification of Hansen's thesis was severe: "All that the third generation of the Italian or Polish group, for example, could, as Americans, remember was the religion of the grandfather; the immigrant language and culture and way of life were, of course, irretrievably gone."[12] In the see-saw of attitudes toward and apprehensions about a third generation return to its grandparental roots that followed Hansen's original statement of his thesis, Margaret Mead voiced a particular concern: too great an interest in ancestral matters might cause members of the third generation to lose interest "in the race toward success"; she exhorted her fellow Americans to move "onward and upward, towards the world of Washington and Lincoln," in effect to accept as an "essential part of American culture" the "odd blending of the future and the past, in which another man's great-grandfather becomes the symbol of one's grandson's future."[13] But, if Hansen supposed that the third generation would not only salvage the heritage that the second generation had thrown away but accomplish even more than its grandparents had in this regard,[14] while Herberg saw only the possibility that a religious resurgence would replace an irretrievable cultural legacy, and Mead fretted over nostalgia's potential to pull people away from America's mainstream of incentive and achievement, Michael Novak wondered how his Slovakian culture had been dissolved so completely by the 1970s, the time that his own third generation cohort had come to maturity: "What has happened to my people since they came to this land nearly a century ago? . . . Did our grandparents choose for us, and our posterity, what they should have chosen?"[15] And, although his earlier study of Jewish ritual innovation had convinced him that "Americans increasingly perceive themselves as undergoing cultural homogenization, and . . . they are constantly looking for new ways to establish their differences from each other,"[16] Herbert Gans concluded—after essaying the findings of a socio-historical study of Polish immigrants to California—that the data do "not provide any evidence that the rest of the third generation is more interested in its ethnic origins than the first or second."[17] Other historians have reached similar conclusions. In terms of the strictures of science, then, it would seem that Hansen's "law" fails to pass the requisite empirical tests; however, it also evokes considerable ambivalence and social concern when it threatens to succeed in doing so.

Hansen's thesis would not appear to be valid as a historical principle, law, or theory; nevertheless, it has considerable value as a *sensitizing* conceptualization. A sensitizing concept, as Herbert Blumer has pointed out, provides an initial orientation toward a cluster of happenings; although it is necessarily imprecise and tentative, it proves its value to research and understanding in terms of its reasonableness, plausibility, and illumination.[18] There can be no doubt that Hansen's hypothesis meets at least the minimum requirements of reasonableness, and it certainly is plausible; where it arouses our interest is in its capacity to illuminate a significant aspect of racial and ethnical life in America. Hansen's "law" sensitizes us to differences in intergenerational thought and activity, but in the process conflates particularistic history and shared group memory; in this combination it also necessarily evokes our concern about that which proceeds against them—social amnesia[19] and national homogenization. The complex cluster of memory and forgetfulness, history and integration are opened up to our investigations by considering the implications of Hansen's provocative proposal for racial groups in America, and especially for black Americans.

Memory and History: Convergence and Divergence

Let us, after the fashion of Maurice Halbwachs,[20] consider remembering. Hansen tells us, "what the son wishes to forget the grandson wishes to remember." Crucial to this formulation, however, is the thesis that the memory of the grandchild is turned toward recalling experiences that are not his or her own. Even more significant, Hansen gives as one example of this appropriation by the living of the experiences of their dead ancestors the reawakening of southern patriotism among third generation descendants of the Reconstruction era. Speaking of the historiography that developed after the

Civil War, he writes, "The Southerners who survived the four years of that struggle never forgot." But, the "second generation made little effort to justify the action of their fathers." However, Hansen goes on to rejoice in the fact that "now the grandsons of the Confederates rule in the place of the sons and there is no apologizing for the events of 1861; instead, there is a belligerency that asserts the moral and constitutional justice of their grandfathers' policy."[21]

But in what sense can this supposedly praiseworthy recollection be called memory? We must first see that the activity described is a peculiar variant of *collective* memory—the reconstruction and re-evaluation of group identity and a shared heritage. In "symbolic interaction," that paradigm of sociology that proceeds according to the perspective outlined by George Herbert Mead, Herbert Blumer, and their school, the individual or the group is perceived as capable of making an object of itself and attaching cognitive and cathectic, experiential and historical referents to it. The person or group expresses mature selfhood by utilizing this capability to employ cognitive, evaluative, and affective orientations toward the construction and reconstruction of itself.[22] Taken in this light, what Hansen is describing in his Civil War example is a complex act of self and group enhancement that proceeds by reconstructing a portion of the history of a self-referencing group—in this case, white southerners—and attaching new and positive evaluations to that reconstruction.

The operation of Hansen's law permits appropriating and substantially reordering the group's identity while adding a new cathectic orientation to it. As a central feature of the present-day group's collective self identity, it allows and indeed calls for each self-proclaimed member of the group to adapt his or her own self concept to the new definition. Much more is involved in such an activity than the word *remembering* connotes, at least, in its ordinary usages. In Hansen's descriptions of third generation return, there is entailed a creative employment of the intellectual imagination as well as a redisciplining of the passions. It is, thence, appropriate that Hansen cites as a crowning achievement of the third generation return of the grandchildren of the Confederacy a work of fiction: "The great novel of the Civil War and Reconstruction era was not written by one who had participated in the events or witnessed the scenes. It did not come from the pen of one who had listened to a father's reminiscences. *Gone With the Wind* was written by a granddaughter of the Confederacy, in the year 1936, approximately sixty years after the period with which it dealt had come to an end."[23] An aroused collective memory had transposed an earlier generation's experiences first into a new history[24] and then into an imaginative tale. From both the history and the tale, the white legatees of the Confederacy could take on a new and proud identity and employ that identity in the pursuit of their own current interests.

Collective historical memory requires the incorporation of the experience of one's predecessors into one's own group and into one's own individual self-consciousness. Such an incorporation places emphasis on one of the four reference groups toward which any generation might orient itself. Competing with one's predecessors for the predominant place in the identity framework are contemporaries, consociates, and successors.[25] For "the third generation return" to triumph in this competition, it must win out over the quite varied and many demands and exigencies of those who share global space and contemporaneousness with us, those with whom we are intimately acquainted and with whom we identify on a primary group basis, and those to whom, though they will come after us, we owe an obligation of some significant kind. Hansen's thesis rests on the assumption that the members of America's third generations find insufficient solace in, élan among, or sentimental attachment to their fellow humans, whether they be kin, friends or strangers, and are less concerned about dying culturally intestate than they are about living within the resuscitated dream world of their own group past. Or, on a more practical level, it provides the basis for a selective exploration of salient elements of a group's past to prosecute goals of interest to the group's immediate present and near future.

The revival of interest in the history and mythology of the antebellum South, the Civil War, and the Reconstruction periods presents a fine example of the attendant processes. Hansen and others, notably Herberg, have suggested that Americans experience their twentieth-century *presentness* as a contemporaneity devoid of significant and self-enhancing content. Those who can find, or imagine, their grandparental roots in a different culture will seek to do so as an act that provides them not merely with an intergenerational biography, but more significantly with a personal and group identity that functions to differentiate their selves from those of their all too one-dimensional fellow citizens. In the case of white southerners, that problem has taken on a special and characteristic form.[26] Of all the divisions among Americans, that between white southerners and all others has had a marked noticeability. The eleven states that make up "the South" have constantly struggled to effect a solution to the pushes toward sectional or national independence from, and the pulls back to regional recognition and absorption within, the United States.

The historical conflict that was supposed to settle the issue was fought between 1861 and 1865, but, rather than ending the matter, the Civil War and its aftermath set it on a new and perhaps permanent course of irresolution. In the six decades that separate the ending of the Reconstruction era and the publication of Margaret Mitchell's classic of Redemptionist thought, the South had been pictured as having either a distinctive social character, an especially powerful and institutionalized regime of color-caste and class, and a continuity in its culture and politics; or, as a region subject to vast economic changes, receiving a few new peoples from Europe[27] and Asia[28] while losing a great many more working class blacks[29] and black and white intellectuals[30] to the better opportunities and higher culture of the North, and undergoing a technological industrialization that would willy-nilly propel it into the mainstream of America.[31] The South found itself trapped between the prideful claim that it was ever enduring and the doleful lament that it was slowly vanishing.[32] Caught in the flux of these contradictory perspectives, white southerners found it difficult to become Americanized in Hansen's sense of the term, that is, to make a "treaty of peace with society."[33] Understood in this light, the founding of the Southern Historical Society in 1934[34]—an event hailed by Hansen as an important instance of non-ethnic third generational return—is also an example of the South's continuation, by another means, of the War Between the States. Publication of the novel *Gone With the Wind*, together with its selection for the Pulitzer Prize in 1936 and its widely acclaimed film version in 1939, constitute important victories in that war. Advertised in the *American Historical Review* as the greatest historical novel ever written by an American,[35] the book, and the movie that followed it, provided popular literary legitimation for the "moonlight-and-magnolia school of history."[36] According to James Temple Kirby, "Margaret Mitchell's Scarlett O'Hara . . . , macho beau Rhett Butler, frail-noble Melanie, sensitive-romantic-tragic Ashley Wilkes, and Hattie McDaniel's Mammy—were stark stereotypes. . . . House servants are toms, mammies, and pickaninny types. Tara's overseer is a rogue, later a scalawag, implying a direct link from slavery's own sinister side to Reconstruction."[37] In a generational sense, Mitchell's novel was the lineal descendant of Thomas Dixon's negrophobic 1904 treatment of the same era, a melodrama entitled *The Clansman*;[38] while David O. Selznick's film version was a later generation's screenplay of the theme that D. W. Griffith had explored two decades earlier in his film translation of Dixon's novel, retitled and released as *Birth of a Nation*.[39] Indicative of how much the Confederacy had won in its seven decade struggle since Appomattox is the fact that the National Association for the Advancement of Colored People, which had pressed for banning Griffith's film,[40] after persuading Selznick to cut some of the most offensive scenes from his screenplay, did not join in the fight against the showing of Gone With the Wind.[41] That was left to such dissident groups as the National Negro Congress and the Communist Party. Yet, some "critics felt that where Birth of a Nation ended, Gone With the Wind began." However, by 1936–39 sympathy for the "lost cause" of the Confederacy and indifference toward the plight of the Negro had so penetrated American social consciousness that Mitchell's novel and Selznick's film version of it "completed the job of wiping out of the public mind the 'Northern' view of slavery, Civil War, and Reconstruction, replacing it with the traditional 'Southern' view."[42] What justification the Confederacy had lost in 1865, its third generation descendants had recovered seventy years later.

In stark testimony to his selectivity of third generation returns, Hansen makes no mention of blacks or of slavery's third generation descent group's attempts to recover their history in the Civil War, Reconstruction, and Redemption eras. Despite his warnings about excessive pride and false filiopietism, there is no air of criticism in Hansen's designation of the revived southern attitude as "a belligerency that asserts the moral and constitutional justice of their grandfather's policy," nor does he evince any apprehension about his own conclusion on the matter: "The South has been revived. Its history is taught with a fervid patriotism in the universities and schools."[43] But, as was surely evident then, that revived and fervidly patriotic history was partial and one-sided. Moreover, although it spawned many intriguing internal disputes, much valuable research, the discovery of previously overlooked facts, and many imaginative interpretations of some aspects of the era, it subjected the Negro either to distorted and demeaning stereotypy or to a less than benign neglect.

In point of fact, Carter G. Woodson had founded the Association for the Study of Negro Life and History and the Journal of Negro History in 1915–16, fifty years after the Civil War had ended and two decades before Mitchell published her novel. However, the disciplinary gatekeepers of official American history looked askance at the subject of Negro history and confined its teachers and practitioners to Negro colleges. Professional American historians relegated its expression to arenas outside the mainstream.[44] The need to revive Negro history had been urgent. In 1916, the noted black historian,

Charles Harris Wesley, exhorted his compatriots: "An interest should be awakened among Colored America in its history, and encouragement should be given to its general reading, study and investigation."[45] Nevertheless, with perhaps a few exceptions, black history did not achieve the goal that Hansen had envisioned for third generational return historiography—becoming accepted "as one chapter in the larger volume that is called American history . . . [its] historical [society's] activities . . . merged with the activities of other societies of the same nature and finally within the main line of American historiography itself."[46] Assessing the struggle of Woodson's and Wesley's generation to crack the color line in America's historical disciplines, John Hope Franklin pointed to its peculiar character, one that required blacks first to establish that they had a history worth recognizing, and then to convince their white brethren that it might be accepted as a significant part of Americans' history of themselves: "Their fight to integrate Afro-American history into the mainstream was part of the fight by Afro-American students to break into the graduate departments of history in every predominantly white university in the southern states and in very many such institutions outside the South. . . . They also did so in order to support their argument that Afro-American history should be recognized as a centerpiece—an adornment if you will—of the history of the United States."[47] But, as late as 1970, at least one popular historian of Afro-Americans claimed that that people's history still remained either lost, stolen, or strayed.[48] And, two decades later, Vincent Harding wondered whether entrance and integration might have come too late. He asked how and in what sense successor generations should remember black Americans at all, given the need for present-day scholars to work to prevent a worldwide nuclear annihilation that threatened to end the very continuity of all human history and its subjects.[49]

Black History and Afro-American Self-Esteem

History as collective memory is inextricably related to the problematics and vicissitudes of self and group esteem. Certainly Hansen saw it in this light. In the case of the Afro-American, however, the issues are compounded by the three-fold allegation that blacks have no history, or have no history of which they might be proud, or have no history that they and non-black fellow Americans need rightfully respect. Much of the effort of the group that John Hope Franklin identifies as the second generation of Negro historians[50] was dedicated to the refutation of that tripartite allegation. To that end these historians subjected each era of American history to a searching investigation, uncovering the variety of roles that blacks had played in building up American civilization and culture.[51]

However, of all the many statuses occupied by Negroes, none seemed so incapable of refuting the still operant demeaning stereotypy than that summed up in the ethnophaulism "sambo," a term that identified blacks with a supposedly deserved status as bond servants. "Slavery," wrote Allan Nevins and Henry Steele Commager, "brought manual labor into contempt."[52] Worse, to some historians, it seemed to fasten on to the Negro a docile, childlike character and an only occasional unwillingness to submit to menial servitude, rude surroundings, a poor diet, a virtually familyless existence, and an interminable future of craven servility. In 1942, Henry Steele Commager and Samuel Eliot Morison included the following statement in volume 1 of their *Growth of the American Republic:* "As for Sambo, whose wrongs moved the abolitionists to wrath and tears, there is some reason to believe that he suffered less than any other class in the South. . . . Although brought to America by force, the incurably optimistic negro [sic] soon became attached to the country and devoted to his white folks."[53] Commager and Morison went on to describe antebellum blacks as members of "a race with exasperating habits" and to depict the typical slave as "childlike, improvident, humorous, prevaricating, and superstitious."[54] Although by 1950 these statements were sufficiently controversial to evoke an unsuccessful call from the City College of New York's chapter of the National Association for the Advancement of Colored People to remove *Growth of the American Republic* from the list of approved texts, and, one year later, for the history department at Queen's College to ban the book altogether from its curriculum,[55] the demeaning of the historical Negro was not so easily erased from either the black or white collective mind of the mid-twentieth century. From 1932 through 1939, the black historian Charles Harris Wesley had labored mightily to prove that, in direct response to their enslaved condition, "Negroes worked to improve their own status and to advance the cause of emancipation," and to demand that "In light of . . . historical facts no one . . . say . . . that the Negroes . . . did nothing for the emancipation of themselves and the group to which they belonged."[56] Although a new era, revising the historiography that Hansen had praised in 1938, was beginning to dawn in the late 1940s, blacks would continue to suffer for years thereafter the disesteem that the previous era's conceptions had loaded onto them.

The collective memory of blacks in the twentieth century draws as it must on the psychological fact that the individual's as well as the group's sense of identity establishes itself by relating and referencing the self with respect to "all other individuals, *known and unknown*, who have the same defining features."[57] When, in 1959, Stanley Elkins attempted to find some truth value in the "sambo" imagery and to attribute the existence of a psychosocial sambo personality to the infantilizing effects that American slavery's total institutionalization had had on both the Negro psyche and the black person's morale,[58] he was met by a chorus of critics accusing him of reinvigorating a pernicious stereotype that generations of black scholars had struggled so valiantly to overcome.[59]

For this reason there would appear to be at least an incentive for some blacks to retreat from history, to embrace forgetfulness rather than revival of the historical memory, should the latter prove capable only of deepening stigmatization and reinforcing degradation. By couching his criticism of the second generation's rejection of its own history in terms of an escape from its potential for humiliating both the individual and the generational group with which he or she is identified,[60] Hansen pointed to the possibility that a historical return, or the reactivation of the group's collective memory, could inflict harm on both the remembering individual and on the living members of the common descent group whose grandparental history is thereby recalled. In the case of the American Negro, three or more generations removed from slavery and its heritage of stereotypy and oppression, there sometimes seems to appear a painful choice: to forget heritage altogether, and, like Mircea Eliade's mythical "archaic man," abolish history altogether and begin life de novo;[61] or, as in fact has been the case with four generations of black historians, to plunge into that heritage not merely to gather and order its data, but to arrange its interpretation so that guilt, shame, embarrassment, and any other degrading sensibility is removed from its interpretation. However, accepting the latter mission carries with it its own dilemmas and contradictions, not the least of which is encountered in establishing a sound basis for integrating black with general American history.

Genitors and Myth-History: American Blacks and the Founding Fathers

When the collective memory of one group is reconstituted as part of that of already assimilated Americans it finds powerful expression in acknowledging a symbolic inheritance from the "founding fathers." That the American nation-state claims to have been "born" by a bellicose "Caesarean section" from the "womb" of another entails the symbolic transfiguration of certain of the revolutionary era's leading men. Present and participating at the creation, these men have become genitors in a supremely important myth-history of national procreation. As America's "founding fathers," they are invested with a posthumous charisma that tends toward converting them from ordinary mortals into supramundane monuments. Among such figures perhaps none is more important to the beginnings of the United States and to the fact that its value system emphasizes both liberty and equality than Thomas Jefferson. Author of the Declaration of Independence and *Notes on the State of Virginia*, third president of the United States during the period when the slave trade came to an end, and an uneasy holder of slaves, Jefferson's life and thoughts are so riddled with ambivalence and anxiety about matters of race and civil order that he may well embody what Gunnar Myrdal later termed the "American dilemma." To the heritage of Jefferson, later generations of settlers, immigrants, and immigrant descendants are invited to be legatees, to become virtual scions of this and the other founding fathers. By willingly accepting this new paternity, they renounce the national patriarchic claim of any other fictive mythohistorical parentage group. They merge *civitas* with *patria*.

In the case of American Negroes, however, this form of mythohistorical re-patriarchalization takes on a special poignancy. Black citizenship has been conferred on the ex-slaves and their descendants by the post–Civil War Amendments; yet their civic and symbolic heritage from the founding fathers is haunted by the possibility of a real matriarchate that threatens to disinherit them as descendants of a morganatic union. Since 1802, Thomas Jefferson and his family, friends, admirers and biographers have attempted to stave off the accusation that he maintained an illicit relationship with one of his slaves, Sally Hemings, and that the paternity of the several children born of this affair was never acknowledged by Jefferson.[62] It is quite likely that the truth of the matter will never be proven to the satisfaction of any of the parties to this historic and historical dispute.[63] However, as Nathan I. Huggins points out, "It does not matter whether or not it was *actually* true. It is *symbolically* true. The story, like so many legitimizing myths, symbolically ties a people (through Sally Hemings) to the founding of the nation."[64] The story links blacks to America's beginnings as a birthright.

Historical myths grant legitimacy to a people. They link the nation to the state, usually by establishing both ancient roots and common descent. The American founding fathers sought their own legitimation through identification with the Roman res publica and annotated their new nation's seals and indicia with Latin phrases, an eagle that hearkened back to the sacred bird of the Roman legions, a heraldry that announced Novus ordo seclorum ("a new order of the ages"), and a motto promising E pluribus unum ("out of many, one").[65] Yet that "one" has not yet materialized. From the beginning, the black population was excluded. Even J. Hector St. John de Creve-coeur did not include Negroes in his amalgram of peoples making up this new man, the American.[66] (His sympathetic concerns about the black condition were expressed in several pages in another part of his book).[67] The frenetic resistance to accepting the possibility that Jefferson fathered Sally Heming's children is not only an illustration of the widespread overvaluation of the virtues credited to a found-ing father, but also, and more significantly, a testimony to the an-guished ambivalence about whether blacks deserve anything more than a mess of pottage as their American heritage.

Hansen's law provides for an enrichment of the American legacy, by adding on to it those aspects of the first generation's experience that helped to build up the complex fabric of the country's institu-tions and culture. Fabric, however, can be strengthened with fabri-cation. The construction of every people's legitimation myth necessarily involves invention, exaggeration, omission, selection, and distortion. In the case of blacks, the quest for a substantive as well as symbolic Revolutionary War era ancestry—one that could secure their group's esteem at the same time that it binds them to Americans of a different hue and a different cultural background—threatens to break through the long established color line and to recognize a more intimate connection than place of Old World ori-gin—a blood relationship.

The situation is reminiscent of the biblical tale (Gen. 25–29) in which the fraternal twins Jacob and Esau compete for their father's recognition, a birthright and a blessing that they and their father be-lieve can only be given to one of them. Although born of the same parents, these children of Isaac's and Rebekah's old age do not re-semble each other. At the time of her confinement the Lord had told Rebekah, "Two nations are in thy womb, and two manner of people shall be separated from thy bowels; and the one people shall be stronger than the other people; and the elder shall serve the younger." The first-born Esau's skin was red and his body hairy; his momentarily younger brother Jacob's fair and smooth. Esau became a hunter, while Jacob "was a plain man, dwelling in tents." While still a youth, Jacob, the fair-skinned and younger twin, cheats his older brother out of both his birthright and his blessing, forcing him when he is starving to sell the former for a bowl of lentils, and later, with the connivance of his mother, disguising himself as Esau and deceiving the nearly blind Isaac into giving him the blessing reserved for the first-born. Jacob thus becomes the last of the three generation trio of founding fathers of the Israelite nation, while Esau becomes the progenitor of a lesser and later-to-be enemy people, the Edomites. Although Jacob and Esau are reconciled after two decades of estrangement, they agree to live apart and to establish their peoples as separate nations.

If Jefferson is considered as a modern Isaac, his establishment of a nation-building myth differs from that in the biblical version precisely in the fact that the two sets of American progeny that descend from him have mothers from different races. In the biblical version Esau takes as his wife a daughter of Hagar, the latter being none other than the concubine of the original patriarch Abraham and the mother of the latter's child, Ishmael, a son also deprived of his paternal inheritance and sometimes imagined to be the forerunner of the African people. Sally Hemings, the stand-in for the conniving Rebekah, cannot behave like the biblical matriarch. Rather, as both a chattel and a concubine, she has no standing to make an effective claim on either the symbol or substance of Jefferson's legacy. Its bequests await the day that the stigma of bondage, concubinage, and illegitimate birth can be removed, and all the progeny of the founding father can be declared as his rightful heirs. The history of immigrants to America is usually presented as a narrative of progressive advance and increasing social acceptance. In sharp contrast, as Huggins has observed, "the Afro-American story has more [often] been told in terms of failed hopes, frustrated and ambiguous victories, dreams deferred."[68] As Langston Hughes once observed, the Negro is the darker brother whose blood relationship goes unrecognized.[69]

Taking Hansen's perspective as our own for a moment, let us examine *Clotel or, The President's Daughter: A Narrative of Slave Life in the United States,* a melodramatic fiction published in 1853[70] and authored by America's first black male novelist, William Wells Brown.[71] In terms of its generational situs, *Clotel* appeared in the era marking the third generation of America's independence, and for that reason it deserves comparison with the novel by Margaret Mitchell. As a third generation novel, *Clotel* breaks new ground, not only serving the cause of abolition, but also identifying eighteenth-century Negroes with America's national procreation myth and contrasting their ignominious status with that accorded to white

European newcomers.[72] Conceived as a result of the illicit union of a slaveholder and a slave, the novel's author Brown, escaped his dreary destiny by becoming a runaway. Years later, he novelized a tale of the tragic death of a person similarly situated—only the eponymous fugitive slave woman in his book is identified as the illegitimate daughter of Thomas Jefferson and a black female bondservant. Unacknowledged by her father, Clotel grows up in the shadow of his steadily advancing career. Fleeing from the desolation that has become her lot in life, Clotel finds herself trapped by slave catchers on a bridge over the Potomac and in sight of the Capitol and her father's presidential mansion. Clasping her hands in front of her and raising her eyes to heaven, she begs "for that mercy and compassion *there*, which had been denied her on earth; and then with a single bound, she vault[s] over the railing of the bridge, and [sinks] for ever beneath the waves of the river!"[73]

Brown's novel returns its readers to the situation affecting the first generation of blacks in the new republic in order to remind the former that, three generations after one of the founding fathers penned the Declaration of Independence and established a society in which the ideals of Christian brotherhood might flourish free from persecution, "it is estimated that in the United States, members of the Methodist church own 219,363 slaves; members of the Baptist church own 226,000 slaves; members of the Episcopalian church own 88,000 slaves; members of the Presbyterian church own 77,000 slaves; members of all other churches own 50,000 slaves; in all, 660,563 slaves owned by members of the Christian church in this pious republic!"[74] The proclamation of liberty, equality, and fraternal Christianity is still but a promise in 1853. Brown's novel is one of third generation return; it seeks recognition and legitimation of the Negro's unfortunately conceived birthright.

Margaret Mitchell's novel made the cruelties inflicted by slaveholders and the depredations carried out by the Ku Klux Klan into acts of paternal benevolence and quests for righteous justice, in effect justifying the actions of historical and present-day protagonists of white supremacy. Brown's novel was far less successful. Whereas *Gone With the Wind* was elevated to the place of a modern American classic, Brown's was consigned to that special oblivion reserved for Afro-American fiction. It occupies no place in the American canon.[75] Until a wave of black consciousness revived interest in neglected masterworks of Negro fiction, it existed outside both collective memory and literary history.[76]

That the fundamental distinction of race that excited most Americans' sympathy for the oppressed European immigrant might also evoke hostility toward the African slave and indifference to the plight of the Negro freedom-seeker was not lost on William Wells Brown. He contrasted the tragedy that befell the fugitive slave Clotel with what would have happened had she been a white woman in flight from Europe:

> Had Clotel escaped from oppression in any other land . . . no honour within the gift of the American people would have been too good to have been heaped upon the heroic woman. But she was a slave, and therefore out of the pale of their sympathy. They have tears to shed over Greece and Poland; they have an abundance of sympathy for "poor Ireland"; they can furnish a ship of war to convey the Hungarian refugees from a Turkish prison to the "land of the free and the home of the brave." They boast that America is the "cradle of liberty"; if it is, I fear they have rocked the child to death.[77]

From Brown's day to the present, historians and sociologists have worked over the comparison of European and Asian immigrants to America's blacks, each scholar seeking to make a different point, but all sure that the comparative approach is valid.[78] In many studies, however, the Negro is made to feel inferior and all too often to become the principal party responsible for the black people's present ignominious condition. Consider, for example, a recent work on the social obligations of citizenship by Lawrence M. Mead, a political scientist teaching at New York University.[79] Mead argues that, since the civil rights movement of the sixties, federal policy had made blacks into its "special objects and beneficiaries." Conceding that "because of slavery and discrimination, blacks in general have special claims on federal attention," that in 1980 "almost a third or 8.6 million [of the 26.5 million of black Americans] were poor,"[80] that the "share of black families headed by women rose from 21 to 41 percent between 1960 and 1982," and that by "1984, 47 percent of black households received welfare benefits of some kind,"[81] Mead nevertheless concludes that the present plight of blacks resides ultimately in his discovery that the poorest among them, the urban youth, "are in Hobbes' phrase, 'masterless men,' living in many ways outside social norms."[82] Blacks have lost the sense of obligation to an authoritative community. He quotes Hobbes's observation that "the prosperity of a people . . . cometh not from aristocracy, nor from

democracy, but from the obedience, and concord of the subjects,"
and then offers a solution to the problem: "Community has indeed
dissolved in the low-wage labor market. For it to be restored, work
must apparently become a duty for the least skilled, not just a matter
of self-interest."[83]

Mead's invocation of the state's duty to enforce work ethics among
America's poorest and least self-admiring blacks is itself an instance
of generational return. For, although Mead does not seem to be aware
of the fact, his proposal for the establishment of a federally regulated
regime of morally uplifting labor echoes the system of "warranteeism" originally put forward in 1854 by Henry Hughes, America's
first sociologist and a foremost apologist-theorist of slavery.[84] Because, like Mead, Hughes believed that everyone must work, but
that some, most notably black field hands and bond servants, were
less inclined to do so than others, he argued that the state ought to
require the lazy, improvident, and unambitious elements of the
black population to submit themselves to a lifetime of obligatory labor in return for which they would be cared for by a stern but benevolent class of "warrantors," backed up by the authority of the
federal government. Like Mead, Hughes feared for the safety and
prosperity of American society should blacks be allowed to roam
free, to be "masterless men."[85] Such thought did not then give promise to Negro self-esteem nor does its rebirth today encourage the free
development of black character and Negro personality.

Hansen's Vision of Black Americans

Hansen's law supposedly functioned to enhance individual self-
esteem by identifying the third generational cohort descended from
immigrants to America (or the third generation descendants of some
identifiable people who are associated with a memorable historical
event) with some favorably interpreted and positively valued activities of their grandparental generation. In some cases, if the third
generational return is to be efficacious it must obviate a stigma that
discredits the acts in question and those who committed them. The
southern school of thought associated with U. B. Phillips and his
disciples constitutes a case in point; it seeks to justify slavery and
exonerate the slaveholders from any moral defaults.[86] In opposition
to that school is one espousing revisionism; associated with such
contemporary historians as Kenneth M. Stampp[87] and John Hope
Franklin[88] and their colleagues and followers, its perspective represents a counterreaction to the former's whitewashing of a sorry

chapter of American history.[89] But even Hansen himself, who was not a party to the debates over the meaning and implications of slavery in southern history, contributed, if only in an incidental way, to the exclusion of blacks from a self-enhancing ethnic history and a positive sense of group identity.

Negroes are not treated as migrants or settlers in Hansen's two books on the settlement of America. Indeed, Afro-Americans hardly appear at all in these works. Neither "Negro," "African," or "slavery" are to be found in the index of Hansen's The Atlantic Migration, 1607–1860. Yet, readers of that important study will learn in passing that "many Negro slaves belonged to the households of the prosperous [New Netherlands], and free blacks and mulattoes already formed a special class";[90] and, in a discussion of the connections that bind the population history of the North American mainland to that of the islands of the Caribbean, that the introduction of sugar cane in the latter led to "large plantations and slaves [taking] the place of white servants."[91] In Hansen's interpretation, blacks exist as a servile people who once elbowed out white smallholders: "The Negroes, numbering sixty-four hundred in 1643, totaled over fifty thousand in 1666, and for nearly every one who came, an Englishman, Scotchman or Irishman had to depart."[92] Blacks are next mentioned as bloody rebels, forcing whites to flee, in Hansen's brief description of how French refugees from strife-torn Haiti reached the United States: "The Negroes of the French colony of Haiti rose in revolt, spreading bloodshed and destruction in their wake. The whites who fled . . . landed in Charleston, Norfolk, Baltimore, Philadelphia or New York. . . . Americans were amazed at the ease with which these Frenchmen accommodated themselves to their new life."[93]

In Hansen's version of the settlement patterns of eighteenth-century Maryland and Virginia, Negroes are merely objects of economic history, never its subjects: the ending of the head rights system of labor recruitment enhanced "the institution of slavery, which had taken possession of the tobacco areas and was now bringing in the first large influx of Negroes."[94] Without mentioning the plight of the new class of freedmen-and-women, or describing the many and varied roles that the peoples who crossed the Atlantic from Africa had played in the social, cultural, economic, aesthetic, and political construction of the United States, Hansen concludes his study of the first 250 years of the Atlantic migration from Europe by pointing out the effects of the Civil War on the latter: "The four years of bloody strife destroyed not only the old South, but also, in a less obvious way, the varied immigrant America of the North. . . . When the war ended, foreign languages and foreign customs had not disappeared, but ideals had changed. All who lived in America, alien-born and native-born, were resolved to become one people."[95] However, the nation-building that Hansen envisions does not seem to extend itself across racial lines or in a racially democratic fashion.

Hansen took brief but significant notice of the moral aspects of Negro life in America, North and South, and of their relation to the subordination and social control of the black population in an essay entitled, "Immigration and Puritanism," first published in 1936.[96] "In a history of Puritanism in America," he writes, "slavery deserves a special chapter because, from the definition that has been adopted, slavery was Puritanism raised to the nth degree."[97] Hansen conceives American Puritanism to be a religio-political philosophy that has as its most distinctive feature "the regulation of the morals and actions of those whom the regulators deemed dangerous to society because they were unable to take care of themselves."[98] Negroes belonged to such a class: "When the labor class (or it may be designated the lower class) consisted of slaves, no code of moral behavior was necessary. The upper ranks of society curbed the lower, not by state law but by personal decree. Every master established the standards of morality to which his Negroes must submit and he determined the punishment to be meted out in case of infraction."[99] Hansen in effect incorporated into his vision of slavery Henry Hughes's ideal of "warranteeism": slaves lived under a stern but paternal regime of watchful superintendence, governed according to a reciprocity of obligations and subsistence and presided over by a Puritanically minded seigneurial aristocracy.

However, Hansen was at pains to point out that the very same Puritanism that deemed it absolutely necessary to maintain magisterial watchfulness over the dangerous and dependent classes of Americans had also inspired the movement to abolish slavery. "The Civil War (which in many ways was an attempt of the South to escape this [Puritan] domination) was a great victory for the [Protestant] ministers and, elated by success, they persisted in their efforts until at last morality was written into the fundamental law of the land in the Eighteenth Amendment."[100] The transition from the privately enforced morality of a slavocracy to the democratic state's surveillance over its citizens' vicious habits had called for special police regulation of both the newly emancipated blacks and the newcomers from Europe. As Hansen conceives of the matter, "What the immigrant was in the North, the Negro was in the South—a laborer whose daily life and mental attitude encouraged overindulgence in the cup that cheers."[101] But, while the bulk of Hansen's writing exonerates the European immigrant from blanket accusations of tippling, vice, and immorality, his silence on the actual condition of Negro life in America leaves their alleged immorality unchallenged. To this limited extent, uncritical acceptance of Hansen's own historical writings on the matter would very likely lead third generation black historians to a less than flattering imagery of their forebears, and white historians to making a moral distinction between the first generation of European immigrants and that of black freedmen-and-women.

The Abolition of History and the Quest for Black Self-Esteem

However, at least one student of the social psychology of oppressed peoples holds that, in the case of black Americans, a liberating self-esteem can and ought to be achieved by the severing of any kind of dependence on either history, anthropology, or the sociology of the present or ancestral situation. "The person of authentic self-esteem," writes Anne Wortham, "is . . . not incapacitated by slavery . . . not impeded by segregation; and . . . not impaired by prejudice." Wortham goes on to claim that there "are thousands of Negroes who exemplify the character of the man of self-esteem." She characterizes such a person as "neither impressed nor incited by racist testimony in his behalf . . . not made indistinct by the assertions of others that his is a collective identity . . . not irresolute in his conviction that he is the captain of his fate—not the genes of his ancestors nor the socioeconomic statistics of his social location." But, Wortham also credits the black person of self-esteem with being "an ordinary human being willing to think and discover the truth on which his life depends."[102] Can such a person succeed in determining the life-dependent truths if he or she proceeds without considerations of the legacy of history or the influence of social conditions?

If the contemporary black life-situation is in fact a consequence of decisions taken or roads not taken in the past, Wortham's belief that an act of independent will can provide the psychic self-sufficiency to overcome both the dread hand of the past and the doleful diagnoses of the present seems unlikely to effect its intended outcome. In the black situation the spirit of Hansen's law, whatever its general validity as science, might have to become a moral and social imperative. If it is to be derived from a reconceptualization of certain events in history, the self-esteem of the black population might have to be purchased at the price of the self-esteem of Margaret Mitchell's white southerners, as well as that of their present-day supporters.

One variant of black third generation return might very well arise among the generation descended from the Reconstruction and Redemption eras. It might seek to answer a question that relates very much to the contemporary Afro-American people's collective and individual self-esteem: Did the Congress and the courts take up and carry into execution the mandate presented to them by the Thirteenth, Fourteenth, and Fifteenth Amendments to the Constitution, namely, the obligation not merely to forbid the re-enslavement of Afro-American (or any other) people residing in or migrating to the United States, but also the command to remove, by appropriate legislation, once and for all, the lingering badges, likely incidents, and lasting indicia of slavery? The contemporary legatees of the Emancipation, Reconstruction, and Redemption eras—now three or more generations removed from the period when their grandparents and their white supporters struggled to unshackle themselves from the effects of more than two centuries of bondage—might want to turn back the historical clock in order to see whether Wortham's conception of a psychological validation of full-fledged black American citizenship—a complete liberation from the debilitating vestiges of racially based involuntary servitude—was prevented from ever arising. Did direct opposition or ineffective actions taken with respect to the comprehensive program of civic inclusion envisioned by the abolitionists and the emancipators of 1865 fail to complete the emancipatory task? If it could be shown that the vestiges of slavery were not only not killed together with the institution of bondage, but in fact permitted to survive, to develop, indeed, to flourish, branch out, and perhaps, engulf other peoples of color in America, entrapping them in an all-encompassing but degrading web of inferior group affiliation, then the new historical understanding might be used to buttress demands for twentieth century Congresses and courts to engage in belated but necessary enforcement of the Civil War Amendments and of all related legislation appropriate to their original purposes.[103] The much-vaunted self-esteem that Wortham describes but most analysts of the black scene have found wanting among the Afro-American people of modern America[104] might be recoverable by means of a search for its historical antecedents and causes—and for the causes that hindered its development. If self-esteem finds its fulfillment in an individual who depends on no ascriptive sodality whatsoever for personal identity, who has emerged not merely from a situation that is beyond the melting pot but one that is socially divorced from self-referencing common descent groups altogether, it behooves those in quest of that self-esteem to search out its roots.

In his path-breaking decision ending public school segregation in the United States, Chief Justice Earl Warren, speaking for a unanimous Supreme Court, observed: "To separate [children in grade and high schools] from others of similar age and qualifications solely because of their race generates a feeling of inferiority as to their status in the community that may affect their hearts and minds in a way unlikely ever to be undone."[105] Certainly that feeling of inferiority, deriving from racially based segregation in public schools, does serious harm to the quality and sense of self-esteem that the black child is in the process of acquiring during the formative years.[106] However, is the esteem-harming segregation, which in 1954 the Court set aside as violative of the Fourteenth Amendment, itself the product of decisions made much earlier? Moreover, might these decisions, that a third generation return to post–Civil-War black history could discover, be interpreted as abdications from the responsibility imposed on Congress and the courts by the Civil War Amendments and the post–Civil War Civil Rights Acts?

These questions are not new. However, in light of the actual method of reasoning employed by the Court in the *Brown* decision, and because of the quarrel over the nature and sources of self-esteem that emerges in a comparison of the views of Hansen and Wortham, it is in order to raise them once again. Chief Justice Warren announced as part of the *Brown* decision that "in approaching this problem, we cannot turn back the clock to 1868 when the [Fourteenth] Amendment was adopted, or even to 1896 when *Plessy v. Ferguson* [the case in which the doctrine of "separate but equal" achieved legitimacy] was written."[107] Warren believed that the Court's earlier reargument hearing, "devoted to the circumstances surrounding the adoption of the Fourteenth Amendment in 1868," had been inconclusive with respect to uncovering the intentions of the framers, their opponents, and the general citizenry: "The most avid proponents of the post–War Amendments undoubtedly intended to remove all legal distinctions among 'all persons born or naturalized in the United States.' Their opponents, just as certainly, were antagonistic to both the letter and the spirit of the [Post–war] Amendments and wished them to have the most limited effect. What others in Congress and the state legislatures had in mind cannot be determined with any degree of certainty."[108] Warren added to this observation another, holding that an examination of the significance of public education at the time of the amendment's adoption was irrelevant because whatever was the case then, "today, education is perhaps the most important function of state and local governments."[109] Having thus disposed of any potential usage for historical arguments, Warren went on to decide the matter on the basis of school segregation's inferiorizing effects, holding these to have been created by a suspect racial classification and to be without any constitutional support. "We conclude that in the field of public education the doctrine of 'separate but equal' has no place. Separate educational facilities are inherently unequal."[110] Despite the undoubted value that Warren's carefully crafted opinion had for securing unanimity from his colleagues on the Court, and for offering up a united judicial front against school segregation,[111] its demurrer about the Civil War Amendment's intent left that matter open for others to determine.[112] The matter is of no small importance, since the present era has been characterized as including a "second Reconstruction period," one that could reinvigorate the process of dismantling slavery that had begun in 1865 and, perhaps, redress the balance of inequities that continues to descend from its vestiges.[113]

Contemporary historical and legal investigations have attempted to show that the makers of the Thirteenth Amendment to the Constitution—declared ratified and in force on December 18, 1865—intended their addition to the supreme law of the land to remove slavery and involuntary servitude from having any place in American law and also to eliminate its "incidents," "badges," and "indicia."[114] Moreover, by its second section, Congress granted to itself the "power to enforce this article by appropriate legislation."[115] The issue debated before the Supreme Court in the first generation of that amendment's existence was the meaning and range of applicability of the terms "badges," "incidents," and "indicia." One consequence of a shifting majority on the Court and of Congress's declining interest in the condition of the emancipated blacks was a constriction of the definition and a restriction of the scope of the amendment and its attendant legislation. In 1883, in the Civil Rights Cases, (109 U.S. 3),[116] a majority of the Supreme Court declared unconstitutional the Civil Rights Act of 1875—a statute that forbade racial exclusion from or segregation in transportation, inns, theaters, and that required racial equality in the selection of juries—holding, inter alia, that the "incidents" of slavery that the Thirteenth Amendment sought to remove included only "compulsory service . . . for the benefit of the master, restraint of . . . movements except by the master's will, disability to hold property, to make contracts, to have a standing in court, to be witness against a white person, and such like burdens and incapacities." Mr. Justice Bradley, speaking for the Court's majority, went on to assert that since "mere discriminations on account of race or color were not regarded as badges of slavery" when directed against free blacks during the slave era, they could not be so regarded after Emancipation. Congress, he concluded, had not taken upon itself an obligation under the Thirteenth Amendment "to adjust what may be called the social rights of men and races in the community."

In a lone dissent, however, Justice John Marshall Harlan argued that since the institution of slavery whose incidents and badges the amendment and the Civil Rights Acts were intended to remove had "rested wholly upon the inferiority, as a race, of those held in bondage, their freedom necessarily involved immunity from, and protection against, all discrimination against them, because of their race, in respect of such civil rights as belong to freemen of other races." In contradistinction to Bradley's opinion, Harlan went on to challenge his colleagues' claim that racial discrimination in transportation, inns, and amusement parks is a purely private matter, beyond the reach of federal statutes: "In every material sense applicable to the practical enforcement of the Fourteenth Amendment," he observed, "railroad corporations, keepers of inns, and managers of places of amusement are agents or instrumentalities of the State, because they are charged with duties to the public, and are amenable, in respect of their duties and functions, to governmental regulation." Therefore, Harlan asserted, "Congress . . . under its express power to enforce that [i.e., the Thirteenth] Amendment . . . may enact laws to protect that people against the deprivation, *because of their race*, of any civil rights granted to other freemen in the same State; and such legislation may be of a direct and primary character, operating upon States, their officers and agents, and, also, upon, at least, such individuals and corporations as exercise public functions and wield power and authority under the State." As to the majority opinion's claim that when a person is delivered from slavery to freedom, that person and his or her fellow ex-slaves must recognize "a stage in the progress of his elevation when he . . . ceases to be the special favorite of the laws"—and its implication that that stage had already been reached in 1883—Harlan retorted that it was "scarcely just to say that the colored race has been the special favorite of the laws" in the eighteen years since the amendment had been ratified. Moreover, he went on to point out that the proponents of the postwar amendments and the supporting civil rights laws had known from the beginning of their endeavors that it would not be enough " 'to help the feeble up, but [that it would also be necessary] to support him after' " by such measures as would secure for the members of the African race "what had already been done in every State of the Union for the white race." However, at every step in that direction, Harlan pointed out, "the nation has been confronted with class tyranny," and he warned that while "today, it is the colored race which is denied, by corporations and individuals wielding public authority, rights fundamental in their freedom and citizenship . . . [tomorrow] it may be that some other race will fall under the ban of race discrimination."

The final blow against the claim that the states had an obligation under the Civil War Amendments to secure the material conditions affecting black and white self-esteem was struck in 1896, when Mr. Justice Brown, speaking for a seven-man majority of the Supreme Court (one justice not participating), upheld a Louisiana statute requiring the segregation in separate or partitioned coaches of colored and white passengers on trains moving within the State (*Plessy v. Ferguson* 163 U.S. 256). One part of Homer Adolph Plessy's argument that Louisiana's law violated both the Thirteenth and Fourteenth Amendment turned on whether the requirement that "colored" persons be seated in racially separate but otherwise equal railroad cars deprived blacks of their *property right* in their own reputations. Conceding for purposes of argument that reputation was a property right, Mr. Justice Brown asserted, "we are unable to see how this statute deprives him of, or in any way affects his right to, such property. If he be a white man and assigned to a colored coach, he may have his action for damages against the company for being deprived of his so-called property. Upon the other hand, if he be a colored man and be so assigned, he has been deprived of no property, since he is not lawfully entitled to the reputation of being a white man" (idem at 260). Hence, the Court's majority inferred that an American's reputation existed largely if not exclusively in terms of his *color* and not in terms of his or her common membership in humanity, in the community, or in the citizenry of the United States.

In the instant case, Mr. Plessy, who was one-eighth "African blood" and seven-eighths "Caucasian," was held to be "colored" by the conductor on the train though "the mixture of colored blood was not discernible in him" (idem at 257). The Court's majority added that "the power to assign to a particular coach obviously implies the power to determine to which race the passenger belongs, as well as the power to determine who, under the laws of the particular state, is to be deemed a white and who a colored person" (idem at 260). Not only were the freedmen-and-women and their descendants reminded that their self-esteem resided in their color, but also they were told that their color was a matter to be determined by the agents of the state where they happened to reside or through which they happened to travel. Indeed, having declared reputation to be a property right protectable within the status spectrum of racial color, the Court went on to admit that, "it is true that the question of the proportion of colored blood necessary to constitute a colored person, as distinguished from a white person, is one upon which there is a difference of opinion in the different states, some holding that any visible admixture of Black blood stamps the person as belonging to the colored race . . . others that it depends upon the preponderance of blood . . . and still others that the predominance of white blood must only be in the proportions of three-fourths." However, in a gesture affirming state's rights over the matter, the Court abandoned the question as one "to be determined under the laws of each state." The Court did concede that "under the allegation of his [i.e., Mr. Plessy's] petition it may undoubtedly become a question of importance whether, under the laws of Louisiana, the petitioner belongs to the white or colored race." However, what race one belonged to, and what indignities might be heaped upon it, were left up to the states, no indignity being recognized as a vestige of slavery so long as any racial separations flowing from it included the provision of equal facilities.[117]

There remained the question of whether Louisiana's legalization of racially segregated railroad coaches constituted an institutionalized conferral of a badge of inferiority on the Negro race and whether, if this be true, it was, thereby, a Constitutionally prohibited continuation, or a vestige, of slavery. In answering this query, Mr. Justice Brown sounded the death knell to Mr. Plessy's request that the Court protect his and his people's hardly won social esteem against public laws that would degrade it:

> We consider the underlying fallacy of the plaintiff's argument to consist in the assumption that the enforced separation of the two races stamps the colored race with a badge of inferiority. If this be so, it is not by reason of anything found in the act, but solely because the colored race chooses to put that construction upon it. . . . The argument also assumes that social prejudice may be overcome by legislation, and that equal rights cannot be secured to the negro [sic] except by an enforced commingling of the two races. We cannot accept this proposition. If the two races are to meet on terms of social equality, it must be

the result of natural affinity, a mutual appreciation of each other's merits and a voluntary consent of individuals. . . . Legislation is powerless to eradicate racial instincts or to abolish distinctions based upon physical differences, and the attempt to do so can only result in accentuating the difficulties of the present situation. . . . If one race be inferior to the other socially, the Constitution cannot put them upon the same plane (idem at 261).

In his lone dissent, Mr. Justice Harlan directly addressed the issue of social esteem and racial pride, observing that there is a distinction between an individual's or group's private notions and rights of action on the matter and the state's right to establish a fixed hierarchy of status by statute. "Every true man has pride of race, and under appropriate circumstances, when the rights of others, his equals before the law, are not to be affected, it is his privilege to express such pride and to take such action based upon it as to him seems proper. But I deny that any legislative body or judicial tribunal may have regard to the race of citizens when the civil rights of those citizens are involved." In Harlan's opinion, not only was Louisiana's statute "inconsistent . . . with that equality of rights which pertains to citizenship, national and state, but [also] with the personal liberty enjoyed by every one within the United States" (idem at 262). Harlan pointed out that the "white race deems itself to be the dominant race in this country," and conceded, "so it is, in prestige, in achievements, in education, in wealth, and in power." And, he added that it would likely "continue to be for all time, if it remains true to its great heritage and holds fast to the principles of constitutional liberty." However, it was precisely in relation to the latter that Louisiana's statute and the Court's majority had run afoul. "There is no caste here," Harlan asserted: "Our Constitution is color-blind, and neither knows nor tolerates classes among citizens. . . . The humblest is the peer of the most powerful. The law regards man as man, and takes no account of his surroundings or of his color when his civil rights as guaranteed by the supreme law of the land are involved" (idem at 263–64). As Harlan concluded on the matter, the Court's approval of the state's right to require racially separate but materially equal accommodations in travel had not only undermined the Civil War Amendment's intended obviation of "the race line from our governmental system" (idem at 262), but also "permit-[ted] the seeds of race hate to be planted under the sanction of law" (idem at 264). The effects of its decisions, Harlan vainly forewarned, "will, in time, prove to be quite as pernicious as the decision made by this tribunal in the *Dred Scott Case*...[i.e., it would assure] that the descendants of Africans . . . could not claim any of the rights and privileges . . . provided for and secured to citizens of the United States" (idem at 264).

From the foregoing sketch of the legalized obstacles put in the way of black advancement during the first generation of their Emancipation, it appears that the situations whose social organization affects esteem were directed toward the degradation of Negroes. This was accomplished by racially discriminatory state laws and by the Supreme Court's approval of them. In the years after *Plessy*, the segregation deemed reasonable for transportation was extended to embrace education, recreation, churches, jobs, professions, and avocations. Ultimately, it defined racial relationships in virtually every avenue and niche of public or quasi-public life. Moreover, until the twenty year campaign—begun in 1948 and successfully completed only in 1967—to have them declared ultra vires, antimiscegenation statutes prohibited marriage across racial lines in thirty-nine of the states of the Union.[118] The separation of the peoples that Isaac's twin sons, Jacob and Esau, had decided was best for their respective development as nations, was reenacted among the black and white "progeny" of Thomas Jefferson—with one significant difference: whereas the biblical Esau was able to establish his people as a free and independent nation on their own land, the "Esaus" of America fell under the dominion of those who had originally appropriated their birthright and then, after a bloody struggle, had grudgingly returned to them its symbols, but not its substance.

□   □   □

We are met today at a conference that celebrates the fiftieth anniversary of the appearance of Hansen's great essay; in the same period, two other celebratory events have occurred. June 30, 1986, marks the half-century since Macmillan Publishers first released Margaret Mitchell's *Gone With the Wind*—the book that Hansen singled out as an instance of southern white third generation return and that already had sold two million copies by the time his essay was published. By 1986, Ms. Mitchell's book was still selling at the rate of 250,000 copies per year, and the eponymous film made from the novel had been seen by more moviegoers than make up the total population of the United States. In his introduction to the fiftieth anniversary edition, Tom Wicker attempts to defend the racist imagery found throughout the book by pointing out that "Margaret Mitchell was born in 1900, when the Civil War was barely 35 years in the past and Reconstruction was even more recent," that she "began work on her novel in 1926 . . . when first generation descendants of the war and the post-war years were all about her and the South itself was by no means economically or politically recovered from those years . . . [and when the] modern civil rights movement was 25 years in the future." Wicker asserts that "Margaret Mitchell was a child of her time, not ours, and is unfairly judged by the current view of racism."[119] However, with the understandings available from Hansen's essay, we may critically evaluate Mitchell's racism as a feature of a particular group's third generation return—her novel is not properly described as a product of her time; it is rather a presentiment of her geo-generational group's last stand in behalf of white supremacy. Wicker's thesis rests on the false assumption that southern white negrophobia was ubiquitous; he overlooks not only the dissents filed by the Tennessean, John Marshall Harlan, but also the South's other forgotten voices, those who spoke up for equality and civil rights during and after the Reconstruction era.[120] The struggle of Afro-American writers and historians to recapture their ancestral heritage—to become creative participants in their own third generation return—entails a fight to overturn the Wicker-Mitchell thesis that white racism was ever justifiable, as well as a search for the lost, stolen, or denied grounds of Negro self-esteem.

The second anniversary of this period celebrates "Negritude" through papers presented at a conference held in March, 1987, in Miami, Florida. Felicia R. Lee, a black journalist who covered the event for the *Miami Herald*, described it as "really a conference about what it means to go home and how one gets there."[121] Aime Cesaire, the French-speaking poet and intellectual who first coined the term, addressed the conference and redefined *Negritude* to refer to "the debris of assassinated cultures." Cesaire went on to pose the same choice that Wortham had: "Either we get rid of the past as a burden . . . or assume it and . . . continue our forward advancement."[122] For him and his fellow conferees, the choice is clear: the debris of those assassinated African cultures must be pressed into service for an all-encompassing black liberation, everywhere that this people is oppressed. A third generation return—such as that recalled in Ms. Lee's reminiscence of her poverty-stricken grandparents in fin de siècle Mississippi—entails a complex redefinition of all the races involved. As Ms. Lee puts it: "So it is up to us, again, to remind whites of who we are and therefore who they are. They did not become 'white' until they came to America, and they became white to define themselves as the norm and blacks as the universal other."[123]

The generational return that Ms. Lee calls for requires America's immigrant descendants to recognize their great grand-parental ethnonational origins in Europe: "The so called white came here as an Irishman, a Pole, a Russian. In assimilating, he cast his history to the winds and pretended that ours began when we stepped off the slave ships."[124] If each people discovers its own ethnonational roots in a continent from which its ancestors were transferred, Lee seems to say, America's *racial* solidarities might lose some of their rigidity— dissolve, perhaps, in the flux of *nationality* and its transformation into *ethnic* identity.

Hansen had entitled his original essay "The Problem of the Third Generation Immigrant." What he may not have realized was that one American problem—a variant of Myrdal's American dilemma— was the conflation of race with ethnicity and nationality, and the confusion of each of these with respect to the achievement of liberty, the establishment of equality, and the promotion of group and self-esteem. In 1979 Oscar Handlin rebuked the new breed of race-conscious historians for grouping the "congeries of [European immigrant] populations sharply divided among themselves" into a single category of "whites": "It may or may not have been correct to speak of 'whites' or of the 'white community' in New York or Chicago of the 1960s; it was grossly inaccurate to do so for those cities before 1930."[125] Like Ms. Lee, Handlin favors remembering the ethnonational distinctions that divided uprooted Europeans from one another and slowed the Americanization process. However, Handlin overlooks the degree to which self-identification as "white" facilitated that process, simultaneously helping to dissolve nationality while giving added vehemence to racism. The European could assimilate in Robert Park's sense of the term—"a process of interpenetration and fusion in which persons and groups acquire the memories, sentiments, and attitudes of other persons or groups, and by sharing their experience and history, are incorporated with them in a common cultural life"[126]—by indicating how much he or she shared with fellow white Americans their prejudice toward blacks. However, since more recent investigations have shown that prejudiced attitudes toward the Negro predate the founding of new societies in the Americas,[127] it is questionable whether a return to self- and group-identity as ethnic aggregates would necessarily reduce interracial hostilities.

A black American generational turn toward "negritude" presents its own problems. Negritude is civilizational in the sense that Durkheim and Mauss used that term;[128] it refers to cultural traits that transcend geopolitical boundaries but are commonly shared by a diasporic people.[129] By redefining negritude as the *debris of assassinated* cultures, Cesaire appears to recognize the difficulties of recovering it, and the partialities that are all that might be expected from such a historical archaeology. For blacks in America this quest is not new; indeed, African return, either through migration or spiritual rebirth, has served as an alluring alternative at each of those historic moments when white America refused full-fledged citizenship to Negroes.[130] However, a realistic ethnic respecification—one that would provide for America's blacks the national equivalent of that which is available to the white man or woman descended from Irish or other European immigrants—seems unlikely. Despite Alex Haley's recent discovery of his Gambian ancestry,[131] few American blacks appear to be possessed of or able to obtain the information necessary to learn their precise ethnic ancestry. We are long past the period when an Equiano Olaudah (1745–1801?) could recall and write about his Ibo childhood,[132] or an enslaved Abd al-Rahman Ibrahima (1762–1829) be returned to his rightful place as a prince in the Fulbe empire.[133] The Black Muslims' employment of an "X" to indicate the unknown family name tells volumes about what Afro-Americans have lost in their four or more centuries in North America.[134] As St. Clair Drake has observed, "however much Negro Americans come to appreciate African cultures for what they are, it is likely that they will continue to think of the African folk and their products as different, non-Western, exotic, strange—as *African*."[135] Nevertheless, the new postcolonial Africa that has formed itself into independent states holds out some capacity for revitalizing American Negro pride: "Seeing successful and forceful Africans winning the respect of *white* Americans—people like Senghor and Azikiwe—will bolster the self-esteem of many American Negroes." Drake went on to observe: "There will be no need for fantasy symbols such as black angels or Madonnas, for attractive black airline hostesses and African beauty queens competing in international contests, as well as the artists and the diplomats, will exist in reality."[136]

Exemplified in a racially divisive work like Margaret Mitchell's *Gone With the Wind*, Hansen's law tends not only to impose a concrete and binding tie on its particular generational group but also to spread out and incorporate other whites, who, though not of the same descent group, nevertheless see in its thesis an expression of their own race-referential ideal and selfish social interest. Within any generation, as Karl Mannheim once pointed out, "there can exist a number of differentiated, antagonistic generation-units." In the case of the black and white third generation descended from the Emancipation-Reconstruction-Redemption eras, there is constituted what Mannheim calls "an 'actual' generation precisely because they are oriented toward each other, even though only in the sense of fighting each other."[137]

Since Hansen presented his thesis as a historical law, historians have pointed out its falsification in the failure of some third generations to make a return to their grandparental roots. However, it was Mannheim who observed that "not every generation location—not even every age group—creates new collective impulses and formative principles original to itself and adequate to its situation."[138] Hansen's law speaks to those generations that do realize the potentialities inherent in their location, that are capable of forming a particular center of configuration around their common descent group and around all who would identify with it. Mannheim calls this capability one that fosters "a new *generation entelechy*."[139] Perhaps, now, blacks and whites are at last in a position to establish such an intellectual formation—to look back honestly to their history of unhappy antagonisms, so that they can look forward to, if not a consensus historiography, at least one that recognizes that racial justice is to be sought as the fruit that has long been ripening on the common American family tree.

NOTES

1. Werner Sollors, *Beyond Ethnicity: Consent and Descent in American Cultures* (New York: Oxford University Press, 1986), p. 214.

2. Marcus Lee Hansen, *The Problem of the Third Generation Immigrant* (Rock Island, Ill.: Augustana Historical Society, 1938). Reprinted in Peter Kivisto and Dag Blanck, eds., *American Immigrants and Their Generations: Studies and Commentaries on the Hansen Thesis after Fifty Years* (Urbana: University of Illinois Press, 1990), pp. 191–216.

3. Ibid., pp. 194–95.

4. See, e.g., Stanford M. Lyman, "Generation and Character: The Case of the Japanese Americans," in Lyman, *The Asian in North America* (Santa Barbara: American Bibliographic Center–Clio Press, 1977), pp. 151–76.

5. For the concept see Stanford M. Lyman and Marvin B. Scott, "On the Time Track" in Lyman and Scott, *A Sociology of the Absurd* (New York: Appleton-Century-Crofts, 1970), pp. 189–212.

6. Maurice Halbwachs, *The Collective Memory*, trans. Francis J. Ditter, Jr., and Vida Yazdi Ditter (New York: Harper and Row, 1980. Original French publication 1950), p. 93.

7. Quoted in English translation of Gustav Ratzenhofer, *Wesen und Zweck der Politik*, in Albion W. Small, *General Sociology: An Exposition of the Main Developments in Sociological Theory from Spencer to Ratzenhofer* (Chicago: University of Chicago Press, 1905; reprint, New York: Arno Press, 1974), p. 256.

8. Hansen, *Problem*, pp. 16–17.

9. Ibid., p. 20.

10. Ibid., p. 19.

11. Marcus Lee Hansen, "The Third Generation in America," *Commentary*, 14 (Nov. 1952), pp. 492–500.

12. Will Herberg, *Protestant-Catholic-Jew: An Essay in American Religious Sociology* (Garden City, N.Y.: Doubleday-Anchor, 1960), p. 186.

13. Margaret Mead, *And Keep Your Powder Dry: An Anthropologist Looks at America*, expanded ed. (New York: Morrow, 1965. Orig. pub. 1942), pp. 53, 49–50.

14. Hansen, *Problem*, p. 9.

15. Michael Novak, *The Rise of the Unmeltable Ethnics: Politics and Culture in the Seventies* (New York: Macmillan, 1975), p. xxxv.

16. Herbert Gans, "Symbolic Ethnicity: The Future of Ethnic Groups and Cultures in America," in *On the Making of Americans: Essays in Honor of David Riesman*, ed. Herbert J. Gans, Nathan Glazer, Joseph R. Gusfield, and Christopher Jencks (Philadelphia: University of Pennsylvania Press, 1979), p. 215.

17. Herbert Gans, "Ethnicity, Acculturation and Assimilation," foreword to Neil Sandberg, *Ethnic Identity and Assimilation* (New York: Praeger, 1974), p. xiii.

18. Herbert Blumer, "The Problem of the Concept in Social Psychology," *American Journal of Sociology*, 45 (Mar. 1940), pp. 707–19.

19. For this concept and its application to second generation Japanese Americans, see Tetsuden Kashima, "Japanese American Internees Return, 1945 to 1955: Readjustment and Social Amnesia," *Phylon: The Atlanta University Review of Race and Culture*, 41 (Summer 1980), pp. 107–15.

20. Maurice Halbwachs, *Collective Memory*.

21. Hansen, *Problem*, pp. 9–10.

22. See S. Frank Miyamoto, "Self, Motivation, and Symbolic Interactionist Theory," in Tamotsu Shibutani, ed., *Human Nature and Collective Behavior: Papers in Honor of Herbert Blumer* (Englewood Cliffs, N.J.: Prentice-Hall, 1970), pp. 271–85.

23. Hansen, *Problem*, p. 10.

24. See E. Merton Coulter, "What the South Has Done about Its History," address presented in Birmingham, Alabama, October 25, 1935. Reprinted in George Brown Tindall, ed., *The Pursuit of Southern History: Presidential Addresses of the Southern Historical Association* (Baton Rouge: Louisiana State University Press, 1967), pp. 163–214.

25. Alfred Schutz, *The Phenomenology of the Social World*, trans. George Walsh and Frederick Lehnert (Evanston: Northwestern University Press, 1967), pp. 163–214.

26. Among many works, see: W. J. Cash, *The Mind of the South* (New York: Vintage Books, 1960. Orig. pub. 1941); Twelve Southerners, *I'll Take My Stand: The South and the Agrarian Tradition* (New York: Harper Torchbooks, 1962. Orig. pub. 1930); Lewis M. Killian, *White Southerners*, rev. ed. (Amherst: University of Massachusetts Press, 1985); William C. Havard and Walter Sullivan, *A Band of Prophets: The Vanderbilt Agrarians after Fifty Years* (Baton Rouge: Louisiana State University Press, 1982); three works by John Shelton Reed, *The Enduring South: Subcultural Persistence in Mass Society* (Chapel Hill: University of North Carolina Press, 1972); *One South: An Ethnic Approach to Regional Culture* (Baton Rouge: Louisiana State University Press, 1982); *Southerners: The Social Psychology of Sectionalism* (Chapel Hill: University of North Carolina Press, 1983); Daniel Joseph Singal, *The War Within: From Victorian to Modernist Thought in the South, 1919–1945* (Chapel Hill: University of North Carolina Press, 1982); Dewey W. Grantham, *The Regional Imagination: The South and Recent American History* (Nashville: Vanderbilt University Press, 1979); *Regionalism and the South: Selected Papers of Rupert Vance*, ed. John Shelton Reed and Daniel Joseph Singal (Chapel Hill: University of North Carolina Press, 1982); George Brown Tindall, *The Ethnic Southerners* (Baton Rouge: Louisiana State University Press, 1976); Louis D. Rubin, Jr., Blyden Jackson, Rayburn S. Moore, Lewis P. Simpson, and Thomas Daniel Young, eds., *The History of Southern Literature* (Baton Rouge: Louisiana State University Press, 1985), pp. 177–606.

27. C. Vann Woodward, *Origin of the New South, 1877–1913* (Baton Rouge: Louisiana State University Press, 1966. Orig. pub. 1951), pp. 297–99.

28. Lucy M. Cohen, *Chinese in the Post–Civil War South: A People Without a History* (Baton Rouge: Louisiana State University Press, 1984); James W. Loewen, *The Mississippi Chinese: Between Black and White* (Cambridge: Harvard University Press, 1971); Robert Seto Quan in collaboration with Julian B. Roebuck, *Lotus among the Magnolias: The Mississippi Chinese* (Jackson: University Press of Mississippi, 1982).

29. George Groh, *The Black Migration: The Journey to Urban America* (New York: Weybright and Talley, 1972), pp. 9–87; Florette Henri, *Black Migration: Movement North, 1900–1920* (Garden City, N.Y.: Doubleday-Anchor, 1976), pp. 1–80.

30. Cf. Albert Murray, *South to a Very Old Place* (New York: McGraw-HIll, 1971); A. Murray, with Willie Morris, *North toward Home* (New York: Dell, 1967).

31. John C. McKinney and Edgar T. Thompson, eds., *The South in Continuity and Change* (Durham: Duke University Press, 1965).

32. See Dewey W. Grantham, *Southern Progressivism: The Reconciliation of Progress and Tradition* (Knoxville: University of Tennessee Press, 1983).

33. Hansen, *Problem*, p. 6.

34. George B. Tindall, "Introduction," in Tindall, ed., *Pursuit of Southern History*, pp. xi–xxi.

35. *American Historical Review*, October, 1936, p. vii.

36. Wyn Craig Wade, *The Fiery Cross: The Ku Klux Klan in America* (New York: Simon and Schuster, 1987), pp. 9–10.

37. James Temple Kirby, *Media-Made Dixie: The South in the American Imagination* (Baton Rouge: Louisiana State University Press, 1978), pp. 72, 73–74.

38. Thomas Dixon, Jr., *The Clansman: An Historical Romance of the Ku Klux Klan* (Phoenix: Associated Professional Services, 1965 [1904]).

39. See Bosley Crowther, "The Birth of *Birth of a Nation*," in Lindsay Patterson, comp., *Black Films and Film-Makers: A Comprehensive Anthology from Stereotype to Superhero* (New York: Dodd, Mead and Co., 1975), pp. 75–83; William K. Everson, *American Silent Film* (New York: Oxford University Press, 1978), pp. 72–89; Thomas Cripps, *Slow Fade to Black: The Negro in American Film, 1900–1942* (New York: Oxford University Press, 1977), pp. 41–69; Peter Noble, *The Negro in Films* (London: Cornhill, 1948; reprint ed., Port Washington, N.Y.: Kennikat Press, 1969), pp. 33–43; Edward Mapp, *Blacks in American Films: Today and Yesterday* (Metuchen, N.J.: Scarecrow Press, 1972), pp. 18–20; James R. Nesteby, *Black Images in American Films, 1896–1954* (Washington, D.C.: University Press of America, 1982), pp. 27–42; Donald Bogle, *Toms, Coons, Mulattoes, Mammies and Bucks: An Interpretive History of Blacks in American Films* (New York: Viking Press, 1973), pp. 10–18; Richard Schickel, *D.W. Griffith: An American Life* (New York: Simon and Schuster, 1984), pp. 212–302.

40. Richard A. Maynard, ed., *The Black Man on Film: Racial Stereotyping* (Rochelle Park, N.J.: Hayden Book Co., 1974), pp. 25–40.

41. Lawrence Reddick, "Of Motion Pictures," in Patterson, *Black Films*, pp. 14–15.

42. Ibid., p. 15.

43. Hansen, *Problem*, pp. 9–10.

44. August Meier and Elliott Rudwick, *Black History and the Historical Profession, 1915–1980* (Urbana: University of Illinois Press, 1986), pp. 1–160.

45. Charles Harris Wesley, "Interest in a Neglected Phase of History," *AME Church Review*, 32 (Apr. 1916), p. 268. Quoted in Meier and Rudwick, *Black History*, p. 77.

46. Hansen, *Problem*, p. 17.

47. John Hope Franklin, "On the Evolution of Scholarship in Afro-American History," in Darlene Clark Hine, ed., *The State of Afro-American History* (Baton Rouge: Louisiana State University Press, 1986), p. 21.

48. Otto Lindenmeyer, *Black History: Lost, Stolen, or Strayed* (New York: Avon Books, 1970).

49. Vincent Harding, "Responsibilities of the Black Scholar to the Community," in Hine, *State of Afro-American History*, pp. 277–84.

50. Franklin, "On the Evolution," pp. 14–16.

51. An exemplar who belongs to the tradition of that generation and exemplifies its spirit in his work is Benjamin Quarles. Among his many works, see *The Negro in the Making of America* (New York: Collier Books, 1964); *The Negro in the American Revolution* (Chapel Hill: University of North Carolina Press, 1961); *Allies for Freedom: Blacks and John Brown* (New York: Oxford University Press, 1974); *Black Abolitionists* (New York: Oxford University Press, 1969); *Frederick Douglass* (New York: Athenenum, 1968. Orig. pub. 1948); *The Negro in the Civil War* (Boston: Little Brown, 1953); *Lincoln and the Negro* (New York: Oxford University Press, 1962).

52. Allan Nevins and Henry Steele Commager, *A Pocket History of the United States,* 7th ed. (New York: Washington Square Press, 1981), p. 38.

53. Samuel Eliot Morison and Henry Steele Commager, *The Growth of the American Republic* (New York: Oxford University Press, 1942), vol. 1, p. 537.

54. Ibid.

55. *Time Magazine,* February 26, 1951, pp. 48–49; Lindenmeyer, *Black History,* p. 15.

56. Charles Harris Wesley, "The Negroes of New York in the Emancipation Movement," *Journal of Negro History,* 24 (Jan. 1939), p. 103. Quoted in Rudwick and Meier, pp. 76–77.

57. Harold Proshansky and Peggy Newton, "Colour: The Nature and Meaning of Negro Self-Identity," in Peter Watson, ed., *Psychology and Race* (Chicago: Aldine, 1974), p. 181. Emphasis supplied.

58. Stanley Elkins, *Slavery: A Problem in American Institutional and Intellectual Life* (Chicago: University of Chicago Press, 1959), pp. 81–139; 2d ed., (1968), pp. 81–139, 239–44; 3d ed., rev. (1976), pp. 81–139, 223–302.

59. Ann J. Lane, ed., *The Debate over Slavery: Stanley Elkins and His Critics* (Urbana: University of Illinois Press, 1971); Kenneth M. Stampp, "Rebels and Sambos: The Search for the Negro's Personality in Slavery," in Stampp, *The Imperiled Union: Essays on the Background of the Civil War* (New York: Oxford University Press, 1980), pp. 39–71.

60. Hansen, *Problem,* pp. 6–9.

61. See Mircea Eliade, *The Myth of the Eternal Return,* trans. Willard R. Trask. Bollingen Series 46 (New York: Random House-Pantheon Books, 1954).

62. For the most comprehensive account of the Jefferson-Hemings affair, see Fawn M. Brodie, *Thomas Jefferson: An Intimate History* (New York, W. W. Norton Co., 1974); for a typical example of the polemical denial, see John Chester Miller, *The Wolf by the Ears: Thomas Jefferson and Slavery* (New York: The Free Press, 1977), pp. 148–76.

63. See the bitter exchange on this matter pitting Justice Bruce McM. Wright against John J. McCartney, in letters to the editor of the *New York Times* (Feb. 7, 1987 and Feb. 15, 1987).

64. Nathan I. Huggins, "Integrating Afro-American History into American History," in Hine, *State of Afro-American History,* p. 163.

65. Ibid., pp. 161–62.

66. J. Hector St. John de Crevecoeur, *Letters from an American Farmer* (New York: E. P. Dutton & Co., 1957. Orig. pub. 1782), pp. 35–82.

67. Ibid., pp. 137, 155–68, 187–89. There is also brief mention of blacks in de Crevecoeur, *Sketches of Eighteenth-Century America: More Letters from an American Farmer*, ed. Henri L. Bourdin, Ralph W. Gabriel, and Stanley T. Williams (New York: Benjamin Blom, 1972), pp. 44, 46, 110–11, 121, 143–44, 148, 160, 168.

68. Ibid., p. 167.

69. Langston Hughes, "I, Too, Sing America," in Langston Hughes and Arna Bontemps, eds., *The Poetry of the Negro, 1746–1949* (Garden City, N.Y.: Doubleday, 1949), p. 97.

70. William Wells Brown, *Clotel or, The President's Daughter: A Narrative of Slave Life in the United States* (New York: Citadel Press, 1969. Orig. pub. 1853).

71. See William Edward Farrison, *William Wells Brown: Author and Reformer* (Chicago: University of Chicago Press, 1969), pp. 215–32.

72. In the tradition of one seeking the legitimation of his people's American identity, Brown would later write *The Blackman, His Antecedents, His Genius, and His Achievements* (Miami: Mnemosyne Publishing Inc., 1969. Orig. pub. 1865); and *The Negro in the American Rebellion: His Heroism and His Fidelity* (New York: Citadel Press, 1971. Orig. pub. 1867).

73. Brown, *Clotel*, p. 219.

74. Ibid., p. 245. The statement is quoted from a contemporary circular: Reverend Edward S. Mathews, "Statistical Account of the Connection of the Religious Bodies in America with Slavery."

75. Robert Bone, an important contemporary critic of black American literature, dismisses *Clotel* as a melodrama whose "intended irony depends upon Brown's allegation that Clotel was the illegitimate daughter of Thomas Jefferson," and whose ironic point is blunted when, in the first American edition of 1867, "an anonymous senator is substituted for Jefferson, and the plot . . . altered accordingly." Robert A. Bone, *The Negro Novel in America*, rev. ed. (New Haven: Yale University Press, 1965), pp. 29–30, 30n.

76. Black critics had recognized Brown's importance by the late 1930s. See Sterling Brown, *The Negro in American Fiction* (Washington, D.C.: Associates in Negro Folk Education, 1937), pp. 39–40; Sterling A. Brown, Arthur P. Davis, and Ulysses Lee, eds., *The Negro Caravan: Writings by American Negroes* (New York: Citadel Press, 1941), pp. 138, 145–51. For the later recognition see Herbert Hill, "Introduction" to Hill, *Anger and Beyond: The Negro Writer in the United States* (New York: Harper and Row, 1966), pp. xix–xx; Philip Butcher, ed., *The Minority Presence in American Literature, 1600–1900* (Washington, D.C.: Howard University Press, 1977), Vol. 1, pp. 421–27.

77. Brown, *Clotel*, p. 220.

78. For a thoughtful discussion see Stanley Lieberson, *A Piece of the Pie: Blacks and White Immigrants Since 1880* (Berkeley: University of California Press, 1980).

79. Lawrence M. Mead, *Beyond Entitlement: The Social Obligations of Citizenship* (New York: The Free Press, 1986).

80. Ibid., p. 23.

81. Ibid., p. 36.

82. Ibid., p. 88.

83. Ibid.

84. Henry Hughes, *Treatise on Sociology, Theoretical and Practical* (Philadelphia: Lippincott, Grambo and Co., 1854; reprint, New York: Negro University Press, 1968), pp. 86–100, 107–18, 165–240, 261–92.

85. Stanford M. Lyman, "Henry Hughes and the Southern Foundations of American Sociology," in Lyman, ed., *Selected Writings of Henry Hughes: Antebellum Southerner, Slavocrat, Sociologist* (Jackson: University Press of Mississippi, 1985), pp. 1–72; see also Arthur J. Vidich and Stanford M. Lyman, *American Sociology: Worldly Rejections of Religion and Their Directions* (New Haven: Yale University Press, 1985), pp. 9–19.

86. See four works by Ulrich Bonnell Phillips: *American Negro Slavery: A Survey of the Supply, Employment and Control of Negro Labor as Determined by the Plantation Regime* (Gloucester, Mass.: Peter Smith, 1959. Orig. pub. 1918); *Life and Labor in the Old South* (Boston: Little, Brown and Co., 1963. Orig. pub. 1929); *The Slave Economy of the Old South: Selected Essays in Economic and Social History*, ed. Eugene D. Genovese (Baton Rouge: Louisiana State University Press, 1968); *The Course of the South to Secession: An Interpretation*, ed. E. Merton Coulter (New York: Hill and Wang, 1964. Orig. pub. 1939).

87. See Kenneth M. Stampp, "The Historian and Southern Negro Slavery," *American Historical Review*, 57 (Apr. 1952), pp. 613–24.

88. See seven works by John Hope Franklin: *The Free Negro in North Carolina, 1790–1860* (New York: W. W. Norton, 1971. Orig. pub. 1943); *The Militant South, 1800–1861* (Boston: Beacon Press, 1964; Orig. pub. 1956); *Reconstruction after the Civil War* (Chicago: University of Chicago Press, 1961); *The Emancipation Proclamation* (Garden City, N.Y.: Doubleday-Anchor, 1963, 1965); *Racial Equality in America: The 1976 Jefferson Lectures in the Humanities* (Chicago: University of Chicago Press, 1976); *From Slavery to Freedom: A History of Negro Americans*, 5th ed. (New York: Alfred A. Knopf, 1980); *George Washington Williams: A Biography* (Chicago: University of Chicago Press, 1985).

89. See Thomas J. Pressly, *Americans Interpret Their Civil War* (New York: The Free Press, 1965); and Kenneth M. Stampp and Leon F. Litwack, eds., *Reconstruction: An Anthology of Revisionist Writings* (Baton Rouge: Louisiana State University Press, 1969).

90. Marcus Lee Hansen, *The Atlantic Migration, 1607–1860: A History of the Continuing Settlement of the United States*, ed. Arthur M. Schlesinger (New York: Harper Torchbooks, 1961. Orig. pub. 1940), p. 39.

91. Ibid.

92. Ibid., pp. 39–40.

93. Ibid., p. 59.

94. Ibid., p. 44.

95. Ibid., p. 306.

96. "Immigration and Puritanism," *Norwegian-American Studies,* 9 (1936), pp. 1–28. Reprinted in Marcus Lee Hansen, *The Immigrant in American History,* ed. Arthur M. Schlesinger (New York: Harper Torchbooks, 1964. Orig. pub. 1940), pp. 97–128. All quotations are from the reprint edition.

97. Ibid., p. 125.

98. Ibid., p. 111.

99. Ibid., pp. 125–26.

100. Ibid., p. 101.

101. Ibid., p. 126.

102. Anne Wortham, *The Other Side of Racism: A Philosophical Study of Black Race Consciousness* (Columbus: Ohio State University Press, 1981), pp. 81–82.

103. See Stanford M. Lyman and Arthur J. Vidich, *Social Order and the Public Philosophy: An Analysis and Commentary on the Works of Herbert Blumer* (Fayetteville: University of Arkansas Press, 1988).

104. See Otto Klineberg, "Experimental Studies of Negro Personality," in Klineberg, ed., *Characteristics of the American Negro* (New York: Harper and Brothers, 1944), pp. 97–140; Abram Kardiner and Lionel Ovesey, *The Mark of Oppression: Explorations in the Personality of the American Negro* (Cleveland: Meridian Books-World, 1962. Orig. pub. 1951); Bertram P. Karon, *The Negro Personality: A Rigorous Investigation of the Effects of Culture* (New York: Springer Publishing Co., 1958), pp. 8–54, 116–73; Martin M. Grossack, ed., *Mental Health and Segregation* (New York: Springer Publishing Co., 1963), pp. 7–182, 227–28; Robert V. Guthrie, *Being Black: Psychological-Sociological Dilemmas* (San Francisco: Canfield Press, 1970), pp. 4–111; Morris Rosenberg and Roberta G. Simmons, *Black and White Self-Esteem: The Urban School Child* (Washington, D.C.: American Sociological Association, 1971), pp. 1–145; E. Earl Baughman, *Black Americans: A Psychological Analysis* (New York: Academic Press, 1971), pp. 37–56.

105. *Brown v. Board of Education of Topeka 347 U.S. 483.* Reprinted in Leon Friedman, ed., *Argument: The Oral Argument before the Supreme Court in Brown v. Board of Education of Topeka, 1952–1955* (New York: Chelsea House, 1969), p. 330.

106. See Edgar G. Epps, "Impact of School Desegregation on Aspirations, Self-Concepts, and Other Aspects of Personality," in Betsy Levin and Willis D. Hawley, eds., *The Courts, Social Science, and School Desegregation* (New Brunswick, N.J.: Transaction Books, 1977).

107. Friedman, *Argument,* p. 329.

108. Ibid., p. 327.

109. Ibid., p. 329.

110. Ibid., p. 330.

111. See Chief Justice Earl Warren, *The Memoirs of Earl Warren* (Garden City, N.Y.: Doubleday, 1977), pp. 2–4, 275–302; Leo Ratcher, *Earl Warren: A Political Biography* (New York: McGraw-Hill, 1967), pp. 321–28, 370–75,

382–83, 470–77; Bernard Schwartz, *Super Chief: Earl Warren and His Supreme Court—A Judicial Biography* (New York: New York University Press, 1983), pp. 72–127.

112. See, e.g., two works by Joseph B. James: *The Framing of the Fourteenth Amendment* (Urbana: University of Illinois Press, 1956); and *The Ratification of the Fourteenth Amendment* (Macon, Ga.: Mercer University Press, 1984).

113. As part of the argument before the Court in the *Briggs* case in 1952—whose decision was consolidated with that of Brown—the following exchange took place between attorney Thurgood Marshall and Justice Felix Frankfurter:

> Justice Frankfurter: Do you think that this law was passed for the same reason that a law would be passed prohibiting blue-eyed children from attending public schools?
>
> Mr. Marshall: No sir, because the blue-eyed people in the United States never had the badge of slavery which was perpetuated in the statutes.
>
> Justice Frankfurter: If it is perpetuated as slavery then the Thirteenth Amendment would apply. Friedman, *Argument*, p. 44.

114. Jacobus ten Broek, "Thirteenth Amendment to the Constitution of the United States: Consummation to Abolition and Key to the Fourteenth Amendment," *California Law Review*, 39 (June 1951), pp. 171–203.

115. "Amendment XIII," in Edward Corwin, *The Constitution and What It Means Today*, revised by Harold W. Chase and Craig R. Ducat (Princeton: Princeton University Press, 1978), p. 459.

116. The following quotations from the *Civil Rights Cases* are taken from Stanley I. Kutler, *The Supreme Court and the Constitution: Readings in American Constitutional History* 3d ed. (New York: W. W. Norton, 1984), pp. 200–208.

117. For the various definitions of membership in a race that prevailed in the several states, see Pauli Murray, ed., "State's Laws on Race and Color," in Robert V. Guthrie, *Being Black*, pp. 175–78.

118. See Andrew D. Weinberger, "A Reappraisal of the Constitutionality of 'Miscegenation' Statutes," Appendix G in Ashley Montagu, *Man's Most Dangerous Myth: The Fallacy of Race*, 4th ed. (Cleveland: Meridian Books-World, 1965), pp. 402–24. See also Robert J. Sickels, *Race, Marriage and the Law* (Albuquerque: University of New Mexico Press, 1972).

119. Tom Wicker, "Introduction," Margaret Mitchell, *Gone With the Wind*, 50th anniversary ed. (New York: Macmillan Publishing Co., 1986), p. xii.

120. See, e.g., Isaac DuBose Seabrook, *Before and After, or The Relations of the Races at the South*, ed. John Hammond Moore (Baton Rouge: Louisiana State University Press, 1967. Originally written, but not published, in 1895); and Charles E. Wynes, ed., *Forgotten Voices: Dissenting Southerners*

in an *Age of Conformity* (Baton Rouge: Louisiana State University Press, 1967). See also Richard N. Current, ed., *Reconstruction in Retrospect: Views from the Turn of the Century* (Baton Rouge: Louisiana State University Press, 1969).

121. Felicia R. Lee, "Negritude: What It Means to Go Home," *Viewpoint: The Miami Herald*, Section C (Mar. 8, 1987), p. 1C.

122. Ibid., p. 6C.

123. Ibid.

124. Ibid.

125. Oscar Handlin, *Truth in History* (Cambridge: Belknap Press of Harvard University Press, 1979), p. 413.

126. Robert E. Park and Ernest W. Burgess, *Introduction to the Science of Sociology*, 3d ed. rev. (Chicago: University of Chicago Press, 1969. Orig. pub. 1921), p. 735.

127. Winthrop Jordan, *White Over Black: American Attitudes toward the Negro, 1550–1812* (Chapel Hill: University of North Carolina Press, 1968), pp. 3–100.

128. Emile Durkheim and Marcel Mauss, "Note on the Notion of Civilization," trans. Benjamin Nelson, *Social Research*, 38:4 (Winter 1971), pp. 808–13.

129. See Jacob Drachler, ed., *Black Homeland/Black Diaspora: Cross-Currents of the African Relationship* (Port Washington, N.Y.: Kennikat Press, 1975); and Joseph E. Harris, ed., *Global Dimensions of the African Diaspora* (Washington, D.C.: Howard University Press, 1982); Graham W. Irwin, *Africans Abroad: A Documentary History of the Black Diaspora in Asia, Latin America, and the Caribbean during the Age of Slavery* (New York: Columbia University Press, 1977).

130. See Sheldon H. Harris, *Paul Cuffe: Black America and the African Return* (New York: Simon and Schuster, 1972); Cyril E. Griffith, *The African Dream: Martin R. Delaney and the Emergence of Pan-African Thought* (University Park: Pennsylvania State University Press, 1975); M. R. Delaney and Robert Campbell, *Search for a Place: Black Separatism and Africa, 1860* (Ann Arbor: University of Michigan Press, 1969); Earl Ofari, *"Let Your Motto Be Resistance": The Life and Thought of Henry Highland Garnet* (Boston: Beacon Press, 1972); William E. Bittle and Gilbert Geis, *The Longest Way Home: Chief Alfred C. Sam's Back-to-Africa Movement* (Detroit: Wayne State University Press, 1964); Edwin S. Redkey, *Black Exodus: Black Nationalist and Back-to-Africa Movements, 1890–1910* (New Haven: Yale University Press, 1969); Amy Jacques Garvey, comp., *The Philosophy and Opinions of Marcus Garvey* (London: Frank Cass, 1967); Adelaide Cromwell Hill and Martin Kilson, eds., *Apropos of Africa: Sentiments of American Negro Leaders on Africa from the 1800s to the 1950s* (London: Frank Cass, 1969); George Padmore, *Pan Africanism or Communism* (Garden City, N.Y.: Doubleday-Anchor, 1972); James R. Hooker, *Black Revolutionary: George Padmore's Path from Communism to Pan-Africanism* (New York: Praeger, 1967); Sterling Stuckey, *The Ideological Origins of Black Nationalism* (Bos-

ton: Beacon Press, 1972); Theodore Draper, *The Rediscovery of Black Nationalism* (New York: Viking Press, 1969).

131. Alex Haley, *Roots* (Garden City, N.Y.: Doubleday, 1976). See the discussion of the authenticity of this work in William L. Van Deburg, *Slavery and Race in American Popular Culture* (Madison: University of Wisconsin Press, 1984), pp. 144–46, 155–56.

132. *Equiano's Travels: The Interesting Narrative of the Life of Olaudah Equiano or Gustavus Vassa the African,* abr. and ed. Paul Edwards (New York: Frederick A. Praeger, 1967. Orig. pub. 1789).

133. Terry Alford, *Prince among Slaves* (New York: Harcourt, Brace, Jovanovich, 1977).

134. C. Eric Lincoln, *The Black Muslims in America* (Boston: Beacon Press, 1961), p. 109–11.

135. St. Clair Drake, "Hide My Face? On Pan-Africanism and Negritude," in Herbert Hill, ed., *Soon One Morning: New Writing by American Negroes, 1940–1962* (New York: Alfred A. Knopf, 1963), pp. 90–91.

136. Ibid., p. 104.

137. Karl Mannheim, "The Problem of Generations," *Essays on the Sociology of Knowledge,* ed. Paul Kecskemeti (London: Routledge and Kegan Paul Ltd., 1968. Orig. pub. 1952), pp. 306–7.

138. Ibid., p. 309.

139. Ibid.

5

Slavery and Sloth:
A Study in Race and Morality

The literature on black slavery in the United States is filled with references to sin. Religious abolitionists denounced the southern system of labor as an abomination to man and an affront to God. White southerners concerned with the salvation of their own souls agonized about and prayed over the divine judgment that might fall upon them for keeping fellow humans in perpetual bondage. Thomas Jefferson—a slaveholder, who, as author of both the Declaration of Independence with its ringing assertion that "all men are created equal" and the *Notes on the State of Virginia*, alleging that blacks were capable of lust but not love, and foolhardiness but not courage, comes closest to personifying the contradictions that comprised what Gunnar Myrdal called the "American dilemma"— feared what the deity might visit upon America: "God is just . . . [and] his justice cannot sleep forever."[1]

As civil war sounded the death-knell to slavery, white southerners, anguishing over the belief that their defeat at the hands of the Unionists was a divine punishment, could still not escape entirely from their own heritage of sin. Although current historians are divided over the extent, depth, and pervasiveness of the southerner's sense of guilt over slavery, enough evidence is available from the writings of Confederate diarists, the sermons of southern preachers, and the editorials of antebellum and wartime journalists to indicate that, as Kenneth Stampp points out, slaveholders' pangs of conscience over their sinfulness affected the very conduct and contributed to the outcome of the war.[2] However, expressions of guilt and feelings of remorse were confined to the *institution* of slavery—and not to the train of evil thought and practice that it had spawned, and that continues its reign of wrongs to the present day.

In the negrophobic racism that constitutes one of the vestiges of slavery, there resides a multiform instance of the survival of the seven deadly sins—and in the justifications for this racism, a rhetoric of their sublimation. Among these is sloth—one of the seven deadly sins, that in this essay shall stand as a synecdoche for its six evil companions. In what follows I shall present a microcosm of the argument relating slavery to sin. Tracing the manner in which a single sin finds its expression in both the slavery and postslavery epochs, I shall chart its path toward one of the world's great evils— race antipathy. This path is not straight; it is strewn with pitfalls in moral judgment, rocky rhetorics of exculpation, vain searches for side roads to remission of sins of commission and omission, and leafy rationalizations of foul thoughts and deeds. And, just as the general considerations of sin and evil were sublimated by latent functional theory in the social sciences, so racism, a vestige of the sins of slavery, has been treated to excuses and justifications for its wrongfulness by those who refuse to see the continuity of evil contained therein.

Slavery and Sloth

The physical expression of the sin of *acedia*—the Latin term from which the English word "sloth" originated—is to be found in lethargy and idleness. As one part of their justification for black enslavement, slavocratic writers urged the rightness of the South's peculiar institution: it was, they said, a deterrent to the Negro's natural and uncivilized tendency to indolence. Slavery, they insisted, was not only *not* a sin against God and humankind—as many abolitionists had charged—it was a specifically devised social and economic support for the virtue of productive and useful effort. As Henry Hughes (1829–62), America's first sociologist and foremost apologist of slavery, put it: "Labor, whether of mind or body, is a duty. . . . To consume and not to produce either directly or remotely is wrong. Idleness is a crime. It is unjust. Every class of society has its economic duty. If it does not do it; if it positively or negatively violates its duty, that is criminal."[3] Slavery in the mind of Hughes and his supporters was an institutionalized moral embodiment of the Protestant ethic of labor, assuring white Americans that their color-caste of black bondsmen and women would comply with their God-given duty to engage in socially useful labor.

That blacks would be given over to sloth unless a higher and powerful authority compelled them to work became a staple argument of the southern slavocratic ethos. Moreover, that thesis survived the abolition of institutionalized slavery and continues to the present day, forming part of the stereotypical imagery of blacks in America and, for some, suggesting the need for some return to a system of supervised labor of blacks. In the late 1830s, the prominent South Carolina magistrate, Chancellor William Harper (1790–1847), asserted as a general maxim that "if anything can be predicated as universally true of uncultivated man, it is that he will not labor beyond what is absolutely necessary to maintain his existence."[4] Because, as William Gilmore Simms (1806–70) put it, labor "is one of the first elements of religion,"[5] Negro slavery had been instituted as an act of divinely ordained benevolence and aimed at the moral cultivation of the African savage. The Negro slave, in the poetic fancy of William Grayson (1788–1863), had in fact been delivered from his sinful nature by slavery's service to Providence:

> In sloth and error sunk for countless years
> His race has lived, but light at last appears—
> Celestial light: religion undefiled
> Dawns in the heart of Congo's simple child
>
> .   .   .   .
>
> And now, with sturdy hand and cheerful heart,
> He learns to master every useful art.[6]

Where artistry was replaced by science, slavery was seen as a tonic "for the enervated muscles" of the slothful African. Fired by his own "scientific" contributions to what we now know to be the American variant of the myth of the lazy native,[7] Dr. Samuel A. Cartwright of Louisiana (1793–1863) believed that blacks received both medicinal and intellectual benefits from enforced field labor: "The compulsory power of the white man, by making the slothful negro [sic] take active exercise, puts into active play the lungs, through whose agency the vitalized blood is sent to the brain to give liberty to the mind and to open the door to intellectual improvement. The very exercise, so beneficial to the negro, is expended in cultivating those burning fields of cotton, sugar, rice and tobacco, which, but for his labor, would, from the heat of the climate, go uncultivated, and their products be lost to the world."[8]

But, if the enslavement of blacks seemed to justify attributing to them the stigma of an allegedly natural but nevertheless sinful slothfulness, the relief from hard labor that Negro bondage provided for their masters and other whites enveloped the latter groups in a veritable subculture of acedia. At the Constitutional Convention of 1787, George Mason of Virginia, in remarks reported by James Madison, observed that "Slavery discourages arts and manufactures. The poor despise labor when performed by slaves." Moreover, he continued, preventing the supposedly natural tendency to indolence among Negroes by imposing ownership and control over their lives as well as their labor power had already had a deleterious effect upon the slaveholder. As Mason put it, "Every master of slaves is born a petty tyrant." Worse, that tyranny would inevitably "bring the judgment of heaven on a Country . . . [for, by] an inevitable chain of causes and effects providence punishes national sins, by national calamities."[9]

To the critics of slavery, the very institutionalization of black bondage had the effect of making work a vice and idleness a virtue— of revoking the moral valences attached to the sin of sloth. Among what the Reconstruction Congress and the Courts would later call its "incidents," black slavery was said to have a tendency to degrade all forms of labor, discourage every useful effort, and to idealize indolence and vice among those not held to involuntary servitude. Hence, in seeking to eradicate the vestiges of slavery that threatened to linger long after the Civil War had ended its institutionalized form, some of the framers of the Thirteenth Amendment sought not only to liberate the Negro from involuntary servitude, but also to elevate the status of white people's labor from the indignities that the blacks' bondage had indirectly heaped upon it. Senator Henry Wilson of Massachusetts supported the addition of the antislavery amendment because, among its many promising features, it would relieve "the wronged victim of the slave system, the poor white man . . . impoverished, debased, dishonored by the system that makes toil a badge of disgrace."[10]

However, it was not merely an opposition to the degradation of the white working classes that evoked considered opposition to black slavery. As the nineteenth century wore on, the southern planter came more and more to be seen as the paragon of a sinfully slothful leisure class, whose very existence boded ill for society's morals and the nation's future.[11] Not only did the owner of slaves appear to do no remunerative or socially valuable work, he also seemed too often to succumb before one of the demons of noontide's temptations: exaggerated assertions of personal honor and an all-too-ready resort to violence when it was besmirched.[12] The lushness of southern land was said to encourage a melancholic sickness of the soul, plunging plantation seigneurs into the depths of *acedia*: restlessness, neurasthenia, and an urge to hedonic excess.[13] As one eighteenth-century promoter of immigration to "The Land of Eden" put it: "Everything will grow plentifully here [in Virginia] to supply the wants or wantonness of man."[14] Slavery, it seemed, had coercively restricted if not altogether eliminated the allegedly natural indolence of the African and his descendants in America, but, in doing so, it had cursed the slaveowners with the very sin that they sought to extirpate.

Of course, pro-slavery advocates sought a casuistic remission from the sin of acedic sloth. In belief of their own absolution they put forward a classic rhetoric of justification: what appeared as laziness, lethargy, and a life of endless if anxious ease was in fact an instance of productive and socially useful labor.[15] Some of the finest examples of this sin-remitting sermonizing are to be found in the writings of Henry Hughes.[16] In one of his "St. Henry" letters, a journalistic series advocating the resumption of the African slave trade, Hughes distinguished southern capital from southern capitalists: "In our system, labor is capital."[17] Such human capital must necessarily be made to be industrious, Hughes observed, but, in consideration of the peculiar character of the African, the South's black bond servants were obliged to labor under their masters' total supervision. Supervision constituted an arduous task. The overseer of blacks could not be an idler.

As Hughes conceived of the matter, the seigneurs of the southern states had at one time utilized Africans as *slave* labor, but this method of organizing the cultivation of crops and the performance of other menial tasks had evolved and was—by the middle of the nineteenth century—a socially and reciprocally beneficent system of reciprocal obligations that he called "warranteeism." Plantation farmers no longer *owned* their "warrantees"; rather, the latter *owed* them their labor power in return for supervision, instruction, food, shelter, clothing, medical services, and old-age assistance.[18] As an even greater incentive against his own indolence, the agricultural capitalist owner of a black servant's "warrant," who had first to perform the mentally difficult task of calculating precisely how much of his own money to invest in the labor power of his warrantee, had also to labor mightily to secure his financial interest by insuring that the warrantee engaged in a profitable performance of his contracted duties: "He who has fifteen hundred or fifteen thousand dollars invested in labor obligations, is by the felicity of the investment, enforced to prevent idleness, except for health, morality and enjoyment or goodwill. . . . Idleness, therefore is bankruptcy."[19]

However, that part of Hughes's argument treated chiefly the labor necessary to prevent the warrantees' alleged tendency to idle away his or her time. What of the accusation that in keeping blacks in bondage the "warrantors" were themselves idlers, sinful servants of sloth? Hughes advanced two interrelated theses in refutation. First, he presented a four-class hierarchy of labor distinguishing the capitalist "mentalists" from the skilled-labor "manual mentalists," the unskilled "manualists," and the "warrantees." The agricultural capitalists were also productive persons, Hughes insisted, and were entitled to respect, recognition, and rewards commensurate with the effectiveness of the calculating and organizing efforts they expended.[20] Second, he located the source for his more refined subclassification of workers into various specialized occupations in each person's possession of an innate talent. Thereby, Hughes combined a moral with a natural and functional theory of occupationally appropriate differentiation: "Talent has rights which must not be overlooked. Nature's grades must be respected. . . . Some grades are natural, and social status should be proportioned to natural grades; the social powers, that is, the grandeurs, should correspond to the grades, and the State should graduate like nature."[21] As for the abolitionists' own version of the moral evaluation of work, and their thesis that slavery attached invidiousness to tasks of lesser ease, Hughes was adamant:

> The general opinion is that menial labor degrades. This is false. All work is sacred; all toils ennoble, and the sweat drops on our brows are the pearls of God. . . . Hard as the worker is the work should be. The craftier craftsmen for the craftier crafts, the finer artists for the finer arts, born sculptors for the chisel, born judges for the bench, born priests for the priesthood, born kings for the kingcraft, and born menials for menial crafts; the bow to him who can bend it, the sceptre to him who can sway it; the gifted according to their gifts, and the powerful according to their powers.[22]

However, despite his and other slavocrats' efforts to supply themselves with a rhetoric of absolution from the sin of sloth, Hughes and his colleagues were unable to overturn altogether the moral judgment on slavery. His own work hints at this worry over the inability to enforce the sacred obligation to work. "Nobody, in any place, can work, without a motive to work. Motives to work, must therefore be produced."[23] Hughes's admiration for the "mentalists"—with whom as a lawyer, journalist, and politician he clearly identified—led him to assert that fear of civil punishment was not necessary to goad them into productive efforts: "If the class of capitalists violate their labor obligation; that also is a misdemeanor. But the punishment of

this, is not forensic or formally civil; because it is a self-remedying
wrong. For if when the simple laborer has begun production; the
other classes do not continue and finish it; the raw produce is lost.
That is the loss of the capitalists and skilled laborers. Thus they are
punished in their property."[24]

Hughes's position arose out of his own adherence to a Protestant
orientation toward the relation of worth to work—an orientation
that had swept over the scientific and religious thought of southern
intellectuals in the first five decades after the American revolution,
replacing the philosophical enlightenment of the Lockean deists
with a Calvinist Baconianism.[25] However, in tandem with the religious obligation that every true believer find a calling and persevere
in some form of productive and useful labor, there coexisted an opposed orientation, a different Old World cultural outlook that justified southern whites not only in their keeping of slaves, but, more
significantly, in their leanings toward leisure, laziness, and licentiousness. That was the Celtic heritage.

The Celtic Culture of the Old South

Standing in normative opposition to one another are the themes that
a man's moral and social worth is derived from his own efforts at
productive work and the idea, as expressed by a nineteenth-century
southerner to a traveler, that "there's luck in leisure."[26] The latter is
a central theme of the Celtic thought that came to predominate in the
lives and activities of one class of white antebellum southerners. It
is in fact the case that, even before the settlement of the colonies, the
cultural orientations of the precursors of the Puritan Yankees and
those of the white settlers of the areas south and west of Pennsylvania were mutually antagonistic.[27] The British Isles emigrant settlers
of what would become the American South hailed from the Celtic
fringe areas, that is, the western and northern uplands of England,
Wales, the Scottish Highlands and Borders, the Hebrides, and Ire-
land. In the South the Celts became known as "crackers," a term that
dates from the seventeenth century. As they swept westward, they
carried the basic themes of their rustic outlook with them, making
them the core of the populist culture of the landless element among
the white southerners.

The elementary forms of Celtic thought in the South celebrated
idleness, sensuality, violence, and gambling; an acceptable subsistence was to be obtained by hunting, fishing, and open-range livestock herding (as opposed to the English pattern of mixed and

rationalized agriculture). The Celtic southerner emphasized nostalgia for the homeland, close family ties, and, ideally, spent his days smoking, drinking, fighting, and loafing. In short, the typical Celtic southerner was a paragon of what both Gregorian Catholics and English Puritans regarded as sloth, but, unlike the latter, the Celt did not regard his way of life as sinful.

According to Grady McWhiney, "Two dominant institutions—black slavery and the open-range system of grazing livestock—made it possible for the most white Southerners to practice a leisurely lifestyle."[28] Hence, although some white southerners protected themselves against the fatigue imposed by arduous field labor by exploiting African slave labor, a great many more entered into animal husbandry to the same end. "Neither Southerners . . . nor their Celtic forebears devoted much time to tillage agriculture."[29] The landless southerner of Celtic background could raise livestock on the open range without great effort. "Aside from marking or branding their animals, [such] Southerners had little more to do than round them up in the fall and either sell them to a local buyer or drive them to market."[30]

When George Fitzhugh, one of the South's most formidable sociologists and slavocrats, attempted to refute the abolitionists' charge—namely, that slavery induced idleness among the slaveowners—by pointing out the arduous personal labors undertaken by smallholding farmers, who, he alleged, worked in tandem with both their slaves and their wives, and contrasted the latter's efforts with those of the northern capitalist, who, he insisted, "lives by mere exploration"[31] of supposedly free labor, he was treading on unsure ground. Indeed, as early as 1799, Duc de la Rochefoucauld-Liancourt, reporting on his travels through Maryland in the previous four years, observed how the widespread desire to do as little work as possible led to enlarged slavocratic development as well as to the economic ruin of the slaveholding but slothful smallholder:

In a country abounding with slaves, the whites do not apply much to labour. Their ambition consists in buying Negroes; they buy them with the first sum of money they get, and when they have two of them they leave off working themselves: this small number is not sufficient to keep their lands in good order according to the tillage of the country, bad as it may be. The small farmers among the whites thus leaving off labour augment their expenses, and their affairs are soon in a bad condition. These, and those who have never been able to purchase

Negroes, find themselves in an inferior situation to their neighbors who have many slaves: displeased with their station, they soon think of establishing themselves in a country whose land is cheaper. . . . So that all these small farms . . . are put to sale, and are bought by the rich planters, and those who have sold them go to establish themselves in Kentucky, in Tennessee, and in the countries of the West.[32]

Although the proponents of Celtic cultural survival in the American South do not emphasize the point, the slave system and cracker slothfulness had a complex and reciprocal influence on one another.

The morals practiced by the southern Celt constitute a veritable catalogue of the train of evils that both the church fathers and the Puritan divines said would follow from the sin of sloth: idle chatter, vice, promiscuity, fighting, and unwarranted melancholy.[33] In the post-Reformation Occident, as Max Weber observed, once ordinary work had been elevated to a calling, that is, to the status of a holy sacrament, such resistance to its imperatives becomes a certain blasphemy. "Waste of time," Weber wrote, "is thus the first and in principle the deadliest of sins."[34] And, among the ways to waste time, those that McWhiney's researches have shown to be regularly engaged in by the southern cracker were just the vices that Weber had listed as particularly proscribed: "Loss of time through sociability, idle talk, luxury, even more sleep than is necessary for health, six to at most eight hours, is worthy of absolute moral condemnation."[35]

The modes of everyday life associated with cracker culture permitted and encouraged indolence and excess. "Celts," McWhiney points out, "loved to talk, preach, orate, tell stories, and to listen to others do the same." So did their southern descendants. "Antebellum Southerners," he goes on, "liked to sit in swings or rocking chairs on breezy porches, at the dining table, or in the 'sitting room.' "[36] But their indolent existence also bred a quest for sportive excitement and eudaemonic thrills: "Southerners and other Celts enjoyed such 'blood' sports as cock fighting and bear baiting, and they often combined these and other amusements with drinking."[37] The leisurely life found other moments of enjoyment in gastronomic excess, indicative of yet another sloth-related sin, gluttony.[38] A Swede, employed as a tutor, described with obvious disdain the table and the table manners at a typical southern party: "The table . . . was completely covered with turkey, ducks, ham, chicken, chicken salad, oyster pate, bread and butter, cloudberry jelly, blancmange, ice cream, cakes, and . . . sugarplums; in addition champagne and other wines. One selects in no special order whatever strikes the fancy, and consequently it happens that many begin with ice cream and end with ham."[39] Finally, the melancholic *tristitia*—that Pope Gregory the Great conceived as the inextricable concomitant of sloth that would in turn give rise to "malice, rancour, cowardice, [and] despair," and which Chaucer felt would engender *wrawnesse*, or peevish anger[40]—found expression in the cracker's unrestrained will to violence. "Whether fights in the Old South were formal duels or simply rough and tumble contests," McWhiney has observed, "they were an intrinsic part of a culture that was as violent as its Celtic progenitor and—what is highly significant—just as unrepentant of its combativeness."[41]

Afro-American and Celtic Cultures

That the slothfulness that was a central theme of Celtic cultural orientations would find its way into the deracinated lifestyle of the slave population is an implication of the thesis presented by McWhiney.[42] Were it to be proved and accepted, it would go far to lift the all-too-benighted blacks from the oft-repeated charge of a constitutional disposition to indolence—but only to saddle them with a new burden, a stigmatized trait resulting from their haphazardous acculturation in the South.

However, the acculturative argument for the allegedly widespread indolence among enslaved blacks has other, competing, explanations. The issue is, in fact, entirely unresolved, and the query into black orientations toward work—including the very question of whether there is such an orientation, and if it does exist, such subsidiary questions as whether it is uniform throughout the race, how it originated, whether it is temperamental, constitutional, cultural, psychopathological, or, rather, a strategic response to their situation in America—constitutes perhaps the single most debated element of current social and economic thought on racial relations. That question will not be resolved in the present essay. Rather, the several attributive theories of black slothfulness will be examined for the light they throw on the nature of sinfulness and absolution in the context of American racist thought. In each case, we shall see that the sin of sloth can be absolved or sublimated, but always at the cost of keeping alive elements of a variegated heritage of racism.

That the religious instruction of slaves—when permitted—consisted largely in hortatory pronouncements against their slothfulness and calls for pious acquiesence to their divinely appointed enslavement is indicated in modern researches on the subject. "The

common denominator of the various white-sponsored religious activities for slaves was the message: God wants you to be good, humble servants, patiently bearing your burdens on earth until your
reward comes in the hereafter."[43] Among the more popular texts chosen for sermonizing the black bondsmen-and-women were, "Servants be obedient to your masters"; "Let as many servants as are
under the yoke count their own masters worthy of all honor"; and
"In the sweat of thy face shalt thou eat bread, till thou return unto
the ground."[44] Slaves were encouraged to remain faithful and ever-
obedient to their masters, and to give honest labor to them. Hard
work under their earthly masters was treated as a debt they must pay
for their original sinfulness.

An African Culture against Work?

In a recent study that brings together the conceptual orientations
of phenomenological sociology with the comparative method of
Comtean anthropology and the facts of documental and archaeological research, Mechal Sobel has sought to depict the coordination of
values that came to prevail among blacks and whites in eighteenth-
century Virginia.[45] Insisting that African cultural orientations and
ways of life survived the Middle Passage and the "seasoning" of
slaves in the West Indies before their arrival in the continental British colonies, Sobel documents the variety of material and moral
elements that were successfully transported across the Atlantic.
Among these was an attitude toward work. Indeed, it is Sobel's contention that "the evidence strongly indicates that most whites in
eighteenth-century Virginia lived in a black world of work."[46] The
character of that workaday world suggests not only the survival of
Africa-originated modes of work but their blending into those or the
southern whites. "Africans came with skills from Africa, blacks
learned trades from other blacks, and white artisans on plantations
trained slaves."[47] However, it was sometimes the case that the white
trainer became the pupil of his slave apprentices. Sobel cites the
instance of George Washington's complaint over the fact that his
white overseer, "finding it a little troublesome to instruct the Negros
[sic], and to compel them to practice of *his* modes, he slided into
theirs."[48] Indeed, it is part of Sobel's argument that African slaves
often rejected the European ways to work that their white masters
and overseers thrust upon them, and introduced their own in place
of them.

The southern white's perception of African styles of doing work
and using tools was influenced by his or her own cultural outlook;

thus Washington lamented that his overseers "fall into the slovenly mode of executing work which is practiced by those [slaves] among whom they are [living and working]."[49] Moreover, Washington invoked the overseer's failure to exert sufficient authority over his slaves as an explanation for the latter's less than efficient performance. "Although authority is given to him," he observed of Thomas Green, his "Overlooker of the Carpenters," "he is too much upon a level with the Negroes to exert it from which cause, if no other, every one works, or not, as they please,"[50] If there is an element of sloth here, Sobel's researches seem to suggest, it would appear to be very much a product of the ethnocentric mote in the observer's eye.

However, since the Reformation, Occidental orientations toward work have been inextricably connected to careful measurements of time; accomplishments and the value of labor are calculated in relation to product moments as indicated in minutes, hours, days, and weeks. With this in mind, it is well to consider the eighteenth-century African's attitude toward time, and to see how this, in turn, affected attributions of indolence toward him. Hedonistic festivals provide a case in point. As involuntary workers in the South's system of plantation agriculture, black slaves regularly partook of the seasonal harvest celebrations that were also a transplanted feature of English rustic life. Although there "is only fragmentary evidence that rites from African harvest festivals were observed in North America," Sobel calls attention to the similarity of northern Nigerian Tiv and Nigerian Ohaffian Igbo harvest rites to those of the English and suggests how blacks might have had their own customary reasons for continuing such celebratory occasions long after white servants in husbandry had become a minority or disappeared altogether from the fields.[51]

The test of slothfulness in Occidental cultures is best applied with respect to the evaluation of labor and its products by clock time. However, the traditional cultures of West Africa observed an attitude toward time measurement that was not dissimilar from that of the Celts. Although time was marked, it was divided by Africans in ways other than those indicated on a clock. Usually the character and duration of a particular task constituted the way of temporal reckoning, but also there were matters counted by market day rhythms, birth cohorts, seasonal changes, lineal genealogies, and metachronological ideas of history. Although several West African cultures emphasized the universal necessity to do work, the measurement of an individual's labors was not taken according to minutes, hours, or days. Rather, as exemplified by the eighteenth-century

Gambians, "The men were occupied for only about two months of the year, at seed time and harvest. . . . The men worked without respite at customary times, when their whole existence might turn on their success, but for the rest of the year, they hardly seemed even to bother to hunt or fish. . . . they . . . lay in the shade, smoking, gossiping, and playing a kind of chess." The Gambians liked to drink, smoke, dance, and fight. "Their only liquors were palm wine, ciboa wine, honey wine, and beer. . . . Eating only once a day, they were able to smoke without interruption. . . . Their social diversions were dancing and wrestling."[52]

Neither work nor leisure proceeded according to durations indicated on a clock. The African practices in this respect bore a close resemblance to those of the southern crackers. As a nineteenth-century traveler in the South observed, "Leisure and ease are inmates of his roof. He takes no note of time. . . . A clock, almanac, and a good fire are hard things to find in a planter's house,"[53] Indeed, Thomas Jefferson, who, despite his professed deism, was himself an adherent of the time and motion morality that Calvinism seemed to require, installed "an enormous clock in the entrance room [at Monticello] that was both the symbol of his concern with time and the very real monitor of the families' days and hours." The clock was intended "to control the work routine of blacks and whites alike" and was reinforced not only with a bell that could be heard in every part of the farm but also with clocks in his bedroom, his study, his living room, and his kitchen.[54] Jefferson dinned into his children's heads the importance of taking care "how your hours are distributed"[55] and warned his daughter—who had expressed outrage over the cruel treatment of slaves and a measure of abolitionist sympathy for their plight—against the sinful effects of an unemployed mind or body. "Ennui [is] the most dangerous poison of life," Jefferson wrote. "A mind always employed is always happy. This is the true secret, the grand recipe for felicity. The idle are the only wretched."[56]

The disdain felt toward African and Afro-American orientations toward time might, hence, be a product of what William James once called that "certain blindness in people"[57] that prevents them from appreciating the ordinary representations of a different way of doing things. However, a recognition of the Afro-Americans' cultural distinctiveness must be seen in relation to its service to the reinforcement of racial prejudices.[58] These prejudices, when not recognized as such, act as rhetorics of justification for the blacks' low place in the American ethos that holds that there is a moral hierarchy of races.

It is one thing to recognize cultural difference under an ideology of racial equality and social justice, quite another to conceive of it within the frame of a slavocratic caste society or a *Herrenvolk* democracy.[59] Sobel's analysis comes at a time when the pressures toward racial equality and the recognition of a relativistic cultural pluralism are high but the economic integration of blacks into the American economy remains largely an uncompleted project. It reads a message of empathy toward the historic plight of the hapless eighteenth-century African slaves in Virginia, who worked out a modus vivendi with their captors and owners amidst a situation of Eurocentric Enlightenment tinged with a largely unacknowledged racism.

However, if the African attitude toward work is a survival of West African culture and one that complements that of the white southerner of Celtic background, it nevertheless can be made to speak to the failure of an *appropriate* acculturation, one that would have (or, in the minds of the benevolent slavocrats of the mid-nineteenth century, should have) guided the West African blacks and their enslaved descendants in America toward industriousness, frugality, and an abhorrence of indolence.[60] As Leo Kuper has pointed out, "the objective cultural differences between races are highly relevant for the structure of their relations . . . but the very nature and extent of these differences affect the structure of the society." More significantly, the perception of the meaning and changeability of these differences is directed and dictated by the ruling elites of that society. The character, content, and kind of justice that prevails in the relations among the races turn on these perceptions. "Cultural pluralism," as Kuper notes, "would thus be an unreliable guide to the nature of their relationship."[61]

The 'Sambo' as a Dehumanized Personality

Quite a different orientation conceives one image of the Afro-American slave—that of the lazy, shiftless, superstitious, and easygoing character, denominated as "Sambo" in numerous nineteenth-century literary, diaristic, and travelers' reports—neither to be a product of Celticization or of West African cultural survival. Rather, the social personality of the "Sambo" is perceived to be the result of a personality-destroying system that operated to sustain American slavery. The latter thesis has been developed by Stanley Elkins,[62] who believes that the American slave plantation resembled nothing so much as a Nazi concentration camp; more significantly, he holds that it had many of the same effects on the personalities of Afro-Americans as Nazidom's arbitrary incarceration and maltreatment had on those of its hapless victims. Whereas the Nazis had had only a few years to work their wicked will on Jews, Gypsies, homosexuals, and radicals, the American slavocracy lasted for more than two centuries. In the process, so the Elkins thesis goes, it had stripped the slave of virtually every vestige of his African heritage and cultural personality and reduced both black men and women to a servile condition of childlike dependency. The Afro-American "Sambo" was a product of American totalitarian dehumanization.

Elkins's attribution of childlike behavior to blacks in bondage laid emphasis on the slaves' much vaunted docility and fidelity; however, critics of Elkins point out that black slaves rose up in rebellion against their masters often enough to cast doubt on his claim that Afro-American personality had been reduced to a uniformly infantile state.[63] However, as George M. Frederickson has pointed out, outbreaks of rebelliousness and disloyalty are not inconsistent with a comprehensive view of a childlike personality.[64] In light of his observation, scholars who accept the Elkins thesis might want to investigate the particular sociopsychological conditions that would produce a docile and loyal acquiescence in some and a rebellious and destructive resistance in other victims of the same process of institutionalized dehumanization.

A further point, however, might be made with respect to the implications of the Elkins thesis for present-day blacks and for the survival of the sin of sloth as a pathology. The picture of the deracinated Negro as either a lazy savage or a lusty brute is not inconsistent with the characterology that the church divines associated with the sin of acedia. Whether southern slaveowners had successfully unmanned their black chattel sufficiently to make them into happy, indolent, children or, inadvertently so abused them as to change them into peevish, sullen, violence-prone, and lusty sensualists, they had, from this point of view, inflicted upon them the entire panoply that follows from the curse of sloth. According to this line of thought, the malevolent nurturance of the Afro-American slave had, in effect, produced a bad seed, the "Sambo." Moreover, by the blind and cunning operation of a mean-spirited sociocultural Lamarckism, present-day blacks had "inherited" the cursed traits inflicted upon their slave forebears and would in turn afflict American society with the habits and practices of that accursed sociopsychological inheritance. An elaborated religious reading of the Elkins thesis in the manner just outlined could shift the blame for the blacks; response to their present ignominious condition onto them, perceiving that condition as a modern and special variant of the curse of Ham whereby their enslavement was justified in the first place.[65]

Sloth as Resistance

In opposition to the claims of a constitutional predisposition to indolence, an acculturative adoption of shiftlessness, or an infan-
tilized reduction to child-savagery, some analysts have treated the
reports of slave slothfulness as evidence of a carefully cultivated
strategy of resistance. Here, it should be noted, the appearance of the
lazy, superstitious, clumsy, and unteachable "darky" constitutes not
a stereotype but rather the last weapon available to a powerless people. When the field slave walked in a shuffling manner, refused to
make haste, broke or misused his master's tools, carelessly allowed
the dry fields to burn, or appeared listless and inattentive to commands, he was engaged in a calculated subversion of a system from
which he could not escape.[66]

If this reading is placed within the acedic tradition, emphasis is
placed on the development of a dramaturgy among the despised, an
artfulness of expression that, simultaneously, silences rebuke while
it slows down production.[67] As the unsung heroes of this passion
play, black slaves deliver themselves from their despoiled masters
while appearing to serve them according to the latters' most cherished beliefs. This amounts to a desublimation of the hated stereotype while living outwardly according to its imperatives—lending it
a dramatic and visible legitimation while covertly undermining its
basic objective. Sloth here becomes the penultimate activity of the
resistants, occuring while they await ultimate deliverance—by divine or human hands.

Sloth after Slavery

The specter of sloth has haunted the condition and the imagery of
the Afro-American from Emancipation to the present day. Essentially the matter has centered on two themes—whether blacks could
or would participate in a "free" market of capitalist labor without
imposed changes in their constitutional, cultural, or sociopsychological makeup; or whether blacks should be entered into the
modern world of multifarious work by some authoritative but non-
meritocratic instauration of their socioeconomic situation.

Race Mixture as Panacea

Those who supposed that blacks were constitutionally incapable of
productive and useful labor outside of slavery, called for their biological reconstruction. Thus, the Comtean intellectual, Joseph Le

Conte (1823–1901), the master of Woodmanston plantation and first professor appointed to the University of California at Berkeley, complained bitterly about the decline in workmanship after Emancipation and asserted that "for the lower races everywhere (leaving out slavery) these is eventually but one of the two alternatives—viz., either extermination or mixture."[68] Sure that the American Negroes were members of one of the lower races and equally sure that their extermination would be inadvisable from the point of view of America's laboring needs, Le Conte proposed instead that the newly constituted freedmen-and-women be interbred with "marginal varieties of the primary races"—being sure, he added, to avoid permitting the blacks to mate with the "Teutons," whose superior racial-cum-social character would have to be preserved at all costs if America was to progress.[69] However, the benefits to agricultural and industrial progress that Le Conte supposed would arise from breeding the former slaves out of their isolated existence was not enough to secure the support of all those who feared what Benjamin Franklin had warned against more than a century earlier—the biological destruction of the "lovely White" people inhabiting America:

> The Number of purely white People in the World is proportionably very small. All *Africa* is black or tawny. . . . And in *Europe*, the *Spaniards*, *Italians*, *French*, *Russians*, and *Swedes*, are generally of what we call a swarthy Complexion; as are the *Germans* also, the *Saxons* only excepted, who with the *English* make the principal Body of White People on the Face of the Earth. I could wish their Numbers were increased. And while we are, as I may call it, *Scouring* our Planet, by clearing *America* of Woods, and so making this Side of our Globe reflect a brighter Light to the Eyes of Inhabitants in *Mars* or *Venus*, why should we in the Sight of Superior Beings, darken its People? why increase the Sons of *Africa*, by Planting them in *America*, where we have so fair an Opportunity, by excluding all Blacks and Tawneys, of increasing the lovely White and Red?[70]

By the time of their emancipation from slavery, blacks were regarded as unsuitable mates for any of the European groups in America; almost all states enacted "miscegenation statutes" prohibiting marriage across racial lines.[71] Moreover, although sexual intercourse between blacks and whites and been a widespread if covert practice during the period of slavery, the emerging population of mulattoes was not usually credited with deriving superior qualities from its mixed parentage nor recognized as a distinctive newly emerging people; its members were all too often assigned the status of Negroes.[72] In addition, some European commentators on the American situation held strongly to the belief that the inferior character traits that were popularly associated with the Afro-Americans could never be eradicated by amalgamation. "Even as by the interbreeding of a horse and a donkey a creature is produced which possesses the qualities of the less noble animal," wrote the Prussian historian Heinrich von Treitschke, "so it is with humans." This leader of the so-called liberal historians in Prussia went on to state, "The Mulatto is a nigger in all but his paler skin; that he is aware of it is shown by his consorting with other blacks."[73]

In the event, Le Conte's proposal was never acted upon; no program of forced or voluntary racial intermixture was ever undertaken in America. Nevertheless, for some Americans, the elimination of the Negro—and with that, the extirpation of his or her supposedly sinful and sensuous traits—through biological means continues to be held out as the only true solution to the race problem. Thus Norman Podhoretz, a writer and editor who grew up in a mixed black, Jewish, and Italian neighborhood in Brooklyn in the 1930s, admits that as a child, he believed that the Negro was, in effect, a veritable model of what earlier generations would have called sloth, and what to him "seemed the very embodiment of the values of the street— free, independent, reckless, brave, masculine, erotic." Such a characterology, of course, also corresponds with that once associated with the southern Celt as well as with the enslaved Afro-American. But Podhoretz believes that, in Negroes, this character type inspires envy, fear, and hatred among whites and must, therefore, be eliminated altogether from the American scene. However, to relieve the Negro from his unfortunate status—"his past is a stigma, his color is a stigma, and his vision of the future is the hope of erasing the stigma by making color irrelevant"—Podhoretz insists that it is necessary to establish the race's complete and total amalgamation with the whites. Although he also believes that "there are even greater barriers to its achievement than to the achievement of integration," Podhoretz firmly holds to "the opinion [that] the Negro problem can be solved in no other way."[74] In effect, he acknowledges the inability to eradicate the sin-laden stigma of racism without obliterating the race itself.

Cultural Uplift and the Remission of Sin

Not all of those who addressed the race and labor question in moral terms believed that color change would remit the sin of sloth, or, for

that matter, any other sin. Timothy Dwight, a poet, preacher, classi-
cist, as well as a veteran of the American Revolution, presided over
the intellectual scene at Yale University when John C. Calhoun was
a student there. He undoubtedly disturbed the future philosopher-
senator of slavocratic racism by insisting that environment rather
than heredity accounted for racial differences and predicting that, in
a temperate climate like that of the United States, the Negroes would
eventually become white, thence revealing for all to see the com-
monalities that made all men and women human—the moral
condition derived from Original Sin: ubiquitous and predestined
depravity.[75] Calhoun could never accept the moral implications of
Dwight's teaching. Years later, while debating the proposed annex-
ation of Texas, he opined that slavery "is consistent with . . . great
improvement to the inferior [race], while . . . abolition of slavery
would (if it did not destroy the inferior by conflict to which it would
lead) reduce it to extremes of vice and wretchedness."[76] For Calhoun
and other ideologues of a seigneurial slavocratic republic only close
control over the life and labor of blacks could withhold them from
submergence in sloth.

Nevertheless, a contrary opinion had arisen, also derived from
the many hermeneutics on the Protestant ethic of work that so dominated American social thought. The emancipated slave, so the argument went, must be both morally induced and educationally
prepared to participate in the workaday world of free market capitalism, or else abolition would not result in emancipation. The Duc
de la Rochefoucauld-Liancourt pointed out that in the instance of
the Negro under slavery, "food of some sort or other was always provided . . . without the least care on his part; . . . he [i.e., the slave]
was aware that no industry, or attention of his, would procure him
either better food or clothing. Labour therefore brought nothing but
fatigue, and he became of course indolent and careless." What would
result if slavery were abolished without some pre-planning, de la
Rochefoucauld-Liancourt went on, would be merely the slaves'
hedonistic joyousness in their relief from unrewarding and lash-
enforced toil: "slavery . . . teaches him to cheat, to steal, to lie; and
he satisfied those wants, for which industry has not provided, by pil-
fering the corn or provisions of his neighbors." Although he believed
that lethargy, licentiousness, and laying about would be a certain result of a general, immediate, and unplanned program of manumis-
sion, de la Rochefoucauld-Liancourt held that this train of evils
"may be avoided, and may at length be entirely prevented, if not in
the present, at least in the future generation" by "a careful and liberal preparation for such a benevolent measure."[77]

However, at least one advocate of slavery believed that the long period of slavery had instilled in the Negro an inherent incapacity to adjust to unmastered labor in a free and competitive society.[78] George Fitzhugh asserted that Negroes, having not been socialized as participants in the struggle to obtain property—having, in fact, as chattel, been led to see themselves as one of the passive objects of that struggle—were not properly conditioned for capitalist society. What was required once abolition had been proclaimed, he argued, was a special system of state-sponsored welfare for the freedmen-and-women, organized under a comprehensive system of regulatory law that would, at one and the same time, shield blacks from the unfortunate effects of the struggle for existence, provide for their subsistence, health, and old age, but coerce their labor in menial and unskilled jobs. In other words, he proposed the reinstitutionalization of slavery under a system that separated ownership from control of the Negroes and that insured that they would not compete for valuable and career-enhancing jobs with whites.

Although they did not take their point of departure from Fitzhugh's thesis, the new labor unions in America adopted a set of practices—documented in the many researches of Herbert Hill on the matter[79]—that virtually accomplished the same result. Evicting blacks from their precariously held places in the industrial workforce, excluding them from their lily-white working men's associations, segregating their hiring when it was allowed, and denying them access to apprenticeship training, the racial practices of organized labor accomplished a veritable continuation of slavery under a post-abolitionist regimen of work.

In behalf of arguments like that of de la Rochefoucauld-Liancourt, schools were set up in the South and other places to bring the allegedly unprepared freedmen-and-women up to moral and industrial par with their white peers. Among these, none is so important in its consequences for the condition and the imagery of black Americans than the Normal and Industrial Institute of Alabama established at Tuskegee under the principalship of the ex-slave, Booker T. Washington. Washington's widely proclaimed pedagogical philosophy embodied more fully than any other the moral basis for a preparatory gradualism in obtaining Negro uplift. His own autobiography bespoke the basic message in its title: Up from Slavery.[80] To the Sage of Tuskegee, the American black was a member of "the semi-barbarous Negro race [that] has been thrown right down in the centre of the highest civilization that the world knows anything about."[81] As such, he told his black and white listeners, "Our greatest danger is that in the great leap from slavery to freedom we may overlook the fact that the masses of us are to live by the productions of our hands, and fail to keep in mind that we shall prosper in proportion as we learn to dignify and glorify common labour and put brains and skill into the common occupations of life."[82] In order to instill the right attitude toward hard work and human worth, Washington had carefully developed a limited and largely vocational curriculum at Tuskegee.

Washington's program was premised upon the belief that precisely because slavery had "impress[ed] upon both master and slave the fact that labor with the hand was . . . disgraceful, that labor of this character was something to be escaped, to be gotten rid of just as soon as possible,"[83] it was imperative to stamp that doctrine out of the hearts and minds of the Negro once and for all. Otherwise, "a large proportion of the race, immediately after its freedom, should make the mistake of confusing freedom with license."[84] His industrial school took as its central purpose to teach that "labor, with the hand or with the head . . . was something . . . that should be sought, loved, and appreciated."[85] Such a pedagogical approach tended, despite the occasional nod in the direction of cultivating "the head," to emphasize the training of "the hand." And, as Washington emphasized, a vocational rather than an academic education "had another value . . . in starting the Negro off in his new life in a natural, logical, [and] sensible manner." It prevented him from succumbing to sloth, from being "led into [the] temptation to begin life in an artificial atmosphere without any real foundation."[86]

However, it was not sufficient that the industrial and vocational curriculum bring blacks into the baseline of the free workaday world. It had also "wonderfully improved the moral and religious life of the Negro race in America."[87] Washington pointed to the facts that no Tuskegee graduate had yet been sent to prison, that its students and alumni led good family lives, that most Tuskegeeans worked six days a week,[88] and that—upon the testimony of a Tuskegee official charged with the task of keeping close contact with the institute's graduates, visiting their homes, talking with their neighbors, and discussing their job performance with their employers— "not ten percent . . . can be found today in idleness in any part of the country."[89] He also insisted that these facts gave practical proof that the strengthening of the blacks' moral and religious life depended on the cultivation in them of habits of industry, thrift, intelligence, and refinement.

That industrial and vocational instruction was inextricably connected to a gospel of material success, moral uplift, and the remission of such sins as sloth and those of the flesh was not only preached to America's blacks by Washington; he also made it the basis of his mission to the blacks of Liberia and of colonialized Africa. The hope that America's former slaves might achieve a social status higher than that warranted by their actual occupations, for example, as field hands or domestic servants, had been carried across the Atlantic and become a basic component of the imperialists' Christian homiletic that manual or agricultural labor, when coupled with a virtuous life, could inspire racial uplift.[90] However, not all advocates of the moral regeneration of black Africa were willing to concede the Negro's racial or cultural heritage as the price for advancement. Washington's and other black leaders' several attempts to export Tuskegee's brand of moral and industrial education to British, French, and German colonies in Africa,[91] as well as the earlier imposition of similar programs by the London-based Church Mission Society and other similarly oriented mission societies, became intertwined with anti-imperialist sentiments and anticolonial uprisings.[92] Such important black proponents of uplift as Edward W. Blyden urged a greater respect for native culture and African institutions, found spiritual support for scientific and material progress in the continent's Islamic religion, and complained that "the European missionary, however ardent his goal in behalf of 'poor benighted Africa' while in Europe, as soon as he comes in actual contact with the Negro, his ardour undergoes a sensible refrigeration."[93]

Whatever assistance Washington's mission school programs did in fact render, they did not succeed in obliterating the American image of the African as an inveterate lazy savage. As late as the 1960s, Dr. Henry E. Garrett, who had for sixteen years chaired Columbia University's Department of Psychology, disputed the positive effects that were said to be likely to attend the court-ordered desegregation of America's public schools by recounting a Eurocentric version of the history of African nonachievement: "Over the past 5000 years, the history of Black Africa is blank. . . . The Black African had no written language; no numerals; no calendar or system of measurement. He did not devise a plough or wheel, nor did he domesticate an animal; he built nothing more complex than a mud hut or thatched stockade. . . . His system of cartage was the human head."[94] But lest his assertion of eons of historyless indolence evoke an imagery of joyous leisure or a pleasure-laden existence, Garrett virtually insisted that his past and present bespoke a judgment on the African's conduct: "Instead of the happy savage basking in the shade of a friendly tree, what we find is a miserable creature wracked by disease, beset by animal and human enemies."[95] To some Americans, then, the African's sloth, whether constitutional or cultural, seemed irremediable.

Moreover, in 1958, to at least one black American scholar, neither the education nor the "progress" of the American Negro had prepared him to offer anything to the new nations of Africa, then just emerging from colonial domination.[96] E. Franklin Frazier pointed out that "although American Negroes had been stripped of their African cultural heritage and had become a biologically mixed group . . . the fact of their African origin has been regarded as a curse." Taught by "Christian preachers that their black complexion was the curse of God upon them and that because of this curse they were destined to be the servants of white men . . . [and] that Africans were savages and cannibals who had hardly taken the first steps toward civilization," the American Negro had "tended to accept the white man's evaluation of everything that was associated with Africa." America's blacks having been "treated as a 'child' race . . . had not been permitted to become dignified human beings and . . . were expected to play the role of a fool or a clown." Indeed, in what might easily be taken as an implicit critique of the Tuskegeean attempt to reconstruct Negro character in the image of thrift, industriousness, and refinement, as well as a condemnation of the refusal of white leaders to give up their commitment to racist caricatures and discriminating occupational restrictions, Frazier wrote, "One might even go so far as to say that in the United States, especially in the South, there has been a process of dysgenesic selection from the standpoint of character building." Given all of this, what could the American black offer to the newly free African nation-builders? Nothing, was Frazier's answer. "American Negroes can not make any contribution to the economic development of Africa because they lack the necessary capital . . . do not have positions of influence in the large financial institutions . . . and lack the managerial experience and skills needed in the modernization of the African economy." As for the field of politics, "American Negroes have scarcely anything to contribute to Africans, who have a long experience of political struggle and are assuming positions of responsibility not open to Negroes in the United States." The same could be said for any projected professional or intellectual contribution; Frazier pointed to the fact that the few American blacks who had reached the heights of these classes possessed an outlook that was "dominated by the provincial and spurious values of the new Negro middle class ... [who] live in a world of make-believe and reject identification with the cultural traditions of American Negroes as well as with their African origin." Hence, he seemed to say, whether viewed as a success or a failure, the Tuskegee experiment and its many imitations had been ultimately alienating and unemancipatory.

Social Reform and the Remediation of Sloth

If post–Civil War America seemed about to become the redeemer nation to many Christian, Eurocentric whites, the nation's treatment of the Negro earned it the sobriquet of barbarism to less sanguine observers. William Graham Sumner asserted that the failure of the federal government to put a stop to the hundreds of lynchings of southern Negroes that were then taking place illustrated the fact that there was greater respect for a dog or a cat in the United States than there was for a fellow human—a sure sign of atavistic degeneration.[97] Bishop Henry McNeal Turner (1834–1915), titular leader of the African Methodist Episcopal Church of the United States, allowed "that the United States has the highest form of civilized institutions that any nation has had," but denied, on the basis of the widespread failure of white people—"who could not stand to kill a brute ... who would not kill a snake or a bug"—to speak out against "the violent and gory outrages which are ... perpetrated ... upon human beings, chiefly because they are of African descent," that "the United States is a civilized nation."[98] He urged Afro-Americans to forsake America altogether and take up residence in the land of their forebears. The "Negro," he wrote in 1902, "can return to Africa, especially to Liberia where a Negro government is already in existence, and learn the elements of civilization in fact; for human life is there sacred."[99]

At the same time, a branch of the largely white Social Gospel—the movement that did hold human life sacred and swept over fin de siècle America, promising national redemption if a collective effort was made at ubiquitous moral uplift—extended its benevolent ministry to the southern blacks. The Methodist Episcopal Church's Woman's Home Mission Movement included a Social Service Bureau, whose chairwoman, Lily Hammond, in 1909 urged her fellow workers "to arouse the women of our auxiliaries to a sense of their personal duty as Christian Southerners, to meet the needs and ameliorate the conditions of those of this backward race who are in their midst by personal service and sympathy." Steeped in the belief that the Afro-Americans were uncivilized and therefore among the most sinful of creatures, Hammond had earlier claimed that "it would be difficult to exaggerate the lack of morals among the mass of negroes." Nevertheless, combining a belief in evolutionary change with a comparative view of the gradual improvement in morality, she noted with optimism that "the whole human race has come up from the depths in this respect; and, remembering how recently their forefathers were savages, the situation is not without encouragement."[100] The "situation" did not include accepting Sumner's definition of America as barbaric, or acknowledging Turner's depiction of America's uncivilized condition; neither did it permit designating savagery as the characterology of those whites who lynched blacks. Rather, the Southern Social Gospelers sought gently to persuade these lawless murderers away from the evil of their acts—usually without success.[101] Indeed, to the Gospelers, it was the blacks who were in need of tutelage. As Mary Helm, author of the widely read tract The Upward Path: Evolution of a Race, wrote, "[Slavery] with its discipline and training was the first great step in the evolution of the African savage, into a citizen of civilization."[102] In the absence of coercive bondage, these benevolently disposed whites looked forward to a form of redemption that would provide, in effect, the moral equivalent of slavery.

The Legacy of the Sin of Sloth

The Afro-American's plight today is in great measure chargeable to being burdened through enslavement with the sin of sloth. The accusation is itself part of the racist ideology that is one of the badges of slavery that survived beyond the institution's demise. Persons charged with a sin are expected to seek remediation and expiation. Blacks, ladened with a propensity to indolence, were first subjected to enforced and involuntary servitude; after abolition, they were obliged to seek their own salvation. Once enslaved, the rhetorics employed to justify that form of degradation adjusted themselves to the ruling ideas of the day; once slavery had been abolished, the rhetorics lent support to the survival of the badges of slavery—racist imagery. Religious rationalizations gave way to those of science. Doctrinal arguments seemed to disintegrate before those of constitutional, cultural, or psychological determinations. Nevertheless, in freedom as in slavery, sloth, that which needed to be expiated as well as explained, remained. Sometimes it was hidden behind less religious terminology, but, all the same, it was said to be operating to retard the black people's progress toward full-fledged emancipation.

So long as the Negro, as a Negro, was said to be morally culpable, a slothful sinner, blacks were obliged to seek redemption by their own efforts. Regeneration could come only if the black man or woman admitted to his or her sinful state and resolved to fight against its doleful effects. In the immediate aftermath of slavery, religiously sponsored ameliorative programs as well as public policies aimed at guiding blacks into a perception of their situation that would accept Christian reconstruction.[103] Later on, social scientific analyses tended toward explaining the failure of blacks to achieve complete equality in the society by referring to the persistence and the survival of one or another of the putative physical, cultural, or psychological retardants.[104]

At the present time, a large segment of the urban black population in the United States forms an impoverished underclass whose economic situation, though improved by the successes of the Civil Rights Movement and the prohibition of public laws creating or enforcing segregation, is nevertheless unpromising.[105] For some analysts, the blacks continue to be perceived as victims of their own characterology; their situation points up the pernicious persistence of sinful sloth among them. Hence, the single parent, the matricentric household, the sexual promiscuity attributed to unwed black teenage mothers, and the violence said to be de rigueur among young black males, are all perceived as symptoms of a deeper malaise—the condition once associated with *tristitia* and acedia. However, just as Henry Hughes insisted that blacks be held under a warrant to work by the civil authority that in modern societies had replaced the church as the enforcer of moral obligations, so today, there are those who see blacks as holding in their attitude toward work the key to their own emancipation. Such persons call for either a personal or a civil ordering of the situation—call in effect, for their enrollment in a moral crusade against sloth.

For some, the new mastery that is to succeed to the morally sovereign place once occupied by the seigneurial master class is embodied in the individual self. Thus, Rev. Jesse Jackson, an unsuccessful candidate for the presidency of the United States, has proclaimed that "self-mastery is a revolutionary concept," and once achieved, it can emancipate the urban black masses. In a litany that has become a popular slogan among his followers, Jackson urges, "Nobody can save us from us for us but us."[106] Despite the claim that he is putting forth a new idea, Jackson is in fact continuing in the tradition of individual Christian endeavor, holding moral rebirth to be the appropriate response to a sinful soul. In this respect his proposals for the solution to black unemployment resemble those of Booker T. Wash-

ington and fall far short of others that hold that the problem is institutional, that is, that the capitalist system is both the culprit and
the obligee. The latter call for a policy of full as well as fulfilling
employment.[107] Moreover, they do not blame the victimized blacks
for their plight.

Still others insist that the state undertake a program not too dissimilar from that first proposed by the slavocrat-sociologist Henry
Hughes—lawfully enforced warranteeism. Perhaps the most candid
of these is the contemporary political scientist, Lawrence M. Mead,
whose book *Beyond Entitlement: The Social Obligations of Citizenship,* perceives present-day urban black youth as a body of "masterless men," disobliged from the responsible duties that go together
with freedom and societal membership. Holding that "a sense of
personal obligation is necessary to freedom,"[108] Mead asserts that
black youths, like certain members of the white counterculture,
"cannot be integrated [into a work-oriented society] unless they become something closer to the disciplined workers the economy
demands."[109] In earlier eras, Mead believes, such disciplinary so-
cialization took place within the family and through the moral authority of the church. However, the disintegration of the Negro
family, so pointedly addressed in the researches of Daniel Patrick
Moynihan,[110] and the shift in some of the current Protestant casuistries toward believing that "the weakest and most deprived members of society [must be given] the freedom to choose how they may
express the meaning of their lives"[111] lead him to demand that "in
some form the government must take over the socializing role."[112]
According to Mead, black youth face "strong disincentives to work
in regular jobs, because they could earn more through illegal work
or crime."[113] Moreover, he implies that inner-city Afro-American
youths are sunk in a slough of slothful despond. Mead asserts that,
"the need to enforce work is clearest in the case of young black men,
the group most central to the work problem."[114] For Mead, as well as
those who share his perspective,[115] the inner-worldly sinfulness of
their situation and its deleterious effects on society and morality,
call for a statist program that will indoctrinate blacks with the appropriate attitude toward labor, but not necessarily provide them
with a job wherein they can exhibit it.

But, suppose that a different orientation would prevail. Imagine
what the scenario of policy toward black progress might be if the
original intention of the framers of the Thirteenth Amendment to the
United States Constitution—to abolish not merely the institution of
slavery but, more significantly, its concomitant and proactive badge

of racial inferiorization[116]—had become the watchword of public law and popular ideology. Then the charge that the ex-slaves and their descendants were predisposed to indolence and its train of evils might have been recognized as nothing more than a rejectable hangover of slavery, a virulent racial prejudice. Then, rather than being culpable for their condition, blacks might be perceived as victims wrongly blamed for the effects of an institutionalized evil upon them. Then, the long history of economic and social deprivation, of residential ghettoization, school segregation, occupational eviction, labor-union exclusion, menial work, or racially motivated joblessness might be seen as indicators of unlawful resistance to a public promise, even a basis for redress or an entitlement. Then, the sin of sloth and any of its post-religious equivalents might be eliminated altogether from the rhetorics of black justification. Then, indolence might be recharacterized altogether for those who bore the yoke— and still wear the badge—of slavery. Then, their situation, rights, and deserts[117] might be recognized as they once were by a Scottish professional soldier who visited the United States in 1833. Noting that slavery had been legislatively abolished in the northern states and that property rights in a Negro's labor power were no longer recognized in law, Thomas Hamilton held that the ostensibly free blacks were, nonetheless, still in bondage. Indeed, he argued, "it may be safely asserted, that this poor degraded caste are still slaves," and went on to show how: "They are subjected to the most grinding and humiliating of all slaveries, that of universal and unconquerable prejudice. The whip, indeed has been removed from the back of the Negro, but the chains are still on his limbs, and he bears the brand of degradation on his forehead. What is it but mere abuse of language to call him *free*, who is tyrannically deprived of all the motives to exertion which animate other men?"[118] To break once and for all the chains of slavery, it would appear, means to abrogate the covenant of slothful sin to which those in bondage have been so long and so wrongfully subjected.

NOTES

This essay originally appeared in *The International Journal of Politics, Culture, and Society*, 5:1 (Fall 1991), pp. 49–79.

1. Thomas Jefferson, *Notes on the State of Virginia* (New York: Harper Torchbooks, 1964), p. 156.

2. Kenneth M. Stampp, *The Imperiled Union: Essays on the Background of the Civil War* (New York: Oxford University Press, 1980), pp. 246–70.

For an excellent discussion on which I have drawn, see Richard E. Beringer, Herman Hathaway, Archer Jones, and William N. Still, *Why the South Lost the Civil War* (Athens: University of Georgia Press, 1986), pp. 336–67.

3. Henry Hughes, *A Treatise on Sociology, Theoretical and Practical* (Philadelphia: Lippincott and Grambo, 1854; reprint, New York: Negro Universities Press, 1968), p. 95.

4. William Harper, "Memoir on Slavery," in E. N. Elliott, ed., *Cotton is King, and Pro-Slavery Arguments: Comprising the Writings of Hammond, Harper, Christy, Stringfellow, Hodge, Bledsoe, and Cartwright, on This Important Subject* (Augusta, Ga.: Pritchard, Abbott, and Loomis, 1860), p. 551. Quotation is from the reprint in Drew Gilpin Faust, ed., *The Ideology of Slavery: Proslavery Thought in the Antebellum South, 1830–1860* (Baton Rouge: Louisiana State University Press, 1981), p. 81.

5. *The Pro-Slavery Argument; as Maintained by . . . Chancellor Harper, Governor Hammond, Dr. Simms, and Professor Dew* (Charleston: Walker, Richards, and Co., 1853), p. 260. Quoted in David Bertelson, *The Lazy South* (New York: Oxford University Press, 1967), p. 199.

6. William Grayson, *The Hireling and the Slave, Chicora, and Other Poems* (Charleston: McCord and Co., 1856), pp. 21–45, passim. Quotation from the abridged reprint in Eric L. McKitrick, ed., *Slavery Defended: The Views of the Old South* (Englewood Cliffs: Prentice-Hall, 1963), p. 63.

7. Cf. S. H. Alatas, *The Myth of the Lazy Native: A Study of the Image of the Malays, Filipinos and Javanese from the 16th to the 20th Centuries and Its Function in the Ideology of Colonial Capitalism* (London: Frank Cass, 1977).

8. Samuel A. Cartwright, "Diseases and Peculiarities of the Negro Race," *DeBow's Review*, 11 (July 1851), pp. 64–69, and (Sept. 1851), pp. 331–36. Quotation from the reprint in Paul F. Paskoff and Daniel J. Wilson, eds., *The Cause of the South: Selections from DeBow's Review, 1846–1867* (Baton Rouge: Louisiana State University Press, 1982), p. 41.

9. James Madison, *Notes on Debates in the Federal Convention of 1787* (New York: W. W. Norton and Co., 1987), p. 504.

10. Quoted in Jacobus ten Broek, *The Antislavery Origins of the Fourteenth Amendment* (Berkeley: University of California Press, 1951), p. 146.

11. See Anne Norton, *Alternative Americas: A Reading of Antebellum Culture* (Chicago: University of Chicago Press, 1987), pp. 234–39.

12. See Bertram Wyatt-Brown, *Southern Honor: Ethics and Behavior in the Old South*, (New York: Oxford University Press, 1982).

13. Bertelson, *Lazy South*, pp. 61–98 et passim.

14. Quoted in ibid., p. 81.

15. For a discussion of the rhetorics of exculpation see chapter 5, "Accounts," in Stanford M. Lyman and Marvin B. Scott, *A Sociology of the Absurd* (New York: Appleton-Century-Crofts, 1970), pp. 111–44.

16. See Stanford M. Lyman, ed., *Selected Writings of Henry Hughes: Antebellum Southerner, Slavocrat, Sociologist* (Jackson: University Press of Mississippi, 1985).

17. St. Henry (pseud. for Henry Hughes), "African Labor Supply-Wealth Argument," no. 9 in the series entitled Reopening the African Labor Supply, in *Jackson Semi-Weekly Mississippian*, April 24, 1860.

18. Henry Hughes, "A Report on the African Apprentice System," paper read at the Southern Commerical Convention, Vicksburg, May 10, 1859. Reprinted in Lyman, ed., *Selected Writings of Henry Hughes*, pp. 167–84.

19. St. Henry, "African Labor."

20. Hughes, *Treatise on Sociology*, pp. 86–88.

21. St. Henry, "Wealth Argument," no. 7 in the series Reopening the African Labor Supply, in *Jackson Semi-Weekly Mississippian*, October 4, 1859.

22. Ibid.

23. Hughes, *Treatise on Sociology*, p. 88.

24. Ibid., p . 97.

25. Theodore Dwight Bozeman, *Protestants in an Age of Science: The Baconian Ideal and Antebellum American Religious Thought* (Chapel Hill: University of North Carolina Press, 1977), pp. 21–31.

26. F. Hall, *Letters from the East and West*, p. 140. Quoted in Grady McWhiney, *Cracker Culture: Celtic Ways in the Old South* (Tuscaloosa: University of Alabama Press, 1988), p. 265.

27. The following draws on McWhiney, *Cracker Culture*.

28. Ibid., p. 51.

29. Ibid., p. 72.

30. Ibid., p. 67.

31. George Fitzhugh, *Cannibals All! or Slaves without Masters*, ed. C. Vann Woodward (Cambridge: Belknap Press of Harvard University Press, 1960, 1973), p. 29.

32. Duc de la Rochefoucauld-Liancourt, *Travels through The United States of North America, the Country of the Iroquois, and Upper Canada, in the Years 1795, 1796, and 1797* (London: R. Phillips, 1799), vol. 3, pp. 263–65, 553–56, 569–73. Excerpt printed in Lenworth Gunther, ed., *Black Image: European Eye-Witness Accounts of Afro-American Life* (Port Washington, N.Y.: Kennikat Press, 1978), p. 38.

33. Stanford M. Lyman, *The Seven Deadly Sins: Society and Evil* (New York: St. Martin's Press, 1978), pp. 5–52.

34. Max Weber, *The Protestant Ethic and the Spirit of Capitalism*, trans. Talcott Parsons (London: George Allen and Unwin, 1930), p. 157.

35. Ibid., p. 161.

36. McWhiney, *Cracker Culture*, p. 112.

37. Ibid., p. 140.

38. Lyman, *Seven Deadly Sins*, pp. 212–31.

39. Quoted in McWhiney, *Cracker Culture*, p. 143.

40. Lyman, *Seven Deadly Sins*, p. 6.

41. McWhiney, *Cracker Culture*, p. 170.

42. Ibid., pp. 20–21, 44–47, 89, 106, 110, 114, 117, 138, 179, 186, 188, 200, 266.

43. Blake Touchstone, "Planters and Slave Religion in the Deep South,"in John B. Boles, ed., *Masters and Slaves in The House of the Lord: Race and*

Religion in the American South, 1740–1870 (Lexington: University Press of Kentucky, 1988), p. 121.

44. Ibid.

45. Mechal Sobel, *The World They Made Together: Black and White Values in Eighteenth-Century Virginia* (Princeton: Princeton University Press, 1987). See also the review of this work by Stanford M. Lyman in *The American Journal of Sociology*, 94:3 (Nov. 1988), pp. 681–83.

46. Sobel, *World They Made*, p. 46.

47. Ibid., p. 50.

48. Ibid., p. 47.

49. Ibid.

50. Ibid.

51. Ibid., pp. 52–53.

52. Douglas Grant, *The Fortunate Slave: An Illustration of African Slavery in the Early Eighteenth Century* (London: Oxford University Press, 1968), pp. 13–14.

53. McWhiney, *Cracker Culture*, p. 45.

54. Sobel, *World They Made*, p. 57.

55. Ibid., p. 59.

56. Ibid.

57. William James, "On a Certain Blindness in Human Beings," in *The Writings of William James: A Comprehensive Edition*, ed. John J. McDermott (New York: Modern Library, 1968), pp. 629–45.

58. See Herbert Blumer, "Race Prejudice as a Sense of Group Position," *Pacific Sociological Review*, 1 (Spring 1958), pp. 3–7.

59. The concept of "Herrenvolk democracy" has been developed by Pierre van den Berghe in his *Race and Racism* (New York: John Wiley, 1967), pp. 77–95.

60. Such seems to be an important part of the thesis about the place of black workers in the American economy put forward by Thomas Sowell. "Cultures," he writes, "are ultimately ways of accomplishing things, and the differing efficiencies with which they accomplish different things determine the outcomes of very serious economic, political and military endeavors." For Sowell, cultural survivals are measured in terms of whether they "have been more technologically or organizationally effective than others during one historical epoch." In the case of Africans brought to America, he believes that their origins were not from among the "more advanced civilization" that had grown up around "the great Niger river," but rather "from other African tribes subjugated by the more powerful Nigerian tribes." For Sowell, advancement among black Americans has been led by the "free persons of color" who were more fully acculturated and imbued with the appropriate incentives toward work and its relation to the Protestant American gospel of success. Thomas Sowell, *The Economics and Politics of Race: An International Perspective* (New York: William Morrow and Co., 1983), pp. 136, 137, 94, 127–28. For a critique of his position, see Rhonda M. Williams, "Culture as Human Capital: Meth-

odological and Policy Implications," *Praxis International*, 7:2 (July 1987), pp. 152–63.

61. Leo Kuper, *Race, Class and Power: Ideology and Revolutionary Change in Plural Societies* (London: Duckworth, 1974), p. 36.

62. Stanley Elkins, *Slavery: A Problem in American Institutional and Intellectual Life*, 3d ed. (Chicago: University of Chicago Press, 1976), pp. 81–139.

63. See Eugene D. Genovese, "Rebelliousness and Docility in the Negro Slave: A Critique of the Elkins Thesis," and Roy Simon Bryce-Laporte, "Slaves as Inmates, Slaves as Men," pp. 43–74 and 269–92, respectively, in Ann J. Lane, ed., *The Debate over Slavery: Stanley Elkins and His Critics* (Urbana: University of Illinois Press, 1971).

64. See George M. Frederickson, "White Images of Black Slaves in the Old South," in Frederickson, *The Arrogance of Race: Historical Perspectives on Slavery, Racism, and Social Inequality* (Middletown, Conn.: Wesleyan University Press, 1988), p. 208.

65. See Winthrop Jordan, *White over Black: American Attitudes toward the Negro, 1550–1812* (Chapel Hill: University of North Carolina Press, 1968), pp. 17–20, 35–37, 41–43, 54–56, 60, 84, 111, 243–46, 308, 525.

66. See two works by Eugene D. Genovese, *Roll, Jordan, Roll: The World the Slaves Made* (New York: Pantheon Books, 1974), pp. 585–660); and *From Rebellion to Revolution: Afro-American Slave Revolts in the Making of the Modern World* (Baton Rouge: Louisiana State University Press, 1979).

67. See Stanford M. Lyman and Marvin B. Scott, *The Drama of Social Reality* (New York: Oxford University Press, 1975), pp. 129–32.

68. Joseph LeConte, *The Race Problem in the South* (Miami: Mnemosyne Publishing, Inc., 1969. Orig. pub. 1892), p. 373.

69. Ibid., pp. 373–75.

70. Benjamin Franklin, "Observations Concerning the Increase of Mankind, Peopling of Countries, etc." (1751). Reprinted in Franklin, *Writings*, ed. J. A. Leo Lemay (New York: Library of America, 1987), p. 374.

71. Andrew D. Weinberger, "A Reappraisal of the Constitutionality of 'Miscegenation' Statutes," Appendix G in Ashley Montagu, *Man's Most Dangerous Myth: The Fallacy of Race*, 4th ed. (Cleveland: Meridian Books—World Publishing Co., 1965), pp. 402–24.

72. See three works by Edward Byron Reuter, *The Mulatto in the United States: Including a Study of the Role of Mixed-Blood Races throughout the World* (New York: Negro Universities Press, 1969. Orig. pub. 1918); *Race Mixture: Studies in Intermarriage and Miscegenation* (New York: Negro Universities Press, 1969. Orig. pub. 1931); *The American Race Problem*, rev. by Jitsuichi Masuoka (New York: Thomas Y. Crowell, 1970), pp. 124–37; and Joel Williamson, *New People: Miscegenation and Mulattoes in the United States* (New York: The Free Press, 1980), pp. 61–140.

73. Heinrich von Treitschke, *Politics*, abr. and ed. Hans Kohn, trans. Blanche Dugdale and Torben de Bille (New York: Harcourt, Brace, and World, 1963), pp. 125–26.

74. Norman Podhoretz, "My Negro Problem—and Ours," *Commentary*, 35 (Feb. 1963), pp. 93–101. Reprinted in *Racial and Ethnic Relations: Selected Readings*, ed. Bernard E. Segal (Thomas Y. Crowell, 1966), pp. 239–50. Quotations from pp. 245, 250.

75. See John Niven, *John C. Calhoun and the Price of Union: A Biography* (Baton Rouge: Louisiana State University Press, 1988), pp. 18–19.

76. Ibid., p. 276.

77. de la Rochefoucauld-Liancourt, *Travels*, p. 37.

78. The following draws on Stanford M. Lyman, "System and Function in Antebellum Southern Sociology," *The International Journal of Politics, Culture and Society*, 2:1 (Fall 1988), pp. 95–108, esp. pp. 99–104.

79. See, among his many studies, two works by Herbert Hill, "The Racial Practices of Organized Labor—the Age of Gompers and After," in Arthur M. Ross and Herbert Hill, eds., *Employment, Race, and Poverty: A Critical Study of the Disadvantaged Status of Negro Workers from 1865 to 1965* (New York: Harcourt, Brace, and World, 1967), pp. 365–402; and *Black Labor and the American Legal System: Race, Work and the Law* (Madison: University of Wisconsin Press, 1985).

80. Booker T. Washington, *Up from Slavery: An Autobiography* (New York: Bantam Books, 1963. Orig. pub. 1901).

81. Booker T. Washington, "The Economic Development of the Negro Race since Its Emancipation," in Booker T. Washington and W. E. B. Du Bois, *The Negro in the South: His Economic Progress in Relation to His Moral and Religious Development. Being the William Levi Bull Lectures for the Year 1907* (New York: Citadel Press, 1970), p. 74.

82. Washington, *Up from Slavery*, p. 155.

83. Washington, "Economic Development," p. 75.

84. Ibid., p. 46.

85. Ibid.

86. Ibid., p. 51.

87. Ibid., pp. 54–55.

88. Ibid., pp. 55–73.

89. Ibid., p. 61.

90. See Louis R. Harlan, "Booker T. Washington and the White Man's Burden," *American Historical Review*, 71:2 (Jan. 1966), pp. 441–67.

91. See, e.g., Horace Mann Bond, "Forming African Youth: A Philosophy of Education," in *Africa Seen by American Negro Scholars* (New York: American Society of African Culture, 1963), p. 247–61.

92. See two essays by George Shepperson, "Ethiopianism and African Nationalism," *Phylon*, 14 (Winter 1953), pp. 9–18; "The Politics of African Church Separatist Movements in British Central Africa, 1892–1916," *Africa*, 24 (Jan. 1954), pp. 233–45.

93. Quoted in Hollis R. Lynch, "The Native Pastorate Controversy and Cultural Ethno-Centrism in Sierra Leone, 1871–1874," *Journal of African History*, 5:3 (1964), p. 399.

94. Henry E. Garrett, *How Classroom Desegregation Will Work* (Rich-

mond, Va.: The Patrick Henry Press, n.d.), p. 24. Quoted in Felix N. Okoye, *The American Image of Africa: Myth and Reality* (New York: Third Press International, 1978), p. 3.

95. Ibid.

96. The following is from E. Franklin Frazier, "What Can the American Negro Contribute to the Social Development of Africa?" in *Africa Seen by American Negro Scholars*, pp. 263–78.

97. William Graham Sumner, "Foreword," to James Elbert Cutler, *Lynch-Law: An Investigation into the History of Lynching in the United States* (Montclair: Patterson Smith, 1969. Orig. pub. 1905), p. v.

98. Bishop H. M. Turner, "Will It Be Possible for the Negro to Attain, in This Country, Unto the American Type of Civilization?" in Adelaide Cromwell Hill and Martin Kilson, eds., *Apropos of Africa: Sentiments of Negro American Leaders on Africa from the 1800s to the 1950s* (London: Frank Cass and Co., 1969), p. 46.

99. Ibid., p. 47.

100. Quoted in John Patrick McDowell, *The Social Gospel in the South: The Woman's Home Mission Movement in the Methodist Episcopal Church, South, 1886–1939* (Baton Rouge: Louisiana State University Press, 1982), pp. 102–03.

101. Ibid., pp. 94–98.

102. Mary Helm, *From Darkness to Light: The Story of Negro Progress*, 2d ed. (New York: n.p., 1909), p. 41. Quoted in McDowell, *Social Gospel*, p. 103.

103. See Joe M. Richardson, *Christian Reconstruction: The American Missionary Association and Southern Blacks, 1861–1890* (Athens: University of Georgia Press, 1986), esp. pp. 235–56.

104. George M. Fredrickson, *The Black Image in the White Mind: The Debate on Afro-American Character and Destiny, 1817–1914* (New York: Harper and Row, 1971), pp. 312–17.

105. See Douglas G. Glasgow, "The Black Underclass in Perspective," in *The State of Black America 1987* (New York: National Urban League, Inc., 1987), pp. 129–44.

106. Quoted in Ken Auletta, *The Underclass* (New York: Vintage Books, 1983), p. 156.

107. See W. Arthur Lewis, *Racial Conflict and Economic Development* (Cambridge: Harvard University Press, 1985), esp. pp. 1–92.

108. Lawrence M. Mead, *Beyond Entitlement: The Social Obligations of Citizenship* (New York: The Free Press, 1986), p. 88.

109. Ibid., p. 87.

110. See Daniel Patrick Moynihan, "Employment, Income, and the Ordeal of the Negro Family," *Daedalus: Journal of the American Academy of Arts and Sciences*, 94:4 (Fall 1965), pp. 745–70.

111. Mead, *Beyond Entitlement*, p. 212.

112. Ibid., p. 87.

113. Ibid., pp. 87–88.

114. Ibid., p. 87.

115. See Charles Murray, *Losing Ground: American Social Policy 1950–1980* (New York: Basic Books, 1984), pp. 69–82.

116. See Jacobus ten Broek, "Thirteenth Amendment to the Constitution of the United States: Consummation to Abolition and Key to the Fourteenth Amendment," *California Law Review*, 39 (June 1951), pp. 171–203.

117. For a fine discussion of rights, deserts and entitlements, see Derek L. Phillips, *Toward a Just Social Order* (Princeton: Princeton University Press, 1986), pp. 341–78.

118. Thomas Hamilton, "Free Black Schools in the North," in Hamilton, *Men and Manners in America* (London: T. Cadell, 1833), pp. 90–101. Excerpt in Gunther, *Black Image*, p. 51.

6

Race, Sex, and Servitude:
Images of Blacks in American Cinema

In the early days of the American film industry, African-Americans were in no position to make or influence movies about Africa, black Americans, or any other subject. However, white European and American moviemakers were not constrained by either their own condition, color, culture, or character—or by their meager knowledge of the realities of African or black American life—from seeking to characterize on film the manners and customs of the Africans and their American descendants. Among the earliest docudramas about Africa made in the United States were those purporting to be films of ex-President Theodore Roosevelt's safaris in East Africa in 1909. Roosevelt's imagery of Africa gave to that continent a Comtean variant of the American pastoral mystique and at the same time lent support to the colonialist mission to civilize the continent's benighted savages. In the book upon which the films were based, he sought to depict a trip on "a railroad through the Pleistocene." As such a geological time traveler, Roosevelt claimed that he had witnessed the "great world movement . . . which . . . has brought into sudden, violent, and intimate contact phases of the world's life history which would normally be separated by untold centuries of slow development."[1]

Like the printing press, the movie camera would also make it possible for modern Americans to travel vicariously, as it were, not merely through space but also through time: Africa would become the setting for a popular culture application of Auguste Comte's "comparative method," providing a cinematic situs for a universal history. Taking scenarios of contemporary African peoples, the movies, like the anthropological texts of the day, assigned dark-skinned people a low place on the linear chronology of geological and cultural time. The trajectory illustrated a presupposed, perhaps preordained, movement from "savagery" through "barbarism" to "civilization."[2]

Roosevelt's version of the African pastoral and its people added a Social Darwinist overlay to the Comtean vision: "In fact," he asserted, the black Africans "were living just as palaeolithic man lived in Europe, ages ago."[3] As a prehistoric people living in the historical world, the Africans were, thence, locatable on the great chain of being, connecting all humankind to its earliest origins and showing the forms it would take as it moved toward its ultimate destiny: "Most of the tribes," Roosevelt pointed out, "were of pure savages; but here and there were intrusive races of higher type; and in Uganda, beyond the Victoria Nyanza, and on the headwaters of the Nile proper, lived a people which had advanced to the upper stages of barbarism, which might almost be said to have developed a very primitive kind of semi-civilization."[4] As the earliest films about Africa would try to document, and such later films as *Sanders of the River* (1935) and *Stanley and Livingstone* (1939) would seek to celebrate, peoples whose cultural cultivation stretched only from savagery through barbarism required a long period of European tutelage. As Roosevelt put the matter, "Over this people—for its good fortune—Great Britain established a protectorate."[5]

In most films about Africa, its people are depicted as inhabitants of fetid, vine-and-snake infested jungles. The early documentaries based on Roosevelt's and other big game hunter's adventures— *Tuaregs in Their Country* (1909); *Theodore Roosevelt in Africa* (n.d.); *Theodore Roosevelt's Camp in Africa* (n.d.); Paul J. Rainey's *African Hunt* (1912); *Capturing Circus Animals in the African Wilds* (1913); *African Natives* (n.d.)—pictured jungle settings as the African norm.[6] Within a very short time, their popularity spawned a host of exotic feature films—*Missionaries in Darkest Africa* (1912); *The Terrors of the Jungle* (1913); *Voodoo Vengeance* (1913); *The Loyalty of Jumbo* (1914); *Forbidden Adventure* (1915); and *A Night in the Jungle* (1915)—exploiting such soon to be standardized themes as "darkest" Africa, jungle "juju," African "primitivism," the tragedy of miscegenation, and heroic if unavailing missionary endeavor. Soon, a leitmotif established by African movies settled on four basic themes: (1) the inherent superiority of Euro-American civilization, the white race, and colonial rule; (2) the sorrow and tragedy of interracial sex and/or marriage; (3) the loyalty and devotion of the African servant; and (4) the altruistic service of white missionaries, doctors, engineers, and wildlife conservationists, who serve as models of civilization and tutors of modernity to grateful African natives.

Eurocentrism in British and American Cinema

Despite the fact that the United States, as the "first new nation," might have served as cinema's eighteenth-century model for the de-colonization movement that would sweep away Europe's overseas empires in the twentieth century,[7] American movies from the beginning lent filmic support to European hegemony over African and other dark-skinned peoples. Theodore Roosevelt's African commentaries had set the terms for this theme so strongly—"The English rule in Africa has been of incalculable benefit to Africans themselves, and indeed this is true of the rule of most European nations. Mistakes have been made, of course, but they have proceeded at least as often from an unwise effort to accomplish too much in the way of beneficence, as from a desire to exploit the natives."[8]—that the demand for national self-determination that characterized Woodrow Wilson's postwar foreign policy (but was not meant to apply to the colonial empires of the victorious powers) could not undermine them.

Although by 1915 the predominant theme of American cinema's African motifs had become "the dull impotence of their blacks,"[9] for the next fifty years pseudohistorical action features would continue to emphasize barbaric atrocities committed by black natives against well-meaning white colonists, honest settlers, and benevolent missionaries. Reprising the "fierce" imagery that had been established in earlier "Zulu" movies, a British film, *Rhodes of Africa* (1935), "depicted the savagery of the Zulu war using Africans, including an African in the role of a chief."[10] Zulus would continue to be prominent in British and American films. One outstanding example is *Zulu* (1964), retelling the story of the battle of Rorke's Drift, in which a small company of British soldiers successfully held off an attack by 4,200 Zulu warriors for twenty-four hours.[11]

A change in the imagery of African Americans permitted a number of "blaxploitation" films to treat Africa in a slightly different way on American movie screens. *Shaft in Africa* (1973) had its eponymous black American hero (Richard Roundtree) go to the former "Dark Continent" to prevent an unscrupulous French entrepreneur from flooding Europe with cheap native labor that would subvert its industrial economy.[12] Treating Africans to the same charges that had been leveled against Asians in nineteenth-century America, this movie failed to treat the issues affecting *Gastarbeiten* being imported into France and Germany from Turkey, Yugoslavia, and Morocco; moreover, it depicted nothing of the poignant perspective on mar-

riage and race relations that in the same year Rainer Werner Fass-
binder had presented in his brilliant study of Moroccan workers in
Germany, *Fear Eats the Soul: Ali* (1973). For American and British
filmmakers, the colonial era remained one for reprising tragic white
missionarianism, docile black subservience, and ungrateful native
resistance to Occidental benevolence.

Sex and the Prohibition of Interracial Marriage

"Stereotyping," writes social anthropologist I. C. Jarvie, "can be interpreted as basically a defense against imagined and real threats."[13]
In the case of the movie stereotyping of African and other dark-
skinned persons as atavistic ape men, tragic mulattoes, or preternatural seducers of white men, Hollywood vicariously and
symbolically reinforced white America's statutory and social barri-
cades against mixing the races. As Gunnar Myrdal was to point out
in 1944, the chief fear of the ordinary white American male was that
the blacks sought "amalgamation" and that Negro men had designs
on "his" woman.[14] One element of this apprehension had to do with
white male fantasies about the alleged sexual superiority of Africans
and blacks and the supposed physical attractiveness of black men to
white women.[15]

Although the racialist theme that pervaded American "exotic"
movies often depicted black people as "natives" in Latin America,
the South Seas, South Asia, and Arabia, it also required them to be
beyond the pale of marriage with white persons. The "forbidden
fruit" of black Africa and its cinematic surrogates—that is, people of
color—was always presented as a basis for either marital or intergenerational tragedy. Although the "tragic mulatto" theme had preceded the writing of film scenarios, having first been presented in
Clotel, or The President's Daughter (1853) by the black American
novelist William Wells Brown,[16] the thesis proclaiming a mixed-
blood's irrevocably threatening claim on a monoracial social order
would be adapted and reworked for many Hollywood films. Depicting star-crossed mulatto lovers, *The Octoroon* (1913), set a filmic
standard that would not be broken until *Guess Who's Coming to
Dinner* (released in 1967, the same year that the Supreme Court
declared the last of the state laws prohibiting racial intermarriage
unconstitutional)[17] put that issue on cinematic hold.

The African and colonial films of the silent era offered opportunities to work numerous plots around the basic miscegenation
theme. In Gauntier's *Missionaries in Darkest Africa* (1912), the re-

morseful daughter of the white Christians who seek to bring civilization to the dark continent commits suicide rather than face up to her erotic interest in the native who kidnapped her.[18] While a black woman might not marry a white man, she might express her love for him by saving his life. In *The Voice of Conscience* (n.d.) the heroine uses voodoo to force another black to confess to the crime for which the white hero has been arrested.[19] *The Leopard Woman* (1920) permitted the eponymous native heroine to sublimate her love for a white hunter by ordering the execution of an innocent Negro (Noble Johnson, essaying a role he would replay in numerous jungle and exotic films for three decades) in his place.[20] Often parodied in later years, *Leopard Woman* and *The Voice of Conscience* had set the terms for contrasting white love with black lust.

When in 1927 Hollywood's Hays Office banned the cinematic presentation of romances between actors of different races and prohibited altogether any positive image of intermarriage—(thirty-nine states of the United States had at one time or another enacted miscegenation statutes)[21]—the scene was set not only for the eviction of the black feature player from his or her paltry opportunities to play frustrated love objects in stereotyped dramas, but also for numerous variations on racial identity mix-ups as screenplay solutions to forbidden romance. Thus, to take one film as an exemplar of many that were to follow, *Volcano* (1926) hints at the idea that an apparently white woman (Bebe Daniels), resident of Martinique, has some "black" blood. The menacing villain of the piece (Wallace Beery) is identified as a "quadroon." In the denouement, the heroine is cleared of the charge of "tainted blood" and is thereby free to marry her white sweetheart (Ricardo Cortez).[22]

The deep-seated fears about a sexual encounter between an African man and a Caucasian woman were graphically illustrated in *Tarzan of the Apes* (1918), when Jane Porter (Enid Markey) had to be saved from a menacing African, a "black ape," who kidnaps and attempts to rape her.[23] The dynamics of race and gender that would become de rigueur in films about Africans and African Americans are here fully anticipated.[24] The lusty African man is in fact the screenplay's replacement of Tarzan-creator Edgar Rice Burrough's "Terkoz," a real ape and Tarzan's short-lived successor as leader of the anthropoids. In the novel, Terkoz, having already been ostracized by his subject-apes, is described as a "horrible man-like beast" who seeks to take Jane, a "hairless white ape," as his mate.[25] In the film, however—exemplifying a thesis that had been debated in religious, literary, and journalistic circles two decades earlier under the heading, "The Negro, a beast?"[26]—Jane is threatened by "a huge, black, bald-headed, paint-faced, diabolically grinning, African buck,"[27] who is pictorially perceived as much more the "ape-man" than her white-skinned muscular saviour-cum-lover, Tarzan (Elmo Lincoln).

Jane's horrified reaction to the advances of the lusty black brute/ape—"One piercing scream escaped her lips. . . . But Jane did not once lose consciousness . . . her brain was clear, and she comprehended all that transpired"[28]—is meant to teach another lesson. Her clearheaded courage was to be contrasted with that of her black, heavyset, handkerchief-headed maid-in-uniform, Esmeralda—"Esmeralda's scream of terror had mingled once with that of Jane, and then, *as was Esmeralda's manner under stress of emergency which required presence of mind*, she swooned."[29] In the film, Esmeralda personifies the comic-mammy-coon character, or, more accurately, caricature, that had originated in the earlier "Jim Crow" minstrelsy.[30] Esmeralda's loyal black maidservant essays the part of a droll, stupid, and superstitious fool, a role that in a later era's movies (e.g., *Gone With the Wind* [1939]) would be elaborated on by Butterfly McQueen.

Although the African American wives lampooned in *Coon Town Suffragettes* (1914)—a blackface travesty on Aristophanes's *Lysistrata*—were permitted to possess some social intelligence, and the formula-enacted domestics played by Louise Beavers, Hattie McDaniel, and Isabell Sanford in numerous movies made from the 1930s through the 1970s were usually compensated for their fawning buffoonery by having a dose of practical wisdom available for their white employers, their characters lent additional support to a complex ideology of white sexual racism. The "wise" black mammy's opposition to miscegenation plummeted to its nadir in Stanley Kramer's *Guess Who's Coming to Dinner?* (1967), a movie widely touted for its liberal outlook and anti-miscegenationist theme. As Tillie, the housekeeper to Matt and Christina Dayton (Spencer Tracy and Katharine Hepburn)—a prosperous white middle-class couple whose daughter Joey (Katharine Houghton) has fallen in love with John Prentice (Sydney Poitier), a black American medical doctor who works for the World Health Organization—Isabell Sanford is made not only to oppose her employer's daughter's marriage to what she calls an "uppity nigger," but also to be such a threat to Dr. Prentice's seemingly liberated libido that he grabs a shirt to cover his bare chest when she bursts in upon him while he is changing clothes.

The early Tarzan films had established an important theme of the African cinematic motif: "good" white women are and ought to be reserved for white he-men. With only an occasional exception, black and other nonwhite women were divided into three types: overweight or elderly maidservants and confidantes to white families; exotic and sensual temptresses who lure unsuspecting white men to depravity and death; and fair-skinned tragic mulattoes who suffered for their parent's transgression of the color line. When compared to white women, black women were always made to appear of less value to either black or white men. In *King Kong* (1932), for example, the dark-skinned savages on an island somewhere southwest of Sumatra are about to sacrifice a light-skinned female member of their own tribe, preparing the virginal beauty to be the "bride of Kong"— a giant ape that was Merian Cooper's and Ernest Schoedsack's enormously enlarged variant of Burrough's "Terkoz." When white filmmakers and sailors arrive unexpectedly at the ceremony, accompanied by Ann, a lovely blonde ingenue (Fay Wray), the tribal chief (Noble Johnson) offers to trade six of his own dark-skinned women for the blonde beauty. Ann's boss (Robert Armstrong) and her lover (Bruce Cabot) refuse to barter a white woman for any number of blacks, so the chief kidnaps her and ties her to stakes for the delectation of the oversized amorous anthropoid.

Movie apes are made to prefer white to black women. Kong takes to the white girl like no other (in one scene he is shown gently stripping off her clothes and licking his paws), and her adventures with and eventual rescue from this smitten simian are constantly described as a love affair between "beauty and the beast." As an oversized man-ape, Kong is moviedom's most graphic characterization of the Occident's apprehensions about the Negro. It is clear that Kong, like Terkoz before him, cannot leave off of his "white ape," and that he would kill other humans, white or black (Rex Ingram has a bit part as one of the sailors attempting to rescue Ann), should they seek to keep him from his anthropomorphic affair. (To be fair, it should be noted that Kong rejects and tosses to her death a young white brunette whom he snatches from her apartment high above New York City's streets. Kong seems firmly attracted to blondes.) The film makes it abundantly clear that Kong merely lusts after the black girls who are supplied to him periodically by the frightened natives, but he loves the white blonde.

The tragedy and impossibility of cross-racial love in the tropics achieved its apotheosis in *White Cargo*, a screenplay by Leon Gordon based on the widely acclaimed Broadway play of the same name and a novel by Vera Simonton, appropriately entitled *Hell's Playground*. Hollywood's Hays Office had virtually proscribed the casting of black actors as screen lovers, especially if miscegenation was to become a theme.[31] *White Cargo*'s setting in the Malayan tropics seemed to offer a way around the prohibition, while reinforcing its basic message. W. E. B. Du Bois had seen the stage production and commented:

> In New York we have two plays: "White Cargo" and "Congo." In "White Cargo" there is a fallen woman. She is black. In "Congo" the fallen woman is white. In "White Cargo" the black woman goes down further and further and in "Congo" the white woman begins with degradation but in the end is one of the angels of the Lord.
>
> You know the current magazine story: A young white man goes down to Central America and the most beautiful colored woman there falls in love with him. She crawls across the whole isthmus to get to him. The white man says nobly, "No." He goes back to his white sweetheart in New York.[32]

By resetting the miscegenation theme outside of Africa and introducing the woman (almost always played by a white actress in brownface) as a racial hybrid, Hollywood found a way to maintain its opposition to intermarriage, cast white actors as black, Oriental, Polynesian, or otherwise dark-skinned characters, and oblige the demands of the censors, who opposed even the presentation of African Americans in intimate scenes with whites. Nevertheless, *White Cargo* at first proved to be too much of a challenge for Hollywood's cautious moviemakers. Its female character, Tondelayo, is described as a "half negro" [sic] whose death in the final scene is deserved because she has committed the miscegenationist's cardinal sin—seducing white men to "go black—to succumb to native life."[33] The Hays Office forbade ever making the film.

A British production of *White Cargo* starring Gypsy Rhouma was imported into the United States in 1930, but it aroused neither admiration nor attack. When, after much wrangling, an American-made version achieved considerable notoriety in 1942, the role of "Tondelayo" was played by Hedy Lamarr, a former leading lady of the Austrian silver screen who had caused a sensation in Europe and America nine years earlier when she appeared nude in the Czech film *Extase*. Among the men whom she leads to destruction by her exotic, erotic ways in *White Cargo* is the white planter (Walter Pidgeon) who personifies the sexual and civilizational dangers that are said to accompany the white man's burden.

The attractiveness of interracial sex in foreign climes—such white silent stars as Mary Pickford, Lenore Ulrich, Pauline Freder-

ick, and Lina Cavalieri had played exotic primitives at least once[34]—
would not die. But in films of the first five decades of the twentieth
century neither real blacks nor blackfaced white men could be allowed to seduce or even appear erotically attractive to white women.
For this reason, it becomes possible to contrast the themes of the
1917 production of *The Slaver*—in which "a tribal chieftain on the
coast of Africa . . . makes a deal with a white sea captain to buy a
white girl," but his nefarious scheme is foiled by the lovesick black
cabin boy, who "saves her, sacrificing himself in the process"[35]—
with the Franco-Camerouns production of *Chocolat* (released in the
United States in 1989)—in which the handsome, muscular black
house servant (Isaach de Bankole) secretly anguishes over the fact
that his love for his employer's wife must never be seen or acknowledged but firmly rebuffs the frustrated French woman's sexual advances. *Chocolat* presents the interracial sex theme as a by-product
of race-conscious colonial domination and allows its African hero
not only to be a sensitive, warm, and intelligent man, better educated than his employers, but also to be physically attractive and to
have his fine physique and powerful musculature presented in full-
frontal nudity.

A finely-honed heroic physique like that of Isaach de Bankole has
not been displayed in leading roles in American films requiring the
presence of African American strong men or "heavies" in interracial
settings. When bare-chested well-muscled black actors were allowed to appear in movies they were usually cast as background figures, obedient servants or frightened natives, as in *White Zombie*
(1932), a thriller set in Haiti in which Murder Legendre (Bela Lugosi)
"commands his flock of mindless but physically superb black zom-
bies who obey his every order with frantic haste."[36] In general, until
the brief reversal of the theme that occurred in the short-lived flurry
of "blaxploitation" movies in the 1970s, Hollywood has treated the
black male physique "as a reminder of what the body can do, its vitality, its strength, its sensuousness; and yet, simultaneously [it has
promoted a] denial of all that bodily energy and delight as creative
and productive." Black male sexuality has been made to appear
"rather hysterically in images of bad (mixed) blood and rape or else
as mere animal capacity incapable of producing civilization."[37]

When in the 1980s movies began presenting black males as heroes
and protectors of civilization (or, at least, of a beleaguered American
urban civil society), they often de-sexed or de-glamorized them.
Hence Danny Glover has complained about the elimination of any
sexual interest in the characterization given to his role as "Detective

Roger Murtaugh," the sensible, intelligent, black cop-sidekick to a near-psychotic colleague "Martin Riggs" (Mel Gibson) in the three-film series Lethal Weapon 1 (1987), 2 (1989), and 3 (1992). As Glover sees the issue, a more sensual quality that might be attached to Murtaugh has been "subconsciously" deleted from these pictures, wasting the voluptuous talents of the actress playing Mrs. Murtaugh (Darlene Love) and neutralizing the sexuality that should be part and parcel of Murtaugh's on-screen character: "'You get a sense, in watching these movies, that these two people do everything but sleep together,' Glover said, 'You know, he could at least be seen kissing her. Or holding her.' " And he concludes that his complaint is not an isolated one: "'It's an interesting dilemma. It happens to [a lot of black actors] in films.' "[38]

Race, Sex, and the Opportunities for Nonwhite Actors: The Case of Dorothy Dandridge

The syndrome of fears encapsulated in African, colonial, and exotic film stereotypy is not exhausted by the sexual-racist fantasies about black male threats to white sexual supremacy. There is also—as the recriminations over White Cargo illustrate so well—the ambivalent lust-fear attached to the exotic black (and also to the equally exotic Oriental, Polynesian, and Amerindian) female. To understand this social and cinematic pathology, it is necessary to reprise its relationship to apprehensions about Occidental civilization's vulnerabilities. The ways of life in Africa, pre-Columbian America, and the tropics have long been envisioned as diametrically opposed to those of civilized Europeans.[39] The former's geotemporal, physical, and cultural "otherhood" is said to be the source of a latent, perhaps subconscious, attraction (especially for white men) that, if allowed to emerge from its properly repressed place in the recesses of both the individual and the collective psyche, will lead to atavism and, eventually, to the destruction of Occidental civilization itself. Of all the icons of this psychic and sociocultural mirage, none is so powerful as that of the savage (read black, Asian, Oceanic, or Amerindian) woman. Such an apprehension, so deeply buried in the core culture, is the stuff of both psychopathology and drama. In movies about jungle princesses (The Jungle Woman, 1926), island native girls (Drums of the Jungle, 1935), Caribbean beauties (Island in the Sun, 1957), and "half-breed" daughters of "squaw men" (One-Eighth Apache, 1920) are to be found not only the warnings against breaking the taboo on interracial sex, but also the admonition that white men take care not to contribute to the subversion of a civilization that has taken so many centuries and so much sexual abstemiousness to forge.

Hollywood's restrictions on the cinematic opportunities open to its fair-skinned but nonwhite actors imitated its artful retelling of the tragic mulatto theme. Light-skinned male actors, such as Noble Johnson,[40] who were classified as Negroes, were permitted to play blacks, Chinese, Spaniards, Cubans, Tibetans, Polynesians, Mexicans, Lascars, Eskimos, and Indians, but never white Anglos. Fair-skinned females classified as Negroes might play a "cinnamon-colored gal" (e.g., Nina Mae McKinney as "an exotic sex object, half woman, half child . . . the black woman out of control of her emotions, split in two by her loyalties and her own vulnerabilities"[41] in King Vidor's *Hallelujah*), but, despite their talents, could never be advanced to stardom playing romantic leads opposite white men.

The tragic career of Dorothy Dandridge epitomizes the plight of the mulatto beauty in Hollywood. Regarded as the most promising successor to the ill-fated Nina Mae McKinney—who in the 1920s had been billed as "a jungle Lorelai,"[42] and "the black Garbo,"[43] but who soon faded into Oscar Micheaux's black film studio and a few black musical shorts, emerging "more a road-company 'Bess' than an African queen"[44] opposite Paul Robeson in *Sanders of the River*, and making her last important film appearance "as a razor-totin', high-strung, high-yeller girl"[45] in Elia Kazan's 1949 melodrama of passing, *Pinky*—Dandridge played out the fantasy of the tragic mulatto in real, as well as reel life. Born into a show business family in 1923, Dandridge had written and performed parodies of Josephine Baker[46] and toured with her sister as part of the Jimmy Lunceford band while still a teenager. She had had some small film roles—*A Day at the Races* (1937), *Lady From Louisiana* (1941), *Bahama Passage* (1942), *Drums of the Congo* (1942)[47]—but then scored a noteworthy triumph as a kidnapped African princess in *Tarzan's Peril* (1951). According to cineast Donald Bogle: "In a crucial episode [of this film], Dandridge . . . was tied to the stakes by a warlike tribal leader. As she lay with legs sprawled apart, heaving and turning to break loose, it was apparent that never before had the black woman been so erotically and obviously used as a sex object. From the way Lex Barker's Tarzan eyed the sumptuous Dandridge, it was obvious, too, that for once Tarzan's mind was not on Jane or boy or Cheetah!"[48]

However, it was precisely Hollywood's recognition of her as a lovely, talented, sensually pleasing, fair-skinned performer that first enhanced and then doomed Dandridge's career. So long as she appeared as only a mild diversion (her scene in an apron and maid's cap with the bare-chested white actor Sterling Hayden in *Bahama Passage* hints visually at eroticism);[49] as a leading lady in all-black films (in *Four Shall Die* she portrays an heiress pursued by two black suitors);[50] in popular musicals (singing "Chatanooga Choo Choo" in *Sun Valley Serenade* [1941]; performing with Count Basie in *Hit Parade of 1943*);[51] as a chaste and kindly disposed schoolteacher (in *Bright Road* [1953] Dandridge aids an insecure black child [Philip Hepburn]);[52] or as a patient housewife keeping her morally weaker husband from going bad (*The Harlem Globetrotters* [1951]),[53] she did not break out of Hollywood's sex-racist casting mold. But, without departing from the genre, Dandridge challenged the caste-ridden place of the fair-skinned female actress when she essayed the title role in Otto Preminger's *Carmen Jones* (1954).

In this World War II revision of the libretto of Bizet's opera, Dandridge portrays a sultry, fair-skinned factory worker, who, true to her divided nature and nurture, seduces a young soldier, "Joe" (Harry Belafonte), entices him into deserting the army, and then deserts him for a black prize fighter, "Husky Miller" (Joe Adams), bringing down on her head the punishment her promiscuous and unpatriotic wickedness so richly deserves.[54] After her notoriously sensuous performance in *Carmen Jones* (once again she is tied and spread-eagled and made to appear as an urban black American variant of the captive African jungle princess), Dandridge discovered that she could not be cast in any role but that of an exotic self-destructive mulatto.[55] And, thus, Dandridge became the obvious choice for the lead in one more Hollywood variation on the tragic mulatto theme, *Island in the Sun* (1957). As "Margot," a Bahamian woman in love with the apparently white scion (John Justin) of an old colonial family, Dandridge does win her lover in the ambiguous finale; however, "David Boyeur," the light-skinned island radical (Harry Belafonte), must give up his love for the "pure" white "Marvis" (Joan Fontaine) in this hackneyed tale of a colonial family that has kept its black ancestry secret.[56]

Because Dandridge, a "black" actress, was permitted to hold hands and dance with Justin, a white actor, ("We had to fight to say the word 'love'," Dandridge later reported),[57] some theater owners threatened to refuse to show the picture, and the South Carolina legislature considered but did not pass a law fining theater owners $5,000 for showing it. For Dandridge, however, the film was the beginning of the end. She appeared as "Bess" opposite Sidney Poitier's

"Porgy" in Hollywood's version of the Dubose and Dorothy Heyward folk-opera, poised disconsolately between the "good" colored cripple (Poitier) and the evil, muscular, dark-skinned "Crown" (Brock Peters),[58] and made no more pictures in America.

Dandridge's subsequent slide into oblivion and death is a real-life story that more than matches her roles as the seductive mulatto who has no secure place in a racist society. Despite her nomination for an Academy Award for *Carmen Jones*, she could find little work as a leading lady in American films. Her marriage to an older white man ended in divorce and bankruptcy. Rumors that she had had love affairs with Tyrone Power, Peter Lawford, Michael Rennie, Abby Mann, Otto Preminger, and Arthur Loew, Jr., were coupled with a report that she had become traumatized on a movie set when a dark-skinned actor was about to touch her, and these stories made her virtually unemployable in the United States.[59] Her last three films were made abroad, each essaying a variant of the tragic mulatto theme. In *The Decks Ran Red* (1958), she played a flirtatious fair-skinned beauty who attracts the erotic attention but not the undying love of the white men (James Mason, Stuart Whitman, Broderick Crawford, and Curt Jurgens)[60] aboard an ill-fated freighter. In *Tamango* (1959), Prosper Merimee's tale of the Africa-to-Cuba slave trade, Dandridge portrayed "Aiche," a black beauty held prisoner on a slave ship and torn between her attraction to its captain (Curt Jurgens) and her loyalty to her own people who are chained in the hold.[61] Her final picture, *Malaga* (1962), released the same year she died a victim of antidepressant drugs and a deep melancholy, pictures her as "Gianni," involved with two double-crossing jewel thieves (Trevor Howard and Edmund Purdom).[62] Fittingly, in light of the cinema's attitude toward mulattoes, the creators of *Malaga's* heroine could not decide on their character's race or nationality[63] and thus could not find her a happy place on this earth. Dandridge was the last important African American actress to be assigned to the role of the tragic mulatto—"the image of the mulatto woman whose white blood makes her beautiful and whose black blood degrades her and who is doomed to die tragically."[64]

In light of how often scholars and publicists have spoken out on how the race problem might be solved by a thoroughgoing racial amalgamation,[65] Hollywood's treatment of mixed marriages and interracial love is instructive. The Supreme Court's declaration of the unconstitutionality of the last of the state antimiscegenationist statutes in 1967[66] did not bring about a rush to intermarry off or on screen. Hollywood did not vary its outlook on the matter very much.

The interracial relationship between white sex-goddess Racquel Welch and black athlete-turned-actor Jim Brown is justified by making her an Indian in *100 Rifles* (1968), but even this modest gesture is undercut—she is killed in the film's finale. Black actor Calvin Lockhart's screen love affair with the young white woman played by white actress Genevieve Waite leaves her pregnant and him in prison in *Joanna* (1968). Sidney Poitier's silver-screened romances with white women are a study in the limitations of the liberal outlook. His affair with Joanne Shimkus ends with both their deaths in *The Lost Man* (1969); a sightless white girl (Elizabeth Hartman) loves him in *A Patch of Blue* (1965), but it comes to nothing when the chaste and kindly black benefactor sends her away to a school for the blind.[67] Poitier's successful winning of a white wife in *Guess Who's Coming to Dinner?* (1967) is undercut not only by the screenplay's emphasis on his membership in the upper professional echelons of the black bourgeoisie but also by the fact that the couple leaves the country immediately after their wedding. The film left its audience guessing as to how its interracial marriage would work out. Moreover, three years earlier, *One Potato, Two Potato* (1964) suggested that the custody of the white child of a woman (Barbara Barrie) whose second marriage is to a good, solid, hardworking and dependable black man (Bernie Hamilton) would still likely be awarded to the white father, a mixed-marriage household being regarded as no place to bring up a Caucasian girl.

The many problems attending interracial unions and their offspring await resolution in fact as well as in fiction, a point given poignant notice recently by historian Joel Williamson's plaintive plea that the twenty-first century make an irrevocable break with America's one person—one race tradition. Imagining a couple, each the progeny of a mixed marriage, coming to adulthood in the year 2000, Williamson writes: "He and she might well be, in fact, the first fully evolved, smoothly functioning model of a people who have transcended both an exclusive whiteness and an exclusive blackness and moved into a world in which they accept and value themselves for themselves alone—as new and unique, as indeed a new people in the human universe."[68] Hollywood has yet to meet the challenge presented by Williamson's sociological imagination.

The Loyal Black Servant of Colonialism:
The Case of Paul Robeson

If black people in films were not permitted to love or marry their white "superiors," they were allowed to serve them loyally, faithfully, and abjectly. The common denominator of all such roles was their popular culture reinforcement of Europe's imperialistic and racial hierarchy. That hierarchy had first positioned whites over blacks wherever they came in contact and then demanded the latter's acquiescence to their supposedly deserved and unmistakably degraded place.

There have been many jungle-, island-, and desert-set movies presenting the African as a loyal servant, but perhaps none so served the colonialist-cum-racist cause than those exploiting the talents of Paul Robeson (1898–1976).[69] During the course of his multifaceted and much-troubled life, Robeson, an enormous talent, enacted the parts of important characters in eleven films made in the United States and Europe. Six of these—*The Emperor Jones* (1933), *Sanders of the River* (1935), *Song of Freedom* (1937), *King Solomon's Mines* (1937), *Jericho* (1937), and *Big Fella* (1938)—explored aspects of imperialist rule in Africa or the Caribbean and reinforced the ideology of Occidental supremacy. Although Robeson starred in each of them and hoped each would contribute to a greater respect for black peoples everywhere in the world, none (with the possible exception of *The Emperor Jones*) succeeded in doing much more than showcasing his talent at the expense of his race's dignity and emancipation.

The screen version of Eugene O'Neill's drama, *The Emperor Jones*, is often regarded as a breakthrough in Hollywood's depiction of the Negro male, giving him classical tragic stature. Robeson reprised his stage performance as "Brutus Jones," a Pullman porter who through a series of remarkable adventures rises from his lowly position to that of Carib King only to suffer the outrage of betrayal, revolt, and eventual death at the hands of his angry and disaffected subjects. In effect this "Brutus" becomes a "Caesar" and then acts as his own "Brutus," having exploited the credulity of his people for his own gain. O'Neill had intended his original theater production to serve as a comment on Anglo-American exploitation of the West Indies and as an allegory of the rise of Jean-Christophe. But it was not perceived that way by American audiences.

As early as 1925 O'Neill had thought of writing what today would be called a "prequel" to the *Emperor Jones*—telling how the crap-shooting, low-down, ghetto Negro had lived before he escaped to the Caribbean island. Such an addition, written by DuBose Heyward, was inserted into the 1933 film version. This insert undercut the original drama's theme and aroused considerable criticism from the black community. *The Emperor Jones* also seemed to question whether the oppressed blacks' quest for self-determination could

ever be effected by a black leader, as well as whether such a liberation could ever establish a free, modern, and truly civil society. As
Robert Stebbins observed in July 1935:

> "The Emperor Jones" maintained unbroken the chain of white
> chauvinism forged in the carbon-arc lights of the Hollywood
> studios. Paul Robeson is presented as a vainglorious braggart, a
> murderer, a tin-foil Napoleon who imposes upon and exploits
> heartlessly members of his own race. And when finally they
> rise against him his false front falls away. He is revealed for
> what he is, and by extension what all Negroes are supposed to
> be, creatures who stand trembling in a murky land of shadow,
> peopled with the ghosts that rise up out of the swamps and jun-
> gles of the primitive mind.[70]

Robeson's "Brutus," having seized control of the island by convinc-
ing the easily hoodwinked "bush niggers" that he cannot be killed
by ordinary bullets, seemed to adopt just the kind of ignoble style
that European imperialists imputed to their subjects. Dilating on the
trappings but not the responsibilities of his newly acquired power,
the new-crowned monarch muses "King Brutus!" But then he recon-
siders: "Somehow that don't make enough noise." He pauses and
then lights up, "The Emperor Jones!" And, by the end of the film,
this boastful emperor is reduced to crawling on his belly, howling in
fear of the ghosts in the swamp, and dying an all-too-craven Negro—
in the words of one critic, "a miserable victim to moral breakdown
and superstitious fears."[71]

In seeking to depict what happens when a member of the servant
underclass becomes a king, the makers of The Emperor Jones did not
shrink from exploiting and then being reprimanded for their exploitation of the animadversions about sex between blacks and whites.
The issue of black sensuality and miscegenation affected the making
and the advertising of The Emperor Jones. Fredi Washington had
been cast as "Undine," a love interest of Brutus. The representatives
of the Hay's Office demanded to preview the first day's rushes, and
when they saw the passionate scenes involving Robeson with Washington, the censors demanded that something be done about the skin
tone of the fair-skinned African American actress, lest audiences assume she was white. Wanting to avoid cutting these scenes, "the producers reluctantly applied dark makeup to Miss Washington for the
daily shoots."[72] Nevertheless, the generalized fear about picturing
sensual blacks still prevailed. Although movie marquees gave top
billing to Robeson, one critic would later complain, "Think back on

the advertising campaign that sold *Emperor Jones* and *Sanders of the River.* No photograph of Paul Robeson was ever used in the advertising of either of these pictures."[73] Such was the apprehension about African American sensuality that not even O'Neill's *Emperor Jones* could break its hold on the collective American psyche.

In the early 1930s Robeson became concerned with the plight of Africans groaning under the yoke of European colonial domination. "A mighty task confronts us," he told a Nigerian reporter in 1934. Someone, perhaps he himself, would have "to go to Africa and reveal to the blacks their own historical mission."[74] That same year he accepted the Korda Brothers' invitation to portray "Bosambo," an African chief, in their film version of Edgar Wallace's novel, *Sanders of the River.* Although the script seemed to promise that this movie would present the peoples of Africa and their cultures, music, and social life in a new and positive light, in fact, the finished film celebrated the rightness, even the necessity, of British rule in Africa. Nancy Cunard dismissed *Sanders of the River* as "pure Nordic bunk."[75] Robeson, who had once been referred to as an "Ebony Apollo," appeared bare-chested and in a leopard-skin loincloth, only to be chided, so Flora Robson recalls, by a real prince of the Ashanti, who happened to be attending Oxford at the time, and who told him that African royalty in fact wore tweeds.[76] Although the movie scenario depicted Bosambo as happily married to Lilongo (Nina Mae McKinney) and raising a young son according to tribal custom, the ballyhoo put out to lure the audience into the theater screamed, "A million mad savages fighting for one beautiful woman! . . .until three white comrades *alone* pitched into the fray and quelled the bloody revolt!"[77]

Sanders of the River argued that white rule was the only basis for law and order among such uncivilized people as the black Africans. Bosambo is ever the loyal lackey of "Lord Sandy" (Leslie Banks), whom he calls "My Lord Sandy . . . the hater of lies . . . the righter of wrongs."[78] Robeson's Bosambo is an object lesson in how to be a true colonial subject. When Sanders tells him that the difference between the British monarch and the African chiefs is that the former is loved by his subjects, Bosambo sings one of Mischa Spoliansky's "authentically-based" African hymns to his white master's wisdom.[79] In the absence of Sanders, the natives—whose leaders were played by African students in London at the time, including Jomo Kenyatta, later first president of independent Kenya; H. O. Davies, later a jurisprudent in Nigeria (where *Sanders* was banned for its offensive portrayal of Africans); and, as a prince to King Molofaba, Orlando Martins, later a Nigerian star in international films about

Africa[80]—become restless, beating out a message on their drums that "Sandy-is-dead" and therefore "there-is-no-law-any-more." Anarchy sets in, a rival group kidnaps Lilongo and her son, the heir-apparent to Bosambo's throne. Sanders returns, puts down the revolt, restores order, and rescues Bosambo's family. In gratitude, Bosambo sends his son off to government house so that he might learn how to become "a great, great chief" like "Lord Sandy."[81]

Although black American critics exploded at Robeson's cinematic capitulation to colonialism, he did not abandon his mission to celebrate the genius of Africa and to bring Western recognition to that continent's aesthetic through cinema. In *Jericho* (1937), Robeson portrayed a World War I sailor falsely accused of a crime. He flees to North Africa, marries a princess of the Tuaregs (played by the light-skinned Sudanese actress Princess Kouka, whose skin, like that of Fredi Washington in *The Emperor Jones,* had to be darkened for the film) and becomes a Tuareg king. Another of the three films that he made abroad in 1937, *Song of Freedom,* seemed to have a better scenario for representing the African people and their aspirations, but its utterly implausible plot and implicit support for Anglocentric culture evoked little emancipatory hope for the empire's dark-skinned subjects. The screenplay took advantage of Robeson's talent as a singer, telling the story of John Zinga (Robeson), an Afro-British dockworker whose recall of African songs speaks to the survival of the racial unconscious and ultimately—through a series of highly improbable events—leads him back to the tribe whose long-lost prince he really is.

As early as 1794, it should be noted, a Scottish apologist for his country's forays into Africa had written, "Societies may be divided into the *civilized* and the *uncivilized*; and the duties of the former to the latter are similar to those of parents to children; for uncivilized nations, like children, are governed by their affections, their understanding being uncultivated."[82] *Song of Freedom* would give a new twist to this late eighteenth-century thesis. Zinga's singing propels him on to the stage, where a white anthropologist not only discerns the precise source of the African chant the black stevedore has sung since childhood, but also deciphers the meaning of the amulet that the singing dockworker wears around his neck. Zinga, it turns out, is not merely an African, he is the long-lost heir to the throne of Casanga. Dressed in pith helmets and the white outfits associated with the cinematic imagery of English missionaries, and accompanied by "a grinning black bearer"[83] (Robert Adams, a Guyanese actor who would do a send-up of Robeson's "Bosambo" role in the 1939 parody, *Old Bones of the River*)[84] Zinga and his wife (Elizabeth Welch) trek through the jungle to his ancestral home, overthrow the tribe's witch doctor despot, and take over the governance of the natives. At movie's end, Zinga proposes a worldwide singing tour to raise money for medicine for his subjects.

If *Sanders of the River* proclaimed the necessity for a Pax Britannica in Africa, while *Song of Freedom* suggested that overseas descendants of black Africans might still serve the civilizing interests of British imperialism though they retained their jungle temperament, *King Solomon's Mines* (1937) called upon Robeson to push these cinematic panegyrics to the rightness of Anglo-Saxon hegemony one step further. The movie is based on the novel of the same name by H. Rider Haggard, a one time British colonial officer in South Africa. The book was first published in September 1885, a bare six months after the Berlin Conference had divided the lands and peoples of Africa among the European powers. As a publishing venture, it was so successful that it went through thirteen United States editions in its first year and had sold more than 650,000 copies by the time of its author's death in 1925. Before Tarzan movies had begun to leave their imprint on the Occident's mental map of Africa, Haggard's fantastic novel had served that popular need.[85]

In the movie version, it again falls to Robeson to play the part of a long-lost African chief, "Umbopa," who is ekeing out a living as the faithful porter to white adventurers (Cedric Hardwicke and Roland Young), unaware that he is in fact the king of the Mashona people.[86] According to Daniel J. Leab, "Robeson saw to it that the character was more than just a splendid savage,"[87] and James R. Nesteby argues that "Robeson's performance is dignified and it effuses the strong presence always felt in his films."[88] Nevertheless, the leitmotif of the film is the African's subservience to his British colonial masters. As one critic put it, "Robeson's ideals were lost in the rough and tumble of the film studio."[89] Umbopa is eventually restored to his throne, but before he achieves full cinematic legitimation as the rightful king of the Mashona people he guides his British protectors to what they want, the rich mines. According to Thomas Cripps, Robeson performs "like a deep-bass teddy-bear, [as he] leads the lagging whites over the mountains singing a booming paean to white ambition: 'Climbin' up, climbin' up, mighty mountain . . . mighty mountain . . . gonna climb you.' "[90]—and it is implied that with the aid of impressed African labor, the white adventurers will exploit the mines to line their own pockets while, of course, serving the interests of the empire.

In 1936, Robeson had recorded a prologue for a documentary originally entitled *Africa Looks Up* but released as *My Song Goes Forth*. Part of that narration stated, "Every foot of Africa is now parceled out among the white races. Why has this happened? What has prompted them to go there? If you listen to men like Mussolini, they will tell you it is to *civilize*—a divine task, entrusted to the enlightened peoples to carry the torch of light and learning, and to benefit the African people. . . . [In fact, however] Africa was opened up by the white man for the benefit of himself—to obtain the wealth it contained."[91] In *King Solomon's Mines*, Robeson, a black American, had essayed the role of a fictional African chief, who not only does not oppose, but in fact aids the whites in their spoliation of Africa's people and resources.

In the last of his feature films to touch on colonialist themes, *Big Fella* (1938), Robeson portrayed "Banjo" in a screenplay loosely based on Claude McKay's eponymous 1929 novel. *Banjo* would soon have enormous influence on such then emerging African poets and political leaders as Leopold Sedar Senghor, Aime Cesaire, and Leon Damas,[92] but, according to McKay's biographer, by "1934, novels such as . . . *Banjo*, which had celebrated the black man's primitive vitality in an increasingly mechanistic world, seemed dated and irrelevant."[93] However, British and American filmmakers had not caught up to the literary world in the latter's depreciation of African primitivism; *Big Fella* presented one more variant of that all-too-popular theme.

In the screenplay, Robeson essays the title role, portraying "Lincoln Agrippa Daily," "a child of the Cotton Belt," known to his workmates on the Marseilles docks as "Banjo" because that instrument always accompanies him on his vagabonding tramp all over the world.[94] The film scenario introduces a homely little story around Banjo befriending a white waif, who follows him all over the drinking, whoring, knife-fighting spots of "The Ditch," the black seamen's name for the Vieux Port area of Marseilles.[95] Sympathetic to the boy's plight, Banjo takes him in charge, protects him from the many dangers of the dockside, and eventually situates him with a white family, returning to his former life of ease on the waterfront.[96] Virtually nothing is said in the film to indict the discriminatory situation that kept African, Caribbean, and American blacks from rising above their mean station in waterfront life. In fact "nowhere in the film does the Negro appear to suffer because of his colour."[97]

Robeson sought, unsuccessfully, in some critics' eyes, to inject a measure of bourgeois respectability to Banjo's character and conduct. The scriptwriters, supposedly under pressure from the star,

made Banjo into "a steady, trustworthy sort of fellow," provided him
with a white buddy, and changed the movie title in order to forestall
any audience expectation that its screen hero is "a sort of 'Uncle
Sambo' of the cotton plantations."[98] Nevertheless, this film failed to
achieve its intended aim. As a kindhearted black man who restores
a lost white boy to his family, Robeson's Banjo illustrated little more
than cinema's image of the "good" Negro, a dedicated supporter of
other people's living according to white, middle-class values—even
if he himself refuses to abide by them. The critic of Lagos's *West African Pilot* gave faint praise to the picture, pointing out that Robeson's "assignment is the usual one depicting him as a scum and a
renegade," but noting that in spite of this fact, "he portrays the type
of virtues which any race on earth would be glad to emulate."[99]

American and British moviemakers explored and exploited the
loyal servant theme in movies made about Africa before and after the
Robeson films. Such silent movies as *The Zulu's Heart* (1908) and
The Kaffir's Gratitude (1915) had treated the black African as either
a faithful bearer or an obsequious domestic. In 1931, the unyielding
loyalty of the African native was brought almost to high art when, in
Trader Horn, the eponymous trader (Harry Carey) and his young
companion (Duncan Renaldo) are ably and nobly assisted by their
African porter (Mutia Omooloo) as they search for a white woman
(Edwina Booth) who has been captured by cannibals.[100] Despite the
fact that Omooloo's performance went far in establishing dramatic
distance from the usual stereotypy, Hollywood filmmakers did not
change their attitude toward or reconsider their usual treatment of
Africans, off-screen or on. Mr. Omooloo, brought to America for further shooting, was treated as an anthropological oddity and subjected to numerous indignities.[101] *Trader Horn* in fact reinforced the
traditional image of white male supremacy. "Trader Aloysius Horn,"
write Alfred E. Opubor and Adebayo Ogunbi in their recent critical
assessment of Africa-centered films, "like the 'invincible' white man
and the 'great explorer,' has the honor of single-handedly encounter-
ing a whole tribe of Isorgi people and vanquishing them, along with
their wild animals, in a mission to save a white girl from the scourge
of 'ferocious savages' and an inhospitable environment."[102]

An African Loyal Servant: The Career
of Orlando Martins

The several variations in the cinematic dichotomization of Africans
as either villainous opponents or willing and eager subjects of their
European colonial overlords are illustrated in the roles essayed by

the Nigerian actor Orlando Martins during his long European and American screen career. Born on December 8, 1899, to one of the elite black families of British-controlled Lagos, Martins ran away to England when he was seventeen. Tall, muscular, and good-looking, he first appeared in a few silent and early sound films (e.g., *If Youth but Knew* [1926]; *Un-Blimey* [1930]; *Black Libel* [1931]); as a Nubian slave in Diaghilev's London ballet performance of 1920; and in the touring company of the London stage revival of *Showboat* (1928).[103] Slightly larger supporting roles came his way in such films as *Tiger Bay* (1933) and *Java Head* (1934)—in each of which he appeared in a vehicle starring Anna May Wong, then at the height of her career as the inevitably tragic but seductive Oriental siren in love with a white man. After appearing in *Sanders of the River* (1935), Martins acted in two more productions with Robeson—*Jericho* and *Song of Freedom*—and then brought his prewar movie career to an end with a bit part in the mystery-thriller *Murder in Soho* (1939).

Martin's postwar movies started with *The Man from Morocco*, a film that gave great promise for a more realistic portrayal of Africans in European and American films. As "Jeremiah," an African who volunteers for service in the International Brigade that fought against the establishment of Franco's fascist dictatorship in Spain, Martins's character is shown to be courageous, honorable, and capable of forming lasting friendships across the color line. In his scenes with the Czech colonel (Anton Walbrook), Jeremiah is treated as an equal to any of the other members of the multinational force. Although the "film was inclined to be romantic and novelettish"[104] and its politics recall one of Hollywood's prewar anti-fascist films, *Blockade* (1938),[105] this British film resisted making any statement other than its visual one about Martins's race: "Nowhere is there any reference to his colour, or any sort of discrimination indicated."[106] However, the color-blindness in *The Man from Morocco* did not lead to an unalloyed sympathy for the anti-colonial movement among Africans in subsequent films made in the English or American studios.

The fact that Martins costarred in the much-acclaimed African theme film, *Men of Two Worlds* (1946)—a pro-colonial screenplay in which he essays the role of Magole, a villainous Tanganyikan witch doctor who uses his extraordinary powers of mind control to oppose the order of the kindly disposed British Commissioner (Eric Portman) that his tribe move away from their tse-tse fly-infested settlement—indicates that his films of the fifties and sixties did not depart from the traditional mold. Events in East Africa aroused American cinematic sympathy for the area's white settlers and their descendants—then in process of displacement. The Mau-mau revolt that eventually would propel Jomo Kenyatta into the presidency of the newly independent state of Kenya was treated in two of Martins's films. In *Simba* (1955), he portrayed an African headman in a screenplay that had been designed to emphasize the savage ferocity of the African rebels. One year later Martins appeared in *Safari* (1956), a remarkably bloody picture in which a noble white man (Victor Mature) is driven to take violent revenge on the men of the Mau-mau who have murdered his wife and son.

Another aspect of the noble-white-man-and-loyal-servant-vs.-uncivilized-savages theme was presented in the two-film series *Ivory Hunters* (1952) and *West of Zanzibar* (1955) in which Martins played a familiar character of the genre. The first picture in the series purported to tell the story of how a white conservationist (Anthony Steel) created Kenya's national park system and continues to manage it with the aid of "Mkwangi," (Martins), the African who oversees the native workers in the reserve.[107] In the sequel, Orlando Martins once more portrays "Mkwangi," described by one Hollywood reporter "as a very black gun bearer . . . [who] gets amiably drunk, goes on the make for a dusky playgirl and caps the climax by kicking a native cop."[108] The plotline pits the native Kenyan reserve workers, led by their clear-eyed, courageous white boss against East Indian ivory poachers. The poachers are depicted not only as "foreign" lawbreakers, but as evildoers motivated by the desire to spend their ill-gotten gains on "used European clothes." In this film such a purpose is deemed so heinous that a native chief (Edric Conner) is roused to enlist himself and his people in the white naturalist's fight against the unwarranted encroachments on Kenya's wildlife.[109]

While making these films, Martins witnessed, experienced, and protested against the indignities heaped upon black Africans by white service and movie personnel.[110] Barred from Cairo's Norfolk Hotel and Bar, where the white cast members were housed and entertained, he was first routed to a local schoolteacher's home and then moved to a roadside inn. At one restaurant he became so incensed over an East Indian bartender's refusal to sell him a drink that he threatened to burn the place down. During the course of shooting *Ivory Hunters,* Martins refused to come onto the set unless the all-white South African crew discontinued its contemptuous treatment of the colored members of the cast and staff. In accordance with the conventional modes of film advertising then in vogue, the lobby posters made for *Ivory Hunters* would not even have listed his

or any other black actor's name in the cast; when he protested the
practice, his and other African actors' names were printed in letters
so small "that one has to strain one's eyes to be able to read them."
Back in London, he discovered he was the only actor not invited to
the royal command performance of the movie. Similar treatment occurred during and after the making of *West of Zanzibar.* Martins was
not invited to the party for the picture's cast and crew given by Zanzibar's Colonial Resident. When he went uninvited, he was insulted
by the local police commissioner, a snub that he sought to repay in
kind at the London showing. Martins discovered that there was little
gratitude for the support his roles lent to the colonial mystique.

In the last two decades of his film career in Anglo-American productions, Martins's roles did not challenge the well-worn colonial
myth of the benevolent white master and his loyal black servant. His
much-praised mime portrayal of "Blossom"—a non-English speaking Basuto soldier who, by his example, helps "Yank" (Ronald Rea-
gan) and the rest of his white fellow-convalescents in a World War II
Burmese hospital to empathize with a dying Scotsman (Richard
Todd)—elevates the theme of the black man's faithful service to an
epiphany (*The Hasty Heart* [1950]).[111] However, despite the sensitiv-
ity of Martins's portrayal, its memorability has been spoiled by one
film historian's reduction of the actor to anonymity: "The scene in
which the black African with no English shows that he likes the Scot
provided a comforting message to the postwar world."[112]

Subsequent roles proved far less fulfilling and offered even less
opportunity for making a socially relevant statement. Martins appeared as the African chief Ogonooro in *Tarzan and the Lost Safari*
(1957), with the usual abject subservience before the white lord of
the jungle (Gordon Scott);[113] as a barman in a British mystery—that
reprised some of the events surrounding the Notting Hill race riots
of the latter years of the 1950s—about the search for the murderer of
a mulatto woman who had passed for white (*Sapphire* [1959]);[114] as
an African native who will benefit from a white engineer's (Robert
Taylor) unstinting efforts to build the first railroad in East Africa
(*Killers of Kilimanjaro* [1960]);[115] as a grinning, much be-feathered,
leopard-skinned savage in a comedy about a fake Africanist (Bob
Hope) pressed into service by the president of the United States to
retrieve a strategic missile's nose cone that has been lost in Africa
(*Call Me Bwana* [1963]);[116] as "Abu Lubaba," a Moslem wise man returning from a pilgrimage to Mecca, one of the many interesting
characters encountered by an orphaned white boy (Fergus McClel-
land) on his way from Port Said to Durban in search of his aunt (*A

Boy Ten Feet Tall [1965]);[117] and, at the end of his long film career, as a Masai chief (in *Mr. Moses* [1965]) who must choose between cooperating with "Joe Moses" (Robert Mitchum), the white expert sent to move his people to a new area because the traditionally occupied tribal land has been scheduled for flooding to make way for a new dam, or joining the resistance, led by the American-educated son of the tribe's witch doctor (Raymond St. Jacques).[118] As might be expected, Martins's character sees the light in the form of the Masai's white benefactor.

Conclusion

Like virtually every other institution of American popular culture, movies have been afflicted by what Gunnar Myrdal called the "American dilemma." As Myrdal, a Swedish economist and sociologist who had been brought to the United States by the Carnegie Corporation in 1937 to study and propose measures that would alleviate the country's race problem, saw the matter:

> The "American Dilemma" . . . is the ever-raging conflict between, on the one hand, the valuations preserved on the general plane which we shall call the "American Creed," where the American thinks, talks, and acts under the influence of high national and Christian precepts, and, on the other hand, the valuations on specific planes of individual and group living, where personal and local interests; economic, social, and sexual jealousies; considerations of community prestige and conformity; group prejudice against particular persons or types of people; and all sorts of miscellaneous wants, impulses, and habits dominate his outlook.[119]

However, Myrdal failed to see that the "ever-raging conflict," whose resolution in behalf of the "higher values" of the American Creed he sought to encourage, might be resolved on the side of "group prejudice against particular . . . types of people," or, worse, that the values he associated with "high national and Christian precepts" might be made consistent with racist imagery and racially discriminatory acts against African Americans.

Myrdal was not unaware of the Negrophobic stereotypy that was ubiquitous in America's mass culture and especially pronounced in its moving pictures. However, his cautious optimism led him to see "a definite improvement, in the last year or so, in the treatment of Negroes in movies" and to voice the assurance that such efforts as

that of the National Association for the Advancement of Colored
People will, "if continued . . . have some effect, especially when further pressure comes from war agencies of the federal government."[120]
In this respect, Myrdal echoed the hopes of all those liberal-minded
critics of Hollywood's treatment of African Americans who periodically predicted the imminence of a new and more honorable screen
presentation of black American "sociotypes" rising to replace film-
dom's outworn and demeaning "stereotypes."[121] In fact, the an-
nouncement of this much-desired breakthrough has become a staple
of sociologically informed film criticism. When, in 1915 and the
years thereafter, such eminent opinion leaders as Booker T. Washington, John Collier, Walter Lippmann, and the NAACP jointly and
separately savaged the racial prejudices that were inflamed by portraying the Ku Klux Klan as a band of Caucasians fighting "in defense of their Aryan birthright,"[122] [D. W. Griffith's *Birth of a Nation*
(a screenplay based on Thomas Dixon's Negrophobic 1905 novel,
The Clansman)],[123] there was some hope that filmmakers would become sensitive to the needs and feelings of their black audiences.[124]
After protests by the Hays Office had forced the makers of *Gone With
the Wind* (1939) to substitute the less than complimentary word
"darkie" for the pejorative "nigger" in the screenplay,[125] and upon
hearing that Hattie McDaniel would become the first black actor to
receive an Academy Award for her role essaying the faithful and
wise "mammy" to Vivien Leigh's Scarlett O'Hara, some followers of
Hollywood's treatment of Negro themes and actors supposed that in
these respects matters would soon improve greatly.[126] As World War
II was coming to an end, L. D. Reddick took heart from the facts that,
in *The Ox-Bow Incident* (1943), the lone Negro (Leigh Whipper) in
this screenplay about a lynching is shown to be on the side of "justice, humanity and civilization"; that, in *In This Our Life* (1942), the
Negro boy (Ernest Anderson) "airs the Negro problem with courage
and dignity"; and that, in *Bataan* (1943), a black soldier (Kenneth
Spencer) is "drawn as naturally and sympathetically as are any of
his half-dozen companions." But Reddick went on to warn that the
pattern of change had not yet reached the plane wherein Hollywood's filmic imagination would "have Negro life admitted to the
full range of human characterization, . . . [would] eliminate the
'race-linking' of vice and villainies, and . . . [would] have Negro actors on the screen treated 'like everybody else.' "[127] Twenty-two
years later, Charles Boren, the president of the Association of Motion
Picture and Television Film Producers publicly thanked the NAACP
and its national labor director, Herbert Hill, for doing his organiza-

tion "a great service in making us aware of the depth of the problems involved" in the employment and characterizations given to black actors, and he went on to express the hope that "if we can do something about this image question we will have done more for race relations than we would by hiring thousands of Negroes, although we know both portrayal and employment issues are vital."[128] And yet another twenty-two years later, cineast and historian Donald Bogle, though more than willing to celebrate the accomplishments of black actors past and present, complained that present-day films showcasing the talents of such black superstars as Richard Pryor, Eddie Murphy, Gregory Hines, Billy Dee Williams, and Danny Glover "much too often . . . failed to uncover the tensions or conflicts of black men in pursuit of some goal or personal aspiration." Their films, Bogle went on to observe, "were tributes to the theme of interracial male bonding." These pictures continued and updated the theme of the loyal black servant—"the tough, assertive white man learns about emotion and the spirit from his good black friend," but also denied these newly discovered mammy-surrogate males a love life or even a strong sexual identity. "Rarely were [Eddie] Murphy or [Richard] Pryor seen in romantic situations with black women, causing the stars sometimes to look, for all their modernity, like asexual pods of the past."[129]

Myrdal, like other optimistic critics of America's race relations, underestimated the depth to which racism and its attendant attitudes, prejudices, and stereotypes had become sedimented within American culture.[130] Such race prejudice as exists in America has taken the form of what Herbert Blumer calls "a sense of group position"—a sense, that is, that the members of the other race are below, beyond, and have unwarranted designs on the culture and civilization of the self-arrogated superior race. According to the tenets of such a cluster of attitudes, opinions, pseudosociologies and conjectural histories, Africans and Afro-Americans are subjected to a multiform inferiorization process. That process locates both their occupations and character within the structure of a biracial caste and class order. As part of the invigoration and reinforcement of that order, the institutions of mass and popular culture, and especially the movies made in Hollywood, contribute the products of a culturally embedded cinematic imagination—a "dream factory" that perpetuates the character of black men as loyal-servant "toms," lusty "bucks," foolish "coons," foolhardy "superspades," ignorant "sambos," or faithful "sidekicks," while demeaning black women as wise but independent "mammies" silly and stupid slaveys, exotic sirens, forbidden "brown sugar," or tragic mulattoes. These characterologies, together with the color of their anatomies, are inextricably connected to the cinematic thesis that black Americans are bound to an irremediably savage African past and consigned to an irrevocably demeaning American destiny. For the most part, America's movies have built upon three centuries of stereotypical imagery to depict an Africa and Afro-America that is consistent with the society's deeply engrained cultural misinformation about the origins and future of dark-skinned people. In the process, they have elaborated on the myopic vision and embroidered upon a mass psychology of racism and cultural prejudice that shows few signs of being undone.

NOTES

This essay originally appeared in *The International Journal of Politics, Culture, and Society*, 4:1 (Fall 1990), pp. 49–77.

1. Theodore Roosevelt, *African Game Trails: An Account of the African Wanderings of an American Hunter-Naturalist* (New York: St. Martin's Press, 1988 [1910]), p. 1.

2. See Kenneth E. Bock, *The Comparative Method* (Ph.D. diss., University of California, Berkeley, 1948).

3. Roosevelt, *African Game*, p. 418.

4. Ibid., p. 2.

5. Ibid.

6. James R. Nesteby, *Black Images in American Films, 1896–1954: The Interplay between Civil Rights and Film Culture* (Washington, D.C.: University Press of America, 1982), p. 18.

7. See Seymour Martin Lipset, *The First New Nation: The United States in Historical and Comparative Perspective* (New York: W. W. Norton, 1979).

8. Roosevelt, *African Game*, p. 120.

9. Thomas Cripps, *Slow Fade to Black: The Negro in American Films, 1900–1942* (London: Oxford University Press, 1977), p. 23.

10. Nesteby, *Black Images*, p. 116.

11. Phyllis Rauch Klotman, *Frame by Frame—A Black Filmography* (Bloomington: Indiana University Press, 1979), p. 594. For the actual history of the Rorke's Drift battle, see Donald R. Morris, *The Washing of the Spears: A History of the Rise of the Zulu Nation under Shaka and Its Fall in the Zulu War of 1879* (New York: Simon and Schuster—Touchstone, 1986), pp. 389–420; Robert B. Edgerton, *Like Lions They Fought: The Zulu War and the Last Black Empire in South Africa* (New York: Ballantine Books, 1988), pp. 92–107.

12. Klotman, *Frame by Frame*, p. 462.

13. I. C. Jarvie, *Movies as Social Criticism: Aspects of Their Social Psychology* (Metuchen, N.J.: Scarecrow Press, 1978), p. 169.

14. Gunnar Myrdal, with the assistance of Richard Sterner and Arnold Rose, *An American Dilemma: The Negro Problem and Modern Democracy* (New York: Harper and Brothers, 1944), pp. 55–56.

15. For powerful discussions of this and related themes as they have pervaded American racism, see four books by Calvin C. Hernton: *Sex and Racism in America* (Garden City, N.Y.: Doubleday and Company, 1965), esp. pp. 55–86; *White Papers for White Americans* (Garden City, N.Y.: Doubleday and Company, 1966); *Coming Together: Black Power, White Hatred, and Sexual Hang-Ups* (New York: Random House, 1971), esp. pp. 2–75, 105–22, 147–81; *The Sexual Mountain and Black Women Writers: Adventures in Sex, Literature, and Real Life* (New York: Anchor Press–Doubleday, 1987), esp. pp. 50–88 et passim. See also Charles Herbert Stember, *Sexual Racism: The Emotional Barrier to an Integrated Society* (New York: Elsevier, 1976), esp. pp. 17–27, 144–95.

16. William Wells Brown, *Clotel or, The President's Daughter: A Narrative of Slave Life in the United States* (London: Partridge and Oakey, 1853; reprint, New York: Citadel Press, 1969). For the life and works of Brown, see William Edward Farrison, *William Wells Brown: Author and Reformer* (Chicago: University of Chicago Press, 1969).

17. *Loving v. Virginia*, 388 U.S.1 (1967).

18. Cripps, *Slow Fade*, p. 23; Klotman, *Frame by Frame*, p. 156.

19. Klotman, *Frame by Frame*, p. 560.

20. William K. Everson, *American Silent Film* (New York: Oxford University Press, 1978), pp. 161–62; Cripps, *Slow Fade*, pp. 127, 129–30; Klotman, *Frame by Frame*, p. 305.

21. See Andrew D. Weinberger, "A Reappraisal of the Constitutionality of 'Miscegenation' Statutes," Appendix G, pp. 402–26 in Ashley Montagu, *Man's Most Dangerous Myth: The Fallacy of Race*, 4th ed. (Cleveland: World Publishing Company, 1965).

22. Nesteby, *Black Images*, p. 118; Klotman, *Frame by Frame*, p. 560.

23. Klotman, *Frame by Frame*, p. 517.

24. Cf. Nesteby, *Black Images*, pp. 137–56.

25. Edgar Rice Burroughs, *Tarzan of the Apes* (New York: Ballantine Books, 1988. Orig. pub. 1912), p. 153.

26. See Rayford W. Logan, *The Betrayal of the Negro: From Rutherford B. Hayes to Woodrow Wilson* (New York: Collier Books, 1965), p. 354; George M. Fredrickson, *The Black Image in the White Mind: The Debate on Afro-American Character and Destiny, 1817–1914* (New York: Harper and Row, 1971), pp. 275–82.

27. Nesteby, *Black Images*, p. 138.

28. Burroughs, *Tarzan*, p. 153.

29. Ibid. Emphasis supplied.

30. For a discussion of black theater and the development of 1890s Broadway "coon" shows, see James Weldon Johnson, *Black Manhattan* (New York: Atheneum, 1968. Orig. pub. 1930), pp. 87–110; and Robert W. Snyder, *The Voice of the City: Vaudeville and Popular Culture in New York* (New

York: Oxford University Press, 1989), pp. 5–6, 44–49, 52–57, 120–23, 159–60.

31. Cripps, *Slow Fade*, p. 119, 125–29.

32. W. E. B. Du Bois, "Criteria of Negro Art," *The Crisis*, 32 (Oct. 1926). Reprinted in Du Bois, *Writings*, ed. Nathan Huggins (New York: Library of America, 1986), p. 1000.

33. Cripps, *Slow Fade*, p. 154.

34. Ibid., p. 128.

35. Klotman, *Frame by Frame*, p. 475.

36. Gary Null, *Black Hollywood: The Negro in Motion Pictures* (Secaucus, N.J.: Citadel Press, 1975), p. 48.

37. Richard Dyer, *Heavenly Bodies: Film Stars and Society* (New York: St. Martin's Press, 1986), p. 139.

38. Pat H. Broeske, "Character Isn't Sexy Enough for Glover," *Palm Beach Post*, July 22, 1989, p. 1D.

39. See Henri Baudet, *Paradise on Earth: Some Thoughts on European Images of Non-European Man*, trans. Elizabeth Wentholt (New Haven: Yale University Press, 1965), pp. 14–19, 45–50, 69–73; Andrew Sinclair, *The Savage: A History of Misunderstanding* (London: Weidenfeld and Nicolson, 1977), pp. 48–101; Brian V. Street, *The Savage in Literature: Representations of 'Primitive' Society in English Fiction, 1858–1920* (London: Routledge and Kegan Paul, 1975); Olive Patricia Dickason, *The Myth of the Savage and the Beginnings of French Colonialism in the Americas* (Edmonton: University of Alberta Press, 1984), esp. pp. 3–88; Ronald Meek, *Social Science and the Ignoble Savage* (Cambridge: Cambridge University Press, 1976), esp. pp. 131–243; and Curtis M. Hinsley, Jr., *Savages and Scientists: The Smithsonian Institution and the Development of American Anthropology, 1846–1910* (Washington, D.C.: Smithsonian Institution Press, 1981).

40. Cripps, *Slow Fade*, pp. 128–32; Peter Noble, *The Negro in Films* (New York: Ayer, 1949; reprint, Port Washington, N.Y.: Kennikat, 1969), p. 179.

41. Donald Bogle, *Toms, Coons, Mulattoes, Mammies and Bucks: An Interpretive History of Blacks in American Films* (New York: Continuum, 1989), p. 33.

42. Cripps, *Slow Fade*, p. 245.

43. Bogle, *Toms, Coons*, p. 33.

44. Cripps, *Slow Fade*, p. 315.

45. Bogle, *Toms, Coons*, p. 33.

46. Cripps, *Slow Fade*, p. 234.

47. Klotman, *Frame by Frame*, pp. 135, 296, 30, 152.

48. Bogle, *Toms, Coons*, p. 168.

49. Null, *Black Hollywood*, p. 129.

50. Klotman, *Frame by Frame*, pp. 186–87.

51. Null, *Black Hollywood*, pp. 128–29.

52. Klotman, *Frame by Frame*, p. 78; Bogle, *Toms, Coons*, p. 168.

53. Klotman, *Frame by Frame*, p. 221.

54. Ibid., p. 95.

55. Bogle, *Toms, Coons*, pp. 168–70.

56. Null, *Black Hollywood*, pp. 178–79; Bogle, *Toms, Coons*, pp. 171–72, 174, 190–91, 193.

57. Bogle, *Toms, Coons*, p. 172.

58. Klotman, *Frame by Frame*, p. 413; Bogle, *Toms, Coons*, pp. 27, 31, 56, 173–74, 183, 189, 193, 204, 207, 210, 214; Null, *Black Hollywood*, pp. 170–72.

59. Bogle, *Toms, Coons*, pp. 171, 175.

60. Klotman, *Frame by Frame*, p. 137.

61. Ibid., pp. 514–15; Bogle, *Toms, Coons*, pp. 172–73; Null, *Black Hollywood*, p. 165.

62. Klotman, *Frame by Frame*, p. 332.

63. Bogle, *Toms, Coons*, p. 174.

64. Null, *Black Hollywood*, p. 169.

65. See, e.g., Joseph LeConte, *The Race Problem in the South* (New York: D. Appleton, 1892; reprint, Miami: Mnemosyne Publishing, Inc., 1969), pp. 373–75; and Norman Podhoretz, "My Negro Problem—And Ours," *Commentary*, 35 (Feb. 1963), pp. 93–101.

66. *Loving v. Virginia*, 388 U.S.1 (1967). For the definitive study of the dynamics of black-white interracial marriage, mulattoes, and passing, see Paul R. Spickard, *Mixed Blood: Intermarriage and Ethnic Identity in Twentieth-Century America* (Madison: University of Wisconsin Press, 1989), pp. 233–342.

67. James Murray, *To Find an Image: Black Films from Uncle Tom to Super Fly* (Indianapolis: Bobbs-Merrill, 1973), p. 54.

68. Joel Williamson, *New People: Miscegenation and Mulattoes in the United States* (New York: The Free Press, 1980), p. 195.

69. For the definitive biography of Robeson, see Martin Bauml Duberman, *Paul Robeson* (New York: Alfred A. Knopf, 1988).

70. Quoted in Noble, *Negro in Films*, p. 57.

71. Duberman, *Paul Robeson*, p. 168.

72. Ibid.

73. Arthur Draper, "Uncle Tom Will Never Die!" *New Theatre Magazine* (Jan. 1936); reprinted in *Black Films and Film-makers: A Comprehensive Anthology from Stereotype to Superhero*, ed. Lindsay Patterson (New York: Dodd, Mead and Co., 1975), p. 32.

74. Duberman, *Paul Robeson*, p. 176.

75. Cripps, *Slow Fade*, p. 316.

76. Duberman, *Paul Robeson*, p. 626 n. 54.

77. Ibid., p. 180; Cripps, *Slow Fade*, p. 316.

78. Cripps, *Slow Fade*, p. 315.

79. David Shipman, *The Story of Cinema: A Complete Narrative History from the Beginnings to the Present* (New York: St. Martin's Press, 1982), pp. 341–42.

80. Takiu Folami, *Orlando Martins—The Legend: An Intimate Biography of the First World Acclaimed African Film Actor* (Lagos, Nigeria: Executive Publishers, Ltd., 1983), p. 30.

81. Cripps, *Slow Fade*, p. 315; Klotman, *Frame by Frame*, pp. 447–48.

82. C. B. Wadstrom, *An Essay on Colonization Particularly Applied to the West Coast of Africa with Some Free Thoughts on Cultivation and Commerce* (London: Darton and Harvey, 1794; reprint, New York: Augustus M. Kelley, 1968), p. 19.

83. Cripps, *Slow Fade*, p. 317.

84. Klotman, *Frame by Frame*, p. 388.

85. William Minter, *King Solomon's Mines Revisited: Western Interests and the Burdened History of Southern Africa* (New York: Basic Books, 1986), pp. 3–4.

86. Klotman, *Frame by Frame*, p. 288; Nesteby, *Black Images*, p. 130; Duberman, *Paul Robeson*, p. 207.

87. Daniel J. Leab, *From Sambo to Superspade: The Black Experience in Motion Pictures* (Boston: Houghton-Mifflin, 1975), p. 114.

88. Nesteby, *Black Images*, p. 130.

89. Leab, *From Sambo*, p. 114.

90. Cripps, *Slow Fade*, p. 317.

91. Quoted, except for the portion in brackets, in Duberman, *Paul Robeson*, p. 203.

92. Wayne F. Cooper, *Claude McKay: Rebel Sojourner in the Harlem Renaissance* (Baton Rouge: Louisiana State University Press, 1987), p. 259.

93. Ibid., p. 293. However, this was precisely the point that McKay (Claude McKay, *Banjo: A Story without a Plot* [New York: Harcourt, Brace Jovanovich, 1957 [1929], p. 324) had made in the original novel: "The more Ray [a black intellectual] mixed in the rude anarchy of the lives of the black boys—loafing, singing, bumming, playing, dancing, loving, working—and came to a realization of how close-linked he was to them in spirit, the more he felt that they represented more than he or the cultural minority the irrepressible exuberance and legendary vitality of the black race. And the thought kept him wondering how that race would fare under the ever-tightening mechanical organization of modern life."

94. McKay, *Banjo*, pp. 11–12.

95. Ibid., p. 9.

96. Duberman, *Paul Robeson*, pp. 207–8.

97. Noble, *Negro in Films*, p. 120.

98. Duberman, *Paul Robeson*, p. 208.

99. *West African Pilot* (Lagos), January 12, 1939.

100. Deems Taylor, Marcelene Peterson, and Bryant Hale, *A Pictorial History of the Movies* (New York: Simon and Schuster, 1943), p. 240; Shipman, *Story of Cinema*, p. 270; Leab, p. 103.

101. Cripps, *Slow Fade*, p. 99.

102. Alfred E. Opubor and Adebayo Ogunbi, "Ooga Booga: The African Image in American Films," in *Other Voices, Other Views: An International*

Collection of Essays from the Bicentennial, ed. Robin W. Winks (Westport, Conn.: Greenwood Press, 1978), p. 364.

103. Folami, *Orlando Martins*, pp. 7, 21, 24–26, 29–30.

104. Noble, *Negro in Films*, p. 127.

105. See Bernard F. Dick, *Radical Innocence: A Critical Study of the Hollywood Ten* (Lexington: University Press of Kentucky, 1989), pp. 54–56.

106. Noble, *Negro in Films*, p. 127.

107. Klotman, *Frame by Frame*, p. 266.

108. Folami, *Orlando Martins*, p. 59.

109. Klotman, *Frame by Frame*, p. 571; Folami, *Orlando Martins*, p. 59.

110. Folami, *Orlando Martins*, pp. 55–61.

111. Ibid., pp. 49–54.

112. Shipman, *Story of Cinema*, p. 798.

113. Klotman, *Frame by Frame*, p. 516; Opubor and Ogunbi, "Ooga Booga," p. 368; Nesteby, *Black Images*, p. 150.

114. Klotman, *Frame by Frame*, p. 448; Folami, *Orlando Martins*, p. 65; Shipman, *Story of Cinema*, p. 1105.

115. Opubor and Ogunbi, "Ooga Booga," pp. 368–69.

116. Folami, *Orlando Martins*, p. 68.

117. Folami, *Orlando Martins*, pp. 66–67; Klotman, *Frame by Frame*, p. 74.

118. Klotman, *Frame by Frame*, p. 362; Bogle, *Toms, Coons*, p. 224.

119. Myrdal, *American Dilemma*, p. xlvii.

120. Ibid., p. 988 n.

121. See Emory S. Bogardus, "Stereotypes versus Sociotypes," *Sociology and Social Research*, 34 (Sept.-Oct. 1949), pp. 286–91.

122. See Everett Carter, "Cultural History Written with Lightning: The Significance of *The Birth of a Nation*," *American Quarterly*, 12 (Fall 1960), pp. 347–57.

123. See John Hope Franklin, "*The Birth of a Nation*: Propaganda as History," in his *Race and History: Selected Essays, 1938–1988* (Baton Rouge: Louisiana State University Press, 1989), pp. 10–23.

124. See Richard A. Maynard, ed., *The Black Man on Film: Racial Stereotyping* (Rochelle Park, N.J.: Hayden Book Co., 1974), pp. 25–40; Bosley Crowther, "The Birth of *Birth of a Nation*," in Lindsay Anderson, ed., *Black Films and Film-Makers* (New York: Dodd, Mead and Co., 1975), pp. 75–83.

125. Leonard J. Leff and Jerold L. Simmons, *The Dame in the Kimono: Hollywood Censorship and the Production Code from the 1920s to the 1960s* (New York: Grove Weidenfeld, 1990), pp. 79–108.

126. Carlton Jackson, *Hattie: The Life of Hattie McDaniel* (Lanham, Md.: Madison Books, 1990), pp. 33–120 passim. See also Hugo Vickers, *Vivien Leigh* (Boston: Little, Brown and Co., 1988), p. 122.

127. L. D. Reddick, "Educational Programs for the Improvement of Race Relations: Motion Pictures, Radio, the Press, and Libraries," *Journal of Negro Education*, 13 (Summer 1944), pp. 367–89. Quotations from pp. 378, 379, 369.

128. *San Francisco Chronicle*, March 16, 1966, p. 48.

129. Donald Bogle, *Blacks in American Films and Television: An Illus-trated Encyclopedia* (New York: Simon and Schuster, 1988), pp. 7–8.

130. See Stanford M. Lyman, *The Black American in Sociological Thought: A Failure of Perspective* (New York: G. P. Putnam's Sons, 1972), pp. 99–120. In a reply to my critique of the Myrdal thesis, David W. Southern, *Gunnar Myrdal and Black-White Relations: The Use and Abuse of "An American Dilemma," 1944–1969* (Baton Rouge: Louisiana State University Press, 1987), pp. 304–5, writes, "Lyman held that since the Afro-American past was so calamitous and discontinuous, predictions about future race re-lations were fatuous. Despairingly, he announced that the black American's 'present is problematic, his past unknown, and his future uncertain.' In an existential funk, Lyman could only talk vaguely about a 'sociology of the absurd.' " Of course, the entire thrust of my book was to point to the failure of sociologists to ground their prognostications and nostrums in the histor-ical record. As to a sociology of the absurd, I am not alone in pointing to its relevance to the condition of African Americans. In addition to Stanford M. Lyman and Marvin B. Scott, *A Sociology of the Absurd*, rev. ed. (Dix Hills, N.Y.: General Hall, 1989), passim, see Esther Merle Jackson, "The American Negro and the Image of the Absurd," *Phylon*, 23 (Winter 1962), pp. 359–71.

PART 3

Asian Peoples in America

In North America . . . the time will come when the population will have become dense. The struggle for existence will have to be more carefully planned. Then the people of America will be forced to stop and reflect. . . . When that situation comes about, the memory of racial extraction may at last be reawakened. The different languages may become the rallying centers for the different interests. Thereupon for the first time will America confront decisively the problem of its national unity.

—Gustav Ratzenhofer
1893

7

Stewart Culin: The Earliest American Chinatown Studies and a Hypothesis about Pre-Columbian Migration

The revival of Chinatown studies in the past twenty-five years can be credited to the revolution of a rising Asian American consciousness and its linkage to renewed scholarly investigations of the origins, character, and struggles of the Chinese minority in the United States. Such studies have concentrated on the diffusion of Southeastern Chinese culture and social organization to the cities of the United States; on the transplantation of clans, *hui kuan*, secret societies, craft and labor guilds, religious practices, recreational pursuits, and the martial arts to the urban enclaves housing Cantonese in America; on the cataloguing of legislative and judicial abuses, occupational discriminations, and Sinophobic prejudices; on the evaluation of the riots, robberies, and murders inflicted on a hapless people; on the agonizing struggles—internal and internecine, external and united—of the Chinese minority to preserve and protect its way of life and to prosper in an alien and almost always hostile land; and on the slow and unsteady acculturation of Chinese Americans. These studies have given both an intellectual character and a certain sociocultural perspective to the investigation of Chinatowns, past and present. And, like every outlook, this one both enlarges our understanding of hitherto neglected facts and features of Chinese history in America and forecloses our attention toward others.

The present essay belongs to the class of thus far neglected outlooks. It seeks to present part of the story of the researches of a lone and adventurous ethnologist of fin de siècle America who saw Chinatown not primarily as a community of beleaguered souls in jeopardy of life and fortune, but rather as a remarkable historical survival, a cultural outpost of the original world civilization. All the more remarkable about his researches is that they were carried on at the time of the most vicious and vociferous anti-Chinese movement in America, that they employed field investigations and participant-observation inside the Chinese quarter of the city, that they appear almost completely free from the prejudice of the period, and—sad to say—that they and the extraordinary hypothesis generated from them have been overlooked by virtually all scholars and partisans from the day of their first proclamation to the present time.

My analysis of this work is not put forth in order to prove the hypothesis set forth in them, nor even to advocate it over its more prevalent and better-argued rivals. Rather, it is presented here in order to illustrate that not all early American ethnographic work on the Chinese is tainted with racial prejudice, and, more important, to show that the study of the art, culture, amusements, and social organization of early American Chinatowns is not merely grist for a chapter in local or regional history, or part of the sorry heritage of American racism; rather, Chinatown once—at least for one analyst of culture—provided a strategic research site for the study of world civilization, and for a shrewd and outrageous hunch as to its origin and spread across oceans and over continents.

Culin's Hypothesis

Speaking before the section on anthropology of the American Association for the Advancement of Science in 1902, Robert Stewart Culin (1858–1929) set forth his hypothesis that America had been the "cradle of Asia," that is, that the civilizations of China, Japan, Korea, and the Asiatic hinterlands had had their origins in Paleolithic America.[1] America, Culin suggested, was in fact an "Old World" out of which civilization had emerged, and not the "New World" that had merely received predeveloped civilizations from Europe and Asia. As an originator of civilization, Old World America had been the site of primordial cultural beginnings and the habitat of the human carriers of this culture across the Pacific to Asia. Moreover, that first civilization had taken root, begun to develop, and continued to spread as different carriers and vehicles brought it over the land masses of Eurasia and Africa. Ultimately it had returned to America as immigrants and settlers brought its many differentiated, developed, and devolved motifs and forms into the United States as part of their own cultural baggage. Among these immigrants, the Chinese were crucially important, Culin asserted, providing in their games, amusements, icons, and other cultural formations recognizable survivals or revivals of the ancient Paleolithic Amerindian originals.

Although unrecognized at the time or afterward, Culin's hypothesis about the American origins of Asiatic civilization was a potentially devastating assault on almost all received ethnological thought. From the time of Columbus's voyages, the flora, fauna, and more especially the peoples and cultures of the Americas had been a challenge for historians and cosmologists to explain. Prohibited by church doctrine from enunciating any theory of multiple creation, the early European "anthropologists" had asserted that the newly discovered lands must be a "new world," populated by human and animal migrations out and away from the original center of human development somewhere in Eurasia. Even after the separation of scientific thought from religious censorship, the diffusionist thesis remained intact: there could have been only one original locus of human and civilizational development, and that place was in Eurasia; the Americas were derivative in both their human and cultural materials.

Eurasian organic and cultural unicentrism continues to be the dominant perspective in prehistory and ethnology today, with the relatively easy addition of Africa and the Olduvai Gorge people as an appendage of the original Eurasian origins thesis. It is generally believed that the Amerindian peoples are descendants of some Asiatic stock or stocks that pushed its ways across Beringia at some yet to be precisely established prehistoric time. For some unaccountable reason the ancient land bridge across the Bering Straits is almost never said to have invited travel westward into Asia, and no scholar to my knowledge has followed up Culin's hunch that some ancient Americans moved into Asia bringing with them a valuable culture and both sacred beliefs and secular ways. Instead a quite different debate over pre-Columbian transpacific migration has broken out over the past four centuries and continues unabated to the present day.[2] This debate is over the origins and development of the so-called high cultures of America, those of the Aztec, the Maya, and the Inca. The contretemps is one between the claimants of autochthonous cultural invention within the Americas or transpacific cultural borrowings from Asia. Discoveries of pottery, carvings, shards, art motifs, and navigational devices provide irregular but insistent resources for renewals of this fascinating disagreement.

The claims of pre-Columbian Chinese in America have been one regularly reappearing aspect of this debate. The Legend of Fusang, according to which a Buddhist monk journeyed to California sometime during the fifth century A.D. is the most remarkable but by no means the only case in point.[3] As recently as August 1980, discoveries and researches by archaeologist James Robert Moriarty in San Diego and paleoanthropologist Jia Lanpo in China gave further evidence of the possibility that an ancient Chinese ship—perhaps that carrying the fifth century monk, Faxian, bound from India to China and blown far off course near present day Sri-Lanka—could have dropped anchor in the shallow water off Palos Verdes Peninsula in California.[4] A most exhaustive case for Asian influence on pre-Columbian art has been made by art historian Paul Shao, whose careful studies and unusually sharp photographs provide both scholarly and visual support for the argument that Chinese reached the Americas long before Columbus.[5] China's art, artifacts, and foodstuffs, and its ancient navigational tradition, have in fact been made the basis for several claims of early Chinese contacts with the Americas, including Neolithic Southeastern Chinese vessels and peanuts, possibly from Kiangsu and Chekiang, in the Mesoamerican Preclassic era; Shang China influences on Olmec civilization; Chou motifs on Classic and Postclassic Mesoamerican pottery and on Northwest Coast Indian art; Dong-son metal workings on early northwestern South American metallurgy and possibly on Andean and southern Mexican developments as well; Han Chinese ceramics, metal works, and lacquer objects on Middle American art; and Han linguistic, town-planning, and artifact influences on Teotihuacan, Mexico and Chan Chan, Peru.[6] The continuing pile-up of evidence and the ingenius historical and meteorological reconstructions of pre-Columbian sailing traditions and oceanic current shifts from Asia make it difficult to reject the thesis that some voyagers from the Asian mainland reached America before the end of the Han period.

No similar body of evidence has been accumulated for pre-Columbian western migrations from America to Asia. Archaeology in China has emphasized the near absence or relative unimportance of non-Chinese influences on the origin and development of Chinese civilization.[7] Thor Heyerdahl's sea voyages from Peru into Oceania have established the navigational possibility of a westward migration, but no work seems to have been pursued beyond such hypothetical reconstructions.[8] Whereas the Fusang legend and other possibilities of pre-Columbian Asians in the Americas have invited persistent archaeological searches and ethnological researches, the possibility of Paleolithic Indians in Asia has aroused no similar rush of field or documentary investigations. Culin's hypothesis—forgotten as quickly as it was proclaimed in America—remains untested, a neglected monument of early ethnologic inspiration.[9]

Culin's Reasoning and Method

Culin's orientation was that of an ethnohistorical civilizational analyst, much like the later approach of Emile Durkheim and Marcel Mauss, on whom he and even more extensively his colleague, Frank Hamilton Cushing (1857–1900), had some significant influence.[10] Specifically, Culin, amplifying Cushing's insightful researches on the religious ritual and recreations of the Zuni Indians, insisted on the religious and, more especially, the divinatory foundations of all early games and asserted that "many games were not only the product of primitive conditions, but represent the means by which man endeavored to bring himself into communion with and to penetrate the secrets of the natural powers that surrounded him." Precisely because "many early games were sacred and divinatory . . . unless we can trace them back to these conditions . . . we have not obtained the clew to their origin." As artifacts indexical of the earliest religious ceremonies and thus to the beginnings of civilizations, games, for Culin, were the most useful kind of historical data: "They have not, like religions, been the object of a propaganda, and yet we find them distributed, comparatively unchanged in form, among the various races of the earth."[11] That distribution—the collection, arrangement, and classification of which formed the greater part of Culin's professional life-work—could be explained either by insisting on the psychic unity of mankind, which everywhere under like conditions would produce like artifacts, or by the diffusion of forms and ideas from some originating people who carried them abroad and introduced them into the cultures of aliens.

At first Culin seemed content to rest his claims on the principle of the psychic unity of mankind and to eschew the controversial issue of diffusion. The key issue in the debate was the Mexican game of *patolli*, which the English anthropologist Edward Burnett Tylor had traced back to the Hindustani game of *pachisi* and used as his principal evidence for a claim of pre-Columbian diffusion from Asia to America.[12] In 1894 Culin pointed to the researches of Cushing that had shown that *patolli* "was born and developed in America, just as much else so puzzlingly like the culture of the Old World." Moreover, Culin went on, "Mr. Cushing has found it here [i.e., America] in every stage of its development not only in Old Mexico, but among practically every tribe on the Northern Continent, and also in the Southern." The autochthonous character of *patolli* in the Americas, together with the fact of an identical game, *pachisi*, in Asia, led

Culin to claim then "only additional confirmation on its correspondence of that great truth to which all investigation seems to lead, namely, the psychological unity of man."[13]

However, other evidences and researches about Asiatic and Amerindian games nagged at Culin's first psycho-philosophical resolution of the problem of civilizational origins. For one thing Korean games, and especially the game of *ute* (or, in later discussions, *nyout*), appeared to be the ancestor of all other Asian games and, further, to have diffused as well as evolved into the Asian hinterlands, the Middle East, Africa, and Europe producing a variety of games using staves, knuckle-bones, dice, and chess pieces. The evolution and changes in *ute* as it moved through time and along the Eurasian-African continents spoke much for the idea of an even wider diffusion and an argument for the documented historical reconstruction of civilization that would embrace the Americas as an early focal point.[14] Another fact was the basic system of primitive classification that Durkheim and Mauss would celebrate in their eponymous book—that of the four cardinal points and the center. This system was not only to be found in ancient China and medieval Korea but among the American Zuni as well.[15] Lastly, the arrow—that Cushing insisted originated in America, preceded the invention of the bow, and had even greater significance for religion and iconography than for wars or hunts[16]—proved to be a common motif that Culin found in Amerindian, Asiatic, and Chinatown games, ornaments, textile designs, and other artifacts. The evidences of his own and Cushing's collections, the burning idea of an original place for America in the history of civilization, and—as we shall see—the pondering over his earlier investigations of Philadelphia's Chinatowners and their games, religious ceremonies, amusements, and divinatory practices, eventually led to Culin's reluctant and cautious abandonment of the psychological unity thesis and his enunciation of ancient America's primary place in the origin and diffusion of civilization.

Culin's Chinatown Studies

Stewart Culin was the first scientific ethnographer of a Chinatown in America. In the late 1880s, beginning with separate reports on religion, medicine, pharmacy, social life, customs, folklore, and secret societies, Culin published virtually the most comprehensive description ever made of Chinese social and cultural life in America.[17] He continued his work on Chinatown materials throughout the 1890s, reporting on the Chinese forms of gambling games, popular literature, opium smoking, divination, and fortune telling found in the Chinese quarters of Philadelphia and occasionally on Chinatowns in New York City and San Francisco as well.[18] Although his papers—discovered in a "secret room" in the Brooklyn Museum in 1974—contain numerous carefully dated and identified newspaper clippings reporting on the outrages against Chinese in America, Culin's own studies are unmarred by the typical prejudices of his day.[19] He does not treat the Chinatown gamblers, opium smokers, or homeless men—all of whom he observed quite closely and knew intimately—as dangerous, depraved, or deviant. Nor does he anticipate or advocate the assimilationist orientation that was to be enunciated by George Seward, Mary Coolidge, and—later—Emory Bogardus, Rose Hum Lee, S. W. Kung, and Betty Lee Sung.[20] Chinese were neither "white men with yellow skins" nor "Westerners from the East" to Culin.[21] Rather, he perceived in their ordinary games, religious ceremonies, secret initiation rituals, and everyday paraphernalia the survivals of and the clues to the most ancient form of civilization. Unmoved either by the clamor for exclusion of the Chinese or the accusation of their unassimilability, Culin took the presence of this culturally unique people in American cities as an unexampled opportunity for investigating the basis and origins of world civilization itself.

Culin's method of investigation was as disarmingly straightforward as it was daring. As he recalled many years later:

> Once in my youth I fell under the spell of a problem which involved a knowledge of the Chinese language. It was, by the way, the elucidation of the origin of the Chinese game which recently has become widely known and popular under the name of mah-jongg. I might have gone to school and taken lessons from a professor. Instead I went to live in one of our Chinese settlements, where in time I came not only to speak the language but, eager and curious, saturated myself with the spirit of these interesting and capable people. It was the direct road to what I wanted to accomplish and I acquired a knowledge of the Chinese that has lasted with me to this day.[22]

Culin's method for saturating himself with the spirit of a people is today known as participant-observation and is regarded as a viable, though still controversial, procedure for sociological and anthropological research.[23] In his own day, it was thought to be both bizarre and unnecessary. Culin, in his twenties, was in fact, following the unorthodox footsteps of fellow ethnologist Frank Hamilton Cushing, who at age nineteen, left the archaeological expedition in the New Mexico territory to which he was attached to join the Zuni tribe, eventually rising to the rank of war chief and becoming an initiate into its sacred mysteries.[24] Culin did not become a clan chief, *hui kuan* leader, or secret society initiate, but he did become intimately acquainted with these Chinatown associations and with the material and spiritual culture that they espoused. Neither the earlier missionary reports nor any current study of an American Chinatown can match the detail, description, and sociocultural understanding of Culin's researches.

However, Culin was also working conceptually and with a theoretical problem in mind. He was not merely an antiquarian nor was he engaged in purposeless ethnographic description. At the time of his Chinatown researches Culin had not yet come to his conclusion about the Amerindian origins of Asian civilization. He was puzzling over the numerous parallels in Asiatic and American artifacts, games, and customs that his own, Cushing's, and other ethnologists' investigations were producing. As late as 1894 he was still content to explain these striking similarities by reference to the recently reintroduced theory of the psychic unity of mankind.[25] In the eight years that separate his enunciation of that explanation and his assertion of the ancient American priority, he reexamined his perspective on the basis of the data and in effect renounced his earlier view in favor of the far more controversial claim of a westward diffusion into Asia. His Chinatown studies are part of his early and transitional period of theoretical development. They formed one crucial empirical element in the making of his major civilizational hypothesis. Together with his and Cushing's researches into primitive American art and amusements, the Chinatown studies formed one major basis for the second stage of his move toward diffusionism, enunciated in 1900: "Man's beginnings were infinitely complex. His art is the product not only of the environment with which economists deal, but also of the interactions of that environment, and man's intellectual nature. The mental processes of man in America are precisely the same as those of man in Europe; *and what we find existing in America underlies all the higher civilization of the other continents.*"[26] And, as we shall see, it was his careful analysis of the *I Ching*, together with Brinton's and Cushing's proofs of the American primacy of *patolli*, that led to his ultimate claim:

> The games of the Eastern continent—and I speak now not so much of the present day, but from what we know of the remote

past—are not only similar to, but practically identical with, those of America, and are not only alike in externals, but, if we may so apply the word, in their morphology as well. And, it may be added, they extend over into Asia from America as expressions of the same underlying culture. They belong to the *same* culture.

Man evidently wandered far and wide over the world before history began. Shall we, with our American explanations in mind—and they hold good not alone for games, which are but the "stalking horse" of the student—shall we not assent to the claim that ancient America may have contributed to an extent usually unimagined, her share of what is now the world's civilization?[27]

Arrows, Dominoes, and the *I Ching*

Two ideas form the background for Culin's hypothesis. The first is the primordial and sacred significance of the arrow. The second and equally important is the fundamental basis of games and primitive classification in divination. Each of these ideas found evidential expression in Culin's examination of Chinatown games, fortune telling practices, and artifacts. Arrow motifs on the dice, dominoes, and cards and divination practices among the customs of Philadelphia's and New York's Chinatowners served as challenges and incentives, moving Culin toward explanations for them that—if not so shamefully ignored—would have revolutionized theory in prehistory and ethnology.

Culin's emphasis on the religious significance of the arrow was borrowed from Cushing's careful and path-breaking researches.[28] The arrow, according to both Cushing and Culin, had originated in America and was treated animistically by primitive man. It also served as the ancient icon of man, and was employed as the principal weapon of the oldest spirit-form, the Divine Twins, deified by the ancient dwellers in the American Southwest. From the arrow Culin located a vast body of descendent artifacts—"the progeny of which are numerous as the stars"[29]—which included numerous game implements including dice, bones, sticks, and counters and also ornamental designs for the body, clothing, weapons, and ordinary objects used in everyday life. The arrow itself and its derivations, including both games and ornaments, originally had a divinatory purpose. Although that primordial purpose had all but died out among contemporary players and decorators, Culin argued, the arrow motif and its variants and offshoots and occasional usages in fortune telling are still to be found in the decoration and practices associated with these commonly used items. Such artifacts and social facts indicate that several peoples—among whom most notably are the Chinatown Chinese—inherited and preserved them from their Paleolithic American originators.

Culin insisted that neither man's amusements nor his aesthetic productions arose out of innate instincts for play or for beauty, but rather had their beginnings in religious and divinatory ceremonials. "These ceremonies," Culin observed in 1900, "repeated often at the same season of the year, after their meaning has been lost, or their necessity past, through man's better understanding of natural phenomena, have become the play of our children, the diversions of our youths and even, indeed, the fierce and irrepressible contests of the gaming table."[30] Central to these ceremonies and rituals was the basic principle of primitive classification whereby the oldest ancestors of contemporary "humanity endeavored to establish the connotation of unrelated facts as the devices through which the gods or the cosmic forces might be led to reveal the unknown or hidden relations that exist between man and his environment."[31] And, as Daniel G. Brinton had demonstrated, "the central idea upon which this classification is based . . . is that of the four quarters of the world." That idea, Cushing and Culin asserted, had originated in prehistoric America. From this classification, in turn, there derives the categorization of the primary colors; further, by "the aid of simple and obvious analogies we may extend the classification to beasts, birds, and men; to human relations, family and communal, secular and sacerdotal; to inanimate nature, the stars, the sentiments, emotions, to everything, in fact, for which the tongue has framed a name."[32] The arrow and the kinds of markings that are carved or painted on its shaftments, the bundles into which it can be tied, and the sticks, staves, bones, dice, cards, and counters to which it can be converted are in turn referable to the original designation of the first arrow and the four world-quarters. "In general," Culin wrote about American Indian games in 1902, "in all the games we find an arrow, or a derivative of the arrow, the predominant implement, and the conception of the four world-quarters, the fundamental idea."[33]

When Culin studied the gambling games, religious ceremonies, fortune telling practices, and printed cards and decorations of the Chinese in Philadelphia he constantly discovered the arrow sign or its derivations. For example, the p'ai ts'im (牌籤) or notice tallies

used to inform members of a meeting of the gamblers' guild "are direct descendants of the arrows used in more primitive conditions for
the same purpose. Their name, ts'im, is almost identical with the
Chinese name for arrow, and their form still retains a suggestion of
their origin." Similarly nin kan (年束). Chinese new year cards ex-
changed among Chinatowners in America "may be regarded as belonging to the same family as the message tally, or arrow, with the
name of a man. Like it they ceremonially stand for the individual
whose name they bear, and as such are preserved as pledges and to-
kens, given each other by members of the same clan and their
friends, for the year."[34] F'an t'an, a popular gambling pastime among
the Chinese sojourners in Philadelphia, dates "back to a time when
it was regarded as sacred, and practised, not as a vulgar game, but as
a means of discovering the past and forecasting the future." Drawing
upon analogies from other games, Culin insisted that "we may justly
regard the square tablet of the f'an t'an board as cosmical, originally
signifying the world and its four quarters." The coins substituted by
the Chinatowners for the bundle of fifty splints used in the game ancestral to f'an t'an suggest that the original implement "was once a
bundle of arrows or arrow shaftments"; moreover, Culin pointed out,
in "many other of the later forms of arrow divination we find coins
substituted for the arrow-derived splints or staves."[35] Tsz' fa, a lot-
tery common among the Chinese in Philadelphia and New York City
in Culin's day was not only the forerunner of European lotteries, but
also a game derived from the elaboration of the original form of
primitive classification and a device employed for divination.[36]

T'in kau, or "Heavens and Nines," a recreation that "is the favorite social game of the Chinese laborers in the United States and is
often played in the shops after dinner" is the one amusement to
which Culin assigns "the first place, both as a game and as an object
of antiquarian research among the many Chinese domino games."
Chinese dominoes, he writes, "are a direct inheritance from primitive conditions and were manifestly inspired by primitive modes of
thought. . . . It is unlikely they were invented as a game. They arose
indeed, like many another games, in the practice of divination, in
which they were implements of magic; implements for determining
numbers and thence places . . . their dots, in orderly permutation,
were the symbols of the world quarters, and of the cosmical powers,
through the interaction of which all things had their being."[37] Culin's derivation of Chinese dominoes from Western Asian dice, and
these dice from I Ching divination ceremonies that in turn ultimately originated among the ancestors of the Zuni living in the

American Southwest, is too long and detailed a line of argument to
be presented here. Suffice it to note for one more example that Culin
observed that *hoi t'ap*, a solitaire domino game "generally known to
the [Chinese] laborers who come to America" was "used in divination," and that the general trajectory of game diffusion, after it
reached Asia, appeared to him to have spread from ancient *I Ching*
necromancers in China into Western Asia and India and then back
again into China in forms derived from the changes undergone in its
travels.[38] Finally, the game that first inspired Culin's researches,
Mah-jong, which as a new parlor amusement swept over white
middle-class America in the 1920s, was, Culin insisted in 1924, "a
reintroduction of a famous old Chinese game which may be numbered with silk, printing type, porcelain, tea and paper money
among China's important material contributions to Western civilization." However, although Culin was quick to point out that "all existing playing cards, whatever their kind, in all countries except
China and Korea, and including Japan, Persia and India, were derived through Europe from the Chinese game," that game itself,
known to Chinatowners and closely related to the domino game of
"Heavens and Nines," was, by a most complicated bit of reasoning,
traceable "to an earlier game in which success was achieved through
the fortuitous association of arrow-derived lots." The deck used in
the Chinese-Korean game of *htou-tjen*, according to Culin the ancestor of *Mah-jong*, shows the "design of a feather . . . drawn on the
backs of these cards, [an important indication that] suggests their
connection with arrow shaftments, from which I believe they were
derived."[39] And, as Culin would insist in 1902, arrow derivation
meant paleolithic American origins.

Culin's study of Chinese religious, ritual, and magical practices in
American Chinatowns was most thorough.[40] Not only did he trace
out the divinatory origins of Chinatown's gambling games, he also
took careful cognizance of various modes of palmistry, fortune telling, stick casting, and other methods of sortilege, finding in each further clues to their ancient origins.[41] Not all the kinds of future-
casting known to Cantonese laborers in America were practiced in
the Chinatowns of Philadelphia and New York, but books and treatises on some of them were to be found in shops in the Chinese quarter. "The universal method of attempting to learn the future is that of
casting lots before the idol of the God of War," Culin observed in
1895. "This is done constantly by gamblers, but the most important
ceremony of this kind is performed at the beginning of the Chinese
year." The *t'sim u*, or splints or slips used in divining answers in this

ceremony, were regarded by Culin "as having originally been arrows, and one of the many forms of the arrow casting which is so
widely distributed, both as a means of divination and then as a
game." A second method of fortune telling in use among the Chinese
in Eastern cities of the United States consisted "in drawing bamboo
splints from a vase." The *kwa ts'im*, or bamboo splints, Culin also
believed to be traceable to arrows and the method of their employment to arrow casting. More important, Culin observed that this system is called *Man Wong kwa* and is believed by Chinese to have
been invented by Man Wong (Wen Wang, B.C. 1231–1135) and derived from the *Yik King* (i.e., the *I Ching*). Through his analysis of
the origins of the *I Ching*, Culin uncovered another master clue to
the origins of Asiatic civilization.

Culin must be numbered among the earliest pioneers of *I Ching*
studies. Although his name is not mentioned in the proliferation of
such studies that have been published recently,[42] he was in fact one
of the first Occidental scholars to delve seriously into the nature and
origin of the *I Ching* and the first, so far as I can tell, to classify it
correctly as divinatory in its fundamental character. More to the
point of the present essay, Culin argued that the methods and implements of the *I Ching* had their origin in ancient American Indian
practices and thus provided more evidence for Amerindian predecessors. Culin noticed that treatises on divination were among the
most prevalent forms of popular literature among the Chinatowners
of Philadelphia and New York. These popular works, in turn, traced
their own descent "from the *Yik King* or 'Book of the Changes,' " Culin observed, "and when an attempt is made to obtain information
concerning the subject from the Chinese here, they always refer the
inquirer to this highly unintelligible book."[43] Inquiring further into
the matter, Culin "became aware that the ancient system, or one imitated from the ancient account, was still practiced in China."[44] With
the aid of a Japanese informant then residing in Philadelphia, Culin
learned much about contemporary Japanese and Chinese derivative
divination and gambling methods. Culin became convinced that the
I Ching was derived from an ancient form of arrow casting, that its
original divining plant stalks, *Ptarmica Sibirica*, were in turn descended from arrow staves not unlike those used in his own day by
the Haida Indians of the American Northwest coast in their stick
games, and that, finally, "America thus furnishes us with a clue to a
correct understanding of the ancient mysteries, which some day, not
far distant, will be revealed in all the fullness of their primal
significance."[45]

Conclusion

Culin's hope for the acceptance of his theory of Amerindian civilization origins has not materialized. In part this is due to the untimely death of his colleague, Cushing, in 1900, without whom Culin felt unable to carry out the mammoth investigations required. Another aspect of his inability to legitimize his hypothesis among fellow ethnologists was undoubtedly the fact that Culin was, throughout most of his life, a museum curator, not a professor, a scholar who proceeded alone, without the aid of students or disciples. Lastly, it should be noted that Culin's idea about the American origins and westward movement of civilization into Asia also embraced a daring explanation of the singular North American Southwest origins of the high cultures of the Aztecs, Mayas, and Incas and, by a long and irregular process of diffusion, of the games of Africa.[46] The ancient inhabitants of the American Southwest were thus the progenitors not only of Asian but of world civilization. His proposal went so against the received ideas of his own time—and of our own—that it aroused no sustained intellectual support.[47] It is today what it was in his own time—an almost unknown and surely neglected iconoclastic hypothesis that has yet to be tested.

And yet, outrageous as it seems, should we not in this era of reexamination of our civilization, its contents and discontents, give pause to honor if not to investigate the Culin thesis? And, in doing so, should we not, paraphrasing Culin, give assent to the claim that Chinatown—through its cultural survivals in the form of religious ceremonies, divinatory practices, and gambling games—contributed to an extent usually unimagined its share of what is now called the world's civilization?

NOTES

I should like to express my appreciation to my research assistants, Yingjen Chang, Cecil Greek, James Cleland, Gary Kriss, Richard Stillman, and Reuben Norman, for gathering materials. The Brooklyn Museum kindly allowed me to inspect, classify, and make copies of the Culin materials contained in the "secret room." Daria Cverna Martin typed the manuscript and kept matters relating to the Chinese Historical Society Conference in order. This essay originally appeared in *The Chinese American Experience: Papers from the Second National Conference on Chinese American Studies (1980)*, ed. Genny Lim (San Francisco: The Chinese Historical Society of America and the Chinese Cultural Foundation of San Francisco, 1984), pp. 117–26.

1. Stewart Culin, "America the Cradle of Asia," an address before the Section of Anthropology, American Association for the Advancement of Science Washington Meeting, December, 1902–January, 1903. *Proceedings of the American Association for the Advancement of Science*, 52 (1903), pp. 493–500. Also published in *Harper's Monthly Magazine*, 106 (March 1903), pp. 534–40.

2. See, e.g., Carroll L. Riley et al., eds., *Man across the Sea: Problems of Pre-Columbian Contacts* (Austin: University of Texas Press, 1971).

3. See Charles G. Leland, *Fusang, on the Discovery of America by Chinese Buddhist Priests in the Fifth Century* (London: Curzon Press, 1973 [1875]); Edward R. Vining, *An Inglorious Columbus; or, Evidence that Hwui Shan and a Party of Buddhist Monks from Afghanistan Discovered America in the Fifth Century A.D.* (New York: D. Appleton and Co., 1885); Frederic J. Masters, "Did a Chinaman Discover America?" *Overland Monthly*, 23 (June 1894), pp. 576–88; Douglas S. Watson, "Did a Chinese Discover America?" *California Historical Society Quarterly*, 14 (March 1935), pp. 47–58; Robert Larson, "Was America the Wonderful Land of Fusang?" *American Heritage*, 17 (1966), pp. 42–45, 106–9; Henriette Mertz, *Pale Ink: Two Ancient Records of Chinese Exploration in America*, 2d rev. ed. (Chicago: Swallow Press, 1972 [1953]); Hendon Mason Harris, *The Asiatic Fathers of America* (Taipei: Wen Ho Printing Co., n.d.); R. A. Jairazbhoy, *Ancient Egyptians and Chinese in America* (Totowa, N. J.: Rowman and Littlefield, 1974), pp. 100–112; Stan Steiner, *Fusang: The Chinese Who Built America* (New York: Harper and Row, 1979), pp. 3–9. For doubts on the Fusang legend see "Fu-Sang," in Samuel Couling, *The Encyclopedia Sinica* (Shanghai: Kelly and Walsh, 1917), p. 199; and L. Carrington Goodrich, "China's first Knowledge of the Americas," *Geographical Review*, 123 (July 1938), pp. 400–411.

4. Fang Zhongpu, "Did Chinese Buddhists Reach America 1,000 Years before Columbus?" *China Reconstructs*, 29 (August 1980), pp. 65–66. See also "Bye Columbus: Did the Chinese Arrive First?" *Time Magazine*, 116 (August 18, 1980), p. 48.

5. Paul Shao, *Asiatic Influences in Pre-Columbian Art* (Ames: Iowa State University Press, 1976).

6. See Stephen C. Jett, "Pre-Columbian Transoceanic Contacts," in Jesse D. Jennings, ed., *Ancient Native Americans* (San Francisco: W. H. Freeman and Co., 1978), pp. 593–650.

7. See three works by Kwang-chih Chang, *Early Chinese Civilization: Anthropological Perspectives* (Cambridge: Harvard University Press, 1976); *The Archaeology of Ancient China*, 3d ed. (New Haven: Yale University Press, 1977); *Shang Civilization* (New Haven: Yale University Press, 1980).

8. See two works by Thor Heyerdahl, *Kon-Tiki: Across the Pacific by Raft*, trans. F. H. Lyon (New York: Pocket Books, 1973 [1950]); and *Early Man and the Ocean: A Search for the Beginnings of Navigation and Seaborne Civilizations* (Garden City, N.Y.; Doubleday and Co., 1979), pp. 151–398. See also Peter Bellwood, *Man's Conquest of the Pacific: The Prehistory of Southeast Asia and Oceania* (New York: Oxford University Press, 1979).

9. See Stanford M. Lyman, "Stewart Culin and the Debate over Trans-Pacific Migration," *Journal for the Theory of Social Behaviour*, 9:1 (March 1979), pp. 91–116.

10. See Stanford M. Lyman, "Two Neglected Pioneers of Civilizational Analysis: The Cultural Perspectives of R. Stewart Culin and Frank Hamilton Cushing," *Social Research*, 49:3 (Autumn 1982), pp. 690–729.

11. Stewart Culin, "The Value of Games in Ethnology," *Proceedings of the American Association for the Advancement of Science*, 43 (1894), p. 355.

12. See three essays by Edward B. Tylor, "On the Game of Patolli in Ancient Mexico and Its Probable Asiatic Origins," *Royal Anthropological Institute Journal*, 8 (1879), pp. 116–29; "Backgammon among the Aztecs," *Popular Science Monthly*, 14 (February 1879), pp. 491–501; "On American Lot-Games as Evidence of Asiatic Intercourse before the Time of Columbus," *International Archives of Ethnography*, supp. to vol. 9 (1896), pp. 55–67.

13. Culin, "Value of Games in Ethnology," pp. 357–58.

14. Ibid.

15. See three papers by Frank Hamilton Cushing, "Manual Concepts: A Study of the Influence of Hand Usage on Culture Growth," *American Anthropologist*, 5 (Oct. 1892), pp. 289–317; "Outlines of Zuni Creation Myths," *Thirteenth Annual Report of the Bureau of American Ethnology, 1891–1892*, (Washington, D.C.: Government Printing Office, 1896), pp. 321–447, esp. pp. 367–77; "Observations Relative to the Origin of the *Fylfot or Swastika*," *American Anthropologist*, 9:2 (Apr. June 1907), pp. 334–37.

16. Frank Hamilton Cushing, "The Arrow," address before the Section of Anthropology, American Association for the Advancement of Science, Springfield Meeting, August 1895. *Proceedings of the American Association for the Advancement of Science*, 44 (1895), pp. 199–240. This essay is also to be found in *American Anthropologist*, 8:4 (Oct. 1895), pp. 307–49; See Stewart Culin, "Games of the North American Indians," *Twenty-Fourth Annual Report of the Bureau of American Ethnology to the Smithsonian Institution, 1902–1903* (Washington, D.C.: Government Printing Office, 1907. Reprinted as *Games of the North American Indians* (New York: Dover Publications, 1975), pp. 33, 213–15, 227–29, 335–36.

17. See the following papers by Stewart Culin: "The Religious Ceremonies of the Chinese in the Eastern Cities of the United States," essay read before the Numismatic and Antiquarian Society of Philadelphia, April 1, 1886 (Philadelphia: privately printed, 1887), pp. 3–23; "China in America: A Study of the Social Life of the Chinese in the Eastern Cities of the United States," essay read before the Section of Anthropology, American Association for the Advancement of Science, New York, 1887 (Philadelphia: n.p., 1887), pp. 3–16; "The Practice of Medicine by the Chinese in America," *Medical and Surgical Reporter*, 56 (March 1887), pp. 355–57; "Chinese Drug Stores in America," *American Journal of Pharmacy* (Dec. 1887), pp. 593–98; "A Curious People: Sketch of the Chinese Colony in Philadelphia," *Philadelphia Public Ledger*, September 22, 1888; "Chinese Folk-Lore: The Habits and Customs of Our Chinese Neighbors," *Philadelphia Public Ledger*, March

1890; "Customs of the Chinese in America," *Journal of American Folk-Lore,* 3 (July-Sept. 1890), pp. 191–200; "The I Hing, or 'Patriotic Rising,' A Secret Society among the Chinese in America," November 3, 1887, *Report of the Proceedings of the Numismatic and Antiquarian Society of Philadelphia for the Years 1887–1889* (Philadelphia: Printed for the Society, 1891), pp. 51–58; "My Friend Herman: A Tale of the Chinese Secret Society of Heaven and Earth," *Philadelphia Press,* August 11, 1889; "Chinese Secret Societies in the United States," *Journal of American Folk-Lore,* 3 (Jan.-Mar. 1890), pp. 39–43; "T'in Ti Ui: The Chinese Heaven and Earth League," *Philadelphia Public Ledger,* August 26, 1890; "I Hing: American Branch of the Heaven and Earth League," *Philadelphia Public Ledger,* August 29, 1890.

18. In addition to the specific articles on gambling games, divination and fortune telling and Chinatown's popular literature cited below see the following by Culin: "Opium Smoking: The Habit among the Chinese in Philadelphia," *Philadelphia Public Ledger,* August 19, 1891; "Social Organization of the Chinese in America," *American Anthropologist,* o.s. 4 (Oct. 1891), pp. 347–52; "Palmistry in China and Japan," *Overland Monthly,* 2d series, 23 (May 1894), pp. 476–80.

19. One exception to this otherwise unblemished record is the cryptic and ambiguous statement about Chinese-Negro marriages in Cuba, which could be interpreted as adherence to the thesis that cross-racial marriages are infertile: "I was especially interested in the Chinese colony in Havana. These people appeared less prosperous than in the United States and to have lost more of their characteristic dress and customs than the Chinese in our American cities. They form unions with negro women—which are commonly sterile, so that the race is dying out without leaving any impression upon the population of the island." Stewart Culin, "The Indians of Cuba," *Bulletin of the Free Museum of Science and Art, Department of Archaeology, University of Pennsylvania,* 3:4 (May 1902), p. 221. As to the character, culture, and survival of Chinese institutions in Havana, Culin was, in this case, quite mistaken. See M.V. Kriukov, "Clan Associations of Chinese Immigrants in Cuba in the Early Twentieth Century (On the Problem of the Structure and Function of Traditional Social Institutions in an Ethnically Alien Environment)," *Soviet Sociology,* 18:L (Summer 1979), pp. 25–46. [This is an English translation of "Klanovye obshchestva kitaitsev-immigrantov na Kube v pervol polovin XX v. (K probleme struktury i funktsii traditsionnykh sotsianykh institutov v inonatsional' noe srede)" that first appeared in *Sovetskaia ethnografiia* 2(1977), pp. 55–67.]

20. See George F. Seward, *Chinese Immigration, in its Social and Economical Aspects* (New York: Charles Scribner's Sons, 1881); Mary Roberts Coolidge, *Chinese Immigration* (New York: Henry Holt, 1909); Emory Bogardus, *Essentials of Americanization,* rev., ed. (Los Angeles: University of Southern California Press, 1920), pp. 201–16; Rose Hum Lee, *The Chinese in the United States of America* (Hong Kong: Hong Kong University Press, 1960); S. W. Kung, *Chinese in American Life: Some Aspects of Their His-*

tory, Status, Problems, and Contributions (Seattle: University of Washington Press, 1962); B. L. Sung, *Mountain of Gold: The Story of the Chinese in America* (New York: Macmillan, 1967).

21. See Amy Uyematsu, "The Emergence of Yellow Power in America (an Excerpt)," *Roots: An Asian American Reader*, ed. Amy Tachiki, Eddie Wong, Franklin Odo, with Buck Wong (Los Angeles: UCLA Asian American Studies Center, 1971), pp. 9–13; and Roger Daniels, "Westerners from the East: Oriental Immigrants Re-Appraised," paper presented to the Fifth Annual Conference of the Western History Association, Helena, Montana, October 15, 1965.

22. Stewart Culin, "Creation in Art," lecture delivered before the evening classes of the Schools of Fine and Applied Arts and of Household Science and Arts of the Pratt Institute, Brooklyn, New York, February 5, 1924 (Brooklyn: Brooklyn Museum, 1924) unpaginated, fourth page.

23. See, e.g., George J. McCall and J. L. Simmons, eds., *Issues in Participant Observation: A Text and Reader* (Reading, Mass.: Addison-Wesley Publishing Co., 1969).

24. See Frank Hamilton Cushing, "My Adventures in Zuni," *Century Illustrated Magazine*, XXC (Dec. 1882, Feb. 1883), pp. 191–207, 500–511, 26 (May 1883), pp. 38–47. See also Raymond Stewart Brandes, *Frank Hamilton Cushing: Pioneer Americanist*, unpub. Ph.D. diss., University of Arizona, 1965 (Ann Arbor: University Microfilms International, 1976), pp. 1–118; Triloki Nath Pandey, "Anthropologists at Zuni" *Proceedings of the American Philosophical Society*, 116 (Aug. 1972), pp. 321–37; Joan Mark, "Frank Hamilton Cushing and an American Science of Anthropology," *Perspectives in American History*, 10 (1976), pp. 449–86; Jesse Green, "Introduction," to his edition of *Zuni: Selected Writings of Frank Hamilton Cushing* (Lincoln: University of Nebraska Press, 1979), pp. 3–36.

25. For discussions of this idea see Frederick J. Teggart, *Theory and Processes of History* (Berkeley: University of California Press, 1941), pp. 95, 105, 113–25; and David Bidney, *Theoretical Anthropology*, 2d augmented ed. (New York: Schocken Books, 1967), pp. 201–9.

26. Stewart Culin, "Primitive American Art," a lecture delivered before the Biological Club, University of Pennsylvania, January 8, 1900. *University Bulletin*, n.v. (April 1900), p. 7. Emphasis supplied.

27. Culin, "America the Cradle of Asia," p. 500. Emphasis in original.

28. In addition to the researches cited above see Frank Hamilton Cushing, "The Zuni Social, Mythic, and Religious Systems," *Popular Science Monthly*, 21 (June 1882), pp. 186–92.

29. Stewart Culin, "The Origin of F'an T'an," *Overland Monthly*, second series (Aug. 1896), p. 155.

30. Stewart Culin, "The Origin of Ornament," *Bulletin of the Free Museum of Science and Art, Department of Archaeology and Paleontology, University of Pennsylvania*, 2:4 (May 1900), p. 236.

31. Stewart Culin, "American Indian Games," *Journal of American Folk-Lore*, 11 (Oct.-Dec. 1898), p. 245.

32. Ibid., pp. 245–46.

33. Stewart Culin, "American Indian Games (1902)," *American Anthropologist*, 5 (Mar. 1902), p. 60.

34. Stewart Culin, *Chess and Playing Cards: Catalogue of Games and Implements for Divination Exhibited by the United States National Museum in Connection with the Department of Archaeology and Paleontology of the University of Pennsylvania at the Cotton States and International Exposition, Atlanta, Georgia, 1895. Annual Report of the Board of Regents of the Smithsonian Institution for the Year Ending June 30, 1896* (Washington, D.C.: U.S. National Museum, 1896; New York: Arno Press, 1976), p. 883.

35. Stewart Culin, "Origin of *F'an T'an*," p. 155.

36. Stewart Culin, "Tsz Fa, or Word Blossoming," *Overland Monthly*, 24 (Sept. 1894), pp. 249–55.

37. Stewart Culin, "Dominoes, the National Game of China," *Overland Monthly*, 2d series, 26 (Nov. 1895), pp. 561, 560, 559. See also three other essays by Culin, "Chinese Games with Dice," paper read before the Oriental Club of Philadelphia, March 14, 1889 (Philadelphia: privately printed, 1889); "The Gambling Games of the Chinese in America," paper read before the American Numismatic and Archaeological Society, New York, January 26, 1888, *Publications of the University of Pennsylvania, Series in Philology, Literature, and Archaeology*, 1:4(1891), pp. 1–17; "Chinese Games with Dice and Dominoes," *Report of the United States National Museum, Smithsonian Institute* (Washington, D.C.: Smithsonian Institution, 1893), pp. 489–537.

38. See Culin, "Chinese Games with Dice and Dominoes," pp. 516–17, 532–37.

39. Stewart Culin, "The Game of Ma-Jong: Its Origin and significance," *Brooklyn Museum Quarterly*, 11:4 (Oct. 1924), pp. 153–68. See also Culin's discussion of this game (and ninety-six others) in his monumental *Korean Games, with Notes on the Corresponding Games of China and Japan* (Philadelphia: University of Pennsylvania, 1895; republished as *Games of the Orient: Korea, China, Japan* (Rutland, Vt.: Charles E. Tuttle Co., 1958), pp. 123–26.

40. See Stewart Culin, "Religious Ceremonies," pp. 1–23.

41. The following quotes from Stewart Culin, "Divination and Fortune-Telling among the Chinese in America," *Overland Monthly*, series, 25 (Feb. 1895), pp. 165–72.

42. *The I Ching: The Book of Changes*, trans. James Legge, 2d ed. (New York: Dover Publications, 1963 [1899]); *The I Ching, or Book of Changes: The Richard Wilhem Translation from Chinese into German, rendered into English*, trans. by Cary F. Banes, 3d ed. Bollingen Series 19 (Princeton: Princeton University Press, 1967); Irene Ebner, "Introduction" to her translation of Richard Wilhelm, *Lectures on the I Ching: Constancy and Change*, Bollingen Series 19:2 (Princeton: Princeton University Press, 1979); Iulian K. Shchutskii, *Researches on the I Ching*, trans. William L. MacDonald, Tsuyoshi Hasegawa, with Hellmut Wilhelm. Bollingen Series 62:2 (Princeton: Princeton University Press, 1979).

43. Stewart Culin, "Popular Literature of the Chinese Laborers in the United States," *Oriental Studies: A Selection of Papers Read before the Oriental Club of Philadelphia, 1888–1894,* (Boston: n.p., 1894), p. 53.

44. Culin, "Divination and Fortune-Telling," p. 171.

45. Ibid., p. 172.

46. See the following essays by Culin: "Mancala, the National Game of Africa," *Annual Report of the Regents of the Smithsonian Institution, The United States National Museum, for the Year Ending June 30, 1894* (Washington: Government Printing Office, 1894), pp. 595–607; "Hawaiian Games," *American Anthropologist,* n.s., 1:2 (Apr. 1899), pp. 201–47; "Primitive American Art," pp. 2–5; "Philippine Games," *American Anthropologist,* n.s., 2 (Oct.-Dec., 1900), pp. 643–56; "A Korean Map of the World," *Brooklyn Museum Quarterly,* 12:4 (Oct. 1925), pp. 183–93.

47. As late as 1924 Culin observed that "no conclusive evidence has yet been offered of the Asiatic origin of early American civilization," "Creation in Art," unpaginated, third page.

8

The Chinese Diaspora in America, 1850–1943

Sociological studies of immigration and its effects on the social organization of the United States have taken a new turn. No longer is "assimilation" assumed to be the ineluctable final outcome of a peoples' settlement abroad. The much vaunted "melting pot" is now being increasingly recognized by sociologists and journalists as an efficacious illusion: part dream, as in the wonderful wish of J. Hector St. John de Crevecoeur, the eighteenth-century "American farmer," that America would dissolve in herself the divisive national identities that had made Europe such a cockpit; part tactic, as in the case of those Jews who supported and celebrated Israel Zangwill's play, *The Melting Pot* (1909), because they thought its homely message would allay widespread fears that Jews in America would remain an alien and subversive people; part ideology, as in the insistence, ritualized in the salutation to the flag, that the American people are "one nation, under God, indivisible, with liberty and justice for all." The general domestic unsettlement of the 1960s, and more especially, the renewal of racial and ethnic consciousness, the revival of nativistic movements, and the retreat of white Anglo-Saxon Protestant hegemony have occasioned a reinvigorated search for the basic social values that underpin social organization in the United States. There is a vague uneasiness surrounding the recent claims that Americans are living in an era of "the decline of the WASP," and "the rise of the unmeltable ethnics." Whereas Gunnar Myrdal sought a solution to the "American dilemma" by appealing to the ultimate capacity of the core values—equality and progress—to end political, social, and economic inequalities, concerned sociologists today are beginning to wonder whether any core values even prevail.

One *intellectual* problem arising out of the current disenchantment with old formulas is the absence of compelling concepts. Concepts can organize the raw reality into a new intelligibility; more important, they can sensitize sociologists to aspects of their subject that have gone hitherto unnoticed. Yet in the sociological analysis of immigration, race and ethnic relations, and minorities concept development has lagged. The very terms of reference are unsettled. In the 1920s, undoubtedly impressed by the condition of stateless but nationalistic people in Europe, American sociologists began to perceive social issues in American society in terms of *majorities* and *minorities*. In this same era, impressed by the birth and maturation of the immigrants' children in America, Robert E. Park and Everett Stonequist, borrowing from the insights of Georg Simmel and Werner Sombart, coined the phrase *marginal man* to describe one who was a product of two cultures and a member of neither. For four decades sociologists have debated the efficacy, dimensions, and correlates of that concept. As different collective experiences were described, the sociological vocabulary appeared always to be inadequate. Race prejudice, racism, institutionalized racism, pluralism, ghetto colonialism, congregation, segregation, and integration are all terms that have bidden for conceptual legitimacy. The rapidity of social change in this arena of American life suggests that the cultural and linguistic lag that has already been noticed will continue.

Immigrants in general, and Asian immigrants in particular, have been among the beneficiaries and victims of this sociological struggle for conceptual dominion and consensus. As new issues and problems have arisen, each people has been subjected or threatened with a reanalysis and reevaluation of its history and present social position. Rarely have the members been consulted about their own categories of identity or experience. Rather, the social scientists, impelled by a belief in their own intellectual superiority and by a distrust of the reason that might prevail among their subjects, unilaterally defined the scope and meaning of these histories and lives.

Perhaps no other people has been subjected to more investigation in reference to an unanalyzed but much vaunted assimilation and the failure to achieve it than the Chinese in America. In 1869 Henry George opened the discussion by insisting that the Chinese were unassimilable; in 1928 Emory Bogardus suggested that the social distance between the Chinese and white Americans might decrease as the former ended their ghetto isolation and entered the middle class, but in 1960 Rose Hum Lee lamented the tardiness of the Chinese in assimilating, accused them of preserving unwarrantable special interests in Chinatown, and urged them to develop the will and strength of character to enter fully into the mainstream of American life. The failure, however, was not that of the Chinese. Rather, there has been a failure of sociological imagination; a faltering of perspective. Assimilation, and its attendant theories and ideologies—that is, the race relations cycle and the melting pot ideology, respectively—suffer from what Robert Blauner has called a "managerial bias," gauging the histories and attitudes of an immigrant people in accordance with the social wishes and group interests of the dominant race.

An alternative approach would seek concepts that translate the actual lived experience of people into a sociology that clarifies it. Such a sociology has not yet been developed, but several steps along the road have already been taken. The philosophical sociology of Alfred Schutz with its emphasis on the common sense understandings of the everyday world, the division of life into routine and crisis, and the significance of temporal and personal perspectives provides a groundwork for conceptual development and new empirical investigations. The ethnomethodology of Harold Garfinkel, Aaron Cicourel, and their followers introduces both a healthy skepticism about absolutism in social scientific explanation and an innovative approach to the rational and social foundations of human accomplishments. Finally, a sociology of the absurd, first presented by Stanford M. Lyman and Marvin B. Scott, promises an existential and phenomenological social science that should avoid the pitfalls of ethnocentrism, managerial bias, and hidden ideological imperatives.

In the orientation of these new schools of thought, borrowing from them indiscriminately and yet not necessarily taking over any one of them wholly, this essay hopes to explore the Chinese experience in America. The analysis is at once historical, sociological, and, in the phenomenological sense of that term, psychological. It is also tentative, suggestive, and in the limiting sense of the term when employed in the historical sciences, experimental. My aim is to sensitize the reader to certain dimensions of the social and psychological condition of a people that arise out of their own experience.

The Chinese Diaspora

Looked at from the perspective of the immigrants, Chinese migrations have created a diaspora, a scattering of a portion of the Chinese people over the face of the earth. A diaspora may be said to exist where group migration has occurred, where acculturation has not taken place, where a people maintain themselves in accordance with the culture of their original homeland, and where there is at least an ideology or strong sentiment calling for an end to exile. In the case of the Chinese it is clear that their migrations were not motivated by plans for colonization, settlement, or permanent residence abroad. Rather they sought the overseas areas as places where, because of accidents of opportunity, a chance was offered to enhance their status when they returned to China. A trip abroad, a few years of work in a foreign land, and a stoic acceptance of the alien land's prejudices and discrimination could, with luck, earn a Chinese sufficient wealth to return to his village in splendor.

From Annam to Zanzibar, Chinese toiled in the hope that they would one day have enough money to retire in the land of their birth. Theirs, then, was not to be an irremediable exile, not to be the diaspora of absurdity described by Camus: permanent exile in a strange land and a life devoid of memories of a homeland left behind (Camus 1955:18). Although they were neither involuntary migrants nor slaves in America, Chinese were excluded as much from a larger society as Negroes. But unlike the blacks, Chinese were not deprived of knowledge about and sentiment for the country of their origin. Nor did they lack hope of a return to the promised land of their past. They did not experience a divorce between themselves and their familiar lives, only a separation. They had only temporarily departed from their existence. They could suffer the exploitation because their hope for return to China served as a source of strength.

But the dream of an honorable return did not usually match the reality of their overseas existence. In alien lands Chinese watched helplessly as the years of toil stretched out over nearly the whole of their lives. The Chinese came as strangers, desired to be homegoers, and all too often lived, and died, as permanent sojourners. Their children became marginal men and women, products of two cultures, members of neither.

The Chinese Immigrant as Stranger

To speak of the Chinese as strangers is to see them in terms of the perceptive conceptualization first employed by Georg Simmel. "The stranger," he wrote in his essay of that title, "is . . . not . . . the wanderer who comes today and goes tomorrow, but rather is the person who comes today and stays tomorrow." The Chinese who journeyed to Southeast Asia, America, Europe, Africa, and Oceania were not wanderers in the strict sense of that term; they had fixed places to go, a definite purpose in mind, and a keen desire to return home to wife and kinsmen in China. Their several courses took them where opportunity beckoned. To the lonely Chinese immigrant the place where he stayed in the diaspora was his *residence;* where he happened to be was his *abode;* but only the place from which he had started out and to which he intended to return was *home.*

The Chinese as a stranger in America was in the society but not *of* it. He imported things into that society that were not native nor original to it. In the most primordial sense we must necessarily recognize that the Chinese brought his body, his physiognomy, his anatomy, and his external appearance with him. In the very act he created a powerful element of his strangeness, for a part of the hierarchy of relevances, the system of priorities—the basic values—of America included the social construction and evaluation of persons as bodies categorizable into "races." It was in America that the man from Canton discovered that he belonged to a "race," that his physical features were an irreducible part of his social identity, and that he would forever exist to his hosts as an undifferentiated member of his racial category. To most Americans Chinese were impenetrable as persons, knowable only as men of "slanted" eyes and "yellow" skin. To be sure his subjective qualities could and did become at least partially known, but, as Robert E. Park's perceptive essay on the Oriental face indicated, his personal and human qualities seemed forever to be hidden "behind the mask," encapsulated within an objective physical frame from which they could not emerge.

Second, the Chinese as a stranger brought with him his language, or rather to be more exact, his languages. The peoples of Kwangtung who made up the bulk of Chinese immigrants in America spoke several dialects of the tongue Occidentals call "Chinese." Although all spoken dialects had a common written script, their verbal forms were frequently unintelligible to those who came from but a few miles away. Linguistically many of the Cantonese were strangers to each other, a phenomenon which found organizational expression in *hui kuan* (speech and territorial associations) that they established soon after their arrival in San Francisco.

However, it must be remembered that the Chinese language appeared to be but one language to Americans. To them Chinese speech seem exotic and incomprehensible, a tongue incomparable to the more familiar languages of Europe from which their own stock had sprung. To the American the Chinese speech melody seemed a cacophony; the accent it imposed on learned English was a cause for mirth and mimicry; and its characters, formed so carefully with a brush, seemed bizarre and utterly remote from the forms of European or American writing. Finally, and most important, it seemed fundamentally to be the case that Americans did not care to learn about the language or to learn to speak it. It was the immigrants' duty to learn English or suffer the consequences of restricted communication.

Third, and derivative from his language and culture, the Chinese stranger brought with him his ways of life, familiar and taken for granted to him, unfamiliar, peculiar, and sometimes frightening to Americans. Even in his absence from hearth and home, the overseas Chinese derived strength and purpose from his family. The Chinese ideal of family loyalty found painful expression in long term bachelorhood abroad, in the association of men of common surname in clans, and in the single-minded purposefulness of returning to wife and village to retire or die. The Chinese ideal of congregation beyond the family revealed itself in the *hui kuan* that united people of common dialect but divided persons who, though racially homogeneous, hailed from different speech communities of the same land. And the subterranean Chinese ideals of resistance, rebellion, and fraternal outlawry transplanted themselves in the form of the secret societies that sprang up wherever large numbers of Chinese settled, forming a parallel system of immigrant institutions inside the ghetto colony. Above all, the central characteristic of early Chinese community life that impressed itself on Americans was the immigrants' adherence to a system of *kadi* justice, traditional law, and partimonial power. Clans, *hui kuan*, and secret societies governed the lives of the immigrants, dispensed justice, adjudicated quarrels, settled disputes, levied fines, punished wrongdoers, and on occasion, meted out capital punishment. To the Americans, Chinese seemed to have established an *imperium in imperio*, a parallel state, and to owe to its institutions and leaders a depth of fealty and allegiance out of proportion to its worth and out of character with what Americans expected of its immigrants. To the Chinese the social system that they established in Chinatown was a familiar form of political and economic organization. It was not universally loved or even uniformly favored, but it was respected and for some revered.

However, it was not only their institutions that puzzled and angered Americans. The personal life and style of the Chinese excited curiosity and, on all too many occasions contempt. The plaited queue in which Chinese men wore their hair was a constant source of amusement and derision. The queue originated as a symbol of subjugation imposed on the Chinese people by the Manchu conquerors in 1645. Gradually it had evolved into the badge of citizenship in the imperial state. In the first half century of their immigration to America, Chinese were taunted about their "pigtails," shaved to the scalp by mobs and miscreants, and, in 1876, ordered by law to have their queues cut off if they served a sentence in prison or were jailed while awaiting trial. To Californians the blue overalls, loose-fitting shirts, and wide-brimmed black hat favored by the Chinese seemed less a costume than a uniform, and tended to encourage the belief that they were serfs and bondmen unfit for settlement in a free society. Further, the practice of binding the feet of women, common among Chinese gentry, but by no means uniform among peasantry and laborers, aroused shock and indignation.[1] Finally, the seemingly loose and dissolute life of Chinese bachelors evoked a chorus of moral imprecations against the immigrants from the Middle Kingdom. Condemned first by Chinese custom then by American law to an almost complete celibacy in the overseas country, the Chinese lived as homeless men, turning to prostitution for sexual outlet, gambling for recreational release, and on occasion smoking opium for surcease from the cares of their lonely sojourn.

As immigrants from a traditional society who had taken up temporary residence in a frontier land to make their fortunes, the Chinese exhibited special characteristics. They were in America not to colonize nor to spread the culture of China. Neither were they there to be absorbed into America's melting pot of races and nations. Rather the special and unique character of their immigration required them to *adapt* America and its ways to their own purposes rather than *adopt* it to the exclusion and surrender of their own values. The experiences to be had in America were bracketed within the all-encompassing goal of the trip itself: to acquire wealth which in the homeland could be used to recoup status lost by flood, poverty, or war, to demand greater esteem, and to enjoy a generally better life. In this sense the familiar context in which contemporary American scholars examine immigration history—in terms of "assimilation," "contributions," and "mobility patterns"—does not describe the Chinese immigrants' own perspective. He was there to earn enough money to leave; he was there in body alone, while his spirit remained in the homeland; he was there because it offered him an opportunity to pursue his aim, not because he desired to stamp its future history with his presence.

The Chinese approached American society with the outlook characteristic of sojourner strangers in general. The most prominent features of this outlook are an enterprising spirit, a willingness to move wherever opportunity beckons, an orientation toward the future that overrides both engrained tradition and current condition, and a freedom from convention. In spite of the hostile prejudices against them, the Chinese persevered and endured. Their efforts are testimony to the unsung genius and enormous capacity of an oppressed immigrant people.

The Chinese Immigrant as Sojourner

Those Chinese who stayed on in the overseas area, postponing their trip home year after year became the sojourner stock of America's pioneer Chinese (Siu 1952:34–44). The special psychological characteristic of the sojourner is manifested in his clinging to the culture and style of the country from which he has come. Despite having been transplanted, he retains the outlook of a Chinese villager, loyal to his family, nostalgic for the Cantonese countryside, friendly to the members of his *hui kuan*, and distant, aloof, and "objective" toward the peoples in the host society. Typically he is neither hostile nor despairing; rather he regards the conditions of his long lonely existence as a challenge to wit and patience. The overseas society exists for him as a job and an opportunity, neither as something to reject, rebuke, or revolt against. To the sojourner his own primary group— kin and friends in China—are the center of things. It is *for* them that he labors so long abroad. It is *to* them that he owes whatever his work may bring. It is *by* them that he will be honored and remembered. The sojourner is a man who remains in an alien country for a very long period of time without being assimilated by it.

As a Chinese wishing to remain Chinese the sojourner characteristically encloses himself in a Chinese world while abroad. "Chinatown," that quarter of the city reserved to Chinese businesses and residences, becomes his basic abode. To be sure his choice in this matter is not entirely voluntary; racial hostility, housing segregation, occupational exclusion, and the general pattern of discrimination in America combine to force ghettoization even on those who have more cosmopolitan outlooks. Nevertheless, in the ghetto, surrounded by compatriots who hail from his native land, the sojourner is in touch with his community and culture. The larger society is physically near but socially remote. Enclosed within the narrow confines of Chinatown, he eats, sleeps, works, and plays under the tutelage of his native values. So long as the outside society does not intrude on his solitude, he remains a Cantonese while abroad.

Even when he is bereft of a Chinese community, the sojourner may be able or be forced to retain his outlook. The lone Chinese laundryman in a white neighborhood, the solitary Chinese restauranteur in a small town, the Chinese cook on a remote ranch in the territory,[2] and the isolated Chinese student in a metropolitan university may keep their minds on their single purpose, their contacts secondary, and their associations brief. Cultural distance from the larger world may be enhanced by the language barrier, while a self-enforced isolation may reduce the possibility that major life adjustments will have to be made. Finally, the ready manner in which race contacts become institutionalized in a formal and rigid way may perforce assist the sojourner, whatever his real desire, to remain a stranger in the society.

For the sojourner life abroad is defined along the narrow lines of a job. It is something that must be done in order that something else shall follow it. Thus the overseas Chinese student studied so that he might assume a post as scientist, engineer, or diplomat in China; the overseas Chinese restauranteur cooked chop suey because that would hopefully make enough money to return home where chop suey was unknown; and the Chinese laundryman washed, ironed, and sewed because that was one of the few occupations open to Chinese men in a frontier society lacking large numbers of women. The job is not a career. It is a preparatory state of existence. But that preparatory state could and often did last the lifetime of the sojourner.

The Chinese laundryman is the sojourner par excellence. His job did not come to him by choice; rather it was gleaned from among the occupational leavings of the American frontier.[3] To be a laundryman in America did not entail a career commitment. Instead it involved the location in a job niche, an acquisition of the skill related to it, and the willingness to continue until fortune had at last smiled. All too often the millenial dream of good fortune receded into an ever-long future. But still the laundryman toiled on. Eventually his condition became ritualized, a thing in itself, rewarded by the small satisfactions of aiding wife and children in China, continued because nothing else seemed to suggest itself. The novelist L. C. Tsung has captured this condition in a passage from his novel, *The Marginal Man*:

> The neon sign of a Chinese hand laundry reminded Charles of the several shirts he had not yet picked up. The sign said Wen Lee, but Charles had never been able to ascertain whether the proprietor's family name was Wen or Lee. He entered the shop and saw the old man still hard at work behind the counter, ironing under a naked electric bulb, although it was already ten o'clock at night . . .
>
> 'How many years have you been in the States? ' Charles asked out of curiosity as he paid the man.
>
> 'Forty years,' the old man answered in Cantonese, and raised his four fingers again. No expression showed on his face.
>
> 'Do you have a family? '
>
> 'Big family. A woman, many sons and grandsons. All back home in Tangshan.'
>
> 'Have you ever gone back since you came out here?'

'No, I only send money,' replied the old man. From underneath the counter he brought out a photograph and showed it to Charles. In the center sat a white-haired old woman, surrounded by some fifteen or twenty men, women and children, of various ages. . . . The whole clan, with contented expressions on their faces, were the offspring of this emaciated old man, who supported not only himself but all of them by his two shaking, bony hands. They seemed to represent the flow of a great river of life, originating from a tiny stream. The stream may dry up some day, but the river flows on. The old man put on his glasses again and identified each person in the picture to Charles Lin. A toothless smile came to his expressionless face. Charles Lin realized that this picture was the old man's only comfort and relaxation. He had toiled like a beast of burden for forty years to support a large family which was his aim of existence, the sole meaning of his life. The picture to him was like a diploma, a *summa cum laude* to an honor student. Behind the facade of sadness and resignation there was the inner satisfaction which made this old man's life bearable and meaningful (Tsung 1963:158–59).

The Chinese Immigrant as Homegoer

Should he fulfill his dream in the overseas country, the Chinese immigrant returned home. To do so was to retranspose memory back into experience. The customs, ways, and institutions of China that he carried away with him into the diaspora were discovered again, life was recreated in its original form, and the joys of the familiar were again a source of everyday happiness. Such at any rate was the ideal. However, two sets of changes marred this wish-fulfilling picture and rendered the dream less of a possibility than the dreamer supposed.

To the Chinese the picture of returning home was clear enough. Pardee Lowe, the son of a Chinese immigrant to America, describes his father's image of what it would mean to return to China: "Father was deeply sensible of the great honors which would be bestowed upon him if he returned to Sahn Kay Sawk. All kinsmen who returned, he remembered, were held in very high esteem. Because of their fortunes they were not treated as ordinary villagers who had never gone abroad. Instead, they were hailed as *Kum Sahn Hock* (Guests from the Golden Mountains). Nothing the village could offer was too good for him. They feasted off the fat of the land, and were treated as mandarins" (Lowe 1943:5).

This image of the return to China presumes that the historical and cultural clock will stand still, that the society that was left behind will remain as it was, that its traditions will not erode, its customs not expire, its fundamental ways not change. So long as the time between departure and the return was short and so long as no major change cracked the cake of custom in traditional China this presumption remained valid. However, for many Chinese what began as a brief and profitable sojourn abroad turned into years of exile. Thus after decades of waiting for his return a Chinese wife wrote to her husband, "You promised me to go abroad for only three years, but you have stayed there nearly thirty years now" (Siu 1952:35–36). As the decades abroad passed China changed. In 1911 the Manchu Empire fell before the onslaught of Sun Yat Sen and his revolutionaries. The warring factions eventually united under Chiang Kai-Shek or joined the growing Communist Movement. A few independent warlords played politics with the scene. In 1949 the Communists succeeded in capturing the state and driving Chiang and his minions to Formosa. Throughout all this period many overseas Chinese held fast to their dream. Those who returned found a different China than the one they had left.

After 1949 the Chinese in America were cut off from remigration. In fact, although few overseas Chinese realize it, the diaspora had ended. For the aged Chinese the sojourn had become a permanent exile. In 1962 William Willmott and I interviewed an aged Chinese in Welles, British Columbia. He told us he had a wife in China he had not seen in forty-five years and a son he had never seen. He said that he received letters from them regularly. When we asked when he planned to rejoin his wife and son, he sighed and said "Maybe, next year." Then he asked if the present regime in China treated old people well; he was afraid, he said, and wondered what would happen to him if he returned.

However, even if the traditional home had not changed during his absence, the immigrant had. The years abroad in the new society could not help but leave their mark. Perhaps he had learned another language and back in his home country found himself thinking— and even occasionally, speaking—in that tongue. More likely he had acquired new skills, interests, and habits which estranged him from his fellow men at home. Some Chinese severed their queues while in America and had so come to favor the tonsorial styles of the Occident that they were embarrassed at the requirement in force until 1911 that they rebraid their hair when they remigrated to China. Abroad the Chinese immigrant had—perhaps unconsciously—

come to incorporate and appreciate some of the fundamental ideas and everyday practices of America as his own. Back home in China he found himself alienated from his own people—not Chinese anymore, but certainly not an acculturated American either.

However, many of those who dreamed of going home one day from the overseas adventure could not make enough money to do so. To assuage their loneliness and, often enough, to marry and sire children, they became birds-of-passage, returning to China every few years to marry, visit with their wife, enjoy the comforts of hearth and home, and then going back to the immigrant colony where they labored in lonely solitude. Pardee Lowe recalls that his father had at one time returned to China to acquire a wife, repay the debts of his family, and retire in luxury. However, "Marriage and redemption of the family homestead soon exhausted Father's meager fortune. He returned to America, not gladly from all I heard, but reconciled. Thousands of Chinese were doing the same thing every year; spending in their native villages a fortune gained abroad, and coming back to this country to toil laboriously to acquire the necessary money to repeat their trip" (Lowe 1945:7).

Even some of those who returned for good did not resume an ordinary life. All too often the "fortune" that they had earned abroad was eaten up by family debts, by bribes to the ubiquitous corrupt magistrates, and by the inevitable feasts, gifts, and ostentatious splendor required of one who had made a success of himself. After funds had been exhausted some new means for making a living had to be found. Sometimes the skills acquired abroad could be turned to use nearer to home. A nice example is found in the recollections of Hosea Ballou Morse, a scholar and administrator who was quite familiar with old China:

> An incident which occurred to the author in 1893 throws some light on the usual result to a returned Chinese emigrant. At a railroad station in Formosa he was addressed in fluent and correct English by the proprietor-cook of the station restaurant; and in answer to a question of astonishment, the Chinese explained why he was there. He had returned from California with a fortune of $2,000.00. He had first to disburse heavily to remain unmolested by the magistrate and his underlings; then he had to relieve the necessities of his aged father; then an uncle, who had fallen into business difficulties, must be rescued from impending bankruptcy; and then he found he had only

enough left to procure himself a wife, with a few dollars margin wherewith to establish himself in his present business, which at most would require $100.00 capital. (Morse 1910:166n).

Marginal Men

If the immigrant who stayed became a permanent sojourner, his children found themselves one step removed from that condition yet not fully a part of the society in which they had been born. They were, in Robert Park's memorable words, marginal men: "The marginal man is a personality type that arises at a time and a place where, out of the conflict of races and cultures, new societies, new peoples and cultures are coming into existence. The fate which condemns him to live, at the same time, in two worlds is the same which compels him to assume, in relation to the worlds in which he lives, the role of a cosmopolitan and a stranger" (Park 1961:xvii).

As marginal men American born Chinese experienced the variety of senses in which they were cultural hybrids. The Chinese Americans were products of two cultures, partial members of two societies. They shared in the cultural traditions and social life of America and of Chinatown intimately at some times, formally at others, on occasion casually, but in some instances with excruciating if silent anguish. Not quite able to break with the manners and customs of their parents, they were still unable to completely join in the ways of America. Racial prejudice kept them at a distance from white America, while Americanization reduced their commitment to Chinatown. The Chinese American, like the second generation of other ethnic groups, "was a man on the margin of two cultures and two societies, which never completely interpenetrated and fused" (Park 1950:354).

One aspect of their condition that differentiated American born Chinese from children of European immigrants was race. So long as America retained its racial prejudice and racist practices, acculturation would not result in acceptance. As late as 1939 William Carlson Smith observed that "Many years will pass before American-born Chinese and Japanese in California will be accepted by the white group, no matter how thoroughly Americanized they become. Skin color and the slant [sic] of eyes categorically classify them with their alien parents" (Smith 1939:369). In their relations with other Americans, the offspring of immigrants from China discovered the ubiquitous intrusiveness of race.

Even when Chinese Americans believed that they had overcome racial prejudices and unfavorable stereotypes they unexpectedly encountered hostilities and antagonisms. A student in a midwestern college reported on an ugly interracial incident that later gave way to friendship:

> In college I was taken into a fraternity. In my second year I took part in the initiation of the new men. We had them lined up and were paddling them with some boards and staves. Several of the fellows had paddled them and then my turn came. After I had given one of the fellows a swat he turned around and said, 'You damned Chink! What business do you have to hit me?' That was a big shock to me. Why should he pick on me? I said nothing and when it came to the election I voted that he be received. After some time we became the best of friends (Smith 1937:193).

But the racial distinction often combined with cultural tradition to stigmatize a Chinese American not only in the country of his birth but also in that of his parents. Such experiences served to drive home the unique position of the second generation Chinese, impressing upon him the fact that he was caught in the middle of a conflict over which he had little control. For example, an Hawaiian-born Chinese girl who had been treated as an American in Honolulu discovered quite a different response in California: "I gradually learned that I was a foreigner—a Chinese—that I would be wiser to admit it and to disclaim my American citizenship, particularly when I was in a Chinese group. I accepted my title as a foreign student more graciously. I became more accustomed to the stares of the American people, to their remarks, and to their sneers. I did not feel inferior to them; I did not feel antagonistic toward them; but I was disappointed and deeply hurt" (Smith 1939:372). But when this girl despaired of America, schooled herself in the Chinese language and culture, and journeyed to the land of her parents' birth, she found that she was still a foreigner, an Americanized Chinese and thus an alien to China's ways: "I gave up trying to be a Chinese; for as soon as the people in China learned that I was an oversea [sic] Chinese, they remarked, 'Oh, you are a foreigner.' Some asked, 'Where did you learn to speak Chinese?' Some thought it remarkable that I spoke Chinese at all. So you see I was quite foreign to China. I wore Chinese clothes and tried to pass as a Chinese, but I could not so I gave up and admitted my foreign birth and education" (Smith 1937:245). As she lived and reflected on her experiences in China, Hawaii, and California, the girl was torn between the questions of identity. To be neither Chinese to people of her lineage nor American to people of her birthplace left her in limbo. But limbo is a land where few care to live and most journey out of it—to compromise and anguish and, perhaps, resignation. The girl concludes:

> I lack very much a Chinese background, Chinese culture, and Chinese manners and customs; I have neither their viewpoint nor their patience. Sometimes I was homesick for America. Where I had friends, I felt better. I got more or less adjusted to some things—one of them was the rickshaw. But most of the time, I had very mixed feelings. I find that unconsciously now I try to avoid the subject of China; I try to put it out of my mind and attention; I don't want to think or feel about China . . . America is really my country and my home (Smith 1937: 243–44).

Marginality is a problem not only vis a vis the dominant racial group but also in relation to the self. It produces one of the cardinal elements of *anomie*—*self estrangement*. Alienation from one's own self is a probability when psychosocial acculturation is accompanied by racial stigma. In such a situation individuals find that their bodies are problematic to them—are issues worthy of both philosophical reflection and worrisome anxiety. To an American-born Chinese the very face he or she presents, masking behind its Oriental visage a half-American mind, may evoke a painful, even excruciating, contradiction. Frank Chin captures this moment of self-estrangement in his haunting novel about Dirigible, a young man of San Francisco's Chinatown: "The clean shaven face, washed and dried, cleanly drily opaque, pinkish, brownish, yellow and vaguely luminescent in the light was grand. Seeing his skin in the mirror, touching his face with his fingers, he sensed color and essence stimulated to movement through his face like petals and leaves stiffening in the sunlight. Pockmarked, lined, shadowed, full of character, like the face of a mudflat dried into a desert of potato chips. Dirigible's real face. . . . The face was forced still, to be looked at in the mirror by him" (Chin 1970:30–31).

Beneath the sense of dual and unresolved identity, and beyond the angst of self-estrangement, the Chinese American senses his or her own nonmembership in the two cultures. Product of both, member of neither, he or she lives between them, participating in the activities appropriate to both but feeling his or her alien identity even as he or she acts. Victor Wong, a Chinese American who grew up in San Francisco's Chinatown in the 1930s, vividly recalls the pain and misunderstanding that arose from his marginal status:

So we *were* all immigrants in those days, no matter where we were born. Between the Chinese and the English education, we had no idea where we belonged. Even to this day, if I wanted to say I'm going to China I would never say it that way; I would say go *back* to China. Because I was taught from the time I was born that this was not my country, that I would have to go to China to make my living as an adult. And I think that if it hadn't been for the Japanese War—that is with the Americans; December 7, 1941—many of us *would* probably have had to go back to China, with our parents (Wong 1970:70).

Until the outbreak of World War II Chinese immigrants retained a sojourner attitude not only for themselves but for their children as well. The sacred duty to be buried in the village of one's father's birth meant little to Chinese born in the United States, but prejudice and discrimination served as a constant reminder of their unequal status and limited opportunities in America. Parents would counsel their children to pay little heed to the daily slights and the legal, occupational, and social restrictions they encountered—except to let those acts of injustice remind them that their ultimate future was in China and, in the interim, in Chinatown. Therefore, parents would advise their children, both a Chinese and an American education was very important. The English schools would provide one with the training, skills, and techniques that would prove useful in China; the Chinese language school would provide one with the language, customs, and traditions that would make it possible to assume a new life in the homeland of their parents. Chinese American youths were encouraged to adopt a diligent but instrumental orientation toward America and what it had to offer. They were to acquire its methods and technics—but they were not to be seduced by its culture, style, and way of life. Though born and reared in America, they were to remain Chinese.

At the same time the schools were interested in Americanizing the offspring of all immigrants, though not necessarily in encouraging all of them to aspire after social equality. Chinese children were required to speak, read, and write English. They were taught to revere American Revolutionary War leaders as the Founding Fathers of *their* country. Chinese Americans absorbed many of the ways of America readily and as a matter of course in school, in the mass media, and in extracurricular activities. As Chinese Americans they found that they could not step into the white American mainstream because of severe racial prejudice and discrimination. But neither

could they acquiesce to a sojourner existence; their own acculturation had progressed too far. Caught between the poles of absorption
and remigration, they managed an existence, carving a way of life
out of the half-a-loaf provided to them by Chinatown and the larger
society, respectively.

The ambiguity of this existence produced a painful and awkward
adjustment for the Chinese Americans. Many found themselves
thinking more and more like their white peers but denied the opportunity to practice an American way of life. Respectful to their parents, they nevertheless could not conform to their wishes.

The remarkable difference in discipline and self-control in the
American public and Chinese language schools is a reflection of the
dual existence that characterized life in general for Chinese Americans. Galen Chow, who studied in San Francisco's afternoon Chinatown schools in the early 1940s, recalls the experience in a vivid
description of children's life among second generation Chinese in
America. Chow's parents had carefully advised him on proper behavior in public school.

> In contrast no pressure was exerted by my parents to do any-
> thing but attend Chinese school. This double standard led to a
> Jekyll-Hyde existence for me on school days. In public school I
> was a model of deportment, studious and courteous. In Chi-
> nese school I was a little terror—baiting the teacher constantly,
> fighting and getting into all kinds of mischief. The reason for
> my parents' attitudes was not lost on me. In public school,
> where all the teachers were white, I had to present my best pos-
> ture in order not to shame the Chinese in general and my family
> in particular. In Chinese school where all the students and
> teachers were Chinese we could revert to normal. However,
> probably due to the strain of my role playing in public school,
> I would react to an extreme when turned loose in Chinese
> school. Generally, I think these actions and reactions were true
> to some extent, more or less, in all the Chinese children.

Helen Lowe summed up this cultural generation gap when she
said, "Father's American ways are not American enough, and as for
his Chinese habits and ideas, they are queer, unreasonable, and humiliating!" (Lowe 1943:175). Her brother, Pardee, has recorded in
minute detail the increasing tide of his own Americanization—the
move to larger quarters for the family, the purchase and installation
of a bathtub to replace the wooden bucket used throughout his childhood, the long struggle to obtain his father's permission to enter

Stanford University, and finally his marriage to a white girl (Lowe 1945:149–61, 174–95, 225–37). However, the Horatio Alger success story did not describe the life of all Chinese Americans. Elmer Wok Wai, born at the turn of the century into the slum of San Francisco's Chinatown, saw his brother and sister sold to meet expenses, was educated in an asylum for wayward youth, and then turned out into the streets. He became a thug and strong-arm man for a Chinese secret society, killed a man, and spent seventeen years in San Quentin prison. After being paroled he ended his days as an overworked and underpaid domestic in the employ of white people (Griggs 1969).

Even when their lives overseas were eventually crowned with success, Chinese Americans suffered because of their marginal status. Pardee Lowe became estranged from his father for two years and spoke to him only when necessary after they had quarreled bitterly over the proper way to live in America (Lowe 1945:176–78). Jade Snow Wong, whose ceramics became internationally renowned in the 1940s, entered into her life's work under a double burden. As a Chinese American she suffered from the prejudices and stereotypes commonly inflicted on members of her race; as a woman she had to overcome the traditional Chinese view that opposed the presence of women in independent professions (J. Wong 1945:211–46). Rose Hum Lee, born into a Montana family of Chinese descent, endured both local and family ostracism and generalized racial discrimination in her efforts to become a leading sociologist specializing in the study of Chinese Americans (Lee 1960). Victor Wong, a Chinese American born and reared in San Francisco, benefited from the greater opportunities for Chinese Americans during World War II and became an engineer. But he anguished so much over his ambiguous status in America that he first repudiated his Chinese background and sought a complete American identity, then, unhappy in that situation, he returned to an all-Chinese setting and resumed a more ethnically exclusive existence (V. Wong 1970:71–72).

Before World War II the likelihood that many Chinese Americans would realize a secure and productive life in America seemed remote.[4] Up until the 1940s the number of Chinese born in America had been low because of the shortage of women in the immigrant group. The few Chinese Americans who reached maturity in the first thirty years of the twentieth century entered into the business established by their kinsmen in Chinatown—restaurants, laundries, curio shops—or went to China to make a living.

The idea of a career in China excited much interest among young American-born Chinese in the 1920s and 30s. However, among those

Chinese Americans who went to China were many who found themselves even more estranged than they had felt in the United States.
Moreover, the social unrest that characterized China's internal condition in the first half of the century did not recommend itself to too
many overseas Chinese. In some Chinatown families brothers divided over how to proceed, one choosing China, while the other
chose Chinatown. In 1926 Winifred Raushenbush, a research associate of Robert E. Park, reported on what she regarded as a Chinese
American success story (Raushenbush 1926:221). An old Chinatown
family had two sons. One had become an engineer, gone to China,
and was, at the time of her research, helping "Sun Yat Sen to work
out his ideas about the harbors of Canton." The other had graduated
from Stanford University where he had been a football player, and
become a businessman and politician conciliating the warring factions in San Francisco's Chinatown. The latter "is a man who, because of his popularity as an athlete, and because of the wide diverse
human curiosities which have made him a politician, finds himself
at home both in America and Chinatown, free to go back and forth
from one to the other. . . . He has solved in his own person a problem
vastly more important to Chinatown than that of the fighting tongs;
he has gotten out of the ghetto."

However, most Chinese could not get out of the ghetto. As late as
the 1930s Chinese parents urged their children to prepare themselves for a life in China. Jade Snow Wong's father "encouraged her
to make the mastery of Chinese her main objective; for he wanted
her to go to China to study after high school graduation. He thought
that a Chinese could realize his optimum achievement only in
China." Her brother was also urged to think of China as his future
home. "Father and son agreed that the study of medicine in China
would prepare Older Brother for his career. Knowing the Chinese
language, he could establish himself where medical personnel was
greatly needed, and he could strengthen his ancestral ties by visits to
Daddy's native village and relatives" (J. Wong 1945:95). Victor Wong
bitterly recalls that in the 1930s "it was always China that we were
taught was home. In those days we were all *immigrants*. Whether
we were born in America, or not, we were all immigrants." (V. Wong
1970:24).

If China seemed uninviting and white America too formidable,
the Chinatown beckoned feebly to some young Chinese Americans.
In 1926 a young American-born Chinese told Winifred Raushenbush, "Just wait until the native-born ride into power here among
the Chinese in San Francisco—which will happen sometime within

the next ten or twelve years—and you will see a different Chinatown" (Raushenbush 1926:221). More Chinese Americans turned to
work in restaurants, laundries, curio shops, and the Chinatown lot-
tery in this period than went to China. But beginning in the 1930s
more Chinese were being born in America and the pressure of Chinatowns to absorb this growing population portended difficulty. In
the same period the Rocky Mountain Chinatowns began to decline,
and Chinese from Montana to Arizona began migrating to San Francisco, Chicago, and New York, centers of Chinese settlement in
America. Chinatown's capacity to house and employ America's Chinese became taxed just as the Great Depression set in.

However successful it was as an arena of employment, the ghetto
contained its American-born Chinese so well that they had little
contact with those white outsiders with whom they might have
shared a common outlook. Galen Chow recalls that during his childhood in San Francisco's Chinatown all his chums were fellow Chinese of the second generation, and with the exception of his white
public school teachers, he had almost no contact with white America: "We all played in and around the streets and buildings of Chinatown with an air of proprietorship. We knew every street, alley,
unusual building, and every nook and cranny of Chinatown. We
were less sure of ourselves when we ventured out of Chinatown either by ourselves or with our parents and at these times would
present our stereotypical personalities of the subdued, unscrutable
Oriental to the white world."

The era of Chinese diaspora in America began to erode in the decade that began with the admission of Chinese to quota status as immigrants and the right of naturalization (1943) and concluded with
the triumph of the communist revolution in China. Since then Chinese have become more and more a national minority in polyglot
America. With the sex ratio coming ever more into balance, the marriage of American-born Chinese to one another increasing, and the
birth and maturation of second and third generations in the United
States, we may speak of the shift from a diasporic people to an ethnic
group. Characteristic of this change is the beginnings of filiopietistic
history, the interest in discovering Chinese "contributions" to America, the search for ethnic origins, and the rise of Asian American
studies. There is also the noticeable difference between the attitudes
of the American-born and the newly arrived immigrants. The new
gangs of American Chinatowns give violent expression to this fact as
they organize along lines that separate the native American from the
youths recently arrived from Hong Kong. And the old institutions of

Chinatown—the clans, *hui kuan*, and secret societies—struggle to maintain themselves in the face of the acculturation and suburbanization of the growing Chinese American middle class and diffidence, hostility, and intractability of the new immigrants.

Paradoxically perhaps, the best evidence of the decline of diaspora is the rise of historical and national consciousness. Membership in the peoplehood of Chinese was a taken-for-granted feature of the immigrant group and the first small cohorts of American-born Chinese. It is among the Americanized generations, the college-bound, and university educated that the gnawing sense of ambivalence and anguish over identity finds anguished expression. Seeking a break away from the brass of America that once seemed like gold to their grandfathers, this generation turns to ethnicity, rediscovers history, defines culture, and attempts to reenter the community. The new Chinese represent America as it is—neither a melting pot nor a mosaic, rather a plurality of interests, values, institutions, and sentiments in less than equal or peaceful coexistence. But that is the story for another essay. For the moment we might dwell on the realities and sentiments of the last era—diaspora and its consequences. It shall not be with us again.

NOTES

This essay originally appeared in *The Life, Influence, and the Role of the Chinese in the United States, 1776–1960*, proceedings/papers of the National Conference of the Chinese Historical Society of America (San Francisco: Chinese Historical Society of America, 1976), pp. 128–47.

1. A Chinese woman in traditional dress and with bound feet had been exhibited as a freak attraction on Broadway in 1834. Missionaries exhorted the Chinese to halt this practice and cited it frequently as evidence of the horrors and immorality that characterized pagan peoples.

2. A poignant example is provided by Frederic Remington's description of a ranch cook at the hacienda of San Jose de Bavicora in a remote part of Mexico: " 'Charlie Jim,' the Chinese cook, has a big room with a stove in it, and he and the stove are a never-ending wonder to all the folks, and the fame of both has gone across the mountains to Sonora and to the south. Charlie is an autocrat in his curious Chinese way, and by the dignity of his position as Mr. Jack's private cook and his unknown antecedents, he conjures the Mexicans and d——s the Texans, which latter refuse to take him seriously and kill him, as they would a 'proper' man. Charlie Jim, in return, entertains ideas of Texans which he secretes, except when they dine with Jack, when he may be heard to mutter, 'Cake and pie no good for puncher, make him fat and lazy'; and when he cross the patio and they fling

a rope over his foot, he becomes livid; and breaks out, 'Da——puncher; da——rope; rope man all same horse; da——puncher; no good that way.' " "An Outpost of Civilization," *Frederick Remington's Own West*, ed. Harold McCracken (New York: Dial Press, 1960), p. 139.

3. In an autobiographical novel, Lin Yutang has presented this idea in a sensitive speech by a Chinatown laundryman to his son: "I did not choose, son. And it is not bad as you can see. I have made a living, and we are now all here. There was no other way. All you have is a pair of hands, and you do what the Americans do not want to do and allow you to do. When they built the railroads in the West, there were no women there. Those American men. They could not cook, and they could not wash. We Chinese cooked and washed better, so they allowed us to cook and wash. Now we wash America and cook America because we wash better and cook better. I would have opened a restaurant if I had the money" (Lin Yutang 1948:27).

4. As the number of Chinese Americans began to grow and their education improved, Chinese community leaders expressed concern for their future. In 1929, Chinatown newspaper editor Ng Poon Chew observed: "Perhaps the future of our American born Chinese will have to look to China for their life work. In this there is much hope. China will open thousands of lines for ambitious modernized young men to utilize their learnings to help develop the country's resources" (Ng 1970:8).

REFERENCES

Blauner, Robert. 1972. *Racial Oppression in America*. New York: Harper and Row.

Bogardus, Emory. 1928. *Immigration and Race Attitudes*. Boston: D. C. Heath.

Camus, Albert. 1955. *The Myth of Sisyphus and Other Essays*, translated by Justin O'Brien. New York: Vintage.

Chin, Frank. 1970. "Goong Hai Fot Choy," from *A Chinese Lady Dies*, in Ishmael Reed, ed., *19 Necromancers from Now*. Garden City, N.Y.: Doubleday.

Chow, Galen. 1972. "Reflections of a Yellow Boy in a White Society *circa* 1938–1950." Unpublished Manuscript.

Cicourel, Aaron. 1974. *Cognitive Sociology: Language and Meaning in Social Interaction*. New York: The Free Press.

Crèvecoeur, J. Hector St. John de. 1957. *Letters from an American Farmer*. New York: E. P. Dutton.

Garfinkel, Harold. 1967 *Studies in Ethnomethodology*. Englewood Cliffs, N.J.: Prentice-Hall.

George, Henry. 1869. "The Chinese on the Pacific Coast." *New York Tribune*, May 1.

Griggs, Veta. 1969. *Chinaman's Chance: The Life Story of Elmer Wok Wai*. New York: Exposition Press.

Lee, Rose Hum. 1960. *The Chinese in the United States of America.* Hong Kong: Hong Kong University Press.

Lin Yutang. 1948. *Chinatown Family.* New York: John Day and Co.

Lowe, Pardee. 1943. *Father and Glorious Descendant.* Boston: Little, Brown and Co.

Lyman, Stanford and Scott, Marvin. 1970. *A Sociology of the Absurd.* New York: Appleton-Century-Crofts.

McCracken, Harold, ed. 1960. *Frederick Remington's Own West.* New York: Dial Press.

Morse, Hosea Ballou. n.d. *The International Relations of the Chinese Empire. Vol. 2: The Period of Submission, 1861–1893.* Taipei: n.p.

Myrdal, Gunnar, with the assistance of Richard Sterner and Arnold Rose. 1944. *An American Dilemma: The Negro Problem and Modern Democracy.* New York: Harper and Brothers.

Ng Poon Chew. 1970. "Letter to Samuel H. Cohn, July 4, 1929," in Edward K. Strong, *The Second Generation Japanese Problem.* New York: Arno Press and the New York Times.

Novak, Michael. 1971. *The Rise of the Unmeltable Ethnics: The New Political Force of the Seventies.* New York: Macmillan.

Park, Robert E. 1950. *The Collected Papers of Robert Ezra Park, Vol. 1.* Edited by Everett Cherrington Hughes et al. Glencoe, Ill.: The Free Press.

———. 1961. "Introduction" to Everett V. Stonequist, *The Marginal Man: A Study in Personality and Culture Conflict.* New York: Russell and Russell.

Raushenbush, Winifred. 1926. "The Great Wall of Chinatown: How the Chinese Mind Their Own Business Behind It." *The Survey Graphic,* 56:3, May 1.

Schrag, Peter. 1970. *The Decline of the Wasp.* New York: Simon and Schuster.

Schutz, Alfred. 1967. *The Phenomenology of the Social World,* translated by George Walsh and Frederick Lehnert. Evanston: Northwestern University Press.

Simmel, Georg. 1950. "The Stranger," in *The Sociology of Georg Simmel,* translated and edited by Kurt Wolff. Glencoe, Ill.: The Free Press.

Siu, Paul C. P. 1952. "The Sojourner." *American Journal of Sociology,* 8, July.

Smith, William Carlson. 1937. *Americans in Process: A Study of Our Citizens of Oriental Ancestry.* Ann Arbor: Edwards Brothers.

———. 1939. *American in the Making: The Natural History of the Assimilation of Immigrants.* New York: D. Appleton-Century Co.

Sombart, Werner. 1962. *The Jews and Modern Capitalism,* translated by M. Epstein. New York: Collier Books.

Stonequist, Everett. 1961. *The Marginal Man: A Study in Personality and Culture Conflict.* New York: Russell and Russell.

Tsung, L. C. 1963. *The Marginal Man.* New York: Pageant Press.

Wong, Jade Snow. 1945. *Fifth Chinese Daughter.* New York: Harper and Brothers.

Wong, Victor. 1970. "Childhood 1930s" and "Childhood II," in *Ting: The Cauldron: Chinese Art and Identity in San Francisco.* San Francisco: Glide Urban Center.

9

Contrasts in the Community Organization of Chinese and Japanese in North America

Race relations theory and policy in North America have for the most part been built upon examination of the experiences and difficulties of European immigrants and African Americans. As a result contrasting ideas and programs, emphasizing integration for the latter and cultural pluralism for the former, have been generated primarily in consideration of each group's most manifest problems.[1] However, relatively little work has been done to ascertain the conditions under which an ethnic group is likely to follow an integration-oriented or a pluralist-oriented path.[2] Two racial groups found in North America—the Chinese and the Japanese—are likely candidates for the focus of such research, since they have superficially similar outward appearances, a long history as victims of oppression, discrimination, and prejudice, but quite different developments in community organization and cohesion.[3] In this essay an attempt is made to ascertain the distinctive features of the culture and social organization of the two immigrant groups that played significant roles in directing the mode of community organization in North America.

There is sound theoretical ground for reconsidering the role of Old World culture and social organization on immigrant communities in North America. Even in what might seem the paradigm case of cultural destruction in the New World—that of the African American—there is evidence to suggest at least vestiges of cultural survival.[4] In those ethnic communities unmarred by so culturally demoralizing a condition as slavery, there survives what Nathan Glazer calls elements of a "ghost nation," so that despite its fires social life goes on at least in part "beyond the melting pot."[5] American ideology has stressed assimilation, but its society is marked by European, Asian, and some African survivals; Canadian ideology has stressed the "mosaic" of cultures, but at least some of its peoples show definite signs of being Canadianized. The immigrants' cultural baggage needs sociological inspection to ascertain its effects on community organization and acculturation. Fortunately, the Chinese and Japanese communities provide opportunities for this research because of new knowledge about the Old Asian World[6] and extensive material on their lives in North America.

The Chinese

In contrast to the Japanese and several European groups, the Chinese in Canada and the United States present an instance of unusually persistent social isolation and preservation of Old World values and institutions.[7] To the present day a great many Chinese work, play, eat, and sleep in the Chinese ghettos known throughout North America as "Chinatowns." The business ethics of Chinatown's restaurants and bazaars are institutionalized in guild and trade associations more reflective of nineteenth-century Cathay than twentieth-century North America. Newly arrived Chinese lads work a twelve to sixteen hour day as waiters and busboys totally unprotected by labor unions. Immigrant Chinese mothers sit in rows in tiny "sweatshops" sewing dresses for downtown shops while infants crawl at their feet. In basements below the street level or in rooms high above the colorfully-lit avenue, old men gather round small tables to gamble at *f'an t'an, p'ai kop piu,* or other games of chance. Above the hubbub of activity in the basements, streets, stores, and sweatshops are the offices of clan associations, speech and territorial clubs, and secret societies. And behind the invisible wall that separates Chinatown from the metropolis the elites of these organizations conduct an unofficial government, legislating, executing, and adjudicating matters for their constituents.

Not every Chinese in Canada or the United States today recognizes the sovereignty of Chinatown's power elite or receives its benefits and protections.[8] At one time San Francisco's "Chinese Six Companies" and Vancouver's Chinese Benevolent Association could quite properly claim to speak for all the Chinese in the two countries. But that time is now past. Students from Hong Kong and Taiwan and Chinese intellectuals, separated in social origins, status, and aspirations from other Chinese, have cut themselves off from their Chinatown compatriots. Another segment of the Chinese population, the Canadian-born and American-born, who have acquired citizenship in the country of their birth, not only exhibits outward signs of acculturation in dress, language, and behavior, but also grants little if any obeisance to Chinatown's elites. Some of this generation now find it possible to penetrate the racial barrier, and pass into the workaday world of the outer society with impunity. Others still work or reside in Chinatown but are too acculturated to be subject to its private law. Still a few others are active in the traditional associations seeking power and status within the framework of the old order.

That North America's Chinatowns are not merely creatures of the American environment is indicated by the relatively similar institutionalization of Chinese communities in other parts of the world.[9] The diaspora of Chinese in the last two centuries has populated Southeast Asia, the Americas, Europe, and Africa with Asian colonies. Should the tourists who today pass along Grant Avenue in San Francisco, Pender Street in Vancouver, and Pell and Mott Streets in New York City, peering at exotic food and art, and experiencing the sights, sounds, and smells of these cities' Chinatowns, be whisked away to Manila, Bangkok, Singapore, or Semarang, or suddenly find themselves in Calcutta, Liverpool, or the capital of the Malagasy Republic, they would discover, amidst the unfamiliarity of the several national cultures, still other "Chinatowns" not unlike their North American counterparts. Recognition of the recalcitrance of overseas Chinese to their surroundings takes different forms in different places. In the United States sociologists marvel at their resistance to the fires of the melting pot; in Indonesia the government questions the loyalty of this alien people; in Malaysia native farmers and laborers resent the vivid contrast between their own poverty and Chinese commercial affluence; in Jamaica Chinese are urged to quit their exclusiveness and become part of the larger community. But everywhere the issue is acculturation. Despite more than a century of migration, the Chinese have not fully adopted the culture, language, behaviour—the ways of life—of the countries in which they have settled. Their cultural exclusiveness—especially as it finds its expression in territorially compact and socially distant communities within the host societies' cities—is a world-historical event deserving far more discussion and research than it has yet been given.

The Japanese

The rapid acculturation of the Japanese in North America has been a source of frequent discussion. The fact that "Japan-town" is not as familiar a term to North Americans as "Chinatown" is an unobtrusive measure of this difference between the two peoples. Such local

names as "Li'l Tokyo" or Li'l Yokohama" have been short-lived references for Japanese communities isolated through discrimination,
but these have rarely been characterized by such peculiar institutions and private government as are found in the Chinese quarter.
Japanese-owned businesses are not organized on the basis of guilds
or zaibatsu; prefectural associations exist primarily for nostalgic and
ceremonial purposes, playing no effective part in political organization in the community; and secret societies like those so prominent
among the Chinese are not found in North American Japanese communities. Neither sweatshops nor gambling houses are established
institutions of Japanese-American or Japanese-Canadian communities. Indeed, in the territorial sense, the North American Japanese
communities show increasing signs of disintegration.

Although overseas Chinese communities exhibit the characteristics of colonization with a superordinate organization to represent
them to the larger society, the Japanese are organized on patterns
closer to that of a reluctant minority group.[10] The earliest associations among immigrant Japanese emphasized defense against prejudice and support for the larger society's laws and customs, and these
organizations have been supplanted by even more acculturation-
oriented organizations in the second generation. Japanese are the
only ethnic group to emphasize geo-generational distinctions by a
separate nomenclature and a belief in the unique character structure
of each generational group. Today the third and fourth generations in
North America (Sansei and Yonsei, respectively) exhibit definite
signs of a "Hansen effect"—that is, interest in recovering Old World
culture—and also show concern over the appropriate allocation of
their energies and activities to things American or Canadian and
things Japanese. Ties to a Japanese community are tenuous and find
their realization primarily in recreational pursuits. Marriage with
whites is at an all-time high for these generations.

Although the situation is by no means so clear, overseas Japanese
communities outside North America exhibit some patterns similar
to and some quite different from those of the continental United
States and Canada. In the most extensive study of acculturation
among Japanese in prewar Kona, Hawaii, the community appeared
organized less along Japanese than Hawaiian-American lines. Other
studies of Japanese in Hawaii have emphasized the innovative food
habits, decline of the patriarch, and changing moral bases of family
life. On the other hand, Japanese in Peru, where Japan's official policy of emigration played a significant role in establishing the colony
and supervising its affairs, had maintained a generally separate

though financially successful and occupationally diversified community until 1942; postwar developments indicate that the Peruvian-born Japanese will seek and obtain increasing entrance into Peruvian society and further estrangement from all-Japanese associations. In Brazil, a situation similar to that of Peru developed: sponsored migration reached great heights during the period of Japan's imperialist development, and, although Brazil welcomed Japanese until 1934, a policy of coerced assimilation motivated by suspicion of Japanese intent led to a closing of many all-Japanese institutions before the outbreak of World War II. In the postwar period, Brazilian-born Japanese indicated a greater interest than their parents had in integration into Brazilian society. However, in recent years, a downturn in the Brazilian economy has led many third-generation Japanese Brazilians to seek work in Japan. In Paraguay, where the first Japanese colony began in La Colmena as recently as 1936, signs of acculturation and community breakdown have been reported by cultural geographers surveying the area.[11] Generally, this cursory survey of overseas Japanese communities suggests that when such communities are not governed by agencies of the homeland and where, as the researches of Caudill and deVos indicate,[12] Japanese values find opportunity for inter-penetration and complementarity with those of the host society (as in the United States and Canada), the speed with which community isolation declines is accelerated.

Contrasts between the Chinese and Japanese have been noticed frequently but rarely researched.[13] As early as 1909 Chester Rowell, a Fresno, California, journalist, pointed to the Japanese refusal to be losers in unprofitable contracts, to their unwillingness to be tied to a "Jap-town," and to their geniality and politeness; in contrast he praised the Chinese subordination to contracts and headmen, their accommodation to a ghetto existence, and their cold but efficient and loyal service as domestics. Similar observations were made by Winifred Raushenbush, Robert Park's assistant in his famous race relations survey of the Pacific coast. More recently the late Rose Hum Lee has vividly remarked upon the contrast between the two Asian American groups. Professor Lee asserts that the Nisei "exhibit within sixty years, greater degrees of integration into American society, than has been the case with the Chinese, whose settlement is twice as long." Other sociologists have frequently commented on the speed with which Japanese adopted at least the outward signs of Occidental culture and attained success in North America. Broom and Kitsuse summed up the impressive record of the Japanese by declaring it "an achievement perhaps rarely equaled in the history of human migration." More recently, Petersen has pointed to the same record of achievement and challenged sociologists to develop a theory that could adequately explain it as well as the less spectacular records of other ethnic groups.

Although the differences between the Chinese and Japanese in North America have excited more comparative comment than concrete investigation, an early statement by Walter G. Beach deserves more attention than it has received. In a much neglected article[14] Beach observed the contrast between the speed of acculturation of Chinese and Japanese and attributed it to those conditions within and extrinsic to the ethnic groups that fostered either segregation and retention of Old World culture traits or rapid breakdown of the ethnic community. Noting that ethnic cultures were an important aspect of the kind of community an immigrant group would form he pointed out that the Chinese came to America "before Chinese culture had been greatly influenced by Western civilization." More specifically, he suggested that "they came from an old, conservative and stationary social organization and system of custom-control of life; and that the great majority came from the lower and least independent social stratum of that life." By contrast, he observed that the Japanese "came at a time when their national political system had felt the influence of Western thought and ambitions." He went on to say: "Japan was recognized among the world's powers, and its people were self-conscious in respect to this fact; their pride was not in a past culture, unintelligible to Americans (as the Chinese), but in a growing position of recognition and authority among the world's powers." It was because of these differences in culture and outlook, Beach argued, that Japanese tended to resist discrimination more vigorously and to adopt Occidental ways more readily, while Chinese produced a "Chopsuey culture" in segregated communities. Stripped of its ethnocentrism, Beach's analysis suggests that acculturation is affected not only by the action of the larger society upon immigrants, but also, and more fundamentally, by the nature and quality of the immigrant culture and institutions.

The present study specifies and clarifies the features of Japanese and Chinese culture that Beach only hinted at, and details the interplay between Old World cultures and North American society. Certain key conditions of life in China and Japan at the times of emigration produced two quite different kinds of immigrant social organization. The responses of the American economy and society to Chinese and Japanese certainly had their effects. But these alone did not shape Chinese and Japanese life. Rather they acted as "accelerators" to the direction of and catalysts or inhibitors of the development of the immigrants' own culture and institutions.[15] Prejudice and discrimination added considerable hardship to the necessarily onerous lives of the immigrating Asians, but did not wrench away their culture, nor deprive them completely of those familial, political, and social institutions that they had transported across the Pacific.[16] The Chinese and Japanese were never reduced to the wretchedness of the first Africans in America, who experienced a forcible stripping away of their original culture, and then a coercive acculturation into selected and subordinated elements of white America. Thus, although both Chinese and Japanese share a nearly identical distinction from the dominant American racial stock, and although both have been oppressed by prejudice, discrimination, segregation, and exclusion, a fundamental source of their markedly different rates of acculturation is to be found in the particular developmental patterns taken by their respective cultures[17] in America.

Emigration

The conditions of emigration for Chinese and Japanese reflected respectively their different cultures. The Chinese migrated from a state that was not a nation, and they conceived of themselves primarily as members of local extended kin units, bound together by ties of blood and language and only secondarily, if at all, as "citizens" of the Chinese empire.[18] Chinese emigration was an organized affair in which kinsmen or fellow villagers who had achieved some wealth or status acted as agents and sponsors for their compatriots. Benevolently despotic, this emigration acted to transfer the loyalties and institutions of the village to the overseas community. In the village, composed for the most part of his kinsmen, the individual looked to elders as leaders; in emigrating the individual reposed his loyalty and submitted his fate to the overseas representative of his clan or village. Loans, protection, and jobs were provided within a framework of kin and language solidarity that stretched from the village in Kwangtung to the clan building in "Chinatown." Emigrants regarded their journey as temporary and their return as certain. Abroad the Chinese, as homeless men, never fully accepted any permanence to their sojourn. They identified themselves with their Old World clan, village, dialect grouping, or secret society whose overseas leaders were recognized as legitimate substitutes for homeland groups.

These institutional leaders further insinuated themselves into the overseas immigrant's life by acting as his representative to white society, by pioneering new settlements, and by providing badly needed goods and services, protection against depredations, and punishment for wrong-doing.

The Japanese emigrant departed from an entirely different kind of society.[19] Japan was a nation as well as a state, and its villages reflected this fact. Village life had long ceased to be circumscribed by kinship, and the individual family rather than the extended kinship group was the locus of loyalty and solidarity. When children departed their homes they left unencumbered by a network of obligations. Unless he had been born first or last, a Japanese son was not obligated as was a Chinese to remain in the home of his parents. After 1868 emigration was sometimes sponsored by the government and certainly encouraged. When Japanese departed the homeland they, like the Chinese, expected only to sojourn, but they were not called back to the home village by the knowledge that a long-patient wife awaited them or that kinsmen fully depended on their return. Moreover, the men who inspired Japanese emigration were not pioneer leaders but exemplary individuals whose singular fame and fortune seemed to promise everyone great opportunity abroad. They did not serve as overseas community leaders or even very often as agents of migration, but only as shining examples of how others might succeed.

Marital Status

The respective marital situation of these two Asian peoples reflected fundamental differences in Chinese and Japanese kinship and profoundly influenced community life overseas. Custom required that a Chinese man sojourn abroad without his wife. A man's return to hearth and village with thus secured, and he labored overseas in order that he might some day again enjoy the warmth of domesticity and the blessings of children. Abroad he lived a lonely life of labor, dependent of kinsmen and compatriots for fellowship and on prostitutes and vice for outlet and recreation. When in 1882 restrictive American legislation unwittingly converted Chinese custom into legal prohibition by prohibiting the coming of wives of Chinese laborers it exaggerated and lengthened the separation of husbands from wives and, more significantly, delayed for nearly two generations the birth in America of a substantial "second generation" among the immigrant Chinese. Canadian immigration restrictions had a similar consequence.[20] Barred from intermarriage by custom and law and unable to bring wives to Canada or the United States, Chinese men sired children on their infrequent return visits to China, and these China-born sons later partially replenished the Chinese population in North America as they joined their fathers in the overseas venture. Like their fathers, the sons also depended on Chinatown institutions. Their lack of independence from the same community controls that had earlier circumscribed the lives of their fathers stood in sharp contrast to the manner of life of the Canadian and American born.

Neither custom nor law barred the Japanese from bringing wives to Canada or America.[21] Within two decades of their arrival the Japanese had brought over enough women to guarantee that, although husbands might be quite a bit older than their wives, a domestic life would be established in America. Japanese thus had little need for the brothels and gambling halls that characterized Chinese communities in the late nineteenth century and that, not incidentally, provided a continuous source of wealth and power to those who owned or controlled them. Japanese quickly produced a second generation in both Canada and the United States, and by 1930 this Nisei generation began to claim a place for itself in North America and in Japanese-American and Japanese-Canadian life. The independence and acculturation of the Nisei was indicated in their social and political style of life. They did not accept the organizations of their parents' community and established ad hoc associations dedicated to civil rights and penetration beyond Canada's and America's racial barrier. Some Japanese immigrants educated one of their children in Japan. These few Japan-educated offspring (Kibei) did not enjoy the same status in North America as Nisei, and in their marginality and problems of adjustment they resembled the China-born offspring of Chinese immigrants. Educated in Canadian or American schools and possessed of Canadian or American culture and values, the Nisei found that prejudice and discrimination acted as the most significant obstacles to their success.

Occupations and Locations

Jobs and settlement patterns tended to reinforce and accelerate the different developmental patterns of Chinese and Japanese communities in America.[22] Except for a small but powerful merchant elite the Chinese began and remained as wage laborers. First employed in the arduous and menial tasks of mining and railroad building, the

Chinese later gravitated into unskilled, clerical and service work inside the Chinese community. Such work necessitated living in cities or returning to cities when unemployment drove the contract laborers to seek new jobs. The city always meant the Chinese quarter, a ghetto set aside for Chinese in which their special needs could be met and by which the white population could segregate itself from them. Inside the ghetto Old-World societies ministered to their members' wants, exploited their needs, and represented their interests. When primary industry could no longer use Chinese and white hostility drove them out of the labor market and into Chinatown, the power of these associations and their merchant leaders was reconfirmed and enhanced. The single most important feature of the occupations of Chinese immigrants was their tendency to keep the Chinese in a state of dependency on bosses, contractors, merchants—ultimately on the merchant elite of Chinatown.

The Japanese, after a brief stint as laborers in several primary industries then on the wane in western America, pioneered the cultivation of truck crops.[23] Small-scale agriculturalists, separated from one another as well as from the urban anti-Orientalism of the labor unions, Japanese farmers did not retain the kind of ethnic solidarity characteristic of the urban Chinese. Whatever traditional elites had existed among the early Japanese immigrants fell from power or were supplanted. In their place ad hoc associations arose to meet particular needs. When Japanese did become laborers and city dwellers they too became segregated in "Li'l Tokyos" presided over by Old-World associations for a time. But the early concentration in agriculture and the later demands of the Nisei tended to weaken the power even of the city-bred immigrant associations.

Community Power and Conflict

Finally, the different bases for solidarity in the two Oriental communities tended to confirm their respective modes of social organization. The Japanese community has remained isolated primarily because of discriminatory barriers to integration and secondarily because of the sense of congregation among fellow Japanese. The isolated Chinese community is, to be sure, a product of white aversion and is also characterized by congregative sentiments, but, much more than that of the Japanese, it rests on communal foundations. Political life in Chinatown has rarely been tranquil.[24] The traditional clans and Landsmannschaften controlled immigration, settled disputes, levied taxes and fines, regulated commerce, and meted out punishments. Opposition to their rule took the form it had taken in China. Secret societies, chapters of or modeled after the well-known Triad Society, took over the functions of law, protection, and revenge for their members. In addition the secret societies owned or controlled the gambling houses and brothels that emerged to satisfy the recreational and sex needs of homeless Chinese men and displayed occasional interest in the restive politics of China. Struggles for power, blood feuds, and "wars" of vengeance were not infrequent in the early days of Chinatown. These conflicts entrenched the loyalties of men to their respective associations. More important with respect to nonacculturation, these intramural fights isolated the Chinese from the uncomprehending larger society and bound them together in antagonistic cooperation. Since the turn of the century, the grounds of such battles have shifted on to a commercial and political plane, but violence is not unknown. Chinatown's organizational solidarity and its intracommunity conflicts have thus acted as agents of nonacculturation.

Position and Prospects of the Asian in North America

The conditions for the political and economic integration of the Chinese appear to be at hand now.[25] This is largely because the forces that spawned and maintained Chinatown are now weakened. The near balancing of the sex ratio has made possible the birth and maturation in America of second and third generation Chinese. Their presence, in greater and greater numbers, poses a serious threat to Old-World power elites. The breakdown of discriminatory barriers to occupations and residency brought about by a new assertion of civil rights heralds an end to Chinatown economic and domestic monopoly. The relative openness of Canadian and American society to American-born and Canadian-born Chinese reduces their dependency on traditional goods and services and their recruitment into communal associations. Concomitantly, the casus belli of the earlier era disappears and conflict's group-binding and isolating effect loses force. What remains of Chinatown eventually is its new immigrants, its culturally acceptable economic base—restaurants and shops— and its congregative value for ethnic Chinese. Recent events in San Francisco suggest that a portion of the young and newly arrived immigrants from Hong Kong, Taiwan, and, Vietnam as well as the American-born Chinese school dropouts are estranged from both the

Chinatown elites and white America. Some of their activities resemble those of protesting and militant black groups; others are of a criminal character.

The Japanese are entering a new phase of relations with the larger society in North America. There is a significant amount of anxiety in Japanese circles about the decline of Japanese values and the appearance of the more undesirable features of Canadian and American life—primarily juvenile delinquency but also a certain lack of Old World propriety that survived through the Nisei generation—among the Sansei and Yonsei.[26] Moreover, like those African Americans who share E. Franklin Frazier's disillusion with the rise of a black bourgeoisie, some Japanese-Americans are questioning the social and personal price paid for entrance into American society. Scholars such as Daisuke Kitagawa have wondered just how Nisei and Sansei might preserve elements of Japanese culture in America. At the same time one European Japanophile has bitterly assailed the Americanization of the Nisei.[27] Nothing similar to a black power movement has developed among the Japanese, and, indeed, such a movement is extremely unlikely given Japanese-American and Canadian material success and the decrease in social distance between Japanese and white Americans. At most there is a quiet concern and a press for a greater measure of ethnic consciousness in college and university programs devoted to Asian American studies. But even such mild phenomena are deserving of sociological attention.

Theoretical Considerations

This survey of Asian American community organization suggests the need to take seriously Robert Park's reconsideration of his own race relations cycle. Park at first had supposed that assimilation was a natural and inevitable outcome of race contact marked off by stages of competition, conflict, and accommodation before there occurred the eventual absorption of one people by another.[28] In addition to its faults as a natural history, a criticism so often discussed by other sociologists,[29] Park's original statement of the cycle took no account of what, in a related context, Wagley and Harris refer to as the "adaptive capacity" of the immigrant group.[30] However, Park himself reconsidered the cycle and in 1937 wrote that it might terminate in one of three outcomes: a caste system as was the case in India; complete assimilation, as he imagined had occurred in China; or a permanent institutionalization of minority status within a larger society, as was the case of Jews in Europe. Park concluded that race relations occur as phases of a cycle "which, once initiated, inevitably continues until it terminates in some predestined racial configuration, and one consistent with the established social order of which it is a part."[31] Park's later emphasis on alternative outcomes and his consideration of the peculiar social context in which any ethnic group's history occurs implicitly recall attention to the interplay between native and host society cultures. As Herskovitz's researches on West African and Afro-American cultures indicate, the immigrant group, even if oppressed in transitu, does not arrive with a cultural tabula rasa waiting to be filled in by the host culture. Rather it possesses a culture and social organization that in contact with and in the several contexts of the host culture will be supplanted, inhibited, subordinated, modified or enhanced. Kinship, occupations, patterns of settlement, and community organization are each factors in such developments. Assimilation, or for that matter pluralism, is not simply an inevitable state of human affairs, as those who cling to "natural history" models assert, but rather is an existential possibility. Social factors contribute to the state of being a people and to changes in that state. The Chinese and Japanese communities in America illustrate two modes of development and suggest the need to refine even further our knowledge of the factors that affect whatever mode of development an immigrant group chooses.

NOTES

This essay originally appeared in The Canadian Review of Sociology and Anthropology, 5:2 (May 1968), pp. 51–67.

1. Cf. Horace M. Kallen, Culture and Democracy in the United States (New York, 1924) with Gunnar Myrdal, An American Dilemma (New York, 1944).

2. See Clyde V. Kiser, "Cultural Pluralism," The Annals of the American Academy of Political and Social Science, 262 (March 1949), pp. 118–29. An approach to such a theory is found in William Petersen, Population (New York, 1961), pp. 114–49.

3. For an extended analysis see Stanford M. Lyman, "The Structure of Chinese Society in Nineteenth-Century America," (unpublished Ph.D. diss., University of California, Berkeley, 1961).

4. Melville Herskovitz, The Myth of the Negro Past (Boston, 1958). See also Charles Keil, Urban Blues (Chicago, 1966), pp. 1–69.

5. Nathan Glazer, "Ethnic Groups in America: From National Culture to Ideology," in Morroe Berger, Theodore Abel, and Charles H. Page, eds. Freedom and Control in Modern Society (New York, 1954), pp. 158–76; Nathan

Glazer and Daniel Patrick Moynihan, *Beyond the Melting Pot: The Negroes, Puerto Ricans, Jews, Italians and Irish of New York City* (Cambridge, 1963).

6. The "knowledge explosion" on China has been prodigious since 1949 despite the difficulties in obtaining first-hand field materials. Much research was inspired by interest in the Chinese in Southeast Asia. See Maurice Freedman, "A Chinese Phase in Social Anthropology," *British Journal of Sociology*, 14:1 (March 1963), pp. 1–18.

7. Sources for the material reported are Lyman, "The Structure of Chinese Society in Nineteenth-Century America, passim; Leong Gor Yun, *Chinatown Inside Out* (New York, 1936), pp. 26–106, 182–235; Calvin Lee, *Chinatown, U.S.A.: A History and Guide* (Garden City, 1965); Stuart H. Cattell, *Health, Welfare and Social Organization in Chinatown, New York City* (New York, August, 1962), pp. 1–4, 20–68, 81–85. For the origins of organized labor's hostility to the Chinese see Herbert Hill, "The Racial Practices of Organized Labor—The Age of Gompers and After," in Arthur Ross and Herbert Hill, eds., *Employment, Race and Poverty: A Critical Study of the Disadvantaged Status of Negro Workers from 1865 to 1965* (New York, 1967), pp. 365–402. For a detailed description of Chinese games of chance see the several articles by Stewart Culin, "Chinese Games with Dice" (Philadelphia, 1889), pp. 5–21; "The Gambling Games of the Chinese in America," *Publications of the University of Pennsylvania, Series in Philology, Literature, and Archaeology*, 1:4, 1891; "Chinese Games with Dice and Dominoes," *Report of the United States National Museum, Smithsonian Institution*, 1893, pp. 489–537. The sweatshops of San Francisco's Chinatown are described in James Benet, *A Guide to San Francisco and the Bay Region* (New York, 1963), pp. 73–74.

8. See Rose Hum Lee, *The Chinese in the United States of America* (Hong Kong, 1960), pp. 86–131, 231–51, 373–404. See also *Chinese Students in the United States, 1948–1955: A Study in Government Policy* (New York, March, 1956). For a Canadian-Chinese view of his own generation's adjustment to Chinese and Canadian ways of life see William Wong, "The Younger Generation," *Chinatown News*, 11:13 (March 18, 1964), pp. 6–7.

9. Material for the following is drawn from Maurice Freedman and William Willmott, "Southeast Asia, with Special Reference to the Chinese," *International Social Science Journal*, 13:2 (1961), pp. 245–70; Victor Purcell, *The Chinese in Southeast Asia* (London, 1965), 2d ed.; Jacques Amyot, S. J., *The Chinese Community of Manila: A Study of Adaptation of Chinese Familism to the Philippine Environment* (Chicago, 1960); Richard J. Coughlin, "The Chinese in Bangkok: A Commercial-Oriented Minority," *American Sociological Review*, 20 (June, 1955), 311–16; Maurice Freedman, *Chinese Family and Marriage in Singapore* (London, 1957); Donald Willmott, *The Chinese of Semarang: A Changing Minority Community in Indonesia* (Ithaca, 1960); Shelland Bradley, "Calcutta's Chinatown," *Cornhill Magazine*, 57 (Sept. 1924), pp. 277–85; Christopher Driver, "The Tiger Balm Community," *The Guardian* (Jan. 2, 1962); Tsien Tche-Hao, "La vie sociale des Chinois à Madagascar," *Comparative Studies in Society and History*, 3:2 (Jan.

1961), pp. 170–81; Justus M. van der Kroef, "Chinese Assimilation in Indonesia," *Social Research*, 20 (Jan. 1954), pp. 445–72; Leonard Broom, "The Social Differentiation of Jamaica," *American Sociological Review*, 19 (April 1954), pp. 115–24.

10. Material for the following is based on Michinari Fujita, "Japanese Associations in America," *Sociology and Social Research* (Jan.–Feb. 1929), pp. 211–28; T. Obana, "The American-born Japanese," *Sociology and Social Research* (Nov.–Dec. 1934), pp. 161–65; Joseph Roucek, "Japanese Americans," in Francis J. Brown and Joseph S. Roucek, eds. *One America: The History, Contributions, and Present Problems of Our Racial and National Minorities* (New York, 1952), pp. 319–84; Forrest E. La Violette, "Canada and Its Japanese," in Edgar T. Thompson and Everett C. Hughes, eds. *Race: Individual and Collective Behavior* (Glencoe, 1958), pp. 149–55; Charles Young, Helen R. Y. Reid, and W. A. Carrothers, *The Japanese Canadians* (Toronto, 1938), ed. H. A. Innis; Ken Adachi, *A History of the Japanese Canadians in British Columbia* (Vancouver (?) 1958); T. Scott Miyakawa, "The Los Angeles Sansei," *Kashu Mainichi* (Dec. 20, 1962), part 2, p. 1; Harry Kitano, "Is There Sansei Delinquency?" *Kashu Mainichi* (Dec. 20, 1962), Part 2, p. 1.

11. For the Japanese in Hawaii, see John Embree, "New and Local Kin Groups among the Japanese Farmers of Kona, Hawaii," *American Anthropologist*, 41 (July 1939), pp. 400–407; John Embree "Acculturation among the Japanese of Kona, Hawaii," *Memoirs of the American Anthropological Association*, no. 59; supplement to *American Anthropologist*, 43, 4:2 (1941); Jitsuichi Masuoka, "The Life Cycle of an Immigrant Institution in Hawaii: The Family," *Social Forces*, 23 (Oct. 1944) pp. 60–64; Masuoka, "The Japanese Patriarch in Hawaii," *Social Forces*, 17 (Dec. 1938), pp. 240–48; Masuoka, "Changing Food Habits of the Japanese in Hawaii," *American Sociological Review*, 10 (Dec. 1945), pp. 759–65; Masuoka, "Changing Moral Bases of the Japanese Family in Hawaii," *Sociology and Social Research*, 21 (Nov. 1936), 158–69; Andrew M. Lind, *Hawaii's Japanese: An Experiment in Democracy* (Princeton, 1946). For the Japanese in Peru see Toraji Irie, "History of Japanese Migration to Peru," *Hispanic-American Historical Review*, 32 (Aug.–Oct. 1951) pp. 437–52, 648–64; (Feb. 1952), pp. 73–82; Mischa Titiev, "The Japanese Colony in Peru," *Far Eastern Quarterly*, 10 (May 1951), pp. 227–47. For Japanese in Brazil see J. F. Normano "Japanese Emigration to Brazil," *Pacific Affairs*, 7 (Mar. 1934), 42–61; Emilio Willems and Herbert Baldus, "Cultural Change among Japanese Immigrants in Brazil in the Ribeira Valley of Sao Paulo," *Sociology and Social Research*, 26 (July 1943), pp. 525–37; Emilio Willems, "The Japanese in Brazil," *Far Eastern Quarterly*, 18 (Jan. 12, 1949), pp. 6–8; John P. Augelli, "Cultural and Economic Changes of Bastos, a Japanese colony on Brazil's Paulista Frontier," *Annals of the Association of American Geographers*, 48:1 (Mar. 1958), pp. 3–19. For Paraguay see Norman R. Stewart, *Japanese Colonization in Eastern Paraguay* (Washington, D.C., 1967).

12. William Caudill, "Japanese American Personality and Acculturation, *Genetic Psychology Monographs*, 45 (1952) pp. 3–102; George de Vos, "A

Comparison of the Personality Differences in Two Generations of Japanese Americans by Means of the Rorschach Test," *Nagoya Journal of Medicine*, 17:3 (Aug. 1954), 153–265; William Caudill and George de Vos, "Achievement, Culture and Personality: The Case of the Japanese Americans," *American Anthropologist*, 58 (Dec. 1956), pp. 1102–26.

13. Materials in this section are based on Chester Rowell, "Chinese and Japanese Immigrants—a Comparison," *Annals of the American Academy of Political and Social Science*, 24:2 (Sept. 1909), pp. 223–30; Winifred Raushenbush, "Their Place in the Sun," and "The Great Wall of Chinatown," *The Survey Graphic*, 56:3 (May 1, 1926), 141–45, 154–58; Rose Hum Lee, *The Chinese in the United States of America*, 425; Leonard Broom and John I. Kitsuse, "The Validation of Acculturation: A Condition of Ethnic Assimilation," *American Anthropologist*, 57 (1955), pp. 44–48; William Petersen, "Family Structure and Social Mobility among Japanese Americans," paper presented at the annual meetings of the American Sociological Association, San Francisco, August 1967).

14. Walter G. Beach, "Some Considerations in Regard to Race Segregation in California," *Sociology and Social Research*, 18 (March 1934), pp. 340–50.

15. See the discussion in Lyman, "Structure of Chinese Society," pp. 370-77.

16. One difference with respect to hostility toward the Chinese and Japanese had to do with whether either was perceived as an "enemy" people. Although the Chinese were occasionally accused of harboring subversive intentions toward America—see, e.g., P. W. Dooner, *Last Days of the Republic*, (San Francisco, 1880)—it was the Japanese who suffered a half-century of such suspicions. See Jacobus ten Broek, Edward N. Barnhart, and Floyd Matson, *Prejudice, War and the Constitution* (Berkeley, 1954), pp. 11–99; Forrest E. La Violette, *The Canadian Japanese and World War II* (Toronto, 1948); Rev. Yoshiaki Fukuda, with a commentary by Stanford M. Lyman, *My Six Years of Internment: An Issei's Struggle for Justice*, trans. Konko Church of San Francisco and the Research Information Center of the Konko Churches of North America (San Francisco, 1990). Undoubtedly these deep-seated suspicions led Japanese to try very hard to prove their loyalty and assimilability. In this respect see Mike Masaoka, "The Japanese American Creed," *Common Ground*, 2:3 (1942), p. 11; and "A Tribute to Japanese American Military Service in World War II," Speech of Hon. Hiram Fong in the Senate of the United States, *Congressional Record*, 88th Congress, 1st sess., May 21, 1963, pp. 1–13; "Tributes to Japanese American Military Service in World War II," Speeches of Twenty-four Congressmen, *Congressional Record*, 88th Congress, 1st sess. June 11, 1963, pp. 1–16; Senator Daniel Ken Inouye (with Lawrence Elliott), *Journey to Washington* (Englewood Cliffs, 1967), pp. 87–200.

17. In the tradition of Max Weber, religion might properly be supposed to have played a significant role in the orientations of overseas Chinese and Japanese. However, certain problems make any adoption of the Weberian

thesis difficult. First, although Confucianism was the state religion of China, local villages practiced syncretic forms of combining ancestor worship, Buddhism, Christianity, and homage to local deities. Maurice Freedman, *Lineage Organization in Southeastern China* (London, 1958), pp. 116. Abroad Chinese temples were definitely syncretic and functioned to support a nonrationalist idea of luck and the maintenance of merchant power. See A. J. A. Elliott, *Chinese Spirit Medium Cults in Singapore* (London, 1955), pp. 24–45; Stewart Culin, *The Religious Ceremonies of the Chinese in the Eastern Cities of the United States* (Philadelphia, 1887); Wolfram Eberhard, "Economic Activities of a Chinese Temple in California," *Journal of the American Oriental Society*, 82:3 (July–Sept. 1962), pp. 362–71. In the case of Japanese, the Tokugawa religion certainly facilitated a limited achievement orientation. Robert Bellah, *Tokugawa Religion: The Values of Pre-industrial Japan* (Glencoe, 1957), pp. 107–32. But both in Japan and the United States Japanese exhibit a remarkable indifference to religious affiliation, even countenancing denominational and church differences within the same nuclear family and relatively little anxiety about religious intermarriage. See Kiyomi Morioka, "Christianity in the Japanese Rural Community: Acceptance and Rejection," *Japanese Sociological Studies. The Sociological Review*, monograph 10 (Sept. 1966), pp. 183–98; Leonard D. Cain, Jr., "Japanese American Protestants: Acculturation and Assimilation," *Review of Religious Research*, 3:3 (Winter 1962), pp. 113–21; Cain, "The Integration Dilemma of Japanese-American Protestants," paper presented at the annual meetings of the Pacific Sociological Association, April 5, 1962.

18. For information of nineteenth-century Chinese social organization in the provinces from which North America's immigrants came see Maurice Freedman, *Chinese Lineage and Society: Fukien and Kwangtung* (New York, 1966); Kung-Chuan Hsiao, *Rural China: Imperial Control in the Nineteenth Century* (Seattle, 1960). On the Chinese as sojourners see Paul C. P. Siu, "The Sojourner," *American Journal of Sociology*, 8 (July 1952), pp. 32–44, and Siu, "The Isolation of the Chinese Laundryman," in Ernest W. Burgess and Donald Bogue, eds. *Contributions to Urban Sociology* (Chicago, 1964), pp. 429–42. On the role of immigrant associations see William Hoy, *The Chinese Six Companies* (San Francisco, 1942); Tin-Yuke Char, "Immigrant Chinese Societies in Hawaii," *Sixty-First Annual Report of the Hawaiian Historical Society* (1953), pp. 29–32; William Willmott, "Chinese Clan Associations in Vancouver," *Man*, 64:49 (Mar.–Apr. 1964), pp. 33–37.

19. Material for the following is based on George B. Sansom, *Japan: A Short Cultural History* (New York, 1943); Takashi Koyama, "The Significance of Relatives at the Turning Point of the Family System in Japan," *Japanese Sociological Studies. Sociological Review*, 10 (Sept. 1966), pp. 95–114; Lafcadio Hearn, *Japan: An Interpretation* (Tokyo, 1955), pp. 81–106; Ronald P. Dore, *City Life in Japan: A Study of A Tokyo Ward* (Berkeley, 1958), pp. 91–190; Irene Taeuber, "Family, Migration and Industrialization in Japan," *American Sociological Review* (Apr. 1951), pp. 149–57; Ezra F.

Vogel, "Kinship Structure, Migration to the City, and Modernization," in R. P. Dore, *Aspects of Social Change in Modern Japan* (Princeton, 1967), pp. 91–112.

20. For discussions of United States restrictive legislation see Mary Coolidge, *Chinese Immigration* (New York, 1909), pp. 145–336; S. W. Kung, *Chinese in American Life: Some Aspects of Their History, Status, Problems and Contributions* (Seattle, 1962), pp. 64–165. A discussion of both American and Canadian restrictive legislation will be found in Huang Tsen-ming, *The Legal Status of the Chinese Abroad* (Taipei, 1954). See also Tin-Yuke Char, "Legal Restrictions on Chinese in English Speaking Countries," 1," *Chinese Social and Political Science Review*, (Jan. 4, 1933), pp. 479–94. Careful analyses of Canadian legislation are found in Duncan McArthur, "What is the Immigration Problem?" *Queen's Quarterly* (Autumn 1928), pp. 603–14; three articles by H. F. Angus, "Canadian Immigration: The Law and its Administration," *American Journal of International Law*, 28:1 (Jan. 1934), pp. 74–89; "The Future of Immigration into Canada," *Canadian Journal of Economics and Political Science*, 12 (Aug. 1946), pp. 379–86; Jean Mercier, "Immigration and Provincial Rights," *Canadian Bar Review*, 22 (1944), pp. 856–69; Hugh L. Keenleyside, "Canadian Immigration Policy and Its Administration," *External Affairs* (May 1949), pp. 3–11; Bora Laskin, "Naturalization and Aliens: Immigration, Exclusion, and Deportation," *Canadian Constitutional Law* (Toronto, 1960), pp. 958–77. In general see David C. Corbett, *Canada's Immigration Policy: A Critique* (Toronto, 1957).

21. For Japanese immigration see Yamato Ichihashi, *Japanese in the United States* (Stanford, 1932), pp. 401–09; Dorothy Swaine Thomas, Charles Kikuchi, and J. Sakoda, *The Salvage* (Berkeley, 1952), pp. 3–18, 571–626; H. A. Millis, *The Japanese Problem in the United States* (New York, 1915); K. K. Kawakami, *The Real Japanese Question* (New York, 1921); T. Iyenaga and Kenosuke Sato, *Japan and the California Problem* (New York, 1921); Iichiro Tokutomi, *Japanese-American Relations* (New York, 1922), pp. 65–88 (translated by Sukeshige Yanagiwara); R. D. McKenzie, *Oriental Exclusion* (Chicago, 1928). For Japanese immigration to Canada see Young, Reid, and Carrothers, *Japanese Canadians*; A. R. M. Lower, *Canada and the Far East—1940* (New York, 1941), pp. 61–89; H. F. Angus, *Canada and the Far East, 1940–1953* (Toronto, 1953), pp. 99–100. For a statement by a pessimistic Nisei see Kazuo Kawai, "Three Roads, and None Easy," *Survey Graphic*, 56:3 (May 1, 1926), pp. 164–66. For further discussions see Tsutoma Obana, "Problems of the American-Born Japanese," *Sociology and Social Research*, 19 (Nov. 1934), pp. 161–65; Emory S. Bogardus, "Current Problems of Japanese Americans," *Sociology and Social Research*, 25 (July 1941), pp. 562–71; For the development of new associations among Nisei see Adachi, *A History of the Japanese in British Columbia, 1877–1958*, pp. 11–14; *Better Americans in a Greater America*, booklet published by the Japanese American Citizens' League, undated (1967), 24 pp. For an ecological analysis of the distribution and diffusion of achievement orientations among Japanese in America see Paul T. Tagagi, "The Japanese Family in the

United States: A Hypothesis on the Social Mobility of The Nisei," revision of an earlier paper presented at the annual meeting of the Kroeber Anthropological Society, Berkeley, California (April 30, 1966).

22. For information on occupations and settlement patterns see Lyman, "Structure of Chinese Society," pp. 111–27; Milton L. Barnett, "Kinship as a Factor Affecting Cantonese Economic Adaptation in the United States," *Human Organization*, 19 (Spring 1960), pp. 40–46; Ping Chiu, *Chinese Labor in California: An Economic Study* (Madison, 1963).

23. For the Japanese as agriculturalists see Masakazu Iwata, "The Japanese Immigrants in California Agriculture," *Agricultural History*, 36 (Jan. 1962), pp. 25–37; Thomas et al., *The Salvage* 23–25; Adon Poli, *Japanese Farm Holdings on the Pacific Coast* (Berkeley, 1944). For farming and fishing communities in Canada see Tadashi Fukutake, *Man and Society in Japan* (Tokyo, 1962), pp. 146–79. For the rise and decline of urban ghettos among Japanese in the United States see Shotaro Frank Miyamoto, *Social Solidarity among the Japanese in Seattle*, University of Washington Publications in the Social Sciences, 11:2 (Dec. 1939), pp. 57–129; Toshio Mori, "Li'l' Yokohama," *Common Ground*, 1:2 (1941), pp. 54–56; Larry Tajiri, "Farewell to Little Tokyo," *Common Ground*, 4:2 (1944), pp. 90–95; Robert W. O'Brien, "Selective Dispersion as a Factor in the Solution of the Nisei Problem," *Social Forces*, 23 (Dec. 1944), pp. 140–47.

24. On power and conflict in Chinatown see Lyman, "Structure of Chinese Society," 272–369. For secret societies see Lyman, "Chinese Secret Societies in the Occident: Notes and Suggestions for Research in the Sociology of Secrecy," *Canadian Review of Sociology and Anthropology*, 1:2 (1964), pp. 79–102; Lyman, W. E. Willmott, Berching Ho, "Rules of a Chinese Secret Society in British Columbia," *Bulletin of the School of Oriental and African Studies*, 27:3 (1964), pp. 530–39. See also D. Y. Yuan, "Voluntary Segregation: A Study of New Chinatown," *Phylon Quarterly* (Fall 1963), pp. 255–65.

25. For an extended discussion of the progress in eliminating discrimination in Canada and the United States see Stanford M. Lyman, *The Oriental in North America* (Vancouver, 1962), lecture no. 11: "Position and Prospects of the Oriental since World War II." On immigration matters to 1962 see S. W. Kung, "Chinese Immigration into North America," *Queen's Quarterly*, 68:4 (Winter 1962), pp. 610–20. Information about Chinese in Canada and the United States is regularly reported in the *Chinatown News*, a Vancouver, B.C., publication and in *East-West*, a San Francisco journal. For problems of recent Chinese immigrants see *San Francisco Chronicle* (March 18, 1968) p. 2; for those of American born, ibid. (March, 19, 1968), p. 42.

26. On April 15, 1965, in response to a rash of teenage burglaries among Japanese in Sacramento, parents and other interested adults met and discussed how the community might act to prevent delinquency.

27. Daisuke Kitagawa, "Assimilation of Pluralism?" in Arnold M. Rose and Caroline B. Rose, *Minority Problems* (New York, 1965), pp. 285–87.

Fosco Maraini has written "The ni-sei has generally been taught to despise his Asian roots; on the other hand, all he has taken from the west is a two-dimensional duralumin Christianity, ultra-modernism, the cultivation of jazz as a sacred rite, a California veneer." *Meeting with Japan* (New York, 1960) (translated by Eric Mosbacher), p. 169.

28. Robert E. Park, "Our Racial Frontier on the Pacific," *Survey Graphic*, 56:3 (May 1, 1926), p. 196.

29. Seymour Martin Lipset, "Changing Social Status and Prejudice: The Race Theories of a Pioneering American Sociologist," *Commentary*, 9 (May, 1950), pp. 475–79; Amitai Etzioni, "The Ghetto—a Re-evaluation," *Social Forces*, 37 (Mar. 1959), pp. 255–62.

30. Charles Wagley and Marvin Harris, *Minorities in the New World* (New York, 1958).

31. Robert E. Park, "The Race Relations Cycle in Hawaii," *Race and Culture* (Glencoe, 1950), pp. 194–95. For an extended discussion of the race cycle see Stanford M. Lyman, "The Race Relations Cycle of Robert E. Park," *Pacific Sociological Review*, 11:1 (Spring 1968), pp. 16–22.

10

Generation and Character: The Case of the Japanese Americans

When the first Japanese Embassy arrived in the United States in 1860, the *Daily Alta Californian,* a San Francisco newspaper, reported with mingled approval and astonishment: "Every beholder was struck with the self-possessed demeanor of the Japanese. Though the scenes which now met their gaze must have been of the most intense interest for novelty, they seemed to consider their display as due the august position they held under their Emperor, and not one of them, by sign or word, evinced either surprise or admiration."[1]

Thus, with their first major debarkation in the New World,[2] the Japanese appeared to Americans to lack emotional expression. Indeed, San Francisco's perceptive journalist went on to observe: "This stoicism, however, is a distinguishing feature with the Japanese. It is part of their creed never to appear astonished at anything, and it must be a rare sight indeed which betrays in them any expression of wonder."[3]

In the eighty-five years that passed between Japan's first embassy and the end of the Second World War, this "distinguishing feature" of the Japanese became the cardinal element of the anti-Japanese stereotype. Characterized by journalists, politicians, novelists and filmmakers as a dangerous, enemy people, the Japanese were also pictured as mysterious and inscrutable.[4] Supposedly loyal to Japan, cunning and conspiratorial, most of the Japanese Americans were evacuated and incarcerated throughout the Second World War. This unusual violation of their fundamental civil rights was justified in the minds of a great many ordinary Americans by the perfidious character they imputed to Japanese.[5]

The anti-Japanese stereotype was so widespread that it affected the judgments of sociologists about the possibilities of Japanese assimilation. Thus, in 1913 Robert E. Park had been sufficiently depressed by the orgy of anti-Japanese legislation and popular prejudice to predict their permanent consignment to minority status: "The Japanese . . . is condemned to remain among us an abstraction, a symbol, and a symbol not merely of his own race, but of the Orient and of that vague ill-defined menace we sometimes refer to as the 'yellow peril.' "[6] Although Park later reversed his doleful prediction, his observations on Japanese emphasized their uncommunicative features, stolid faces, and apparently blank characters. The Japanese face was a racial mask behind which the individual personality was always hidden. "Orientals live more completely behind the mask than the rest of us," he wrote. "Naturally enough we misinterpret them and attribute to disingenuousness and craft what is actually conformity to an ingrained convention. The American who is flattered at first by the politeness of his Japanese servant will later on, perhaps, cite as a reproach against the race the fact that 'we can never tell what a Japanese is thinking about.' 'We never know what is going on in their heads.' "[7]

Since the end of World War II recognition of the evils of racism has reduced the negative and pejorative effects of racial stereotypes, but it has not brought about an end to their popular usage or academic study. Recent scholarship, while eschewing antipathetic and hostile stereotypes, has begun to lay great emphasis on the role of character and character formation for achievement and assimilation. Thus, in one study, the success of Jews in America is attributed in part to their belief "that the world is orderly and amenable to rational mastery"; to their willingness "to leave home to make their way of life"; and to their "preference for individualistic rather than collective credit for work done."[8] Another study points out that the child rearing practices of Jews, Greeks, and white Protestants lay the emphasis on independence and achievement, while those of Italians, French-Canadians, and African Americans emphasize cooperation and fatalistic resignation.[9]

The remarkable record of achievement by Japanese Americans has been noted frequently in reports of both journalists and sociologists. As early as 1909, Chester Rowell pointed to their refusal to accept unprofitable contracts, their commercial advancement beyond the confines of the ghetto and to their geniality and politeness.[10] Seventeen years later Winifred Raushenbush, Park's assistant in his race relations survey of the Pacific Coast, admonished the Japanese of Florin, California, for their impatience with racial restrictions and praised the Japanese community of Livingston, California, for its propriety.[11] More recently, Rose Hum Lee vividly contrasted the Chinese Americans with their Japanese counterparts, noting that the Nisei "exhibit greater degrees of integration into American society, than has been the case with the Chinese, whose settlement is twice as long."[12] Broom and Kitsuse have summed up the impressive record of the Japanese in America by declaring it to be "an achievement perhaps rarely equaled in the history of human migration."[13] The careful statistical measures of Schmid and Nobbe indicate that present-day Japanese in America have outstripped all other "colored" groups in America in occupational achievement and education.[14]

Analyses of Japanese American achievement have laid stress on the same character traits that once made up the notorious stereotype. Thus, Caudill and de Vos have pointed out that the Nisei appeared to be more acculturated than they are in fact because of "a significant compatibility (but by no means identity) between the value systems found in the culture of Japan and the value systems found in American middle class culture."[15] "What appears to have occurred in the case of Japanese-Americans is that the Nisei, while utilizing to a considerable extent a Japanese set of values and adaptive mechanisms, were able in their prewar life on the Pacific Coast to act in ways that drew favorable comment and recognition from their white middle class peers and made them admirable pupils in the eyes of their middle class teachers."[16]

The experiences of prewar California were repeated in Chicago during the Second World War. Personnel managers and fellow workers admired the Nisei. "What has happened here," wrote Caudill and de Vos, "is that the peers, teachers, employers and fellow workers of the *Nisei* have projected their own values into the neat, well-dressed and efficient *Nisei* in whom they saw mirrored many of their own ideals."[17] What were these ideals? They included patience, cleanliness, courtesy and "minding their own business,"[18] the same ideals capable of distortion into negative characteristics. Thus, Japanese patience has been taken to be silent contempt; cleanliness and courtesy, as matters for comic ridicule or dark suspicion; minding their own business as unwarranted aloofness and "clannishness."[19] What was once caricature is now recognized as character.

The fact that the same, or very nearly identical, traits can be used to denigrate the Japanese, as well as account for their unprecedented success, suggests the possibility that behind these traits there exists a unique character structure. Indeed, the Japanese Americans themselves believe this and, as we shall presently show, they regard each generation of Japanese Americans as possessed of a unique character.

That there should exist a correspondence between a racist stereotype and culturally created character should not cause too great a concern. The haters of a people have often scrupulously searched out elements of their enemies' character and spun webs of viciousness out of them. Indeed, one reason for the survival of a stereotype through time and other changes is its origin in a kernel of fundamental truth that it distorts for evil purposes.

Recently a great advance in the understanding of the nature of slavery and Afro-American personality has been suggested by Elkins's recognition of the truth value of personality elements in the "Sambo" stereotype and his attempt to discover just how such a personality could arise.[20] Progress in the social analysis of culture and personality might be enhanced by sociologists and social psychologists undertaking the unpalatable task of assuming for the sake of research that the worst statements made about a people have their origins in some fundamental truth that needs first to be abstracted from its pejorative context and then subjected to behavioral and cultural analysis.

This essay presents an analysis of Japanese American character. Data for this analysis was obtained by the method known as participant observation. The author conducted this research as an active member of an all-Nisei group in the San Francisco Bay area during 1951–66. Direct observations were made at homes, churches, schools, and recreational areas. A conceptual framework first developed by Alfred Schutz[21] and effectively employed by Clifford Geertz to study the Balinese[22] is here used to analyze Japanese American character. A somewhat similar formulation of concepts by Clyde Kluckhohn has been applied to Japanese character by Caudill and Scarr.[23] Although this essay relies heavily on Schutz, the conceptual schema of Kluckhohn and the findings of Caudill and Scarr will be noted when appropriate. In addition, the findings of numerous researchers on Japan and the Japanese Americans have been employed and interpreted throughout.

Time Person Perspectives

In every culture and in many subcultures there is a predominant time-person perspective. This perspective organizes the relevant temporal and personal categories in order to structure priorities with respect to past, present, and future, and to structure orientations with respect to intimacy or impersonality. Any culture may be viewed then with respect to its priorities of predecessors, contem-

poraries, consociates, and successors.[24] *Predecessors* are all those
who have lived in some past time, in history, and about whom no
contemporary can have direct subjective knowledge. *Successors* are
all those who shall live in some future time and with whom no contemporary can share a mutual intersubjective identity because they
have not yet lived. *Contemporaries* are all those fellow humans who
share the same spatiotemporal environment. Among contemporaries
are those about whom one has only categorical but not intersubjective knowledge, and those whom one knows intimately and in regular association. The latter are *consociates*. Now, for any culture or
subculture, we may ask how these distinctions appear—not merely
as analytic features, but rather as members' understandings of their
own world. Note that it is possible for any one of these time-person
perspectives to be experienced subjectively by members as prior to,
having precedence over, or exclusive from any one or group of the
others. The relative subjective weight placed on any one or more of
these perspectives over and against the others has profound consequences for the organization of behavior and is, in turn, reciprocally
related to other elements of culture and the institutional order.

In the case of the Japanese in America, time and person are perceived in terms of geographic and generational distance from Japan.
With the possible exception of the Koreans, the Japanese are the only
immigrant group in America who specify by a linguistic term and
characterize with a unique personality each generation of descendants from the original immigrant group.[25] In contrast, for example,
to the United States Census[26] and the Chinese,[27] the Japanese do not
merely distinguish native-born from foreign-born but rather count
geogenerationally forward or backward with each new generational
grouping. Moreover, from the standpoint of any single living generational group, the others are imputed to have peculiar and distinctive personalities and attendant behavior patterns that are evaluated
in positive and negative terms. Each generation removed from Japan
is assumed to have its own characterological qualities, qualities that
are derived at the outset from its spatiotemporal position, and are
thus not subject to voluntaristic adoption or rejection. Thus, each
generation is living out a unique, temporally governed lifetime that
shall not be seen again after it is gone.

Immigrants from Japan are called Issei, literally "first generation," a term referring to all those who were born and nurtured in
Japan and who later migrated to the United States. The children of at
least one Issei parent are called Nisei, literally "second generation,"
and this term encompasses all those born in the United States of

immigrant parentage. The grandchildren of Issei are called Sansei, literally "third generation," and include all those born of Nisei or Kibei parentage. The great-grandchildren of Issei are called Yonsei, literally "fourth generation" and include all those born of Sansei parentage. The great-great grandchildren of Issei are called Gosei and include all those born of Yonsei parentage. In addition, there is both terminological and characterological distinction imputed to all those persons who were born in the United States of Issei parentage, educated in Japan and then returned to the United States. These are called Kibei,[28] literally "returned to America," and their American-born children, as mentioned, are considered Sansei.

Age and situation may modify the strictness of membership in these generational groups, but while persons might be informally re-assigned to a group to which they do not belong by virtue of geo-graphical or generational criteria, the *idea* of the groups remains intact as a working conception of social reality. Thus, a young Jap-anese American friend of the author's who enjoys the social status of a Nisei jokingly refers to himself as an Issei since he was born of Nisei parents during their temporary residence in Japan. Older Nisei whose social and personal characteristics are similar to those of Issei are sometimes treated as if they were the latter.[29] Sansei age peers of Nisei are treated as the latter if they behave accordingly. But Nisei who appear to their fellow Nisei age peers as "too Japanesy" are sometimes associated in the minds of their more Americanized friends with Kibei, while those who are "too American" are associ-ated with Sansei. Finally, the offspring of geogenerationally mixed parentage—for example, Issei-Nisei, Nisei-Sansei, Nisei-Yonsei, and so on—and of racially mixed parentage are not easily classifiable. In practice they tend to demonstrate the sociological rule that status is as status does; that is, they enjoy the classification that social rela-tions and personal behavior assign to them and that they assign to themselves.[30]

In terms of the temporal categories with which we began this dis-cussion, the Japanese in America lay great emphasis on contempo-raries. This does not mean that they have no sense whatsoever of predecessors, successors, and consociates. Rather, their ideas about these categories—in practical terms about the past and history and the future of other generations, as well as about intimates—are vague and diffuse, or in the case of consociates, deemphasized and deprecated. From the point of view of the Nisei—and especially those Nisei who grew up on the West Coast and received cultural and group reinforcement from the Japanese American communities—Issei, other Nisei and Sansei, white Americans, blacks, Chinese Americans, and other persons whom they encounter are contemporaries in the formal sense since they are capable of being known to one another and of sharing similar, but not especially identical, situations. Moreover, while individuals live through an age-demarcated life cycle with *rites de passage* to mark off birth, marriage, death, and certain ceremonies, for the Nisei it is the common lifetime of the whole generational group that circumscribes social and personal orientations. The generational group has a life cycle of its own, internally indicated by its appropriate behavior patterns and externally bounded by the temporal duration of the whole group.

To the Nisei—and for the balance of this essay it is this group's perspective we shall be examining—the world of their predecessors is known through whatever their parents have told them about old Japan and what they have learned in afternoon "language" schools, college history courses, and Japanese movies. Nisei parents are concerned about their own children in particular and the Sansei and Yonsei successor generations in general, partly in terms of achievement and advancement—which Nisei efforts have facilitated—but more significantly they are worried about the future generations' character. Sansei and Yonsei do not exhibit Nisei character, and Nisei regard this fact as both inevitable and unfortunate.

It is as and with contemporaries that Nisei feel both pride and apprehension. The basic conception of the Nisei phenomenon ultimately depends on the objective existence of their own generational group. The Nisei geogenerational group inhabits time and space between that of the Issei and the Sansei. The Japanese American community in general and the Nisei group in particular provides a Nisei with emotional security and a haven from the turbulence and unpredictable elements of the outer world.[31] But the Nisei group is threatened by both centripetal and centrifugal forces, by individual withdrawal and acculturative transcendence.[32] Should collective identity be dissolved by the overarching precedence of atomized individuals, dyadic relationships, or small cliques, then Nisei would lose both its objective existence and its subjective meaning. Should individuals transcend the generational group by moving out into the world of their non-Japanese contemporaries, by "validating their acculturation,"[33] then too would both the objective and subjective senses of Nisei identity lose their compelling force. Thus, Nisei must worry on two fronts about the risks of intimate association. On the one hand, the very close contacts inherent in the segregated yet secure Japanese community allow for intimate association "below" the level of the generational group; on the other hand, the break-down of prejudice and discrimination threatens to seduce the Nisei individual away from the confines of the ethnoracial group.[34] Hence, it follows that for Nisei social and interpersonal relations are governed by a permanent interest in maintaining an appropriate social distance, so that individuals do not "escape" into integration or withdraw themselves from group solidarity. Either of these would jeopardize if not destroy the Nisei as a group and an idea.

Nisei do not speak of their social and personal life in this fashion; rather, they exhibit in numerous ways a quiet but deep and pervasive pride in their Nisei identity. This pride is not rooted in their material success, as it might be among other ethnic groups in America, but instead in their character. Nisei believe that they combine in themselves a perfect balance of Japanese and American traits. They are not "too Japanesy" as are the Issei by definition and the Kibei by virtue of imposed culture and education; they are not "too American" as are their white American contemporaries and the Sansei. Nisei character at its best is exhibited in cathectic management and by control over and suppression of spontaneity, emotionalism, and inappropriate expressiveness. It is this character itself, in which the Nisei take so much pride, that reacts back on the Nisei group to maintain its objective existence. It is this character that operates to orient behavior in such a manner that contemporaries are not converted to consociates, that fellow Nisei are not brought *too close* into the intimate circle.

Manners, Mores and Meanings

For the Nisei to preserve the objective identity of its own generational group, to deemphasize the biological aging of its members in favor of preserving the single moment-to-moment simultaneity of the generational group, it is necessary to move interpersonal relations away from the intimate or consociate level and push them back toward the formal or contemporary plane. In behalf of this objective, the Nisei have a built-in aid, Japanese culture, especially as it had developed by the late Meiji–early Taisho eras, the periods in which the bulk of Issei came to America. Although this culture had its origins in an environment far different from that which the Nisei experienced, it served the goal of anonymization of persons and immobilization of individual time through its emphasis on etiquette, ceremony, and rigid status deference.

The emphasis on etiquette in Japanese culture has been such a frequently mentioned feature that it hardly needs demonstration here.[35]

The Japanese language itself is one of social forms, indicative polite-ness, and status identifiers.[36] Moreover, Japanese language is one of indirection, removing the subject (speaker) in a sentence from direct relation to the predicate, and utilizing stylistic circumlocutions so that the intended object of the particular speech is reached by a cir-cular rather than linear route.[37] The net result of these forms is that individuals are held at arm's length, so to speak, so that potential consociates remain contemporaries—quasi-strangers, quasi-friends.

The Issei were able to transmit the basic ideas of this culture to their offspring, but its manifestation took place in an American id-iom interpenetrating the only society with which Nisei were famil-iar. Thus, Japanese etiquette appeared in the form of a sometimes seemingly Victorian politeness. Although the bow, whose rigid rules the Japanese imposed upon themselves while exempting all foreigners,[38] did not survive the generational passage, except in a limited vestigial form,[39] other forms especially verbal ones, could be translated into English. Thus, Japanese Americans are likely to pay careful attention to titles, to employ the terms of genteel propri-ety, to avoid obscenity and to use the passive voice.[40] In all this the Nisei succeed simultaneously in keeping associations under man-agement and emotions under control.

The primary concern of a Nisei male is the management and con-trol of his emotional economy. He truly cannot countenance an emo-tional economy governed, or should we say ungoverned, according to principles of behavioristic laissez-faire; he desires ultimately a "socializing" of that economy, and in the absence of complete "so-cialization," he introduces a constant "Keynesian" watchfulness over it. The human state that is idealized is that of inward quies-cence—that is lauded, is an outward appearance of emotional equa-nimity. An outward appearance that is boisterous, excessively emotional, visibly passionate, obviously fearful, unabashedly vain, or blushingly embarrassed, is distasteful and itself shameful, fit per-haps only for children and foreigners.

"Etiquette," as Clifford Geertz has pointed out in his study of Java, provides its user "with a set of rigidly formal ways of doing things which conceals his real feelings from others. In addition, it so reg-ularizes behavior, his own and that of others, as to make it unlikely to provide unpleasant surprises."[41] The manner in which Nisei at-tempt to employ tonal control, euphemisms, and circumlocution forms in speaking English illustrates the role of etiquette in lan-guage. Although English-speaking Europeans and most native-born Americans employ tonal change for emphasis and object indication, the Nisei strive after a flatness of tone and an equality of meter in their speech. For those who are unfamiliar with this style—as are a great many white Americans—it becomes difficult to distinguish the important from the insignificant items in any speech encounter. For the Nisei, it provides a continuous demonstration of the proper state of emotional equanimity; for the uninitiated "foreigner," it presents the Nisei as a blank slate. Since no one believes that a fellow human is in fact a blank state, it causes wonder about what "really" is being said and in some instances arouses suspicion of ulterior motives.[42]

Nisei employ euphemisms whenever the simpler and more direct form might indicate a state of emotional involvement or evoke an undesirable emotional response from others. Euphemisms and roundabout expressions are especially employed when the direct and precise term would or could be insulting or otherwise emotionally provocative. Where no English euphemism is available, or where one is so awkward as to introduce an embarrassment by its very usage, a Japanese term may be employed. This is especially the case in using nouns to designate racial or ethnic groups. Nisei rarely say "white man," "black," "Chinese," or "Jew" in their everyday speech. Nisei understand that race is a touchy subject in America with ambiguous meanings and ambivalent feelings deeply embedded in the subterranean value structure. To avoid possible emotional entanglements, they employ substitute and usually neutral terms derived from Japanese. This is the case despite the fact that Nisei tend not to speak Japanese to their peers. For "white man," the term "Caucasian" is sometimes used, but one is more likely to hear *Hakujin*, literally "white man," and occasionally one might overhear the pejorative *Keto*, literally a "hairy person," but freely translated as "barbarian." For "black," the Nisei, who combine a culturally derived, mild antipathy to blackness[43] with an unevenly experienced and ambivalent form of the American Negrophobic virus, almost never employ such vulgar terms as "nigger," "coon," "jigaboo" or "black boy." Rather, they use the denotatively pejorative *Kuron-bo*, literally "black boy," usually in a neutral and unpejorative sense, at least on the conscious level. For "Chinese," another people toward whom Nisei are ambivalent, the mildly pejorative Hawaiian term, *Pakē*, is quite commonly employed.

For "Jew" the terminology is especially interesting and provides an unusual example of trans-Pacific linguistic transmogrification. Anti-Semitism was almost unknown in Japan at the time the Issei came to America, and neither they nor their offspring readily adapted to this essentially European prejudice.[44] While growing up, however, Nisei learned of the special attitude held by other Americans toward Jews, and in their own inimitable way invented a term whereby they could express one central *idea* of the anti-Jewish stereotype without using the emotion-laden English term, "kike." Nisei employ the "Japanese" neologism *ku-ichi* to express this idea. Now, ku-ichi in its everyday use among Nisei does not refer so much to the Jews as such but rather to the idea of stinginess and miserliness and the representation of "cheapskate." The etymology of ku-ichi is the combination of the Japanese numbers "ku," meaning "nine" and "ichi" meaning one. Nine plus one is ten, and the Japanese term for ten is "Ju," the homonym for the English word "Jew." This Nisei linguistic innovation is not used or even widely known in Japan. The denotative word for Jew in Japan is *yudaya-jin*.[45] Nisei do not apply ku-ichi exclusively to Jews, but rather to fellow Nisei or to anyone who openly displays an attitude of cheapness or stinginess.

Circumlocutions and indirect speech are regular features of Nisei conversations serving to mute one's own feelings and prevent the eruption of another's. In the Chicago researchers employing the Rorschach test, Nisei males resorted to a significant amount of "confabulatory" responses when faced with a perplexing or emotionally troubling perception.[46] Indirect speech is a regular feature of conversations in Japan and is matched there by the circular placing of household furniture and the use of open space in streets and homes.[47] It also effects the quality of translations from Japanese to another language.[48] Among the Nisei, English usage is preferred, except when propriety dictates otherwise,[49] and circumlocutions and indirections are not too difficult to develop. Abstract nouns, noncommittal statements, and inferential hints at the essential meaning are regular features.

Indirection is also effected by the use of go-betweens to mediate in delicate situations. Anthropologists have emphasized the role of the marriage-arranger (*nakyo-do* or *baishakunin*) in traditional Japan, and some Nisei are prevailed upon to employ a baishakunin to ceremonialize an engagement *after* it has been effected in the American pattern.[50] On a more personal level, intermediaries may be employed to inform one male friend that another wishes to borrow money from him and to sound out the former on his willingness to loan it. In this manner the would-be borrower is prevented from having to go through a direct face-losing refusal should the hoped-for creditor decide not to loan the money, and the borrowee is saved from the mutually embarrassing situation that would arise if he had to refuse his friend the money. An intermediary is also employed, occasionally, to warn someone that he will receive an invitation to a social affair or to inform someone quietly that a "surprise party" is going to be given for him. In the former case, the affective linkage hinted at by the extension of an invitation is blunted, the embarrassment of a refusal to attend is reduced, and the invitee is given the opportunity to mobilize himself for the receipt of the formal invitation. In the latter case, the "surprise" is rendered unprovocative of an undesirable, excessive, emotional display.

Bluntness of speech is not a virtue among Nisei. Here again the trait is also found in Japan where it is accompanied by a high tolerance for lengthy monologues and a polite indifference to complete comprehension.[51] Among the Nisei as among their forebears in Japan, the main point of a conversational episode is not approached immediately. Moreover, as mentioned earlier, the monotonal flatness of affect prevents it from being readily identifiable to those who, like Europeans and white Americans, are accustomed to a tonal cue which indicates that what is being said now is more important than what has preceded or will follow it. Indeed, conversations among Nisei almost always partake of the elements of an information game between persons maintaining decorum by seemingly mystifying one another.[52] It is the duty of the listener to ascertain the context of the speech he or she hears and to glean from his or her knowledge of the speaker and the context just what is the important point.

Violations of this tacit ritual speech relationship occur fairly often, sometimes among Nisei themselves, but more often in encounters between Nisei and Hakujin, Nisei and Sansei, and Nisei and other Gaijin. Exasperation with the apparent pointlessness of talk, frustration with vain attempts to gauge the meaning of sequential utterances, and the desire to reach a conclusion sometimes lead these non-Nisei to ask a pointed question directed at the heart of the matter. Nisei are troubled by this; they may refuse to answer, change the subject or, more subtly, redirect the conversation back to its concentric form. The idealized aim in a conversation is to maintain the appropriate ritual and calm state of speaker and audience. To do this, important items (that is, those charged with potential affect and those likely to disturb speaker-audience homeostasis) are buried beneath a verbal avalanche of trivia and, in the most perfected of conversations, are never brought to the surface at all—they are silently *apprehended* by the listener.

This emphasis on calmness and composure lends itself to unstated but widely held norms of conversational propriety appropriate to different social occasions. Since it is at informal social occasions—parties, dinners, tête-à-têtes—that one's speech partners and oneself are vulnerable to conversion from contemporaries to consociates, it is precisely such occasions, seemingly just the ones for intimacy and spontaneity, that require careful monitoring for excessive affect.[53] Nisei "rules" for social gatherings, therefore, include (1) an emphasis on "democratic participation" in speech; that is, no one should speak too long or too much and everyone should have an opportunity to speak; (2) circulation; that is, small clusters of conversationalists are permissible but these should be governed by fusion and fission, regularly decomposing and reforming with new elements; lengthy dyadic conversations at a gathering of ten or twenty people are discouraged; (3) unimportance; that is, the content of conversations should be restricted to trivial matters, things that can always be kept "external," items that do not reflect directly on either the speaker's or listener's inner life. The most fruitful items for conversation are sports, stocks and bonds, and fashion, technical subjects, for all of these can be kept "outside" the inner domain of individual personhood and every speaker can be fairly confident that he or she is not likely to be importuned or embarrassed.[54]

Further exemplification of Nisei emotional management is seen in their handling of the erotic and their emphasis on form over function. The erotic is everywhere emotionally exciting and thus is a source of potential emotional discomfiture to Nisei. Two examples—that of wedding receptions and pornographic movies—illustrate modes of mitigation and neutralization of the erotic. One "survival" of the rural customs of Japan among current Nisei is the employment of a "master of ceremonies" at wedding receptions. Originally, this role was usually enacted by the baishakunin,[55] but among Nisei a good friend of the groom is often requested to assume this post. At the banquet or reception following the wedding, the master of ceremonies formally introduces the bride and groom and their families to the assembled company, presents one or several toasts to the newlywed couple, calls people out of the audience to perform as comedians, storytellers, or singers, and tells jokes, droll anecdotes, and humorous incidents about the groom. In the rural prefectures of traditional Japan, this part of the reception was often accompanied by ribald jokes and risqué stories.[56] When Issei participate in such a reception, they sometimes introduce humorous obscenities into them. However, Nisei usually instruct their appointed masters of ceremonies to "keep it clean" and to refrain from any drolleries that would "embarrass" bride, groom, or company.

Watching pornographic films constitutes one instance of "watching the unwatchable" since they depict activities usually carried out in private with no audience except the participants. Viewing them is not governed by well-known ubiquitous norms.[57] Pornographic films are typical fare at an American stag party for a groom-to-be and his male friends. When Nisei are watching such films two kinds of response are prevalent. On the one hand, jibes and catcalls will tease one or another of the assembled company about his excessive interest in the films, alleged similarities or dissimilarities in his behavior and that depicted on the screen, or his remarkable quietness in the presence of an obviously stimulating event. On the other hand, it sometimes happens that a Nisei will verbally transform the meaning of the activities on the screen, emphasizing their form irrespective of content. Thus, the nude bodies copulating on the movie screen can be treated in terms of their physical anatomy, aesthetic quality, or gymnastic innovation.

Emphasis on form over and against content is not only a protective device against possible emotional disturbance in the presence of the erotic, but also a generally utilized mechanism in the presence of anticipated or actual performance failure. Thus, Nisei golfers and bowlers who are performing poorly, or who believe they will do so, may justify their bad scores by pointing out that they are working on their stance, body form, follow-through, and so on. Since it is widely accepted that form and content are analytically separable but related aspects of a variety of activities, the claim to be emphasizing the former irrespective of the latter is an acceptable account.[58] Moreover, it prevents any effective referral of the poor scores to the inner or actual state of the performer. Thus, inner equanimity may be maintained and outer calmness may be exhibited even in the presence of apparently contradictory evidence.

Social and Personal Controls

The ideal Nisei is one who has mastered the art of personal control. This requires management of body, mind, and feelings.[59] If these are properly under control the outward appearance is that of a calm, collected, blasé sophisticate.[60] This state is rarely reached in fact, but Nisei have mechanisms of impression management and mutual monitoring that keep any appearance approximating the ideal from being damaged too much by emotional breakdowns. Among these mechanisms are face controls, dissimulation, and avoidance.

The face, as Simmel observed long ago,[61] is the most significant communicator of the inner person. This is especially true of the eyes, nostrils, and mouth, and of the color exhibited by the face.[62]

For Nisei the face is a most vulnerable object in any interpersonal encounter, for its uncontrolled expression, if met by the searching gaze of another, may lock them into a consociative relationship from which extrication would be both difficult and embarrassing. Nisei faces tend to be "set" at the expressionless level or at least to strive after that effect. This is achieved more easily in America perhaps because of the stereotypical interpretation of Japanese faces by Caucasians and Negroes, and because the epicanthic eye fold and smooth skin make face "readings" difficult. However, some Nisei are disturbed over their vulnerability to facial disclosure; they avoid facing others for any length of time or erect barriers and involvement shields against another's gaze.[63] Newspapers and magazines provide objects for scanning during a conversation, and, although too close attention to these might be considered rude, a deft employment of them will serve to reduce eye contact. Finally, the fact that Nisei share a common concern over face management facilitates a mutual avoidance of staring or fixed gaze, and a tendency to avert one's eyes.

Dissimulation is a regular feature of everyday life among Nisei. Its most elementary form is the self-imposed limitation on disclosure. Nisei tend not to volunteer any more information about themselves than they have to. Thus, to a listener, a Nisei's autobiographical statements appear as a series of incompletely presented episodes, separated by voids that are not filled in with events or information unless it is unavoidable.

Beyond silence about much of personal life is the half-truth or "little white lie" that bridges the gap between information requested and personhood protected. Thus, Nisei will sometimes not tell about an important event, or will casually dismiss it with a denial or only a partial admission, suggesting by style and tone that it was not important at all. Direct questions are usually answered with vague or mildly meretricious replies.[64] Still another element of dissimulation is concealment of feelings, opinions, or activities, especially in the presence of employers, colleagues, and guests. As Nisei have been promoted into middle-management and other decision-making posts, their colleagues and superiors have sometimes been astonished at their silence during conferences or executive meetings. And, as with the Javanese practice of *etok-etok* (pretense),[65] the Nisei do not feel the need to justify these omissions, "white lies," or evasions; rather, the burden would appear to be on the listener to demonstrate why such tact and tactics should not be employed.[66]

Nisei men attempt to avoid those persons and situations that are likely to evoke embarrassment, personal disorganization, and loss of self-control. When a new line of endeavor is undertaken, especially if it requires learning a new skill or taking a risk, it is usually entered into in secret or with those persons whom the Nisei does not know well or wish to know. After it has been mastered, or after the risk has been evaluated as worthwhile, or sometimes after the endeavor has already begun, a Nisei will inform his close associates in a casual manner that he thinks he *might be about to* undertake the line of action in question. To fellow Nisei this will be understood not as a probablistic statement, but as an absolute one, and they will further understand that all preparations, rehearsals, and calculations have already been made. Later, if his associates see a performance of the new skill, they remain silently aware that it is in fact an exhibition of an already perfected ability.

Persons who are importunate, who demand too much display of interpersonal commitment, or who violate norms of emotional propriety are an ever-present threat to the cathectic equanimity of a Nisei. A concept usually employed with respect to Japanese child rearing practices is relevant here.[67] Japanese speak of *amaeru*, an intransitive verb by which they mean "to depend and presume upon another's benevolence." Not only children but adults suffer from too much *amae*, and their behavior toward those whom they wish to express affection toward them is regarded as overly demanding and excessive. A person suffering from too much amae feels himself to be *kodawaru*; that is, he feels inwardly disturbed over his personal relationships. A recognition of one's own feeling of *kodawari* leads to *sumunai*, guilt over one's failure to do as one should. Behind many Japanese people's feeling of sumunai, as Professor Doi has pointed out, lies "much hidden aggression engendered by frustration of their wish to *amaeru*."[68] Nisei do not employ this terminology generally, but several studies have pointed to a complex of dependency needs and consequent personal difficulties in Nisei individuals, needs that have their roots in the wish to be loved, and the guilt over this wish or the shame over its expression.[69]

For Nisei males, the entire complex of amae-kodawari-sumunai is rarely admitted to be a personal problem; rather it is most frequently perceived to be a problem in another's interpersonal relations. When a Nisei recognizes a close associate's excessive amae toward him, he may become upset by this fact, retreat even further behind a formal facade of etiquette and attempt to establish greater social distance. Or he might hope, or even clandestinely request, that a third party, recognizing the difficulty between the two friends, tactfully explain the problem to the defalcating party and urge upon him an approach to his friend that is less demanding and less obviously a display of excessive amae. Still another alternative is to gently but firmly tease the offending party until he realizes that he has overstepped the bounds of propriety. Finally, another tactic is to make sure that all contacts with the offending party will take place with other friends present, so that his excessive affection will be "diffused" among the whole body of friends rather than centered on just one person.[70]

Building Nisei Character

There can be little doubt that one fundamental source of Nisei character is to be found in the samurai ethic that developed from the Tokugawa through the Meiji Eras (c. 1601-1912). Nisei find representative expression of this ethic in the brilliant epic films made in Japan to celebrate the feats and character of warriors of that period.[71] At one time shown in basements and church social halls in *Nihonmachi* (the Japanese quarter of the city), these movies are now known to many non-Japanese Americans because of their general popularity when exhibited at public theaters. *Chambara* (samurai) stories always emphasize the stoic character of the solitary and often tragic warrior who, though beaten about on every side by personal or clan enemies, political misfortunes, and natural disasters, nevertheless retains an outward appearance suggesting inner psychic strength and emotional equanimity.[72] Such characters—poignantly portrayed on the screen in reent years by such actors as Toshiro Mifune and Tatsuya Nakadai—serve as ideal character models and reminders of the appropriate presentation of self.

The patterns of hierarchical society, rigid formalism, etiquette, and shame were routinized features of the early life of the Issei, who grew up in a time of great technological and political—but little ethical or interpersonal—change in Japan.[73] The modernization of Japan, actually begun in the Tokugawa Period, was achieved not by overturning the old cultural order but rather by adapting western industrial, educational, and military forms to the framework of that order. "Within this general context," writes Reinhard Bendix, "the samurai were transformed from an estate of independent landed, and self-equipped warriors into one of urbanized, aristocratic retainers, whose privileged social and economic position was universally acknowledged. They remained attached to their tradition of ceremonious conduct, intense pride of rank and the cultivation of physical prowess."[74] The educational system fostered not only study of classics and, later, the more technical subjects, but also, and more importantly, directed its major attention to the development of virtue, humble modesty before superiors, self-control, and etiquette.[75] Thus, the Issei bore the cultural marks that had been part of the Japanese tradition for at least two centuries.

Few of the Issei were of samurai rank,[76] but in the two hundred years before emigration began, a complex melding process had helped to "nationalize" the samurai ethic and remove it from encapsulation within a single status group. First, after 1601 many samurai became displaced *ronin* (masterless warriors) obliged to sell their services to other lords, to cities as policemen or magistrates, even to commoners on occasion or, as a last resort short of suicide, they felt compelled to give up official samurai status entirely and become merchants.[77] All of these acts caused a certain filtering of the samurai ethic through the social order. Second, the educational system founded in the Tokugawa period, and universalized in 1873, though undecided about whether heredity or merit was more conducive to learning, admitted increasing numbers of commoners to the schools, thus affording them direct access to samurai indoctrination.[78] Third, samurai status itself was muddied by the practice, begun after 1700, of selling the right to wear a sword and bear a surname (the status symbols of samurai) to commoners.[79] Finally, it would appear that a significant portion of America's Issei came from prefectures in southeastern, central, and western Japan, prefectures in which the "democratization" of "ethical" education had been well advanced at the time of emigration.[80]

In addition to the samurai ethic, elements of the rural farmer's outlook also helped forge the orientation with which the Issei reared their children. The *ie* system, by which Japanese farmers represented both the contemporary physical house and the permanent family household, operated through this notion of preservation and continuity to forestall the development of individualism.[81] In Japan's rural villages the *honke-bunke* (stem-branch family system) allowed nuclear families to split off from one another in a partial sense, so that nothing like the extended Chinese clan system developed,[82] but atomization below the *ie*, or household, level was strongly discouraged. Village people spoke of the *iegara*, or *kakaku*; that is, the "reputation" or "standing" of a family, rather than the *hitogara* or *jinkaku*, the "personality" or social "standing" of individuals. The *ie* "was also far more important than the individuals who at any one time composed it, and hence if 'for the sake of the *ie*' the personal wishes and desires of those individuals had to be ignored or sacrificed, this was looked on as only natural."[83] The *ie* "required its members each to keep their proper place under the authoritarian direction of the household, resigning themselves to the suppression of personal desires unbecoming to their position. Thus, was order within the *ie* preserved and its harmony guaranteed—a harmony not of liberated cheerfulness, but of smouldering reserve and the frustration of still incompletely repressed desires."[84]

In America the Issei men, often married by proxy to women whom they had only seen in pictures *(shashin kekkon)* and who were sometimes quite a bit younger than they,[85] applied the principles of late Tokugawa–early Meiji child rearing to their Nisei offspring. In certain respects—notably for the Issei, in the lack of Japan's bath houses and geisha for outlet; for the Nisei, in the inhibitions on physical expression and open sensuality, and because of the absence of an indulgent grandmother to assuage the harshness of parental authority—child rearing was more harsh than in Japan.[86] Physical punishments were rarely used, although the *moxa* treatment was sometimes practiced by Issei parents not only for punishment and moral training, but also as a curative.[87] In one instance known to the author, an Okinawan Nisei reported that his father purposely cut his ears when giving him a haircut. When the boy screamed in pain, his father would slap him across the face with the stern admonition: "You don't scream. Japanese boys do not scream." However, resort to physical punishment is rare among Issei-Nisei families. Much more likely is the use of ridicule and teasing.

Several reports on Japanese child rearing have emphasized the role of ridicule.[88] Among these is the common theme of teasing a recalcitrant, noisy, emotionally upset, or otherwise obstreperous boy about behaving like a little girl. That a young man should be ashamed of his emotional expressions because they remind him of behavior associated with women is a frequent theme in Japanese biographies.[89] Nisei boys were also reprimanded by their parents for acting like little girls.[90] In addition, they were reminded that they were *Japanese* and therefore obligated to avoid arai (crudeness); to speak "good" Japanese and not zuzu (the dialect characteristic of northern Japan);[91] and to avoid any association with or even mention of *Eta* (Japan's pariah caste, some of whose members had unobtrusively settled in Florin, California, and a few other places).[92]

Moreover, emphasis was placed on individual superiority, achievement, and education as a criteria for both individual and group maturity.[93] Thus, Nisei children were not invited to discuss family matters at the dinner table, but rather were instructed to withdraw from participation until age and achievement had demonstrated their worth. Nisei children and adolescents were admonished with the statement, *Nisei wa mada tsumaranai;* that is, they were told that the Nisei generation was still worthless. Until adulthood had been achieved, an adulthood indicated not merely by coming of age but, far more importantly, demonstrated by independent status achieved through steadfastness, determination, and single-minded purposefulness, the Nisei were treated as immature but developing children.

Central to the demonstration of maturity among growing Nisei was self-control. Although independence and real achievement could not be actually demonstrated until adulthood, emotional management was always worthy of exhibition and often tested for its own sake. Issei tended to be oriented toward their children in terms of the latter's position in the birth order and their sex.[94] A line of direct authority extended down from the father through the mother to the first-born, second-born, third-born, and so on. A line of obligation extended upward from the youngest to the eldest. The authority system was not infrequently tested by an elder brother harshly rebuking his younger brother, sometimes for no apparent reason. Younger brothers learned that if they could "take" these rebukes with an outwardly calm detachment, they would ultimately be rewarded with a recognition of their "maturity." First-born sons received similar treatment from their fathers, and daughters sometimes found that they had to live up to both the precepts of manhood maturity and womanliness.[95] Brothers who threw tantrums or gave way to violent emotional expression were regarded as "immature" and were teased or otherwise maneuvered into conformative cathectic quiescence.

In the case of the Nisei, teasing and ridicule are characteristic not only of parent-child discipline but also of intragroup relations. They function to monitor behavior. Among Nisei, peer groups begin to share authority over the individual with parents with the onset of adolescence, and they begin to supersede parental authority, though not parental respect, in late adolescence and early adulthood. No one who has not been intimately associated with adolescent second generation Japanese groups can testify adequately to the remarkable, pervasive atmosphere and social effect of ridicule among Nisei teenagers. A veritable barrage of "cuts," "digs," "put-downs," and embarrassing stories are the stuff of verbal life. Moreover, as if a survival of the cultural collective unconscious,[96] Nisei youth, like their Japanese forebears across the sea, have a facility and interest in the organization of clubs, cliques, and gangs.[97] These associations are the units through which Nisei character is manifested, sustained, and reinforced.

Nisei teasing is not randomly directed. Targets for the verbal "cuts" are those fellow Nisei and other close friends who exhibit outward signs of tension, embarrassment, excessive emotional display, or boisterousness. Persons who blush, tremble, give way to tears, or raise their voices too often in anger or too much for emphasis are the "victims" and recipients of jibes and cajolery designed to bring them back into line. Many Nisei are self-consciously aware of the didactic purpose of this teasing, and regular "victims" have on occasion reported to me their heartfelt gratefulness for it.

In addition to its teaching and control functions, two other "rules" appear to govern Nisei teasing. First, the status position of any particular Nisei vis-à-vis his fellow Nisei may render him or her ineligible or preferable for teasing. For instance, in the joking relationship there is a tendency for Nisei whose parents hail from peasant and poor prefectures not to tease those whose parents are from urban and socioeconomically better-off areas; for Nisei from rural parts of California to be somewhat awed by those from San Francisco or Los Angeles; and for clique leaders to be less eligible for "cuts" than ordinary members. The "inferior" statuses are themselves the butt of jokes that earmark offensive behavior and gauche ways as stemming from poor, peasant, and rural origins. Thus, Nisei whose parents came from Shiga, Kagoshima, and a few other prefectures, and those whose parents are from Okinawa and Hokkaido, are often teased mercilessly about their culturally acquired agrestic characters, or are perceived as persons incapable of realizing the Nisei characterological ideal. More mild in form, but no less felt, are the ridicule and humor directed at Nisei from rural America by their urban compatriots. An informal avoidance and segregation sometimes set boundaries between Nisei of different status groups and prevents confrontations that would be mutually embarrassing.[98]

The second so-called rule governing man-to-man teasing is that Nisei ridicule and joking must steer a careful course between the Scylla of ineffectiveness and the Charybdis of associative breakup. If jokes and "cuts" are too mild, too obscure, usually misunderstood or always mitigated by apologies and explanations, then the intended objective is frustrated and the defalcating party is not brought to heel. If, on the other hand, the jokes are too damning, too pointed, if they cut to the very heart of a person and leave him no room to maneuver or retreat, then the defalcating party may withdraw from the group in unredeemed shame or anger and be lost, perhaps forever, to its benefits and protections. To indicate that a person has gone too far in his teasing, a Nisei "target" may warn him of his offense by directing a telling remark at a third party in earshot of the two. Thus, watching two youthful Nisei friends of mine escalate their reciprocal "cuts," I became the third party in such a situation. The offended party turned to me and said, "Man, he's a chilly dude, isn't he?" The warned person recognized the rebuke for what it was and proceeded to deescalate his humorous assaults on the other. And so the appropriate relationship—not too harsh, not too soft—was maintained.

The characterological ideal of any Nisei male is best realized when others do not know his emotional state. To achieve this, he must, as one Nisei put it to me, build a wall around his emotions so that others cannot see what they are. Their "authoritarian" upbringing on the one hand, and the "samurai" code of stoicism and endurance on the other, helped them to construct this social and psychic edifice. The functions of this wall have been described by Geertz in his study of Java where he found an identical ideal: "If one can calm one's most inward feelings . . . one can build a wall around them; one will be able both to conceal them from others and to protect them from outside disturbance. The refinement of inner feeling has thus two aspects: the direct internal attempt to control one's emotions . . . and secondly, an external attempt to build a [wall] around them that will protect them. On the one hand, one engages in inward discipline, and on the other in an outward defense."[99] However, while this impregnable "wall" is the ultimately desired objective, most Nisei point out that few can fully attain it.

The character displayed or aimed at by Nisei in everyday life is not unfamiliar to other Americans. Indeed, while at one time it was thought to be the unique trait of aristocrats, Orientals, and urbanites, mature industrial societies seem to require it of everyone today.[100] Ordinary people describe it by such adjectives as "blasé," "sophisticated," and, in more recent times, "cool." Other related terms describing aspects of this character are "self-possessed," "detached," "aloof," "sang-froid," and "savoir-faire." What is referred to is the "capacity to execute physical acts, including conversation, in a concerted, smooth, self-controlled fashion in risky situations, or [the capacity] to maintain affective detachment during the course of encounters involving considerable emotion."[101] Ideally for the Nisei, this means combining courage, a willingness to proceed on a course of action anticipated to be dangerous without any manifestation of fear; gameness, sticking to a line of action despite set-backs, injury, fatigue, and even impending failure (*Yamato damashii*);[102] and integrity, the resistance of temptations that would reduce the actor's moral stance. Finally, Nisei character places its greatest emphasis on composure, including all its ramifications of physical and mental poise during any act, calmness in the face of disruptions and embarrassing situations, presence of mind and the avoidance of "blocking" under pressure, emotional control during sudden changes of situation, and stage confidence during performances before audiences.[103]

As has been intimated, Nisei males find it difficult to live up to this ideal. However, there are strategies and tactics whereby its appearance can be generated and its failures avoided or hidden. Thus, courage is balanced by a realistic appraisal of risks and opportunities. Studies of Nisei estimates of first salaries, for example, show that they almost always guessed the salary to the nearest dollar,[104] suggesting perhaps a procedure whereby face could be protected from the loss it would suffer by a rejection of an incorrect estimate of self-worth. Gameness is partially mitigated by choosing lines of action—such as jobs, sports, games, and so on—in which one has secretly tested oneself for potentiality and ability. Violations of absolute integrity are neutralized by the practice of situation ethics and the invocation of a layman's version of the international legal principle *rebus sic stantibus*. Composure, as has been mentioned, is guarded by self-discipline, protected by barriers and involvement shields, and tested and supported by teasing and ridicule. Finally, disasters and misfortunes, either personal or collective, may be accepted with equanimity by assigning them to fate (or as the Japanese would say, *shikata-ganai*).[105]

Consequences of Nisei Character

The everyday practice of the Nisei way of life has certain consequences that both reflect its essential nature and react back upon Nisei as sources of pride or problems. These consequences may be discussed under the headings of perception and projection, communication confusion, stage fright, and real and imagined illnesses.

In everyday discussions with Nisei any non-Nisei listener would be impressed by their pointed perceptions and shrewd observations of others. These perceptions and observations are made about absent third parties and are never uttered in the presence of the party under discussion. Many people would be surprised at how keenly quite ordinary Nisei have paid attention to the minute details of interpersonal situations, placed brackets around particular sets of events, and interpreted words and gestures in light of the general "theory" of Nisei character. Most Nisei analyses of fellow Nisei concentrate on the degree to which the latter fail to carry off the appropriate presentation of self and attribute any failings to some inner-lying maladaptation or maladjustment. Parlor "Freudianism" is quite common in these analyses, and one Nisei may speak of another in terms of the latter's essential inability to mask his or her "inferiority complex," "fear of failure," or "feelings of inadequacy."

It is my impression that these "perceptions" are in fact "projections." Nisei tend to function as one another's mirror images, showing up the defects in each other's character. This is possible because the "wall" that Nisei have built to prevent others from seeing their own emotions is actually only a set of personal blinders keeping the individual from introspection. To put it another way, the Nisei have attempted to separate personal feeling from particular action and in doing so have "alienated" their emotional from their behaving selves.[106] This "alienation" gives Nisei the peculiar advantage of self-detachment and an angular vision of their fellow Nisei not shared by those not so detached from self. But the angle of perceptive advantage, reinforced by the similarity of life styles among Nisei results, as I see it, in the imputation to others of the perceiver's own partly recognized failings. Thus, their common life and general self-alienation permit projections and perceptions to coincide without the latter necessarily being seen as having derived from the former.

Nisei character is an ideal that few Nisei in fact ever feel they have achieved. In trying to live up to the ideal, many Nisei find they are confused or are confusing to others. These confusions occur over mutual misreadings of intentions or meanings, misunderstandings of jokes and ridicule, and problems arising out of the episodic nature of Nisei life. Because tonal cues are not used as indicators of significance, Nisei sometimes fail to grasp the relevant item in a conversation; more often their non-Nisei colleagues or friends miss the important point and fail to act appropriately. Since Nisei often take it for granted that those with whom they converse will automatically understand them and will be able to separate the chaff from the wheat of their speech, they are frustrated and exasperated when this fails to happen.[107]

Mention has already been made of the role of jokes and ridicule in Nisei social control. Despite their importance, or perhaps because of it, these "cuts" and "digs" create problems. Discussing the problem of what a humorous jibe at another Nisei really means, a Nisei friend and I distinguished analytically three kinds of barbs: (1) those that are given just in fun; that is, "pure" humor having neither intent nor consequences beyond the ensuing laughter; (2) those that are didactic; that is, having as their objective the redirection of another's behavior so that it is no longer embarrassing or inept; and (3) those that are intentionally destructive having as their object another's degradation.

Nisei tend to disbelieve that many jokes can have no object at all, preferring instead to believe that some intent must lie behind the ostensibly humorous utterance. However, they experience difficulty in ascertaining whether a jibe is didactic or destructive, because, in fact, the line between them is difficult to draw. Witty repartee is a well-developed and highly prized art among Nisei, but precisely because skill at it is differentially distributed, no Nisei can feel entirely comfortable in an encounter.

Beyond adolescence, Nisei occasionally confess discomfiture about being permanently locked into a system of competitive relations with fellow Nisei. Social visits are occasions for the reciprocal giving and receiving of humorous remarks calling attention to invidious distinctions. Birth, sex, and growth of children, richness and style of furniture, occupational advancement, skill at leisure time activities, and many other everyday things may become grist for the wit's mill. Indeed, a young Nisei told the author that one reason Nisei oppose the continuation of the Japanese residential ghetto is that they "just know" that they would be constantly "looking in each other's windows."

Individual Nisei encounters with acquaintances and new colleagues tend to be cathectically episodic rather than developmental. (However, it is important to emphasize that among Nisei, friendships cliques are long-lasting and that non-Nisei [including the author of this essay] have maintained decades-long intimate association with Japanese Americans without any noticeable difficulty.) Non-Nisei, however, often assume a developmental sequence to be the operative norm in continued interactions. Thus, among non-Nisei Americans a sequence of social encounters usually proceeds upon the assumption that each new encounter will begin at the emotional level or feeling-state reached at the end of the last meeting. Among Nisei, however, there is a limit to expressed feeling-states that is quickly reached and may not be deepened without loss of inner equanimity or outer poise. Hence, Nisei tend to treat each such encounter almost as if the participants were meeting for the first time. This permits the limited range of feeling-states to be reached again each time but not transcended. For those content with a friendship based in a permanently established line beyond which interpersonal relations may not go, this pattern may go unnoticed. However, those who expect that each new encounter will bring increased "depth," or those who expect to open any "second" encounter with a Nisei with a reciprocated expression of the warmth often indicated in Occidental friendships, may be startled or exasperated by what appears to them to be a coolness of response. Episodic encounters function to keep potentially consociative relationships at the contemporaneous level, and thus, to protect the integrity of the Nisei group.

Unlike many middle-class Occidentals in America, Nisei are more conscious of being on display, so to speak, before a hypercritical audience. "A simile is useful in pointing up the similarities and differences between Japanese American and white middle-class achievement orientations: the ultimate destinations or goals of individuals in the two groups tend to be very similar; but Japanese Americans go toward these destinations along straight, narrow streets lined with crowds of people who observe their every step, while middle class persons go toward the same destinations along wider streets having more room for maneuvering, and lined only with small groups of people who, while watching them, do not observe their every movement."[108] People who believe that their every move is under scrutiny are liable to suffer from "stage fright."[109] In the case of Nisei this would appear to be an inevitable consequence of their need to exhibit an appearance of poise and equanimity in the face of a constantly intrusive and challenging world. Moreover, an exhibition of "stage fright" is itself a flaw in Nisei character management and must be avoided if the illusion of composure is to be maintained. Among Nisei one finds a fear—usually mild, occasionally quite intensive—that an encounter will be spoiled by a collapse of formality and a revelation of the actual personality hidden behind the facade of etiquette. Nevertheless, Nisei lend support to the belief system that generates this fear by observing in quite ordinary conversations, and insisting in their reprimands given to fellow Nisei, especially to siblings, that the entire community is watching them, and that they must, therefore, behave with circumspection.[110]

It sometimes occurs that ceremony and etiquette collapse and Nisei find themselves locked in the mutually embarrassing relationship of consociates. More often this happens to one party who during an encounter is, for some reason, unable to sustain appropriate emotional equipoise. When this does occur, the other parties present will try to repair the psychic bridge that has kept them at the proper social distance from one another by studied non-observation of the other's embarrassment, by aversion of the eyes from the other's discomfiture in order to allow the latter time to repair his or her social front, or by a warm but unmistakably triumphant grin that simultaneously signals a "victory" in the ever-played "game" of social testing and also the social reinstatement of the "losing" player. Social life for Nisei is a contest something like tennis: a single faux pas is a "game" victory; an evening full of them may be a "set," but it takes an entire lifetime to play out the "match."

Many observers have pointed to the noticeable hypochondria in the Japanese character,[111] and at least one has stated that it indicates a remarkably compulsive personality.[112] It is questionable whether, or to what extent, hypochondria is a feature of Nisei life; for a sociologist the very question raises problems for which an unambiguous answer is difficult if not impossible.[113] Disease, or the outward signs of disease, threatens the equanimity so cherished by Nisei. On the other hand, admission that one has a disease is also potentially damaging. In traditional Japan a history of disease in a family was sufficient reason to cancel a marriage, and it was the task of the nakyo-do to discover if such a history existed.[114] Shame over illness is found to some degree among Nisei men and extends also, with numerous individual variations, of course, to cover any involuntary loss of control over body stasis such as occurs when vomiting or in a state of intoxication. A Nisei is vulnerable to "attacks" from his body, which enjoys for him something of the sociological status of the stranger as conceived by Simmel:[115] it is ever with him but mysterious and not quite subject to perfect control.

It is my impression that the Nisei suffer from an unusual amount of that kind of psychosomatic disease—ulcers, colitis, psoriasis, falling hair, and so on—that results from permanent unresolved tensions.[116] That the tensions are real should be clear not only from what I have written thus far, but also from the findings of clinical studies.[117] Proof of the actual existence of these diseases is more difficult to obtain, not only because of the desire on the part of Nisei to conceal and deemphasize sickness in themselves, but also because of the structural arrangements in current America that aid them in their efforts. Many of my Nisei friends have informed me of the abdominal pains from which they silently suffer. Others are startled by and ashamed of their seemingly incurable mottled fingernails or falling hair. Few Nisei, however, visit doctors to have their symptoms analyzed. Instead, they rely on Nisei pharmacist friends and colleagues, of whom in California there are a great many, to diagnose their symptoms and prescribe a remedy or a relief. Seeing a Nisei pharmacist friend is not too threatening apparently since it keeps the information localized and requires far less elaborate explanation by either "patient" or pharmacist than would or might be required by a physician. The suffering Nisei need only hint at his or her ailment, and the pharmacist, who may suffer from the same problem, will know what not to say and what medicine to prescribe. By eliminating the "middle man"—in this case, the physician—the Nisei sufferer preserves poise while at the same time protecting his or her health. Moreover, the sufferer avoids that source of potentially embarrassing or frustrating information, the doctor or psychiatrist, who might show that the pain and discomfort arise directly out of the unresolved problems created by the patients subcultural outlook. That ultimate revelation might be too much to bear; one logical conclusion to be drawn from it is that abandonment of the Nisei way of life is the price for permanent relief from pain.

The Crisis of the Future

The geogenerational conception of time and person that predominates in Nisei life evokes the recognition that any generation with its attendant character structure will eventually decline and pass away. Although the Issei generation has by no means passed out of existence, its influence began to decline after 1942 when the enforced incarceration of all persons of Japanese ancestry propelled the Nisei into positions of prison camp and community leadership.[118] At the present time, as the Sansei generation comes to maturity and establishes its independent existence and special group identity in America, the Nisei group is beginning to sense its own decline and eventual disappearance.

The Nisei can clearly see the end of their generational existence in the not too distant future. The census of 1960 reported that 82 percent of all Japanese in thirteen western states were born in the United States, its territories or possessions; in other words, a little more than eight-tenths of the persons of Japanese descent in that area are Nisei, Kibei, Sansei, Yonsei, and Gosei. The manner of taking the census prohibits any further breakdown of these figures into respective geogenerational groupings. However, by looking at age distribution, we can arrive at a crude approximation. In California, where 159,545 persons of Japanese descent live, the 1960 census recorded 68,015 of these between the ages of zero and twenty-four. Most of these are the children, grandchildren, or occasionally great-grandchildren of Nisei, and thus will soon equal and then outstrip the latter in number.

The inevitable end of the Nisei group has provoked a mild crisis in the *Lebenswelt* ("life-world") of the Nisei.[119] Nisei are coming to realize with a mixture of anxiety, discomfort, and disillusion—but primarily with a sense of fatalistic resignation—that the way of life to which they are used, the presentation of self that they have always taken for granted, the arts of self-preservation and impression management that they have so assiduously cultivated and so highly prized, will soon no longer be regular features of everyday existence among the Japanese in America. Thus, Nisei perceive that what has been a valid way of living for so many years will not continue to be so, and that what they have accomplished by living this way will no longer be accomplished this way or perhaps at all. The Sansei and, for that matter, the other successor generations will be different from the Nisei in certain fundamental respects. Moreover, some of these respects are viewed with considerable misgivings by contemporary Nisei.

Nisei have always seemed to recognize the sociocultural and psychic differences between themselves and the Sansei. Some of these differences are based on clearly distinguishable generational experiences. Few of the Sansei are old enough to remember or have experienced the terrible effects of imprisonment during World War II; most Sansei have not grown up in homes marked by a noticeable cultural division between America and Japan; most Sansei have benefited from the relative material success of their parents and have received parental support for their educational pursuits without difficulty; finally, few Sansei have borne the oppressive burden of racial discrimination or felt the demoralizing agony of anti-Japanese prejudice. In all these respects Nisei recognize that the Sansei are the beneficiaries of Issei and Nisei struggles and perseverance, and they acknowledge that if, because of these things, the Sansei do behave differently than an immigrant or oppressed people, then it is only right and proper for them to do so.

There is one aspect of Sansei behavior, however, that worries and disappoints Nisei: it is their lack of appropriate (that is, Nisei) character. Some Nisei see this characterological loss as a product of increased urbanization and Americanization; others emphasize the loss of Japanese "culture" among the third generation. Whatever the explanation, many Nisei perceive a definite and irremediable loss of character in their successor generation. To illustrate this point, note that Nisei often use the term Sansei to indicate at one and the same time the existence and cause of social impropriety. Thus, in the face of an individual's continued social errors in my presence, a Nisei explained to me, "What can you expect? He's a Sansei."

Ironically, Nisei child rearing and parental practices contribute to the creation of the very Sansei character that disappoints them, just as their own Issei parents helped to lay the groundwork for Nisei character.[120] Despite the great general respect and personal deference which the Nisei pay to their parents, they tend to see them as negative role models when it comes to rearing their own children. The isolation, loneliness, harshness, and language and communication difficulties of their own childhoods are vividly recalled, and a great many Nisei have vowed that their children will not experience any of that. As a result, the ethics of samurai stoicism and endurance and the discipline associated with them are rarely emphasized by Nisei parents. Rather, they choose to order their child rearing by following the white middle-class ethos of love, equality, and companionship. The principles of *Bushido* gave way to those of Dr. Spock; the idea of age-graded obligation is supplanted by the age-cohort theory of Gesell; the social distance that separated parent and child is replaced by the idea that parents and children should "grow up together."

The resultant product of this upbringing is, of course, quite different from that of its parents. Worse, from the point of view of most Nisei, it is a disappointing one. Nisei complain that Sansei seem to lack the drive and initiative that was once a hallmark of the Japanese; that they have no interest in Japanese culture, especially its characterological elements; that they are prone to more delinquency and less respect for authority than were the Nisei; and that they are "provincial" and bound to the "provincialisms" of Los Angeles, perhaps the city that encloses the single largest aggregate of Sansei.[121] Nisei often complain about the lack of psychological self-sufficiency and independent capacity for decision making among Sansei. Thus, a Nisei scoutmaster pointed out to me how his scout troop, mostly Sansei, became emotionally upset and homesick when away for but a week's camping trip, and how their projected wiener roast would have been ruined if he had not stepped in and directed the planning for food purchases. He attributes these "failings" to their Sansei background, and he admitted that his own intervention in assisting the scouts in their plans was a distinct departure from what his own parents would have done in a similar situation during his childhood. Issei parents, say many Nisei, would probably have "let" their children "fail" in such an endeavor in order to help them cultivate responsibility and initiative. But such a seemingly cold and unfeeling response to their own children is anathema.

Sansei indicate an ambivalence and a mild anxiety over their own situation. They do exhibit a certain "Hansen effect"—that is, a desire to recover selected and specific elements of the culture of old Japan[122]—but in this endeavor itself they discover that their own Americanization has limited the possibility of very effective recovery. If juvenile delinquency among them is on the rise—and the evidence is as yet inconclusive[123]—they attribute it in small part to parental misunderstandings and in greater part to the effects of the great social changes taking place in America. Their parents often appear "old-fashioned" to them, unprepared to understand their "hang-ups" and unwilling to offer sufficient love and understanding to them.[124] Finally, they seem at times to be about to claim the right to dissolve their own geogenerational identity and that of their successor generations in favor of both deeper intimate associations below the level of the generational group and interracial intimacies transcending them.[125] Yet, they also wonder how and in what manner they can or should retain their "Japanese" identity.[126]

Unlike many groups, the Nisei do not stand at a crossroads. Their fate is sure and their doom is sealed by the moving hands of the generational clock. They have not merely survived the hatred and oppression of America's racism, they have triumphed over it. In nearly every "objective" measure they outstrip their minority "competitors," and in education they have surpassed the white majority.[127] They have turned almost every adversity into a challenge and met each with courage and cool judgment. In all this their own subcultural character has been an invaluable aid as well as an ever-present source of pride. Now they see the coming of the end of their own generation and of this character, and they can only wonder what psychic supports will provide mental sustenance for future generations. In one sense the Nisei are the last of the *Japanese* Americans; the Sansei are American Japanese. As Jitsuichi Masuoka observed over four decades ago, "It is the members of the *Sansei* who, having been fully acculturated but having been excluded by the dominant group because of their racial difference, really succeed in presenting a united front against exclusion by the dominant group. A genuine race problem arises at this point in the history of race relations."[128] Ironically, in the 1990s, this generation is coming into its maturity at the same time that a revival of anti-Japanese and anti-Asian sentiment in America threatens its hard-won personal and social security.

NOTES

1. Quoted in Lewis Bush, *77 Samurai: Japan's First Embassy to America* (Tokyo: Kodansha International, 1968), p. 132. (Based on the original

manuscript in Japanese by Itsuro Hattori.) Bush does not give the date of this newspaper article. It would appear to be April 2, 1860, or thereabouts.

2. The embassy was not the first visit of Japanese to America. It is possible that a Japanese ship was wrecked off the coast of South America in 3000 B.C. Betty J. Meggers, Clifford Evans and Emilio Estrada, *Early Formative Period of Coastal Ecuador: The Valdivia and Machalilla Phases* (Washington, D.C.: Smithsonian Institution, 1965), pp. 167–78. The Hashikura Embassy arrived in New Spain in 1614 and some of its members remained until 1615, not returning to Japan until 1620. William Lytle Schurtz, *The Manila Galleon* (New York: E. P. Dutton, 1959), pp. 99–128. Moreover, twenty-four Japanese ships were wrecked off western North America in the period between 1613 and 1850 and some of the survivors resided temporarily among Occidentals. Charles Wolcott Brook, *Japanese Wrecks Stranded and Picked up Adrift in the North Pacific Ocean* (Fairfield, Washington: Ye Galleon Press, 1964. Origin. publ. 1876); Shunzo Sakamaki, "Japan and the United States, 1790–1853," *The Transactions of the Asiatic Society of Japan,* 18 (1939), 2d series, pp. 3–204. See also J. Feenstra Kuiper, Ph.D., "Some notes on the Foreign Relations of Japan in the Early Napoleonic Period (1798–1805)," Ibid., 1 (1923–24) 2d series, pp. 55–82.

3. Bush, 77 Samurai, p. 132.

4. See Jacobus ten Broek, Edward N. Barnhart, and Floyd Matson, *Prejudice, War, and the Constitution, Japanese American Evacuation and Resettlement,* vol. 3 (Berkeley: University of California Press, 1954), pp. 11–98.

5. See Anne Reeploeg Fisher, *Exile of a Race* (Sidney, British Columbia: Peninsula Printing Co., 1965); Morton Grodzins, *Americans Betrayed: Politics and the Japanese Evacuation* (Chicago: University of Chicago Press, 1949), pp. 1–230, 400–422. For a typical example of the rhetoric of that period see Alan Hynd, *Betrayal from the East: The Inside Story of Japanese Spies in America* (New York: Robert M. McBride & Co., 1943).

6. Robert E. Park, "Racial Assimilation in Secondary Groups with Special Reference to the Negro," in *Race and Culture* (Glencoe, Ill.: The Free Press, 1950), p. 209.

7. Robert E. Park, "Behind Our Masks," *Survey Graphic,* 56 (May 1, 1926), p. 137. This essay emphasized its point with photographs of *Noh* masks on each page.

8. Fred L. Strodtbeck, "Family Interaction, Values, and Achievement," in Marshall Sklare, ed. *The Jews: Social Patterns of an Ethnic Group* (New York: The Free Press, 1958), pp. 162–63.

9. Bernard C. Rosen, "Race, Ethnicity, and the Achievement Syndrome," *American Sociological Review,* 24 (Feb. 1959), pp. 47–60.

10. Chester Rowell, "Chinese and Japanese Immigrants—A Comparison," *Annals of the American Academy of Political and Social Science,* 24 (Sept. 1909), pp. 223–30.

11. Winifred Raushenbush, "Their Place in the Sun," *Survey Graphic,* 56 (May 1, 1926), pp. 141–45.

12. Rose Hum Lee, *The Chinese in the United States of America* (Hong Kong: Hong Kong University Press, 1960), p. 425.

13. Leonard Broom and John I. Kitsuse, "The Validation of Acculturation: A Condition of Ethnic Assimilation," *American Anthropologist*, 57 (Feb. 1955), p. 45.

14. Calvin F. Schmid and Charles E. Nobbe, "Socioeconomic Differentials among Nonwhite Races," *American Sociological Review*, 30 (Dec. 1965), pp. 909–22.

15. William Caudill and George de Vos, "Achievement, Culture, and Personality: The Case of the Japanese Americans," *American Anthropologist*, 58 (Dec. 1956), p. 1107.

16. Ibid., p. 1116.

17. Ibid.

18. Alan Jacobson and Lee Rainwater, "A Study of Management Representative Evaluations of Nisei Workers," *Social Forces*, 32 (Mar. 1953), pp. 35–41.

19. See, e.g., Wallace Irwin, *Letters of a Japanese School Boy* (New York: Doubleday, Page, 1909), pp. 172–73 et passim. So powerful was Irwin's caricature of the Japanese that the distinguished Negro novelist and statesman, James Weldon Johnson, felt he could not be sure whether a letter he received from a Japanese student offering to assist in the Negroes' struggle for equality was genuine or a product of Wallace Irwin's mischievous hand. After a conference attended by Chinese and Japanese diplomats, Johnson noted: "I myself reacted differently to these two peoples; the Japanese left me rather cold. Not during the time I was at the Conference did I form cordial relations with warm friendships." James Weldon Johnson, *Along This Way* (New York: Viking, 1968), pp. 399–401.

20. Stanley M. Elkins, *Slavery: A Problem in American Institutional and Intellectual Life* (Chicago: University of Chicago Press, 1959), pp. 81–139.

21. Alfred Schutz, *The Phenomenology of the Social World*, trans. George Walsh and Frederick Lehnert (Evanston: Northwestern University Press, 1967), pp. 139–214.

22. Clifford Geertz, *Person, Time, and Conduct in Bali: An Essay in Cultural Analysis* (New Haven: Yale University Southeast Asia Studies, Cultural Report series no. 14, 1966).

23. William Caudill and Henry A. Scarr, "Japanese Value Orientations and Culture Change," *Ethnology* (Jan. 1962), pp. 53–91.

24. Schutz, pp. 142–43, 194–214.

25. Cf. Edward Norbeck, *Pineapple Town, Hawaii* (Berkeley: University of California Press, 1959), pp. 5, 86–104.

26. See the interesting discussion in Clyde V. Kiser, "Cultural Pluralism," *The Annals of the American Academy of Political and Social Science*, 262 (Mar. 1949), pp. 118–29.

27. Chinese prefer to distinguish by a common "middle name" all persons born in the same generational cohort of a single lineage, but they do not continue a genealogical measurement of geo-generational distance from

China. See Maurice Freedman, *Chinese Lineage and Society: Fukien and Kwangtung* (New York: Humanities Press, 1966), pp. 44–45, 179–80.

28. The Kibei have been the most frequently discussed group among the Japanese Americans because of their sociocultural marginality and because of their alleged disloyalty to the United States during the Pacific War. See E. K. Strong, Jr., *The Second-Generation Japanese Problem* (Stanford: Stanford University Press, 1934); Andrew W. Lind, *Hawaii's Japanese: An Experiment in Democracy* (Princeton: Princeton University Press, 1946), pp. 33–34, 183–88, 212–13, 245; Carey McWilliams, *Prejudice: Japanese Americans: Symbol of Racial Intolerance* (Boston: Little, Brown, 1944), pp. 321–22; An Intelligence Officer, "The Japanese in America: The Problem and the Solution," *Harper's Magazine*, 185 (Oct. 1942), pp. 489–97; "Issei, Nisei, Kibei," *Fortune*, 29 (Apr. 1944), pp. 8, 21, 32, 74, 78–79, 94, 106, 118; Bradford Smith, *Americans from Japan* (Philadelphia: J. P. Lippincott, 1948), pp. 253–55, 275, 315–21; Dorothy Swaine Thomas and Richard Nishimoto, *The Spoilage, Japanese American Evacuation and Resettlement*, vol. 1 (Berkeley: University of California Press, 1946), pp. 3, 69, 78–81; Dorothy Swaine Thomas, with the assistance of Charles Kikuchi and James Sakoda, *The Salvage, Japanese American Evacuation and Resettlement*, vol. 2 (Berkeley: University of California Press, 1952), passim; ten Broek, Barnhart, and Matson, *Prejudice, War*, pp. 142, 177, 275–85; Alan Bosworth, *America's Concentration Camps* (New York: W. W. Norton, 1967), passim.

29. Norbeck, *Pineapple Town*, p. 94.

30. For a poignant account of the social and personal adjustment of the daughter of an Irish-American mother and an Issei father, see Kathleen Tamagawa, *Holy Prayers in a Horse's Ear* (New York: Ray Long and Richard R. Smith, 1932).

31. See Daisuke Kitagawa, *Issei and Nisei: The Internment Years* (New York: Seabury Press), pp. 26–31.

32. The phenomena discussed here are analogous to the issues involved in romantic love and incest on the one hand and group dissolution through loss of function on the other. For perceptive theoretical insights, see Philip Slater, "Social Limitations on Libidinal Withdrawal," *American Journal of Sociology*, 67 (Nov. 1961), pp. 296–311 and Talcott Parsons, "The Incest Taboo in Relation to Social Structure," *British Journal of Sociology*, 5 (June 1954), pp. 101–17; Parsons, "The Superego and the Theory of Social Systems," *Psychiatry*, 15 (Feb. 1952), pp. 15–25.

33. Broom and Kitsuse, "Validation."

34. Discussions of this group breakdown through withdrawal or transcendence usually focus on juvenile delinquency, although the issues clearly go beyond this element of behavior. See, e.g., Harry H. L. Kitano, "Japanese-American Crime and Delinquency," *Journal of Psychology*, 66 (1967), pp. 253–63.

35. See, e.g., Ruth Benedict, *The Chrysanthemum and the Sword: Patterns of Japanese Culture* (Boston: Houghton Mifflin, 1946); Nyozekan Ha-

segawa, *The Japanese Character: A Cultural Profile* (Tokyo: Kodansha International, 1966); Fosco Maraini, *Meeting with Japan* trans. Erie Mosbacher (New York: Viking Press, 1960), pp. 22–23, 217–18.

36. Joseph K. Yamagiwa, "Language as an Expression of Japanese Culture," in John W. Hall and Richard K. Beardsley, eds. *Twelve Doors to Japan* (New York: McGraw-Hill, 1965), pp. 186–223.

37. Hajime Nakamura, *Ways of Thinking of Eastern Peoples: India–China–Tibet–Japan* ed. Philip P. Wiener (Honolulu: East-West Center Press, 1964), pp. 409–10.

38. See Benedict, *Chrysanthemum,* pp. 48–49. Professor Shuichi Kato informs me that *gaijin* (i.e., foreigners) will be automatically exempted from the rigid requirements of the Japanese bow. Nisei in Japan, however, may suffer loss of face for their lack of knowledge in this area of etiquette, especially if they are not recognized as American-born.

39. Among Nisei I have observed a quick jerk of the head in genuflection before elders, Issei, and visitors from Japan, but this vestigial bow is far from the careful employment of body idiom required of traditional Japanese.

40. Among my Nisei associates it is widely professed that the Japanese language contains no obscenities, and many Nisei utter English scatological phrases softly and under their breath. In contrast, Chinese Americans of the same generation, especially those who speak Sz Yup dialect, employ a rich variety of epithets, curses, and obscenities.

41. Clifford Geertz, *The Religion of Java* (London: Collier-Macmillan, 1960), pp. 241–42.

42. As a general phenomenon of human behavior, this suspiciousness has been described by Erving Goffman. See *The Presentation of Self in Everyday Life* (Edinburgh: University of Edinburgh Social Science Research Centre, Monograph no. 2, 1958), pp. 1–46.

43. See Hiroshi Wagatsuma, "The Social Perception of Skin Color in Japan," *Daedalus,* 96 (Spring 1967), pp. 407–43.

44. Jews had reached China as early as the twelfth century, and the synagogue at K'ai-feng was still standing in 1851. See William Charles White, *Chinese Jews: A Compilation of Matters Relating to the Jews of K'ai-feng Fu* 2d ed. (New York: Paragon Book Reprint Corp., 1966) pp. 9–204. A few Jews came to Japan in the ninth century, and another group in the sixteenth, but it was not until the nineteenth century that the Jewish religion had even a small establishment there. In the early twentieth century Kobe became a center for European Jewish merchants, and this colony was enlarged by refugees from Nazi Germany. See Abraham Kotsuji, *From Tokyo to Jerusalem: The Autobiography of a Japanese Convert to Judaism* (New York: Bernard Geis, Random House, 1964), pp. 58–59, 159–61. The Nazis had a difficult time converting their Japanese allies to anti-Semitism. Kotsuji (*From Tokyo,* pp. 131–200) provides a personal report of his own activities in behalf of Jews in Manchuria and Japan. See also Marvin Tokayer and Mary Swartz, *The Fugu Plan: The Untold Story of the Japanese and the Jews during World*

War II (New York: Paddington Press Ltd., 1979); and Norman Cohn, *Warrant for Genocide: The Myth of the Jewish World Conspiracy and the Protocols of the Elders of Zion* (New York: Harper and Row, 1966), pp. 242–43.

45. I am indebted to the Rev. Taro Goto and Mr. Nobusuke Fukuda for explaining this term and its origins to me.

46. George de Vos, "A Quantitative Rorschach Assessment of Maladjustment and Rigidity in Acculturating Japanese Americans," *Genetic Psychology Monographs*, 52 (1955), p. 66.

47. Edward T. Hall, *The Hidden Dimension* (Garden City, N.Y.: Doubleday, 1966), pp. 139–44.

48. Bernard Rudofsky, *The Kimono Mind* (Garden City N.Y.: Doubleday, 1965), pp. 159–61.

49. Japanese, like English, is a language that betrays the speaker's social and regional origins. Japanese Americans, highly conscious of the poor quality of their spoken Japanese and wary lest it betray peasant origins, tend to rely on English whenever possible.

50. See Erza Vogel, "The Go-Between in a Developing Society, the Case of the Japanese Marriage Arranger," *Human Organization*, 20 (Fall 1961), pp. 112–20. For the go-between among Japanese in America, see Shotaro Frank Miyamoto, *Social Solidarity among the Japanese in Seattle* (Seattle: University of Washington Publications in the Social Sciences, vol. 12 [Dec. 1939], pp. 87–88; Robert H. Ross and Emory S. Bogardus, "Four Types of *Nisei* Marriage Patterns," *Sociology and Social Research*, 25 (Sept. 1940), pp. 63–66; John F. Embree, "Acculturation among the Japanese of Kona, Hawaii," Memoirs of the American Anthropological Association. Supplement to *American Anthropologist*, 43 (1941), pp. 74–77; Toshio Yatsushiro, "The Japanese Americans," in Milton Barron ed., *American Minorities* (New York: Alfred A. Knopf, 1962), p. 324.

51. Rudofsky, *Kimono Mind*, pp. 161–63.

52. For a discussion of information games, see Stanford M. Lyman and Marvin B. Scott, "Game Frameworks," in *Sociology of the Absurd*, rev. ed. (Dix Hills, N.Y.: General Hall, 1989), pp. 157–80.

53. For the most perceptive theoretical analysis of social occasions, and one that is applicable to the Japanese American scene, see Georg Simmel, "The Sociology of Sociability," trans. Everett C. Hughes, *American Journal of Sociology*, 55 (Nov. 1949), pp. 254–61.

54. See also David Riesman et al., "The Vanishing Host," *Human Organization*, 19 (Spring 1960), pp. 17–27.

55. John Embree, *The Japanese* (Smithsonian Institution War Background Studies Number 7. Washington, D.C.: Smithsonian Institution, 1943), p. 25.

56. John Embree, *A Japanese Village: Suye Mura* (London: Kegan Paul, Trench, Trubner, 1946), pp. 155–56.

57. See Lyman and Scott, "Stage Fright and the Problem of Identity," in *Sociology of the Absurd*.

58. See Marvin B. Scott and Stanford M. Lyman, "Accounts," *American Sociological Review*, 33 (Feb. 1968), pp. 46–62.

59. See also Edward Gross and Gregory P. Stone, "Embarrassment and the Analysis of Role Requirements," *American Journal of Sociology*, 70 (July 1964), pp. 6–10; Erving Goffman, "Embarrassment and Social Organization," *American Journal of Sociology* 62 (Nov. 1956), pp. 264–71; Stanford M. Lyman and Marvin B. Scott, "Coolness in Everyday Life," in Marcello Truzzi, ed. *Sociology and Everyday Life* (Englewood Cliffs, N.J.: Prentice-Hall, 1968), pp. 92–101.

60. Cf. Georg Simmel, "The Metropolis and Mental Life," in *The Sociology of Georg Simmel*, ed. and trans. Kurt Wolff (Glencoe, Ill: The Free Press, 1950), pp. 409–26.

61. Georg Simmel, "The Aesthetic Significance of the Face," in *Georg Simmel, 1858–1918*, ed. Kurt Wolff (Columbus: Ohio State University Press, 1959), pp. 276–81.

62. Georg Simmel, "Sociology of the Senses: Visual Interaction," in Robert E. Park and Ernest W. Burgess, *Introduction to the Science of Sociology* (Chicago: University of Chicago Press, 1921), pp. 356–61.

63. Cf. Erving Goffman, *Behavior in Public Places: Notes on the Social Organization of Gatherings* (London: Collier-Macmillan, 1963), pp. 38, 42.

64. Cf. Maraini, *Meeting with Japan*, p. 23.

65. See Jerry Enomoto, "Perspectives: Enryo-Syndrome?" *Pacific Citizen*, 64 (June 16, 1967), p. 1; "Perspectives: Enryo," Ibid., 65 (July 7, 1967), p. 1. In 1953 John H. Burma wrote: "There is evidence that Nisei leaders are not so aggressive and consistent in their leadership roles as are Caucasian leaders. In their thinking Nisei leaders seem very often to be liberal, progressive, or radical, but these attitudes are often not carried over into aggressive action because such behavior will call down censure from the by-no-means impotent Issei, and because of the tradition that no Japanese leader should assert himself too strongly or too often or place himself in the limelight too frequently. Nevertheless, the leader is expected to be able to speak on his own initiative in keeping things running smoothly, and to speak out when Nisei rights are being infringed upon. The problem involved here is that Nisei are likely to be much concerned with 'doing the proper thing,' meeting requirements placed upon them, and being careful not to do anything which would too much disturb the Japanese community or disrupt the *status quo*. This tends to penalize initiative and aggressiveness and to slow down the dynamics of leadership as the Caucasian knows it." "Current Leadership Problems among Japanese Americans," *Sociology and Social Research*, 37 (Jan. 1953), p. 162.

66. Geertz, *Religion of Java*, pp. 245–47.

67. See three essays by L. Takeo Doi, "Japanese Language as an Expression of Japanese Psychology," *Western Speech*, 20 (Spring 1956), pp. 90–96; " 'Amae': A Key Concept for Understanding Japanese Personality Structure," in Robert J. Smith and Richard K. Beardsley, eds. *Japanese Culture: Its Development and Characteristics* (Chicago: Aldine, 1962), pp. 132–39; "Girl-Ninjo: An Interpretation," in R. P. Dore, ed., *Aspects of Social Change in Modern Japan* (Princeton: Princeton University Press, 1967), pp. 327–36.

68. Doi, " 'Amae', " p. 133.

69. See Charlotte E. Babcock and William Caudill, "Personal and Cultural Factors in Treating a Nisei Man," in Georgene Seward, (ed., Clinical Studies in Culture Conflict (New York: Ronald Press, 1958), pp. 409–48; Charlotte E. Babcock, "Reflections on Dependency Phenomena as Seen in Nisei in the United States," in Smith and Beardsley, Japanese Culture, pp. 172–88. See also Katharine Newkirk Handley, "Social Casework and Intercultural Problems," Journal of Social Casework, 28 (Feb. 1947), pp. 43–50; Mamoru Iga, "The Japanese Social Structure and the Source of Mental Strains of Immigrants in the United States," Social Forces, 35 (Mar. 1957), pp. 271–78.

70. For this last point I am indebted to Hideo Bernard Hata.

71. See Joseph L. Anderson and Donald Richie, The Japanese Film (New York: Grove Press, 1960), pp. 63–71, 223–28, 315–31.

72. Cf. Robert Frager, "The Psychology of the Samurai," Psychology Today, 2 (Jan. 1969), pp. 48–53.

73. Douglas G. Haring, "Japanese National Character: Cultural Anthropology, Psychoanalysis, and History," in Personal Character and Cultural Milieu 3d ed., comp. and ed. Douglas G. Haring (Syracuse: Syracuse University Press, 1956), pp. 424–37; George A. de Vos, "Achievement Orientation, Social Self-Identity, and Japanese Economic Growth," Asian Survey, 5 (Dec. 1965), pp. 575–89.

74. Reinhard Bendix, "A Case Study in Cultural and Educational Mobility: Japan and the Protestant Ethic," in Neil J. Smelser and Seymour Martin Lipset, eds., Social Structure and Mobility in Economic Development (Chicago: Aldine, 1966), pp. 266–67.

75. Herbert Passin, Society and Education in Japan (New York: Bureau of Publications, Teachers College, East Asian Institute, Columbia University, 1965), pp. 149–60; R. P. Dore, Education in Tokugawa Japan (London: Routledge and Kegan Paul, 1965), pp. 124–51.

76. The early student migration to America was of samurai rank, a fact attested to by their each having two swords. See Charles Lanman, The Japanese in America (London: Longmans, Green, Readers, and Dyer, 1872), pp. 67–79. See also Charles F. Thwing, "Japanese and Chinese Students in America," Scribner's Monthly, 20 (July 1880), pp. 450-53; John W. Bennett, Herbert Passin, and Robert K. McKnight, In Search of Identity: The Japanese Overseas Scholar in America and Japan (Minneapolis: University of Minnesota Press, 1958), pp. 18–46. Although students, some of whom were of samurai rank, continued to migrate to the United States thereafter, the settler and sojourner immigrants who came after 1880 were largely of peasant, handicraft, and merchant origin. Some of these undoubtedly descended from noble lineage or ronin (masterless warrior) backgrounds. See Hirokichi Mutsu, "A Japanese View of Certain Japanese-American Relations," Overland Monthly, 32 (Nov. 1898), pp. 406–14; Yosaburo Yoshida, "Sources and Causes of Japanese Emigration," Annals of the American Academy of Political and Social Science, 24 (Sept. 1909), pp. 157–67. The Japanese Ameri-

can History Project now carrying on research at UCLA may produce more data on the social origins of Issei.

77. George Sansom, *A History of Japan, 1334–1615* (Stanford: Stanford University Press, 1961), pp. 333, 398; Sansom, *A History of Japan, 1615–1867* (Stanford: Stanford University Press, 1963), pp. 32–34, 54–58, 79, 92–93, 133–38; Sansom, *Japan: A Short Cultural History*, rev. ed. (New York: Appleton-Century-Crofts, 1943), pp. 356, 496–98.

78. Passin, *Society*, pp. 117–21, 177–79, 190, 191, 226–28; Dore, *Education*, pp. 214–51.

79. George B. Sansom, *Japan: A Short Cultural History*, pp. 520–21.

80. Paul T. Takagi, "The Japanese Family in the United States: A Hypothesis on the Social Mobility of the Nisei," revised version of a paper presented at the annual meeting of the Kroeber Anthropological Society, Berkeley, California, April 30, 1966.

81. Tadashi Fukutake, *Japanese Rural Society*, trans. R. P. Dore (Tokyo: Oxford University Press, 1967), pp. 39–59, 212–17.

82. Chie Nakane, *Kinship and Economic Organization in Rural Japan* (New York: Humanities Press, 1967), shows a distinct difference between Japanese rural social structure and that of China described in Maurice Freedman, *Lineage Organization in Southeastern China* (London: Athlone Press, 1958), and *Chinese Lineage and Society*. See also Stanford M. Lyman, "Contrasts in the Community Organization of Chinese and Japanese in North America," *Canadian Review of Sociology and Anthropology*, 5 (May 1968), pp. 51–67.

83. Fukutake, *Japanese Rural Society*, p. 40.

84. Ibid., p. 212. See also Robert J. Smith, "The Japanese Rural Community: Norms, Sanctions, and Ostracism," *American Anthropologist*, 63 (June 1961). Reprinted in Jack M. Potter et al., *Peasant Society: A Reader* (Boston: Little, Brown, 1967), pp. 246–55.

85. Sidney L. Gulick, *The American Japanese Problem* (New York: Charles Scribner's Sons, 1914), pp. 90–96; T. Iyenaga and Kenoske Sato, *Japan and the California Problem* (New York: G. P. Putnam's Sons, 1921), pp. 109–19; Thomas et al., *The Salvage*, pp. 7–8, 10–12. For a poignant account of the meetings between young brides and their older husbands, see Sessue Hayakawa, *Zen Showed Me the Way* (Indianapolis: Bobbs-Merrill, 1960), pp. 84–88. Accounts of the adjustments to proxy marriages may be found in *Our Christian Testimony*, comp. and trans. Rev. Taro Goto (Loomis, Calif.: First Methodist Church, 1967). See also Mei Takano, *Japanese American Women: Three Generations, 1890–1990* (Berkeley: Mina Press and the Japanese American Historical Society, 1990), pp. 21–102.

86. See William Caudill, "Japanese American Personality and Acculturation," *Genetic Psychology Monographs*, 45 (1952), p. 32. In rural areas and in some of the ghetto residences of urban *Nihonmachi*, the hot bath was transplanted from Japan. I have taken a "Japanese bath" in a traditionally operated boarding house in the Japanese community of Walnut Grove, California. Sake, Japanese rice wine, was also manufactured or purchased by

the Issei. Drunkenness was a common complaint among the wives of Issei settlers. *Our Christian Testimony.*

87. Benedict, *Chrysanthemum,* pp. 266–267. Personal interviews with Nisei indicate that *moxa* was used or threatened against naughty, overly excited, tantrum-throwing children. See also Monica Sone, *Nisei Daughter* (Boston: Little Brown, 1953), p. 28.

88. Douglas G. Haring, "Aspects of Personal Character in Japan," in *Personal Character and Cultural Milieu,* pp. 417–419; Betty B. Lanham, "Aspects of Child Care in Japan: Preliminary Report," in Ibid., pp. 565–83; Edward and Margaret Norbeck, "Child Training in a Japanese Fishing Community," in Ibid., pp. 651–73; Benedict, *Chrysanthemum,* pp. 261–64.

89. See, e.g., *The Autobiography of Yukichi Fukuzawa,* rev. translation Eüchi Kiyooka (New York: Columbia University Press, 1966), pp. 113–14.

90. Caudill, "Japanese American Personality," p. 30.

91. Takagi, "Japanese Family."

92. For the *Eta* in Florin see Winifred Raushenbush, "Their Place in the Sun," *Survey Graphic,* 56 (May 1, 1926), pp. 154–58; Hiroshi Ito (pseud.), "Japan's Outcastes in the United States," in George de Vos and Hiroshi Wagatsuma, eds., *Japan's Invisible Race: Caste in Culture and Personality* (Berkeley: University of California Press, 1966), pp. 200–221.

93. Takagi, "Japanese Family."

94. Cf. Edward Norbeck, "Age-Grading in Japan," *American Anthropologist,* 55 (June 1953), pp. 373–84.

95. Caudill, "Japanese American Personality," p. 30. On the other hand, in Meiji Japan girls were expected to observer certain proprieties—including a proper body position when sleeping—from which boys were exempted. See Etsu Inagaki Sugimoto, *A Daughter of the Samurai* (Rutland, Vt.: Charles E. Tuttle, 1966), p. 24; Baroness Shidzue Ishimoto, *Facing Two Ways: The Story of My Life* (New York: Farrar and Rinehart, 1935), pp. 13–76.

96. See Edward Sapir, "The Unconscious Patterning of Behavior in Society," in David G. Mandelbaum, ed., *Selected Writings of Edward Sapir in Language, Culture, and Personality* (Berkeley: University of California Press, 1963), pp. 544–59.

97. George A. de Vos and Keiichi Mizushima, "Organization and Social Function of Japanese Gangs: Historical Development and Modern Parallels," in R. P. Dore, Ed., *Aspects of Social Change in Modern Japan,* pp. 289–326.

98. Takagi, "Japanese Family"; Stanford M. Lyman, "The Nisei Personality," *Pacific Citizen,* 62 (Jan. 7, 1966), p. 3.

99. Geertz, *Religion of Java,* p. 241.

100. Lyman and Scott, "Coolness in Everyday Life."

101. Ibid., p. 93.

102. Caudill, "Japanese American Personality," pp. 66–68.

103. For an excellent discussion of these phenomena in general, see Erving Goffman, *Interaction Ritual: Essays on Face-To-Face Behavior* (Chicago: Aldine, 1967), pp. 218–26.

104. William Petersen, "Success Story, Japanese-American Style," *New York Times Magazine*, January 9, 1966, p. 40.

105. Professor Harry H. L. Kitano has suggested that most Japanese Americans did not resist incarceration in detention camps during World War II because of their ingrained sense of fateful resignation. Joe Grant Masaoka, "Japanese tailor-made for Army order, says Kitano," *Pacific Citizen*, 64 (June 9, 1967), pp. 1–2.

106. There is cultural support for this phenomenon, summed up in the Buddhist ideal of *muga*, carrying on activities effortlessly; that is, having eliminated the observing self in one's acts. The observing self is seen as a hindrance to smooth performance. See Benedict, *Chrysanthemum*, pp. 247–51.

107. Cf. the remark by Sapir: "We do not really know what a man's speech is until we have evaluated his social background. If a Japanese talks in a monotonous voice, we have not the right to assume that he is illustrating the same type of personality that one of us would be if we talked with his sentence melody." "Speech as a Personality Trait," *Selected Writings* p. 539.

108. Caudill and de Vos, "Achievement," p. 1117.

109. Geertz, *Person, Time, and Conduct in Bali* pp. 53–61; Goffman, *Interaction Ritual*, pp. 226–33; Lyman and Scott, "Stage Fright and Social Identity."

110. The Japanese term *jicho* sums up this sense. Literally "a self that is weighty," it refers to circumspection in social relations. A person loses *jicho* when he or she commits an impropriety. See Benedict, *Chrysanthemum*, pp. 219–22. A nice example is found in the autobiography of a daring, youthful Japanese sailor. Writing of an older sailor whom he admired very much, he tells of his surprise when his "idol" actually spoke to him: "Takeuchi was a man with a superb record as a yachtsman at Kansai University. He was always one of my idols. . . . He seemed like a big shot to me, so much so that I never even used to say 'hello' to him because he might not recognize me or return my greeting. But on this day there was something different about him, because he spoke to me first. I was sure that I hadn't done anything wrong, but I still wondered why Takeuchi would want to talk to me." Kenichi Horie, *Kodoku: Sailing Alone across the Pacific*, trans. Takuichi Ito and Kaoru Ogimi (Rutland, Vermont: Charles E. Tuttle, 1964), pp. 26–27.

111. George de Vos and Hiroshi Wagatsuma, "Psycho-Cultural Significance of Concern over Death and Illness among Rural Japanese," *International Journal of Social Psychiatry*, 5 (Summer 1959), pp. 5–19; George de Vos, "Social Values and Personal Attitudes in Primary Human Relations in Niike," *Occasional Papers*, Center for Japanese Studies, University of Michigan, 1965; Babcock and Caudill, "Personal and Cultural Factors," pp. 436–37; Marvin K. Opler, "Cultural Dilemma of a Kibei Youth," *Culture and Social Psychiatry*, (New York: Atherton Press, 1967), pp. 360–80.

112. Weston LaBarre, "Some Observations on Character Structure in the Orient: The Japanese," in Bernard S. Silberman, ed., *Japanese Character*

and Culture (Tucson: University of Arizona Press, 1962), pp. 325–59, esp. pp. 349–51.

113. See Thomas S. Szasz, The Myth of Mental Illness: Foundations of a Theory of Personal Conduct (New York: Dell-Delta, 1967), pp. 100, 110, 129–30, 139–43, 248–58.

114. Erza Vogel, "The Go-Between."

115. Georg Simmel, "The Stranger," pp. 402–8.

116. See Franz Alexander, "The Psychosomatic Approach in Medical Therapy," The Scope of Psychoanalysis: Selected Papers of Franz Alexander, 1921–61 (New York: Basic Books, 1961), pp. 345–58.

117. George de Vos, "A Comparison of the Personality Differences in Two Generations of Japanese Americans by Means of the Rorschach Test," The Nagoya Journal of Medical Science, 17 (Aug. 1954), pp. 153–261. Recent medical evidence lends support to my observations. The British psychiatrist Dr. H. H. Wolff reports that psychosomatic illness may be a substitute for "healthy" discharge of aggression impulses, impulses that arise from fear of loving or being rejected. San Francisco Chronicle, November 25, 1968, p. 7.

118. See five articles by Emory S. Bogardus: "Current Problems of Japanese Americans," Sociology and Social Research, 25 (July 1941), pp. 562–71; "Culture Conflicts in Relocation Centers," Ibid., 27 (May 1943), pp. 381–90; "Relocation Centers as Planned Communities," Ibid., 28 (Jan. 1944), pp. 218–34; "Resettlement Problems of Japanese Americans," Ibid., 29 (June 1945), pp. 218–26; "The Japanese Return to the West Coast," Ibid., 31 (Jan. 1947), pp. 226–33. See also Leonard Bloom, "Familial Adjustments of Japanese-Americans to Relocation: First Phase," American Sociological Review, 8 (Oct. 1943), pp. 551–60; Bloom, "Transitional Adjustments of Japanese-American Families to Relocation," American Sociological Review, 12 (Apr. 1947), pp. 201–9; Robert W. O'Brien, "Selective Dispersion as a Factor in the Solution of the Nisei Problem," Social Forces, 23 (Dec. 1944), pp. 140–47; Richard A. Niver, "Americanizing the Issei," Free World, 11 (Mar. 1946), pp. 31–34; John H. Provinse and Solon T. Kimball, "Building New Communities during War Time," American Sociological Review, 11 (Aug. 1946), pp. 396–410; Bernard L. Hormann, "Postwar Problems of Issei in Hawaii," Far Eastern Survey, 15 (Sept. 11, 1946), pp. 277–80; John H. Burma, "Current Leadership," pp. 157–63.

119. For this concept, see Alfred Schutz, "Some Structures of the Life-World," Collected Papers 3: Studies in Phenomenological Philosophy, ed. I. Schutz (The Hague: Martinus Nijhoff, 1966), pp. 116–32.

120. Studies of Issei with teenage children in the 1950s suggest that these Issei were relaxing their standards and grudgingly accepting the fact of their children's "Americanization." See Dennie L. Brigges, "Social Adaptations among Japanese American Youth: A Comparative Study," Sociology and Social Research, 38 (May-June 1954), pp. 293–300; Melvin S. Brooks and Ken Kunihiro, "Education in Assimilation of Japanese: A Study in the Houston

Area of Texas," *Sociology and Social Research*, 37 (Sept. 1952), pp. 16–22; Mamoru Iga, "Japanese Social Structure," p. 278.

121. See T. Scott Miyakawa, "The Los Angeles Sansei," *Kashu Mainichi*, holiday supplement, Christmas edition, December 20, 1962, part 2, pp. 1, 4.

122. For the "Hansen Effect," see Marcus Lee Hansen, "The Third Generation in America," *Commentary*, 14 (Nov. 1952), pp. 492–500; Eugene I. Bender and George Kagiwada, "Hansen's Law of 'Third-Generation Return' and the Study of American Religio-Ethnic Groups," paper presented at the annual meeting of the Pacific Sociological Association, Vancouver, B.C., Canada, April, 1966. For its application to Japanese Americans, see George Kagiwada, "The Third Generation Hypothesis: Structural Assimilation among Japanese-Americans," paper presented at the annual meeting of the Pacific Sociological Association, San Francisco, March, 1968.

123. See Harry H. L. Kitano, "Is There Sansei Delinquency?" *Kashu Mainichi*, p. 1.

124. See "A Sansei's Opinion," *Kashu Mainichi*, p. 2; Ken Yoshida, "Contra Costa Youth Trade Views with Nisei Parents," *Pacific Citizen*, 64 (Mar. 3, 1967), p. 4; Donald Kazama, "On Focus: The Sansei and Nisei," *Pacific Citizen*, 64 (May 26, 1967), p. 4.

125. World War II Nisei air ace Ben Kuroki observed that "We're losing our Japanese heritage through intermarriage." His public "blast" at intermarriage [*Pacific Citizen*, 64 (Feb. 17, 1967), p. 1] was criticized in letters to the editor [Ibid., 64 (Apr. 14, 1967), p. 6] and by a young columnist: Ken Kuroiwa, "Mampitsu: Interracial Dating," [Ibid., 64 (Mar. 24, 1967), p. 5].

126. "Sansei in California divided on Integration, FEPC Told," *Pacific Citizen*, 64 (May 19, 1967), p. 1; Jeffrey Matsui, "Sounding Board: Anonymously Integrated," Ibid., p. 4; Bill Strobel, "Japanese Heritage in the United States," *Oakland Tribune*, March, 1966. Reprinted in *Pacific Citizen*, 62 (Apr. 1, 1966), pp. 1, 3, 4. See also Daisuke Kitagawa, "Assimilation or Pluralism?" in Arnold M. Rose and Caroline B. Rose, eds., *Minority Problems* (New York: Harper and Row, 1965), pp. 285–87.

127. Isao Horinouchi, *Educational Values and Preadaptation in the Acculturation of Japanese American*, Sacramento Anthropological Society paper no. 7, Fall 1967.

128. Jitsuichi Masuoka "Race Relations and Nisei Problems," *Sociology and Social Research*, 30 (July 1946), p. 459.

11

Asians, Blacks, Hispanics, Amerinds: Confronting Vestiges of Slavery

An analytical as well as practical separation of the situations, rights, opportunities, privileges, and immunities of blacks on the one hand and immigrants on the other has been part of American social thought at least since 1782, when Hector St. John de Crèvecoeur defined "the American" as an amalgam of the several European strains together with those of the indigenous Indians but confined mention of the Africans in the new nation to a solicitous concern for their slave status.[1] The same distinction found its way into William Wells Brown's *Clotel* (1853), the first novel written by an American black man, when the author contrasted the deadly fate that overtook his eponymous heroine, a fugitive slave and the illegitimate daughter of Thomas Jefferson, with the initial welcome and social acceptance that would have been hers had she been a white woman in flight from Europe's despotisms.[2] The amendments added to the Constitution in the five years following the Union victory intentionally if only by implication continued the distinction not only by abolishing slavery but also by granting citizenship specifically to persons of African descent and seeking to remove from them the entire complex of "badges," "incidents," and "indicia" of their two centuries of involuntary servitude. Although the first quarter century of their life witnessed the Supreme Court's constriction of the applicable scope of the amendments to a prohibition on Negro reenslavement,[3] and though the Court permitted the doctrine of separate-but-equal to rule with respect to virtually all "colored"-white institutional arrangements from 1896[4] to 1954,[5] a more recent Court in 1968 reaffirmed the original broader meaning and extended the application of the amendments[6] and their supportive legislation. Moreover, the Congress has seen fit to legislate a requirement of affirmative action affecting not only the equal opportunities of blacks but also those of certain other minorities.[7]

However, the groups now eligible for the benefits that affirmative action programs confer cut across the old division separating blacks from immigrants and include descendants of nonwhite and non-Anglo members of the latter while excluding the others. Opponents of affirmative action have called the new class of eligibles into question, referring to it as an instantiation of "reverse discrimination."[8] Defenders of the new approach to equality have had to search out a justification for the new division and show it to be within the purview of reason and of the Constitution.[9]

This essay is directed toward confirming the legal rectitude of the new division and redeeming it from the charge of reverse discrimination. Substantively, this a study in the historical sociology of American Constitutional law; methodologically, it proceeds in accordance with an approach to classificatory matters that arose originally from Durkheim's and Mauss's formulation,[10] has moved through that of Herbert Blumer and the symbolic interactionalists,[11] and been combined for purposes of the present investigation with that employed in conventionalized jurisprudential classificational procedure.[12]

Recently litigated affirmative action programs have extended their benefits not only to blacks but also to certain nonwhite and non-Anglo peoples. Although the industrial craft training program sustained by the Supreme Court in the *Weber* case established its special school exclusively for blacks, the category of persons eligible for eighteen reserved seats in the medical school under the University of California at Davis's Constitutionally unsuccessful experiment in affirmative action embraced self-designated members of such "disadvantaged minority groups" as blacks, Chicanos, Asians, and American Indians; the ethnoracial limitation on layoffs concluded in the judicially disapproved collective bargaining agreement signed by the Jackson, Michigan, Board of Education protected black, American Indian, Asian, and Hispanic teachers; the Court-approved consent decree entered into by the City of Cleveland with respect to the hiring and promotion of firefighters required special affirmative action procedures with respect to black and Hispanic firemen and women; and a New York City sheet metal workers' union local was ordered to institute a percentage admission plan positively affecting the job chances of blacks and Hispanics. Common to almost all these plans—both those that meet and those that fail the test of judicial scrutiny—is a classification of eligibles that includes nonwhite, non-Anglo peoples and by implication excludes members of white Anglo and European descent groups.

Critics of affirmative action insist that these programs are instances of reverse discrimination in that they grant educational privileges and/or open up job and career opportunities to one group but deny these same privileges and opportunities to all those not included in the beneficial plan. Because they believe that advantages in education and opportunities for employment should be granted in accordance with a strictly individualized meritocratic policy, the most consistent critics of affirmative action should oppose any program that modifies such an ideal. However, neither the Supreme Court, the federal government, nor all enemies of affirmative action advocate an unmodified meritocracy for the United States. Racial classifications have been held to be "suspect" by the Supreme Court but not absolutely forbidden to the accomplishment of an otherwise lawful public purpose.[13] In a case decided before he retired from the bench, Chief Justice Burger pointed out that although the Court must "recognize the need for careful judicial evaluation to assure that any congressional program that employs racial or ethnic criteria to accomplish the objective of remedying the present effects of past discrimination is narrowly tailored to the achievement of that goal . . . we reject the contention that in the remedial context the Congress must act in a wholly 'color-blind' fashion."[14] By the same token, both state and federal governments have enacted such Court-sustained laws as those granting a monopoly on becoming Mississippi river pilots to the sons of river pilots,[15] a restriction on being a female bar employee unless one is the wife or daughter of the bar owner,[16] a subsidy to attend college or university and unearned points on a Civil Service Examination to all those who served in the military during the Second World War and the Korean and Vietnam Wars, while excluding those who served the government in a nonmilitary capacity during the same wars.

It should be noted that one of the currently most active opponents of affirmative action, Nathan Glazer, denied from the outset of his protests on the matter that the United States had ever been—except in its own dreamy-eyed ideology about itself—a single "American community . . . in [which] . . . heritage, ethnicity, religion, [and] race are only incidental and accidental personal characteristics." Glazer insists that "liberal principles—[including] . . . the newer ones arguing the democracy of merit— . . . are being increasingly accepted by everyone . . . nowadays under the pressures of a technological world," but that the pressure exerted by blacks to break down ethnocultural barriers to their own education, employment, and economic opportunity threatens "institutions which are the true seats of Jewish exclusiveness—the Jewish business, for example, th_ Jewish union, or the Jewish (or largely Jewish) neighborhood and school."[17] Hence, it can be concluded that a proposal to confer special privileges or particular immunities upon racial or ethnic sodalities does not in and of itself constitute a prima facie violation of the pattern of American educational, residential, occupational organization; nor does every legislatively constructed ethnic, racial, or gender classification violate the guaranty of equal protections of the law that the Constitution provides for each person in the United States.

"It is clear," observes the Constitutional scholar Jacobus ten Broek, "that the demand for equal protection cannot be a demand that laws apply universally to all persons." Legislatures, when they act to eliminate an evil practice or promote some aspect of the public welfare "must impose special burdens upon, or grant special benefits to, special groups or classes of individuals."[18] Legislatures, thence, are the architects engaged in a legal and equitable construction and reconstruction of public reality. In so doing they, ideally, pursue the public interest in freedom, justice, and equality by so distributing the burdens and benefits of civil life in America that none shall be denied or deprived of the rights and opportunities that flow therefrom. The classification made by a legislature, or by any agency charged with the task of assuring a just distribution of items of positive value, are not "natural," nor must they necessarily be congruent with any categorizations or groupings that exist in the world outside of lawful legislative intent. Rather, a legislative classification meets the test of equal protections required by the Fourteenth Amendment when it is made in furtherance of a permissible public purpose and when, "within the sphere of its operation, it affects alike all persons similarly situated"[19] and none who are not.[20] Hence, the classifications made by affirmative action proposals are subject to objective assessment. They can be evaluated with respect to whether they serve a lawful public purpose in a manner that embraces only those who deserve the benefits they seek to confer.

As a first step in this examination, the public purpose that affirmative action programs serve must be determined. Generally, they are alleged to remedy past discriminations, but such is not sufficient to clarify the propriety of their classificatory limitations, prescribe classificatory exactitude, or even to insure their lawful character. Here, it will be suggested that these programs ought to be perceived as policies in service to the mandate imposed on the post–Civil War national and state governments by the Thirteenth Amendment: to remove the "badges," "incidents," and "indicia" of slavery from all

those affected by them.[21] Race discrimination against the emancipated blacks was at first recognized as the most significant of the
badges of slavery, in that such discrimination reinforced and gave
manifest expression to the allegation that Afro-Americans belonged
to an inferior caste of human beings. However, in the first three decades that followed the adoption of the Thirteenth, Fourteenth, and
Fifteenth Amendments to the Constitution, the Supreme Court restricted the meaning, scope, and application of their promise to a
simple prohibition on reenslavement and involuntary servitude[22]
and virtually abandoned judicial support for the legislative removal
of the badges, incidents, and indicia of slavery. Judge Loren Miller
has summarized the Supreme Court's role in this constriction of the
freedmen's and women's rights:

> In the *Slaughter-house Cases*, it restored the *Dred Scott* doc-
> trine that there are two categories of citizenship, national and
> state, and gutted the privileges and immunities clause of the
> fourteenth amendment of all meaning. In *United States v.
> Cruikshank*, it restored control of civil rights to the states. In
> *United States v. Reese*, it severely restricted the scope and
> reach of the fifteenth amendment. In the *Civil Rights Cases*, it
> further cabined the meaning of the fourteenth amendment with
> its ruling that Congress could not proscribe an individual's
> discriminatory conduct. In *Virginia v. Rives*, it validated the
> indictments of all-white juries in the absence of specific ob-
> jections and proof by a Negro defendant of systematic and
> purposeful racial exclusion, and thus it set up a rule which al-
> lowed extensive discrimination in jury selection. In *Williams
> v. Mississippi*, and later in *Giles v. Harris* and *Giles v. Teasley*,
> it gave its blessing to state constitutional and statutory provi-
> sions deliberately and professedly designed to circumscribe the
> franchise. In *Plessy v. Ferguson*, it approved a state's racial clas-
> sification, undertaken to establish the separate-but-equal rule
> in the use of state facilities or public utilities. In *Berea College v.
> Kentucky*, it approved state statutes proscribing interracial as-
> sociation for innocent purposes.[23]

Throughout the era of constriction, one dissenting judicial voice
was raised in behalf of the original intent and range of application of
the postwar Amendments. In 1883, Justice John Marshall Harlan reminded his brethren that their majority decision in the *Civil Rights
Cases* would permit race "discrimination [to be] practiced by corporations and individuals in the exercise of their public or quasi public

functions," and he asserted that such discrimination was "a badge of servitude the imposition of which Congress may prevent under its power, by appropriate legislation, to enforce the Thirteenth Amendment."[24] Thirteen years later, Harlan dissented from the Court's majority decision upholding Louisiana's law requiring racially separate-but-equal coaches for passengers on interstate railroads, pointing out that "arbitrary separation of citizens, on the basis of race, while they are on a public highway, is a badge of servitude wholly inconsistent with the civil freedom and the equality before the law established by the Constitution."[25] He concluded that if other states were to enact similar segregative legislation, even though the institution of slavery had disappeared, "there would remain a power in the states, by sinister legislation, to interfere with the full enjoyment of the blessings of freedom; to regulate civil rights, common to all citizens, upon the basis of race; and to place in a condition of legal inferiority a large body of American citizens, now constituting a part of the political community called the people of the United States."[26] Moreover, Harlan was of the opinion that the amendments not only commanded the government to protect the freedmen-and-women from all of the proactive vestiges of slavery but that it had an affirmative obligation to do so. In his dissent in the *Civil Rights Cases*, he rebuked the Court's majority for suggesting that the emancipated blacks had been "the special favorite of the laws," pointing out that in their behalf it would be necessary not merely " 'to help the feeble up, but to support him after.' " However, he observed at "every step, in this direction, the nation has been confronted with class tyranny."[27]

A return to something approximating Harlan's broader understanding of the spirit animating the Amendments did not occur until after 1954, when the Warren Court declared public school segregation inconsistent with the equal protections of the law guaranteed by the Fourteenth Amendment.[28] Subsequent orders to desegregate schools with all deliberate speed led to reconsideration of the worthiness, rectitude, and constitutionality of various compensatory policies proposed to redress the host of past inequities. "The critical question," wrote Judge Miller in 1966, "is whether the color-blind constitution which equalitarians have always demanded will tolerate such compensatory measures." Reminding his readers that the Reconstruction Congress had had "no constitutional qualms about enactment of remedial legislation such as the Freedmen's Bureau Acts, which were designed to assist Negroes and newly freed slaves," Miller supposed that "compensatory legislation designed to benefit

Negroes as a class is constitutionally permissible."[29] Here, it should be noted, the implication was that the affirmative benefits were to be conferred upon the descendants of the Afro-American slaves insofar as they were present-day victims of the lingering effects of slavery.

That the mandate to remove the vestiges of slavery was still Constitutionally viable was asserted by the Supreme Court two years later. In a decision upholding a Congressional statute (42 U.S.C. 1982) requiring that "all citizens of the United States shall have the same right, in every State and Territory, as is enjoyed by white citizens thereof to inherit, purchase, lease, sell, hold, and convey real and personal property," the Court held the law to be a valid exercise of Congress's power to implement the original intent of the framers of the Thirteenth Amendment. Citing the speech of Illinois Senator Lyman Trumbull, who had chaired the judiciary committee that had brought the Thirteenth Amendment to the Senate floor in 1864, the Court's majority pointed out that "Congress has the power under the Thirteenth Amendment rationally to determine what are the badges and the incidents of slavery and the authority to translate that determination into effective legislation."[30] Race discrimination against twentieth-century blacks was held to be a badge of slavery, and Congress was recognized as serving a valid public interest when it enacted laws that forbade it. Three years later,[31] in the words of Herbert Hill, the Supreme Court held "that the use of tests by employers to make hiring and promotion decisions violates Title VII [of the Civil Rights Act of 1964] when such tests have no relationship to successful job performance and operate to disqualify blacks at a substantially higher rate than white applicants."[32] When, in 1976, the Court refused to invalidate a verbal ability, vocabulary, and reading comprehension test for police officers in Washington, D.C., that resulted in disqualifying a high proportion of black applicants, it nevertheless recognized that the "central purpose of the Equal Protection Clause of the Fourteenth Amendment is the prevention of official conduct discriminating on the basis of race," and went on to observe that even when a discriminatory intent is not written into the text of a law, "an invidious discriminatory purpose may often be inferred from the totality of the relevant facts."[33]

That neither the Congress nor the judiciary is required to be color-blind in relieving blacks from the heritage of slavery and the discriminatory vestiges thereof is clear from the record of recent Supreme Court decisions. A more pressing question—one that informs the charge of "reverse discrimination" against many affirmative action programs—is whether such remedial programs may be reasonably and Constitutionally extended to benefit Asians, Hispanics, and Amerinds, but be restricted from aiding white Anglo descendants of European immigrants. The matter depends on whether the bar of inclusion-exclusion meets the test of reasonable relationship to the valid public purpose for which the programs are established.

In order to meet this requirement it should be able to be shown that the racial and ethnic discriminations suffered by Asians, Hispanics, and Indians are vestiges of the system of black slavery, while those obstacles to opportunity and advancement that affected the life-chances of European immigrants and their American-born descent groups stem from some other source or sources. Should it be indicated that there are several trajectories of thought and practice that produce racial and ethnic discrimination, that one of them arose out of the imposition of a racially based system of involuntary servitude while the other stemmed from one or several aspects of a particularized and selective xenophobia, then it would seem to follow that legislative programs designed to eradicate the effects of the first, that is, the badges of slavery, should not only be recognized as such, but also crafted to embrace all those persons and groups who are properly shown to have been victimized by the heritage of bondage and none who have not. Although much work has been done to compare the conditions of work and life of immigrants with those of blacks, little effort has been made to see whether the ancillary and vestigial effects of slavery had a "horizontal" as well as a temporal dimension, whether, that is, they reached out to engulf select groups among the Native American and immigrant peoples and tarred them as well as the freedmen-and-women with the brush of inferiorization while leaving other sectors of the immigrant population unblemished. In what follows, I suggest a body of evidence supporting this hypothesis and invite further research on the topic.

Pluralized versus Plural Societies

In his reconceptualization of how the race problem arose in America, Benjamin Ringer offers implicit support for a claim on the mandate of the Thirteenth Amendment by blacks, Asians, and Hispanics. He points out "that the [social organization of the] thirteen colonies created two different kinds of pluralized societies. . . . One kind, a pluralistic society, reflected the instability and fluidity that operated within white colonist America. The other kind, a plural society, reflected the stabilized structure of repression that had come to characterize relations between black and white by the end of the colonial period. There seems to be no doubt that one version was built on the back of the enslaved black."[34] His thesis is in accordance with that of the framers of the Thirteenth Amendment: that the inferiorization of blacks had arisen out of their enslavement, and that, as a vestige of slavery, inferiorization is the principal element of their condition to be eradicated by any legislation enacted to implement the Thirteenth Amendment. However, Ringer goes on to show that the pattern of racially repressive duality first formulated in slav-ocratic America was not exorcised from the body politic after Emancipation, but instead remodeled and extended to embrace political, social, and economic discriminations against Asians and Hispanics as well as the newly freed Negroes.[35] Although Ringer's thesis includes inter alia, a defense of affirmative actions programs against the claim by Nathan Glazer, Thomas Sowell, and others that they institutionalize "reverse discrimination," he does not utilize the badges of slavery thesis to analyze or justify the classificatory dichotomy that these programs entail. However, other investigations provide evidence and argument that points in that direction.

With respect to the comparability of black with white immigrant situations since 1880, Stanley Lieberson has recently provided evidence that might be employed to justify exclusion of the latter group from affirmative action remediation:

> The situation for new Europeans in the United States, bad as it may have been, was not as bad as that experienced by blacks at the same time. Witness, for example, the differences in the disposition to ban openly blacks from unions at the turn of the century . . . the greater concentration of blacks in 1900 in service occupations and their smaller number in manufacturing and mechanical jobs . . . the higher black death rates in the North . . . and even the greater segregation of blacks with respect to the avenues of eminence open to them. . . . It is a serious mistake to underestimate how far the new Europeans have come in the nation and how hard it all was, but it is equally erroneous to assume that the obstacles were as great as those faced by blacks or that the starting point was the same.[36]

Lieberson goes on to note the distinctive hierarchical ordering of Europeans, blacks, Hispanics, and Asians in public opinion and other polls: "Attitudinal surveys administered in the 1920s confirm the notion that the groups were implicitly ranked on a continuum of inferiority. . . . In a variety of surveys, the American population ranked Northwestern Europeans highest, then the South-Central-Eastern Europeans, in turn the Japanese and Chinese, and finally blacks."[37] Lieberson explains the relatively greater accomplishments of Asian Americans in the employment and educational sectors by referring to the reduction in their "threat" imagery. Such a reduction occurred after their immigration to the United States had been all but cut off, but it was also affected by their concentration in certain regions of the United States where their mutual aid practices shielded them from the worst aspects of American racism, and by their discovery of and entrance into certain narrow occupational niches through which they might achieve a modest economic advance.[38] Although Lieberson has less to say about Hispanics in America, he does point out that the extraordinarily high rate of illiteracy recorded in 1920 for "native whites" of "foreign parentage" in the West-South Central region "reflects the sizable numbers of second-generation Mexicans present."[39] For the year 1960, Lieberson measures the ratio of a people's workforce engaged in craft occupations in relation to those in semiskilled jobs: native whites of native parentage rank highest (.97); second generations white groups of European parentage never fall below—and usually score several points above—that of Greek Americans (.64), while second generations Mexicans score .55, with only blacks (.38) falling below them.

Chinese

There is evidence to suggest that Asians were regarded as surrogates for blacks and as likely candidates for a process of inferiorization similar to that imposed on the latter both before and after Emancipation. Henry Hughes (1829–62), America's first sociologist, proposed to the legislature of Mississippi in 1856 that Chinese might be imported into that state from Cuba and then subjected to enslavement—after their inferiority had been ascertained scientifically.[40] In the first decade after slavery had been abolished, the importation of Chinese contract workers to replace the freedmen-and-women was the objective of the nefarious and unsuccessful "Koopmanschap incident" in Louisiana.[41] Southern plantation owners, eager "to rid themselves of their dependence on blacks," turned to the Chinese.[42] In one not unusual example, a Mrs. Leigh of Georgia "entered into a scheme to employ Chinese workers on McIntosh plantations. As part of this plan, A. S. Barnwell brought in thirty coolies to work General's Island."[43] More indicative of the treatment of Chinese as substitutes for degraded blacks was their employment as night-shift contract laborers in the cotton mills set up inside the Louisiana State Penitentiary, which had been leased to Samuel L. James and Company as an industrial enterprise.[44] Chinese in the South worked as railroad hands, fishermen,[45] and, all to often to suit the purposes of their importers, set themselves up as independent storekeepers.[46] But for purposes of the present analysis, the central point is that they were originally thought to be replacements for the emancipated slaves on sugar, tobacco, and cotton plantations.

A veritable degradation ceremony with respect to Chinese workers was conducted by key members of the United States Senate in 1876, who, even when faced with testimony that contradicted their prejudicial presuppositions, persisted in linking Chinese to Negroes and regarding both as a menace to white laboring interests and to the civilization of the United States.[47] The testimony of Henry George, a forerunner of certain theories about progress and poverty that are still in vogue in some parts of the United States,[48] is instructive in regard to the comparison of Chinese with blacks on the one hand and Southern and Eastern Europeans on the other:

Q. You think that, like the negro, the Chinese are incapable of attaining a high state of civilization?
A. They are incapable of attaining the state of civilization the Caucasian is capable of.
Q. You would make the same objection to the introduction of the negro to civilization as to the introduction of the Chinese on that ground.
A. I would have the same objection to the introduction of the negro as to the importation of the Chinese.[49]

. . . .
Q. Has this influx of Chinese tended to degrade the dignity of labor?
A. Undoubtedly.
Q. Has it had a tendency to bring white labor into the same repute that slavery did in the Southern States?
A. I think its ultimate effects are precisely the same upon the white race as slavery.[50]

. . . .
Q. Why is the Italian immigration preferable to the Chinese?
A. They are of a different race. The Italians are of the same stock as we are, and have come to their present pitch by a slow course of development for thousands of years.
Q. They are a higher civilization?
A. Undoubtedly.
Q. Do you think the same objection would apply to any lower civilization as to the Chinese?
A. Undoubtedly.[51]

. . . .

Q. . . . Do the Italians assimilate with us and become part and portion of our body-politic?

A. Undoubtedly.

Q. Do they become citizens and take upon themselves the duties of citizens?

A. Undoubtedly.

Q. And so of the Irish, the Germans, and all others of the European family?

A. Yes, sir.

Q. In time do they so assimilate with us that they are American?

A. Yes, sir.

Q. We are all of that stock are we not?

A. Yes, sir.[52]

. . . .

Q. Do you think, as a race, they [i.e., the Chinese] would make fit citizens?

A. O, no; I have not the slightest comprehension that they would; it is totally foreign to their ideas.

Q. You do not think they could be made such?

A. O, no.

Q. You think it would be an injury to our civilization to incorporate them with us?

A. It would be utterly destructive.[53]

For those post-Emancipation leaders concerned to establish an agricultural and industrial labor force and enhance American civilization and regenerate its citizenry, most Europeans were welcome as assimilable, while Chinese were regarded as racially and culturally inferior, and unfairly competitive, and civically dangerous people— a people not even fit for citizenship and the franchise that had been granted to blacks by the Fifteenth Amendment.

Japanese

That the Japanese were perceived as a people deserving the kinds of treatment meted out to the ex-slaves, the Chinese, and the American Indians speaks not only to their separation from European immigrants in the minds, hearts and policies, of a majority group Americans, but also to their deserving of a place among the beneficiaries of Thirteenth Amendment benefits. Held to be neither "free white persons" nor "persons of African descent," Japanese immigrants, like the Chinese, were assigned to an ignominious legal status: "aliens ineligible for citizenship in the United States." One Japanese immigrant, aspiring to United States citizenship, unsuccessfully petitioned the Supreme Court to declare his people to be Caucasians.[54] A few years earlier, Robert E. Park, the preeminent sociologist of race and ethnic relations in the United States, had issued a doleful prophecy: "The Japanese, like the Negro, is condemned to remain among us an abstraction, a symbol, and a symbol not merely of his own race, but of the Orient and of that vague, ill-defined menace we sometimes refer to as the 'yellow peril.' "[55]

It was in one of his fulminations against the Chinese that Henry George would propose the policy later used in an attempt to evict the Japanese from their principal occupational niche, the family farm: "Root the white race in the soil," George had exhorted his listeners, "and all the millions of Asia cannot dispossess it."[56] The Chinese had been driven out of California's agricultural fields by a series of strikes in the late 1870s and 1880s. The Japanese smallholder was subjected to the privations of California's and ten other states' alien land laws which—though enacted too late to be fully effective—sought to drive the Japanese off the land.[57] When, early in the twentieth century, Japanese farmers pioneered the production of tropical fruits in Florida, they were classed as a people similar in habits to the freedmen-and-women and subjected to many of the same kinds of prejudices.[58] However, Japanese suffered their most severe material and moral injuries in the years 1942–45, when 120,000 Americans of Japanese descent, 65 percent of whom were citizens of the United States, were imprisoned on wastelands, in specially constructed prison camps and guarded by American military personnel—all of this done without a criminal charge, a presumption of innocence, or a court trial.[59] At the present time, Japanese American survivors of the wartime policy are receiving the redress of payments granted to them by Congress after a presidential commission had reevaluated their treatment during World War II[60] and hailing the outcome of the cases reopened in the 1980s to reverse the Supreme Court decisions of 1943 and 1944 that had justified the curfew, evacuation, and imprisonment that had been imposed on them.[61]

It should be noted that during the course of the Congressional hearings held in February, 1942, both the mayor of Los Angeles and a spokesman for California's Tulare County proposed that Japanese Americans be forcibly removed to uninhabited Indian reservations on the California-Arizona Border.[62] The sequestration of American-born Japanese was regarded as even more important than the removal of alien Japanese, because, according to California Attorney

General Earl Warren, some of the former (that is, the Kibei) had attended school in Japan and become indoctrinated with a "religious instruction which ties up their religion with their Emperor," and because the loyalty of the American educated Nisei could not be established by any known means. It is to be noted that Warren and others believed that the loyalty of German and Italian aliens could easily be established.[63]

Hispanics

Hispanic peoples in America belong to a civilizational body that embraces all those lands and peoples affected by the imperialist advance of the Spanish seaborne empire. For practical purposes, however, the Hispanic groups deemed eligible for affirmative action are of Mexican and Puerto Rican descent. Mexican and Mexican American peoples of the Southwest and California found that their status hung precariously between that of blacks and Anglos, while their economic condition was marked by difficult-to-dislodge but illegal practices of peonage or by their employment as much-exploited migratory labor in California's Confederate-derived system of agribusiness. All too often, their educational opportunities were restricted through segregated and inferior school systems. Deemed to be only slightly higher on the social scale than blacks, Mexican Americans found themselves subjected to the obloquies of group positioning that are characteristic of slavery's legacy of American race prejudice.[64]

Puerto Ricans, Mexicans, and Indians are among those who have had their respective positionings in the American racial order regulated by law. Whereas Mexican residents in the ceded territories had one year to decide whether or not to opt for American citizenship,[65] Puerto Ricans and Indians found their own civic statuses to be governed by novel additions to international law. In the case of the former, the Foraker Act of 1900 established the newly conquered island community as an unincorporated territory whose denizens had no clear right to United States citizenship. As part of its justification for imposing this unusual status, Senatorial Report No. 249 held the Puerto Ricans to be a "people of wholly different character, illiterate, and unacquainted with our institutions, and incapable of exercising the rights and privileges guaranteed by the Constitution." Because of their condition, the Report concluded that it "would be competent for Congress to withhold from such people the operation of the Constitution and the laws of the United States . . . [and to] govern the people thereof as their situation and the necessities of their case might seem to require."[66] That the mind of at least some of the congressmen was turned toward comparing the Puerto Ricans and the Filipinos (whose homeland was also acquired as a result of the Spanish-American War) with the freedmen-and-women and the Chinese is indicated in this statement from the Democratic congressmen from Kentucky: "We are trying to keep out the Chinese with one hand, and now you are proposing to make Territories of the United States out of Puerto Rico and the Philippine Islands, and thereby open wide the door by which the negroes [sic] and Asiatics can pour like the locusts of Egypt into this country."[67] Although the rights, privileges, and immunities of citizenship were eventually granted to Puerto Ricans and a number of their people entered into the middle classes, an even larger number found themselves members of a servile underclass, employed on white-Anglo dominated sugar plantations on the island or crowded into the poverty-stricken slum of Spanish Harlem, an ethnoracial ghetto in New York City. All too often considered to be Negroes, Puerto Ricans in effect bore the stigma of bondage—the badge of inferiority—that had arisen in the age and through the institutionalization of black slavery.

Amerinds

Amerinds owe their unusual status to their identification as Asians,[68] their selection for and resistance to enslavement, and to their subsequent degradation as members of a uniquely conceived "domestic dependent nation." In a concurrence with the paramount decision that has been decisive in determining their rights, privileges, and immunities since 1831, the Supreme Court's Associate Justice, Mr. Johnson, was of the opinion that the Native Americans were not members of foreign states but rather of "Indian tribes—an anomaly unknown to the books that treat of States, and which the law of nations would regard as nothing more than wandering hordes, held together only by ties of blood and habit, and having neither laws or governments, beyond what is required in a savage state."[69] The opinion of the Court, delivered by the Chief Justice, held that "it may well be doubted whether those tribes which reside within the acknowledged boundaries of the United States can, with strict accuracy, be denominated foreign nations. They may, more correctly, perhaps, be denominated domestic dependent nations. . . . Meanwhile, they are in a state of pupilage. Their relation to the United States resembles that of a ward to his guardian."[70] Having been reduced to the collective status of pupils and wards, the Indians were made to resemble the enslaved Negro, insofar as the latter, under the degrading designation of "Sambo," was held to be in a state of perpetual childhood. The conflation of "savage" with "child," completed the cycle of degradation, circumscribing the limits of free action, competitive opportunities, civil rights, and social privileges within which this people might move.

□ □ □

As the twenty-first century approaches, scholarly concerns might well turn to the future of the American dream—especially as that dream affects the various races already settled in the United States, the immigrants presently arriving, and those who in the future will arrive on the shores of these United States. That future in part depends on the resolution of lingering conflicts, conflicts that arose in America's misunderstood racial and ethnic past and that evoke bitter dispute today. America's present and future immigrants, despite their material, moral, cultural, and historical uniqueness, will likely be identified with ethnic or racial elements of the settled American population. They will be seen as new generations of and people deserving the prevalent attitudes and policies toward Europeans, Latin Americans, Asians, Oceanians, or Africans. These heritages are themselves matters of dispute, as are the various proposals for remedies and eligibility for redress for discriminations of the past. In this essay I have suggested a hypothesis that might inform both research and policy with respect to this debate: that, in America, there have been two distinctive and distinguishable trajectories of discrimination, but—although I have not detailed that trajectory that affects Euro-Americans and derives, I believe, from a generalized xenophobia—only one, that descended from the badges of slavery, is remediable under the mandate that flows from the intentions of the framers of the Thirteenth Amendment. It is a special class of eligibles. Should this thesis be accepted, affirmative action programs benefiting the blacks, Asians, Amerinds, and Hispanics would be rid of the accusation that they implement reverse discrimination and welcomed as one remedy that might be employed to mitigate the occupational and educational legacy of Americans erstwhile slavocracy.

NOTES

In different form, this essay originally appeared in *Rethinking Today's Minorities*, ed. Vincent N. Parrillo (Westport, Conn.: Greenwood Press, 1991), pp. 63–86.

1. J. Hector St. John de Crevecoeur, *Letters from An American Farmer* (New York: E. P. Dutton & Co., 1957. Orig. pub. 1782), pp. 35–82, 137, 156–68, 187–89.

2. William Wells Brown, *Clotel or, The President's Daughter: A Narrative of Slave Life in the United States* (New York: Citadel Press, 1969. Orig. pub. 1853), pp. 219–20.

3. *Civil Rights Cases*, 109 U.S. 3 (1883).

4. *Plessy v. Ferguson*, 163 U.S. 537 (1896).

5. *Brown v. Board of Education of Topeka*, 347 U.S. (1954).

6. *Jones v. Alfred H. Mayer Co.*, 392 U.S. 409 (1968).

7. *Title VII of the Civil Rights Act*, 42 U.S.C. sec. 2000e et seq. (1964).

8. See, e.g., Justice Scalia et al., "Dissent," *Johnson v. Transportation Agency of Santa Clara County, California et al.*, no. 85-1129 (Mar. 25, 1987), pp. 1–21.

9. See, e.g., three works by Ronald Dworkin, *Taking Rights Seriously* (Cambridge: Harvard University Press, 1978). pp. 223–39; *A Matter of Principle* (Cambridge: Harvard University Press, 1985), pp. 293–334; *Law's Empire* (Cambridge: Belknap Press of Harvard University Press, 1986), pp. 355–99.

10. Emile Durkheim and Marcel Mauss, *Primitive Classification*, trans. and ed. Rodney Needham (Chicago: University of Chicago Press, 1967. Orig. pub. 1903); *Durkheim on Politics and the State*, trans. W. D. Halls, ed. Anthony Giddens (Stanford: Stanford University Press, 1986), pp. 97–121.

11. Herbert Blumer, *Symbolic Interactionism: Perspective and Method* (Englewood Cliffs, N.J.: Prentice-Hall, 1969), pp. 10–12. See also the discussion of affirmative action in Stanford M. Lyman and Arthur J. Vidich, *Social Order and the Public Philosophy: An Analysis and Commentary on the Works of Herbert Blumer* (Fayetteville: University of Arkansas Press, 1988), pp. 61–91.

12. See Joseph Tussman and Jacobus ten Broek, "The Equal Protection of the Laws," *California Law Review*, 37 (Sept. 1949), pp. 341–81.

13. *Korematsu v. United States*, 323 U.S. 214 (1944), 216.

14. *Fullilove v. Klutznick*, 448 U.S. 448 (1980).

15. *Kotch v. Board of River Pilot Commissioners*, 330 U.S. 552 (1947).

16. *Goesaert v. Cleary*, 335 U.S. 464 (1948). But see *Craig v. Boren*, 429 U.S. 190 (1976).

17. Nathan Glazer, "Negroes and Jews: The New Challenge to Pluralism," *Commentary*, 38 (Dec. 1964), pp. 29–35; Reprinted in Glazer, *Ethnic Dilemmas, 1964–1982* (Cambridge: Harvard University Press, 1983), pp. 29–43. Quotations from pp. 42, 37.

18. Jacobus ten Broek, *Equal under Law*, enlarged edn. (New York: Collier Books, 1965), p. 21.

19. *Yick Wo v. Hopkins*, 118 U.S. 356 (1886).

20. Tussman and ten Broek, "Equal Protection," pp. 344–56.

21. See Jacobus ten Broek, "Thirteenth Amendment to the Constitution of the United States: Consummation to Abolition and Key to the Fourteenth Amendment," *California Law Review*, 39 (June 1951), pp. 171–203.

22. Even this proved difficult to enforce. See Sydney Brodie, "The Federally-Secured Right to be Free from Bondage," *Georgetown Law Review*, 40 (Mar. 1952), pp. 367–98; and Harry H. Shapiro, "Involuntary Servitude: The Need for a More Flexible Approach," *Rutgers Law Review*, 65 (Fall 1964), pp. 65–85.

23. Loren Miller, "Race, Poverty, and the Law," in Jacobus ten Broek and the editors of the California Law Review, eds., *The Law of the Poor* (San Francisco: Chandler Publishing Co., 1966), p. 67.

24. Dissent, *Civil Rights Cases*, 109 U.S. 3 (1883).

25. Dissent, *Plessy v. Ferguson*, 163 U.S. 256 (1896).

26. Ibid.

27. Dissent, *Civil Rights Cases*.

28. *Brown v. Board of Education of Topeka*, 247 U.S. 483 (1954).

29. Miller, "Race, Poverty," p. 81.

30. *Jones v. Alfred H. Mayer Co.*, 392 U.S. 409 (1968).

31. *Griggs v. Duke Power Co.*, 401 U.S. 424 (1971).

32. Herbert Hill, *Black Labor and the American Legal System: Race, Work, and the Law* (Madison: University of Wisconsin Press, 1985), p. 61.

33. *Washington, Mayor of Washington v. Davis*, 426 U.S. 229 (1976).

34. Benjamin Ringer, *"We the People" and Others: Duality and America's Treatment of its Racial Minorities* (New York: Tavistock Publications, 1983), p. 80.

35. Ibid., pp. 157–1097.

36. Stanley Lieberson, *A Piece of the Pie: Blacks and White Immigrants since 1880* (Berkeley: University of California Press, 1980), p. 383.

37. Ibid., p. 31.

38. Ibid., pp. 5–7, 30–31, 207, 365–82.

39. Ibid., p. 134.

40. See Stanford M. Lyman, "Henry Hughes and the Southern Foundation of American Sociology," in Lyman, ed., *Selected Writings of Henry Hughes: Antebellum Southerner, Slavocrat, Sociologist* (Jackson: University Press of Mississippi, 1985), pp. 24–25.

41. See two works by Stanford M. Lyman, *The Structure of Chinese Society in Nineteenth-Century America* (Ph.D. diss., University of California, Berkeley, 1961), pp. 399–404; and *Chinatown and Little Tokyo: Power, Conflict, and Community among Chinese and Japanese Immigrants in America* (Millwood, N.Y.: Associated Faculty Press, 1986), pp. 240–42. See also Gunther Barth, *Bitter Strength: A History of the Chinese in the United States, 1850–1870* (Cambridge: Harvard University Press, 1964), pp. 191–97; and Lucy M. Cohen, *Chinese in the Post-Civil War South: A People without a History* (Baton Rouge: Louisiana State University Press, 1984), pp. 67–70, 89–95, 120–23, 180–82.

42. See, e.g., Michael Wayne, *The Reshaping of Plantation Society: The Natchez District, 1860–1880* (Baton Rouge; Louisiana State University Press, 1983), pp. 60–61, 68–72. See also Lyman, "Henry Hughes, pp. 51–54; and Cohen, *Chinese* pp. 46–81.

43. Russell Duncan, *Freedom's Shore: Tunis Campbell and the Georgia Freedmen* (Athens: University of Georgia Press, 1986), p. 60.

44. Cohen, *Chinese*, pp. 93–94.

45. Roger Shugg, *Origins of Class Struggle in Louisiana: A Social History of White Farmers and Laborers during Slavery and After, 1840–1875.* (Baton Rouge: Louisiana State University Press, 1972. Orig. pub. 1939), pp. 254–255, 311–12.

46. Cohen, *Chinese*, passim; James W. Loewen, *The Mississippi Chinese: Between Black and White* (Cambridge: Harvard University Press, 1971), pp. 32–57; Robert Seto Quan in collaboration with Julian B. Roebuck, *Lotus among the Magnolias: The Mississippi Chinese* (Jackson: University Press of Mississippi, 1982), pp. 68–99.

47. United States Senate. Forty-fourth Congress, *Report of the Joint Special Committee to Investigate Chinese Immigration* (Washington, D.C.: Government Printing Office, 1877), pp. 82, 289, 293–94, 942, 953–56, 969, 1004, 1036–37, 1133–35.

48. See six works by Henry George: *Progress and Poverty: An Inquiry into the Causes of Industrial Depressions and of Increase of Want with Increase of Wealth*, fiftieth anniversary ed. (New York: Robert Schalkenbach Foundation, 1942); *The Land Question* (New York: Robert Schalkenbach Foundation, 1965. Orig. pub. 1881); *Protection or Free Trade: An Examination of the Tariff Question, with Especial Regard to the Interests of Labor* (New York: Robert Schalkenbach Foundation, 1966. Orig. pub. 1886); *Social Problems* (New York: Robert Schalkenbach Foundation, 1966. Orig. pub. 1883); *A Perplexed Philosopher: Being an Examination of Mr. Herbert Spencer's Various Utterances on the Land Question, with Some Incidental Reference to His Synthetic Philosophy* (New York: Robert Schalkenbach Foundation, 1965. Orig. pub. 1892); *The Source of Political Economy* (New York: Robert Schalkenbach Foundation, 1968. Orig. pub. 1897). For a discussion with much original material of George's views on the Chinese question, see Henry George, Jr., *The Life of Henry George* (New York: Robert Schalkenbach Foundation, 1960. Orig. pub. 1900), pp. 191–203.

49. United States Senate. Forty-fourth Congress, p. 289.

50. Ibid., p. 282.

51. Ibid., p. 286.

52. Ibid.

53. Ibid., pp. 287–88.

54. *Ozawa v. United States*, 260 U.S. 178 (1922); for particulars of this case see the Consulate-General of Japan, *Documental History of Law Cases Affecting Japanese in the United States, 1916–1924* (San Francisco: Consulate General of Japan, 1925; reprint, New York: Arno Press, 1978), vol. 1, pp. 1–121.

55. Robert E. Park, "Racial Assimilation in Secondary Groups with Particular Reference to the Negro," in Park, *Race and Culture: The Collected Papers of Robert E. Park*, vol. 1, ed. Everett Cherrington Hughes et al. (Glencoe, Ill.: The Free Press, 1950), p. 209.

56. Henry George, "Why Work is Scarce, Wages Low, and Labour Restless," address presented in the Metropolitan Temple in San Francisco, March 26, 1878. Quoted in Henry George, Jr., *Life*, p. 203.

57. Consulate-General of Japan, 2, pp. 1–1051; *Oyama v. California*, 332 U.S. 633 (1947); Audrie Girdner and Anne Loftis, *The Great Betrayal: The Evacuation of the Japanese Americans during World War II* (London: Collier-Macmillan, 1969), pp. 428–32.

58. George E. Pozzetta and Harry A. Kersey, Jr., "Yamato Colony: A Japanese Presence in South Florida," *Tequesta: The Journal of the Historical Association of Southern Florida*, 36 (1976), pp. 66–77.

59. Jacobus ten Broek, Edward N. Barnhart, and Floyd W. Matson, *Prejudice, War, and the Constitution* (Berkeley: University of California Press, 1954).

60. *Personal Justice Denied: Report of the Commission on Wartime Relocation and Internment of Civilians* (Washington, D.C.: December, 1982); *Personal Justice Denied: Report of the Commission on Wartime Relocation and Internment of Civilians-Part 2: Recommendations* (Washington, D.C.: June, 1983). Rockwell Chin et al., "The Long Road: Japanese Americans Move on Redress," *Bridge: Asian American Perspectives*, 7 (Winter 1981–82), pp. 11–29; Judith Miller, "Wartime Internment of Japanese was 'Grave Injustice,' Panel Says," *New York Times* (Feb. 25, 1983), pp. A1–A2.

61. Minoru Yasui, " 'Coram Nobis' to the Supreme Court," *Pacific Citizen*, 94 (Apr. 16, 1982), pp. 2, 5; "3 Japanese-Americans Ask Court to Overturn Wartime Convictions," *New York Times* (Jan. 31, 1983), p. A14; "Bad Landmark: Righting a Racial Wrong," *Time* (Nov. 21, 1983), p. 51; David Margolick, "Legal Legend Urges Victims to Speak Out," *New York Times* (Nov. 24, 1984), pp. 25, 26; Aaron Epstein, "Japanese Internment Cases to be Heard," *Miami Herald* (Nov. 18, 1986), p. 15A; and two articles by Robert Shimabukuro, "Min Yasui Dies at 70; Services Held in Denver," and "Coram Nobis Attorney Says Yasui Appeal Will Continue," both in *Pacific Citizen*, 103 (Nov. 21, 1986), pp. 1, 8. See also Gordon Hirabayashi, "Good Times, Bad Times: Idealism is Realism," Sunderland P. Gardner Lecture, Canadian Yearly Meeting, August 14, 1985. Canadian Quaker Pamphlet no. 22 (Argenta, B.C.: Argenta Friends Press, Sept. 1985); Peter Irons, *Justice at War: The Story of the Japanese American Internment Cases* (New York: Oxford University Press, 1983); and Irons, ed., *Justice Delayed: The Record of the Japanese American Internment Cases* (Middleton, Conn.: Wesleyan University Press, 1989).

62. *National Defense Migration. Hearings Before the Select Committee Investigating National Defense Migration*. House of Representatives. Seventy-Seventh Congress, 2d sess. (Washington, D.C.: Government Printing Office, 1942; reprint, New York: Arno Press, 1978), pp. 11648–50.

63. Ibid., pp. 10973–11023.

64. "The . . . minority groups mentioned here have lived in this region under social and economic conditions that are commonly associated with the fate of the Negro in the United States. The Indian, the Spanish Surnamed, the Oriental, the Negro—all of whom are of significant number in the region's population—can match among themselves their experiences with segregated housing, segregated schools, discriminating social treatment, repressed civil rights, and limited employment opportunities. . . . That so many . . . were seen as spicks, greasers, pepper bellies, niggers, japs, chinks, red skins, or as persons deserving some other contemptuous name . . . made it relatively easy to sort and segregate the non-Anglo. Those so sorted were not considered proper members of the dominant society." Fred H. Schmidt, *Spanish Surnamed American Employment in the Southwest.* A Study Prepared for the Colorado Civil Rights Commission under the Auspices of the Equal Employment Opportunity Commission (Washington, D.C.: Government Printing Office, 1970), pp. 76–77.

65. Robert F. Heizer and Alan J. Almquist, *The Other Californians: Prejudice and Discrimination under Spain, Mexico, and the United States to 1920* (Berkeley: University of California Press, 1971), pp. 96, 197. But see Paul S. Taylor, *Mexican Labor in the United States* (Berkeley: University of California Press, 1930; reprint, New York: Arno Press and the *New York Times,* 1970), pp. 242–48.

66. Ringer, "We the People," pp. 968–69.

67. Ibid., p. 973.

68. *People v. Hall.* 4 Cal. 399 (Oct. 1, 1854). See Stanford M. Lyman, "Asian American Contacts before Columbus: Alternative Understanding for Civilization, Acculturation, and Ethnic Minority Status in the United States," in Sohken Togami, ed., *Japanese Americans: Iju Kara Jiritsu Eno Ayumi* (Kyoto: Mineruva Shobo, 1985), pp. 341–92.

69. *Cherokee Nation v. State of Georgia,* 5 Peters 1 (1831), at 34.

70. Ibid., at 16.

PART 4

Assimilation, Pluralism,
and the Postmodern Challenge

People, I just want to say, can we all get along? Can we stop making it horrible for the older people and the kids? . . . It's just not right; it's not right. And it's not going to change anything. We'll get our justice. . . . We'll have our day in court, and that's all we want. . . . I'm neutral. I love everybody. . . . We're all stuck here for a while. Let's try to work it out.

Rodney King
Los Angeles, May 1, 1992

12

Between *Ecriture* and *Thymos*: Dilemmas and Contradictions of Racial, Ethnic, and Minority Culture Expression in the Twenty-first Century

Race, Culture, and Anomie

As the twentieth-century fin de siècle draws near, the very ability to discourse on color, culture, and nation has been thrown into flux by the counterposed positions of an allegedly fading modernism and an emerging but as yet inchoate postmodernism. Such important sociological theorists as Anthony Giddens, Rose Laub Coser, and Stjepan G. Meštrović have addressed aspects of this problem. Giddens recognizes that one fundamental issue of the time is how to define and determine the relationship of self and society in what he calls the "late modern age."[1] For Giddens the "life-politics" of the late modern era are characterized by an emancipatory perspective that will liberate "social life from the fixities of tradition and custom," reduce or eliminate altogether "exploitation, inequality, or oppression," and obey "imperatives suggested by the ethics of justice, equality and participation."[2] The thrust of this line of thought would seem to be toward a dynamic, individualist, and, as far as the race question is concerned, an assimilationist orientation. However, the matter is not quite so clear when we find Giddens writing that "in all cases the objective of emancipatory politics is either to release *underprivileged groups* from their unhappy condition, or to eliminate the relative differences between them."[3]

Rose Laub Coser writes in defense of modernity in part because she believes it is the occasion and situs for role and status demarcations *within* the individual, permitting him or her to inhabit multiple worlds—some that are evidences of the survival and perseverance of racial heritages or of the several immigrant folk cultures, others that are instantiations of a cosmopolitan civil society—in the ıe life-space and life-time.[4] But still another position is advanced by Stjepan G. Meštrović, who insists that social fragmentation is the leitmotif of both modernism and postmodernism, that the fin de siècle of each is characterized by a gnawing *anomie*, and that both represent a quest for the irrational bases of social order.[5] Meštrović is intent on showing that postmodernism is merely the logical successor to modernist thought. For him, postmodernism "is the institutionalization of anomie in the core of culture and across many social institutions, from religion to the family."[6]

Postmodernists, however, as well as some of their critics, conceive of their perspective as far more radical—as a repudiation of the entire modernist orientation and its project. Thus Stephen Crook observes that for French postmodernisms the " 'classical' projects of the nineteenth and early twentieth centuries which came to define the nature and tasks of modern social theory, the projects of Comte, Marx, Durkheim and the rest, are held to be anachronistic in a strong sense."[7] Indeed, Mike Featherstone goes further in this argument, suggesting that the postmodern perspective is sufficiently revolutionary to threaten the basis of sociology itself, especially insofar as that discipline conceives of itself as a systematizing, generalizing, social science.[8] According to a hotly disputed interpretation of the works of Jacques Derrida by John M. Ellis, postmodernism is even more formidable, capable of subverting not merely the social sciences, but the entire tradition of Occidental philosophy as well.[9]

Nevertheless, some social scientists are more sanguine. One recent convert, the sociologist Norman Denzin, holds that the postmodern perspective opens up a new way to examine the narrative structures of American popular culture and to metatheorize on such recently revisited ethnographic classics as William F. Whyte's study of Italian American urbanites, *Street Corner Society*.[10] Indeed, the decentering of the subject in postmodernist thought, as Denzin conceives of it, places the very project of conventional ethnography under suspicion by its insinuation of doubt about whether any outside observer could succeed in "somehow prevail[ing] upon this subject to reveal her inner world of experience to the kindly knowing scientist."[11] Thereby, it raises the possibility of an ultimately irreducible "other," whose internalized culture and sensibilities are irrevocably hidden not only from the investigator but also from the never-fully-present subject as well. Under such a regime of nonintersubjective thought, there is more at stake than academic ethnography—the very possibility of cooperative and coordinative race *relations* are threatened too. Such a fragmentation, if real, not only denies the possibility of that coordination of sentiments that Robert E. Park treated as the sine qua non of assimilation,[12] but also bids fair to destroy any chance for formulation of the noncontractural basis of the democratic civic covenant that pluralism presupposes.[13]

However it is conceived, postmodernism has already had and will continue to have a profound if unsettling effect on the social sciences in Europe and America in general and, especially in the United States, on questions of culture and its roots—on the problem of assimilation and pluralism—in particular.

Pluralism and Assimilation in Postmodern Thought: Baudrillard and Lyotard

In what has become a classic of postmodernist writing, Jean Baudrillard calls attention to:

> The beauty of the Black and Puerto Rican women of New York. Apart from the sexual stimulation produced by the crowding together of so many races, it must be said that black, the pigmentation of the dark races, is like a natural make-up that is set off by the artificial kind to produce a beauty which is not sexual, but sublime and animal—a beauty which the pale faces so desperately lack. Whiteness seems an extenuation of physical adornment, a neutrality which, perhaps by that very token, claims all the exoteric powers of the Word, but ultimately will never possess the esoteric and ritual potency of artifice.[14]

By making a color aesthetic an important part of his text on culture in the United States—and by referring en passant to Mexicans, Japanese, and Indians in a related manner throughout the work—Baudrillard seems to be celebrating the physical basis of the ethnoracial diversity that makes up one central aspect of American pluralism. But, in fact, his perspective transcends that thesis and embraces a vision that, while accepting the realities of each, ironicizes both pluralism and assimilation. For example, as his tour across America progresses, Baudrillard takes note of "the Mexicans [who have] become Chicanos [and who] act as guides on the visit to El Alamo to laud the heroes of the American nation so valiantly massacred by their own ancestors," in order to show that "history is full of ruse and cunning. But so are the Mexicans who have crossed the border clandestinely to come and work here."[15] Even this multilayered perception does not grasp the whole of Baudrillard's postmodern outlook on the United States, however. For to this French intellectual,

America represents the triumph of technocentric artifice over what was once nature's awe-inspiring grandeur: "America is a giant hologram," he asserts, "in the sense that information concerning the whole is contained in each of its elements. . . . The hologram is akin to the world of phantasy. . . . Everything is destined to reappear as simulation."[16]

For Baudrillard the realities of race and ethnicity in America are neither melted down by the fires of the melting pot nor preserved intact by the powers of nostalgia and the pull of the Old World. On the one hand, Baudrillard believes that "in America, each ethnic group, each race develops a language, a culture in competition with and sometimes superior to that of the 'natives,' and each group symbolically rises to the top."[17] On the other, Baudrillard calls attention to the fact that this "top" is itself a Tocquevillian celebration of status and value equality: "The American world tends both towards absolute insignificance (all things tending to become equal and therefore cancelling each other out in their power) and towards absolute originality. . . . *This is a world that has shown genius in its irrepressible development of equality, banality, and indifference.*"[18] In such a society, races and ethnic groups live on in and at the same time outside of a hollow shell of ethnoracial identity—their "culture" is that which is either marketable to the "natives" as stereotypy or useful for class and status enhancement in a civil society. But such a society is built on conspicuous consumption. Hence, Baudrillard concludes, "the have-nots will be condemned to oblivion, to abandonment, to disappearance pure and simple."[19] To Robert E. Park, the trend toward civilization meant the movement to absorb folk cultures within a global cosmopolis whose urban agglomerations made grudging room for the "human junk" that would neither conform nor die;[20] to Baudrillard, the American "social order is contracting to include only economic exchange, technology, the sophisticated and innovative," while leaving ever smaller portions of its space for "dumping grounds, wastelands, new deserts for the new poor."[21] From this perspective, the nontechnological, preindustrial or anti-commercial ideologies put forward by some advocates of a salvationist ethnoracial pluralism would likely be seen as surplus commodities worthy only of commercial appropriation accompanied by cultural evisceration.

If one takes leave of Baudrillard's America with a sense that this French raconteur takes a certain delight in the *Schrecklichkeit* of America's culture, to move into the world of Jean-Francois Lyotard is, in the words of Arthur Kroker, "to enter a big crash scene after the catastrophe where we live at the end of rational politics, economy, and culture."[22] Lyotard's postmodernism entails a search for the basis of a new identity, one that is somehow constructable from the shards of smashed art and the shrapnel of an exploded science. His perspective is dynamic: there are "no identities, only transformations."[23] In one sense, Lyotard represents postmodernism's rejection of both Freud and Weber, a rejection, that is, of both the psychoanalyst's rationalized future for the illusion of religion and the scholar's prediction of rationality's power to disenchant every aspect of the world. His is a quest for reenchantment in the face of chaos—a reenchantment of the political world by means of an aesthetic. However, for Lyotard it is an aesthetic that owes more to Wittgenstein's conception of discourse as "language games" than to any metanarrative of either art or politics. Essential to Lyotard's postmodernism is an irremediable disconnectedness of every thing to every other thing.[24] For many modernists the chaos of disconnectedness that marked the conception of what is now their century-old fin de siècle served as a spur to reconnect the fragmented pieces by means of some metalanguage, metanarrative, or metatheory. For a postmodernist like Lyotard, on the other hand, fragmentation, ephemerality, discontinuity, and irruptive change are the elementary and unchangeable forms of the human condition. Hence in place of such "totalizing" schemas as that of Freud, Marx, Weber, or Durkheim—indeed, in place, it would appear, of Simmel's tragic sense of culture as the unending struggle of *life* against all *forms* of life—Lyotard poses a plurality of game-empowered discourses and an attitude toward modernism that offers "incredulity towards [all] meta-narratives."[25]

What then of assimilation and pluralism in their American ethnoracial context? Without ever saying so in *haec verba*, Lyotard's vision of the ultimate effects of modernization presents the final product of assimilation as a cracked mosaic—shards of once more constituted peoples, once more firmly established statuses, once more hierarchicalized races and genders, once more courageous captains of industry, once more militant proletarians, now (and perhaps forever) living uneasily together in a kind of relationship that Robert Park once referred to as "symbiotic."[26] However, for Lyotard there is no vital center toward which the old advocates of assimilation (and such more recent ones as Arthur Schlesinger, Jr.)[27] would push the possessors of outworn folk cultures; nor is there an effective or relevant centralized power structure against which the protectors of ethnoracial diversity might struggle. Instead, what survives (or is constructed out) of ethnoracial cultures has—like everything else—become ephemeral and epiphenomenal. There is no "base," as the Marxists liked to imagine, only a "super-structure." The darker races belong to an "otherness' that the limited and exclusive rules of Occidental fraternization have made both permanent, seductive, and perhaps in keeping with Francis Fukuyama's sense that the triumph of capitalism means the end of the Hegelian dynamic of history,[28] a mere object of political and commercial commodification.

Such critics of Lyotard as Jameson[29] and Harvey[30] treat his conception of society and culture as reactionary; nevertheless, his reduction of culture—and, by extension, ethnoracial cultures—to products of an utterly commercialized civilization has its own ring of truth, its own acknowledgment of the condition that Neil Postman calls "technopoly," the surrender of culture to technology.[31] And yet, Lyotard seems to wish to rescue the still surviving ethnoracial cultures from both dismemberment in and exploitation by the burgeoning commercial cosmopolis that he conceives as the post-Kantian legacy bequeathed by modernism to the future. Lyotard hopes to accomplish this emancipation by elevating narrative to authority in its own right, without any authorization by an author. Ethnoracial narratives—the stuff of cultural pluralism for many of its advocates—are conceived by Lyotard to be de-legitimations of "the great narratives of legitimation that characterize Western modernity."[32] However, such an emancipation bids fair to deny to the oppressed minorities the great and universal pronunciamentos on which their claim to a separate and equal dignity is based. For Lyotard holds that such universal declarations have failed in their manifest intent, but at the same time have succeeded in becoming the source for the modernist authorial narrative that is now in process of decentrification. He writes, "It is as though the immense effort, signalled by the name of the Declaration of Human Rights, that has been made to strip peoples of a narrative legitimacy which lies, so to speak, downstream in historical terms, and to make them adopt as their sole legitimacy that Idea of free citizenship, which lies upstream . . . , has ended in failure."[33]

There is an unresolved paradox here. Lyotard admires the narrative structures developed by anticolonial, anti-imperialist, and antiracist "guerillas fighting for independence,"[34] but also believes that the ubiquitous Keynesianism that characterizes the present and future political economies of the world has neither reduced inequality nor fostered the ideal of a universal history. Instead, "cultural differences are . . . being promoted as touristic and cultural commodities at every point on the scale."[35] How, except for those resistant "guerrilla" narratives that remain in the ever-decreasing space of the periphery, ethnoracial cultures will avoid being taken over by the new, seductive, and far-reaching technopoly is unclear.

Ecriture, Assimilation, and Pluralism: Derrida, Toomer, and Gates

Like Baudrillard and Lyotard, Jacques Derrida offers up a world wherein the metanarratives of the late nineteenth century have lost their efficacy. Introducing the term "deconstruction" to the discourse on postmodernity, Derrida regards culture and cultural life as a series of "texts" weaving in and out of one another, yet, as David Harvey points out, each having "a life of its own." "Whatever we write conveys meanings we do not or could not possibly intend, and our words cannot say what we mean."[36] Hence, the deconstructive project aims to examine a text to see how it contains, covers up, or superimposes itself over another, indeed, over many others. However, the ultimate project of postmodernism, Derrida's as well as that of Lyotard and Baudrillard, is to document the end of all privileged texts and all hegemonic narratives—and with that documentation, or so its Marxist critics bitterly complain, to put finis to the hopes of all current and future disprivileged but aspiring texts of emancipation.[37]

In the work of Derrida, authorization is separated from the author of any text; the author's privileged position in determining the meaning of his or her own textual production is laid side-by-side with those of the readers in what amounts to a "Rashomon" structure of multiple, opposed, and nonresolvable understandings. Every established, that is, privileged, text—and, although Derrida does not refer to these terms specifically, this would include every authorialized text defining such signifiers as, or purporting to delineate a discourse on, "Negro," "black," "Afro-American"; "Chinese," "Japanese," "Oriental," "Asian American"; "Mexican," "Chicano," "Hispanic"; and "Indian," "Amerindian," and "Native American"—is now discreditable, an appropriate topic for a "deconstructive" analysis that would both deny the privileged validity of the author's own definition and expose the many meanings upon which the author's has been superimposed.

There is both an "assimilation" and a "pluralism" to be derived from Derrida's version of postmodernism and to be found in postmodern society. Both the "assimilation" and the "pluralism" are

Lyotardean; assimilation contains the plurality of elements—the shards and shibboleths of color, culture, and ethnicity that form the seemingly chaotic mosaic of an over-commercialized civilization. And it is precisely because these elementary forms of postmodern life are shards and shibboleths that Derrida's concept of ecriture is fundamental to the emerging structure of human group differentiation.

Ecriture, in its special Derridean sense, arises as a part of the process whereby every term of a discursive text becomes eligible for a deconstruction that places it, as it were, under erasure, that is, the term is still there, visible beneath the "x" that stands for its placement sous rature. Such placement acts as a warning to the reader to be skeptical about the word, especially about its privileged authorial meaning. In the spirit of this aspect of Derrida's approach, Henry Louis Gates, Jr., has written the following about the term "race": "Scores of people are killed every day in the name of differences ascribed only to race. This slaughter demands the gesture . . . to deconstruct, if you will, the ideas of difference inscribed in the trope of race, to explicate discourse itself in order to reveal the hidden relations of power and knowledge inherent in popular and academic usages of 'race.'"[38]

Gates' demand that the term "race" be subjected to deconstruction is certainly a welcome addition to the projects that might be undertaken by followers of Derrida. Indeed, long before the rise or even the recognition of an age of postmodernism, such critical scholars as Margaret Hodgen,[39] Ruth Benedict,[40] and Ashley Montagu[41] had undertaken what might now be designated as proto-deconstructive assaults on the term. More recently, I have begun an "archaeology," or perhaps more accurately, a "paleontology" of the terms of racial reference and of the ethnoracial signifiers given hegemonic force in American law.[42] Such projects, however, work at what is but the first phase of the postmodern project—they decenter and delegitimize the authorialized texts that have thus far held sway over Occidental thought and justified Occidental praxis. Beyond this phase lies the ever-treacherous space of a plurality of equally disprivileged or disprivilegeable texts—each also eligible for a deconstructive probe.

Derrida introduces the term "paleonymics" to describe the process whereby old names are retained while new meanings are added to them. Certainly all the terms of ethnoracial reference are likely subjects of a paleonymic logic that treats the grafting of an additional meaning onto the old. Such would be, in Derrida's terms, an "intervention"—one that would "give everything at stake in the operations of deconstruction the chance, the force, the power of *communication*."[43] Marcuse once referred to a related phenomenon—a kind of primitive deconstructionism one might say—that prevailed among militant members of America's ethnoracial minorities in the late 1960s who took over or, in Marcuse's words, "desublimated" such hegemonic terms of racial oppression as "nigger" and "yellow peril" remaking them into a rhetoric of intragroup affection and solidarity as well as part of a dialectic of antiracist resistance.[44] However, useful as it might be for the delegitimation of an oppressive culture, the epistemological thrust of deconstruction is applicable to every text—that of the privileged as well as the disprivileged. It is in this latter sense that it has a unique role to play in the struggle between pluralism and assimilation.

In one sense the project of poststructuralism denies at the very moment that it encourages the aims of both assimilationists and pluralists. On the one hand, by deconstructing the oppressive rhetorics of race at work in the Occident since at least the sixteenth century,[45] postmodernism might encourage an integration of the races that permitted equality in the presence of acknowledged anatomical difference. Such a cultural as well as politico-economic cosmopolis, Lester F. Ward prophesied shortly after the turn of the nineteenth century, would arise when the harsh but amalgamative process of *social karyokinesis* had so blended the peoples of America and the world that whatever epidermal pigmentary distinctiveness still remained would form but an aesthetic relief on the cartography of a fully acculturated technocentric civilization.[46] More recently Charles Johnson, author of novels described as philosophical fictions, director of the Creative Writing Program at the University of Washington, and a literary critic of African American writing, has predicted a new "species of black American fiction . . . taking form on the horizon of contemporary practice." This species, he asserts, will herald the end of a discourse of "narrow complaint" in black writing and the beginning of a "broad celebration": "When we have finally crossed this great distance, the prehistory of Afro-American literature will [have to come to an] end. We will not have "black" writers or books long out of print and collecting dust in Black Studies libraries. . . . Rather, we will see a fiction by Americans who happen to be black, feel at ease both in their ethnicity and in their Yankeeness, and find it the most natural thing, as Merleau-Ponty was fond of saying, to go about 'singing the world.' "[47]

However, such feeling at ease in one's ethnicity as well as one's Yankeeness is precisely the kind of bland assimilation that must be overthrown, according to such pluralistically oriented culture critics of canonical literature and African-American letters and life as Henry Louis Gates, Jr.[48] Gates has criticized the earlier and assimilative uses of Negro literature, holding them to be motivated by the desire to give evidence for a thesis that only a racist culture would demand— namely, that blacks were indeed a part of the "humanity" that an Enlightenment-oriented, Eurocentric America might recognize.[49] In its place, Gates puts forward a black cultural aesthetic that seeks "to valorize (and demonstrate in what ways literature can contribute to) a larger political and economic analysis of the position of the black person living in the United States." Moreover, Gates claims that "the Black Aesthetic should repudiate the received terms of academic, or white, literary critical methods and theories."[50] Gates goes even further, appropriating the tools of Derridean deconstruction in order to assault both the Western canon and those African American writers, critics, and activists who have acquiesced to it, but, at the same time, dissociating his own emerging black aesthetic from the full implications of the project of the French postmodernists. "Our pressing question now," he stated when speaking to a conference of black scholars called to debate and to formulate *The Study of Afro-American Literature: An Agenda for the 1990s*, "becomes this: in what languages shall we choose to speak, and write, our own criticisms?"[51]

Gates's complex answer to that question is that of a Lyotardean guerilla fighter secreted within the oppressor's camp: "Learning the master's tongue, for our generation of critics, has been an act of empowerment, whether that critical language be New Criticism, so-called humanism, structuralism, Marxism, poststructuralism, feminism, new historicism, or any other 'ism' that I have forgotten."[52] However, this learning will be ineffective, Gates asserts, if it is not accompanied by the kind of praxis enunciated by Wole Soyinka, the Nigerian Nobel laureate: "And when we borrow an alien language to sculpt or paint in, we must begin by co-opting the entire properties of that language as correspondences to properties in our matrix of thought and expression."[53] Failure to adopt Soyinka's epistemological perspective will result in continued abjection. "To assume we can wear the masks, and speak the languages, of Western literary theory without accepting Soyinka's challenge," Gates concludes, "is to accept, willingly, the intellectual equivalent of neocolonialism, placing ourselves in a relationship of discursive indenture."[54]

Much of Gates's work thus far has been taken up with critically appraising those black (and white) *litterateurs* who still live behind the Eurocentric veil.[55] In this regard he once accused black literary scholar Houston A. Baker, Jr., of limiting his black aesthetic to "race and superstructure criticism," an approach that, Gates insisted, would lock "Black Aestheticians into a Western problematic."[56] Baker, of course, disagreed, pointing out that his own analysis of why and how the Harlem Renaissance poet Countee Cullen desired to be judged as "just a poet" in fact reveals "a unique inscription of the *racial* dynamics of Afro-American expressive culture" and going on to assert that by his mode of analysis "Cullen . . . becomes a veritable sign of struggle, a poet *malgré lui*, encoding inaudible reaches of the low and common valley of *blackness*."[57] This debate evokes a fundamental but so far unnoticed feature of the postmodernist approach to an ethnoracial pluralistic perspective—the inherent "undecidability"[58] in the Derridean sense of that term, of blackness—of its sense as experience and its being as epistemo-epidermal form.[59]

This issue is more precisely met when we turn to one of Gates's finest applications of Derrida's concept of *rature*—his deconstruction of the identity-genealogy of Jean Toomer (1894–1967), the author of *Cane*, [60] a major work associated with the Harlem Renaissance era in African American culture. Toomer, a grandson on his mother's side of the mulatto P. B. S. Pinchback (1837–1921), who had served for forty-three days as a Reconstruction-era governor of Louisiana, [61] is a significant figure for analysis of the problematic of "blackness" because of his lifelong ambivalence over his own racial identity, his respected but ambiguous place in the canon of African American letters, his discipleship with the Armenian mystic, Georges Gurdjieff, and his decision a decade after the publication of his seminal book, to "pass" as a white man.[62] At one point in his life, sometime between 1920 and 1922, Toomer had come to a conclusion about his own ethnonational identity as well as that of all other Americans—one that is strikingly consonant with that of Crèvecoeur:

> I had observed [he wrote] that . . . very few . . . United States citizens were aware of being *Americans*. On the contrary, they were aware of, and put value upon, their hearsay descents, their groupistic affiliations. . . . Yet, underlying what they were aware of, underlying all of the divisions, I had observed what seemed to me to be authentic—namely that a new type of man was arising in this country—not European, not African, not Asiatic—but American. And in this American I saw the

> divisions mended, the differences reconciled—saw that (1) we
> would in truth be a united people existing in the United States,.
> saw that (2) we would in truth be once again members of a
> united human race.[63]

When Toomer shared this bit of reasoning with a friend whom he
described as "a colored fellow of more than ordinary mental grasp,"
his companion dismissed it with a single phrase, "You're white,"
adding to Toomer's plaintive inquiry about his own identity, "[I'm]
colored." Toomer saw his friend's perspective as the product of a
misleading, pervasive, and pernicious "racial conditioning" that he
alone could not "unfix."[64] Gates, however, seizes upon this colloquy
as a singular but exemplary piece of discourse worthy of a Derridean
deconstruction.

Toomer had earlier claimed about his own discovery of the Amer-
icanness of himself and his contemporaries: "I began feeling that I
had in my hands the tools for my own creation."[65] From this statement and from Toomer's autobiographical American credo, Gates
uncovers a subtending rature:

> Toomer's "tools for my own creation," paradoxically, were "but
> words," yet words with which he put his Negro ancestry under
> erasure: his grandfather, P. B. S. Pinchback, Toomer rewrites,
> "passed" or crossed over to being a Negro only to seek and gain
> political office during the Reconstruction: Toomer simply re-
> versed the chiasmus. If Grandfather Pinchback was white, then
> Grandson Jean was Negro.[66]

Having proceeded this far, Gates asserts that "to be a human being . . . Toomer felt that he had to efface his mask of blackness, the
cultural or racial trace of difference, and embrace the utter invisibil-
ity of being an American."[67] And, recalling Derrida's observation
that "the 'matinal trace' of difference is lost in an irretrievable in-
visibility, and yet even its loss is covered, preserved, regarded, and
retarded,"[68] Gates resurrects Toomer's "tell-tale trace of blackness"—no matter what the author claims about his identity or ancestry—from the discourse in his novel Cane.[69]

Although Gates can now claim to have restored the supposedly
complete erasure of blackness that Toomer might have been attempting in his autobiography and in the rest of his life, it is to be noted
that another major African American critic of black letters regards
Cane as "an artistic fusion . . . of Christian myth and elements of the
African and Afro-American experience," and goes on to treat this fu-

sion of cultural forms as that which, together with its usage of black music, "establishes the book as a unique contribution to the tradition of the Afro-American novel."[70] Is "blackness" a separate and independent element that must be resurrected from its hiddenness under an erasure, or is it the emergent product of an intercultural chiaroscuro fusion?

Fusion, it is to be noted, a term usually associated with assimilation, acculturation, and amalgamation, has figured occasionally—but always significantly—in anthropological as well as cultural approaches to African American life. Thus, in one of his early researches in physical anthropology, Melville Herskovitz, the ethnologist most well known for his lifelong insistence—over the vigorous objections of black sociologist E. Franklin Frazier[71]—that features of African culture survived both slavery and emancipation and continued, sometimes in syncretic form, to play a part in the everyday lives of ordinary black Americans,[72] also claimed that the people he wished to designate as "the American Negro" were a uniquely interbred descent group, having been procreated over several generations marked by a significant amount of black and white amalgamation.[73] Indeed, it was just such a fusion that Jean Toomer invoked as justification for his own claim to be an "American":

> Racially, [he observed in 1922], I seem to have (who knows for sure) seven blood mixtures: French, Dutch, Welsh, Negro, German, Jewish, and Indian. Because of these my position in America has been a curious one. I have lived equally amid the two race groups. Now white, now colored. From my own point of view I am naturally and inevitably an American. I have strived for a spiritual fusion analogous to the fact of racial intermingling.[74]

However, Toomer discovered that his attempt to let the several bloods that flowed through his spiritual veins "function as complements . . . [and] live in harmony" was difficult if not impossible to accomplish as a way of life. His visit to Georgia and his decision to give vent to his artistic expression while living and working among the black peasantry of that area "pulled me deeper and deeper into the Negro group. . . . And a deep part of my nature, a part that I had repressed, sprang suddenly to life and responded to them."[75] It is this deep part—what, perhaps, Robert E. Park would have assigned to "temperament," a biosocial element that he designated as the source for the distinctiveness that made for each race's expressive uniqueness[76]—that it seems Gates would have us resurrect as the basis of Toomer's "blackness," and that others (including myself) might designate as the ineffable psychocultural basis of the symbolic estate of an acculturated ethnicity.[77]

There is, however, another way to read Toomer's and Crèvecoeur's Americanist credo, one that bids fair to collapse the polarity of pluralism and assimilation in a dialectical fusion wherein blackness becomes the trace as well as the resource for whiteness. The possibility that blackness might be the color-culture element of whiteness *sous rature*—the thing "absent" that defines the "thingness" of the white "present"—has been suggested recently by the African American novelist and critic Toni Morrison.[78] In Morrison's trenchant deconstruction of the writings of such canonical white American writers as Edgar Allan Poe, she uncovers the trace, or "shadow," as she calls it, of blackness that allows figures with "skin 'the perfect whiteness of snow'" to appear. "Because [such figures] . . . appear almost always in conjunction with representations of black or Africanist people who are dead, impotent, or under complete control," Morrison observes, "these images of blinding whiteness seem to function as both antidote for and meditation on the shadow that is companion to this whiteness—a dark and abiding presence that moves the hearts and texts of American literature with fear and longing."[79]

Morrison, drawing upon Bernard Bailyn's historical researches on the origins of the American people,[80] in effect, and without any acknowledgment that she is engaged in this kind of deconstructionism, takes up the second meaning of Derrida's concept "*differance*," that is, "to defer."[81] In this part of her study, she emphasizes how, for the original white, Anglo-Saxon settlers of America, the new society they were forging seemed to promise them the opportunity to realize four desiderata unavailable to them in the Old World—"autonomy, authority, newness and difference, [and] absolute power." To the extent that these promises were realizable, each was "shaped by, activated by a complex awareness and employment of a constituted Africanism . . . that provided the staging ground and arena for the elaboration of the quintessential American identity."[82] Nevertheless, these promises form the not fully requited "romance" of both white American life and literature, an anguishing affair that on the one hand requires the permanent abjection of blacks—the group without whose subjection the promises could not be fulfilled—but, on the other, denies the reality of its embedded racism. "Eventually," Morrison observes, the sullied ideal of American "individualism fuses with the prototype of Americans as solitary, alienated, and malcontent."[83]

There are, in fact, two separate deferrals implicit in Morrison's deconstructive project: the first, having to do with the unmeasured and uncalculable *duree* that marks the epoch during which the promise of autonomy, authority, novelty, and absolute power to whites in America is not yet consummated, is characterized by the haunting shadow of blackness that serves as a subliminal trace upon the otherwise bright white cultural escutcheon:

> For the settlers and for American writers generally, this Africanist other became the means of thinking about body, mind, chaos, kindness, and love; provided the occasion for exercises in the absence of restraint, the presence of restraint, the contemplation of freedom and of aggression; permitted opportunities for the exploration of ethics and morality, for meeting the obligations of the social contract, for bearing the cross of religion and following out the ramifications of power.[84]

The African trace—the absence that makes the American whiteness possible as a presence—constitutes the essence of what distinguished America from Europe, the New World from the Old: "What was distinctive in the New was, first of all, its claim to freedom and, second, the presence of the unfree within the heart of the democratic experiment."[85] However, although Morrison does not make as much of it as she might, there is a second deferral, one that not only elaborates upon and confounds the first, but also permits us to return to Gates's deconstruction of Toomer's life and work and to perform upon it a deferential deconstruction of our own making.

Let us first, however, proceed to unpack Derrida's second meaning of *differance*. That term incorporates two significations—"to differ" and "to defer." Here we are concerned with the latter signification—the one that, according to Derrida, "makes the movement of signification possible only if each element that is said to be 'present,' appearing on the stage of presence, is related to something other than itself *but retains the mark of a past element and already lets itself be hollowed out by the mark of its relation to a future element.*"[86] This sense of *differance*, then, evokes the dynamic tension of any present element as it both stops, as it were, while still in motion along a time track.[87] It is this temporal but potentially protean sense that Morrison attaches to the term "American": "Deep within the word 'American,' [she writes], is its association with race. To identify someone as a South African is to say very little; we need the adjective 'white' or 'black' or 'colored' to make our meaning clear. In this country it is quite the reverse. American means white, and Africanist people struggle to make the term applicable to themselves with ethnicity and hyphen after hyphen after hyphen."[88] If, to overcome this exclusionary sense of American, we take note of and attach to the term American, the hope, or in this sense, the deferral, expressed by Charles Johnson that the prehistory of Afro-American literature will evolve into a future history in which neither black nor white but only American writers and literature is recognized; or the wish made recently by the African American historian Joel Williamson that in the twenty-first century the offspring of racially mixed marriages will cease to be designated as mulattoes or assigned to the racial status of the lower-caste parent and instead become "the first fully evolved, smoothly functioning model of a people who have transcended both an exclusive whiteness and an exclusive blackness and [have] moved into a world in which they accept and value themselves for themselves alone,"[89] we shall have completed the project of a fully realized *differance* only to find that our efforts place the discovery of a true difference in blackness as a moment of deferral of its ultimate telos—the forging of a new integrated people in a newly emergent nonracial society and culture.

Thus, if we perform a deconstruction on top of Gates's deconstruction of Jean Toomer's belief that though he could not "fix" the matter for others, he, like Crèvecoeur one hundred and thirty-eight years earlier, could sense and see the emergence of a new raceless humankind in America, his recognition of the blackness in his ancestry and his agonizingly qualified erasure of the blackness in himself was not merely an attempt to notice and cover up a difference, but also a promissory deferral, a putting off until a later time what would be the deracinated telos of America. Our second deconstruction of the "blackness" in Toomer's life and work yields the exposure of but a moment in a long unfolding but unidirectional history of white and black Americans, a moment between the past assertion of Pinchback's Negro identity and the future coming to be of Toomer's and others' nonracial sensibility of being American. Unreserved assimilation, acculturation, and amalgamation thence become the final outcome of America's pluralistic dynamic.

Differance, *Thymos,* and Africanity

Gates, of course, has a different project in mind and, as he has said, will employ the tools of any European approach efficacious to its end without necessarily committing himself to its totalizing aim. As a founder-contributor to an instauration in Afro-American letters,

Gates is unique and independent. He subscribes neither to the thesis that Jews are to be blamed for the past and present conditions of Africans, nor to the belief, ascribed to him by Tzevetan Todorov, that only persons of African descent can analyze black literature.[90] Rather, he believes in sound scholarship, and that a theory of Afro-American criticism and culture, like any other such theory, must be faithful to, and derived from the kind of *text* to which it applies. Hence, he asserts, "we must turn to the black *textual* tradition itself to develop theories of criticism indigenous to our literatures."[91] In this sense, Gates's approach reminds us of that of Herbert Blumer, who insisted that the methods appropriate to sociological analysis must be faithful to the nature of its subject matter—and not borrowed from those of the better established and more privileged sciences.[92] However, unlike Blumer, Gates seeks to displace Occidental epistemology—to set an African American canon and its unique mode of criticism side by side with that of Western literary and social thought and its praxis. To Gates and those who share his view, "racism and . . . *logocentrism* marched arm in arm to delimit black people in perhaps the most pernicious way of all: to claim that they were subhuman, that they were a 'different species of men,' as Hume put it so plainly, because they could not 'write' literature."[93] Opposing both racism and its logocentric concomitants, Gates seizes upon Derrida's recognition of the functions of voice.[94] He applies the first designation of the French philosopher's twofold definition of *differance*—to differ—to his own analyses of Afro-American vernacular, argot, and patois as well as to various written texts.

A Derrida-informed pluralist, Gates proposes that an archaeology of texts and discourses be undertaken in order to find the trace of blackness that, he insists, has not been wholly wiped away by the authors' own perhaps unconscious logocentrism, that is, the practice of self-denying, race-denigrating erasure. In a more recent work, he has gone even further, valorizing the rhetoric of black ghetto speech over the semantics of white language. Taking Derrida's invention of the term "differance" as an example of agnominatio, that is, repetition of a word with an alteration of both one letter and a sound, Gates performs a similarly paleonymic act upon the words signification/signifying. Where standard linguistics employs the equation sign = signified/signifier, Gates invokes the black stylized speech term "signifyin(g)," with the "g" intentionally placed in parentheses, in order to indicate the black difference and to call attention to how the black term—which Gates believes emerged "anonymously and unrecorded in antebellum America [when some] black genius or a community of witty and sensitive speakers emptied the signifier 'signification' of its received concepts and filled this empty signifier with their own"[95]—constitutes a virtual "guerilla action" against its white homonym. However, "signifyin(g)" does even more than this, in Gates's treatment: it lays the foundation for a black poetry of signification that, he believes, ought to be elevated to canonical importance.[96]

Gates's concern for how Occidental logocentrism has disprivileged Afro-American life as well as literature leads him to seek to rectify the matter. As a first step, he deconstructs the supervening term "race," observing not only that "within the biological sciences [it] has long been recognized as a fiction," but also, and far more significantly, that the "sense of difference defined in popular usages of the term 'race' has both described and *inscribed* differences of language, belief system, artistic tradition, and gene pool, as well as all sorts of supposedly natural attributes such as rhythm, athletic ability, cerebration, usury, fidelity, and so forth."[97] As a people classified as a race, continental and diasporic Africans have been uniformly subjected to both benevolent and malevolent usages and effects of that trope, and most especially of the Occident's orientation toward writing "as a commodity to confine and delimit a culture of color."[98] In brief, Gates points out that such canonical western philosophers as Hume, Kant, and Hegel had, each in his own words, insisted that "Blacks and other people of color could not write."[99]

As an ironic result of this deliteracization of blacks, Gates claims that "Anglo-African writing arose as a response to allegations of its absence."[100] To prove his or her right to membership in an allegedly universal but in fact Eurocentric humanity, an African or Afro-American would have to erase the black face, covering it with an "authentic black voice," speaking through the text of a "talking book."[101] In so doing, Gates argues, blacks acquiesced to the false promise "that racism would be destroyed once white racists became convinced that we were human, too."[102] Instead of liberation, Gates points out, black writers indentured themselves to a fundamentally racist philosophy and a Eurocentric epistemology exemplified by and instituted in the established (and by that fact, privileged,) canon of western literature.

What is to be done? Gates's proposal is that, rather than mastering the western canon and applying it to their own cultural productions and daily lives, African Americans ought to "turn to the black tradition itself, to develop theories of criticism indigenous to our literatures."[103] Such a turn involves two separate but related praxes.

First, the new theory of criticism might begin by exploiting elements in such recent Occidental philosophic and cultural approaches as those of the post-modernists, but that activity must be guided by Gates's warning that "to attempt to appropriate our own discourses by using Western critical theory uncritically is to substitute one mode of neocolonialism for another."[104] Neocolonialist analysis may be avoided by turning "to the black vernacular tradition . . . to isolate the signifying black difference through which to theorize about the so-called discourse of the Other."[105] Second, and following from the first, it becomes necessary to build up and legitimate an Afro-American canon, one, that, at the very least, would stand equally beside that of the Occident, and at the most displace its hegemonic monopoly over ethnoracial thought and social-economic policy. That canon would envelop a wider range of texts than are included in the conventional list.

The Afro-American canon would embrace the full range implied by the postmodern term "text." It would include not only such forms of written discourses as literature, history, biography, narrative, and memoir, but also those forms (and, possibly, anti-forms) of speech, dialect, patois, vernacular; of instrumental, solo-sung, and ensemble music; of body and facial idiom, "rhythm," and movement that are properly associated with "blackness" and with the African American tradition.

Two problems heretofore associated with canonization of the black culture are: (1) the at one time widespread belief that Afro-Americans had neither a culture, nor a history that anyone, white or black, need respect; and (2) the dilemma of how, in overcoming the belief just enunciated, an authentication of a "black" or "Afrocentric" culture might be realized outside of the hegemonic and Eurocentric rules in force for the recognition of any culture complex. Solving the first problem has been the special mission undertaken by African American historians, at least since the seminal work of George Washington Williams (1849–91),[106] but that project has become divided over whether its aim is the pursuit of a separate black history or a new, "integrated" American history that would take account of the experiences and activities of African-Asian-Oceanian-Amerindian persons of color as well as those of the European whites.[107]

The issues entailed in the second problem were ably summed up as early as 1966 by James T. Stewart, in whose critique of the cosmologies available to Afro-Americans it is trenchantly observed that "existing white paradigms or models do not correspond to the realities of black existence."[108] Stewart went on to call for an artistic revolution that would employ a dialectical method: "The dialectical method, [he pointed out], is the best instrument we have for comprehending physical and spiritual phenomena. . . . And the revolutionary artist must understand this . . . philosophy of reality which exists in all non-white cultures."[109] As to an orientation particularly appropriate for African American culture, Stewart asserted, "We need our own conventions, a convention of procedural elements, a kind of stylization, a sort of insistency which leads inevitably to a certain methodology—a methodology affirmed by the spirit."[110] And to drive home the point he went on:

> That spirit is black.
> That spirit is non-white.
> That spirit is patois.
> That spirit is Samba.
> Voodoo.
> The black Baptist church in the South.[111]

Although Stewart did not say as much, the canonization of that spirit would seem to require the energization made possible by a black-inspired *Thymos*. And without employing the latter term, Gates would appear to be engaged in precisely that project in his quest for the Afrocentric authentication of the black voice—a project that in effect takes its hope for displacement of the Western canon and its point of departure from Derrida's comment to Julia Kristeva: "Now, if one ceases to limit oneself to the model of phonetic writing, which we privilege only by ethnocentrism, and if we draw all the consequences from the fact that there is no purely phonetic writing . . . then the entire phonologist or logocentrist logic becomes problematical. Its range of legitimacy becomes narrow and superficial."[112]

The identification and valorization of the authentic, that is, Afrocentric, black voice requires the deconstructive erasure of the Eurocentric authentication devices that have marked (and from the point of view of Gates and his followers, marred) the hidden but truly authentic Afro-American voice, a strategic research site for which is the body of slave narratives written or dictated before 1865.[113] These works, however, must not only be stripped of their white, Eurocentric, Yankee-abolitionist authenticating devices and paraphernalia, but also "resurrected" and empowered. Performing the latter involves discovering and elevating the generic black voice in the narratives, giving to today's black reader of them a sense of the spiritedness that is in the now uncovered original, involves, that is, an insertion of *Thymos*.

Thymos, a Greek term central to the argument in Plato's *Republic* and given a revival in a recent work by Francis Fukuyama, means, among its family of interrelated definitions, "spiritedness," or in Fukuyama's words, "that part of man which feels the need to place *value* on things—himself in the first instance, but on the people, actions, or things around him as well."[114] *Thymos*, thence is entailed in valorization. And valorization is a necessary part of the project of Gates, et al., in establishing the canon of black life and Afro-American culture, and, beyond that, a true justice for persons of color in America. Indeed, although he makes no reference to Gates's work, Fukuyama virtually recognizes the relevance of *Thymos* to such a project when he deconstructs the word "indignation" while explaining the relation of *Thymos* to justice:

> *Thymos* is something like an innate human sense of justice: people believe that they have a certain worth, and when other people act as though they are worth less—when they do not *recognize* their worth at its correct value—then they become angry. The intimate relationship between self-evaluation and anger can be seen in the English word synonymous with anger, "indignation." "Dignity" refers to a person's sense of self-worth; "in-dignation" arises when something happens to offend that sense of worth. . . . When we are evaluated justly (i.e., in proportion to our true worth), we feel *pride*.[115]

There should be no mistaking one point: Fukuyama is not a pluralist and, with the exception of consigning the current conditions of black Americans to the debilitating and apparently heritable effects of a precapitalist economic formation, he does not address the race question directly.[116] His resurrection of *Thymos*, however, permits us an additional understanding of the dilemmas and contradictions confronting assimilation and pluralism in the postmodernist era. Although Fukuyama treats *Thymos* and its consequences as a phenomenon of individuation, it is necessary for the postmodern pluralist project (as well as all other pluralist discourses) to extend the matter to cover ethnoracial collectivities. Consider a single sentence in which Gates not only indicates his indignation over the fact that black Americans have been "deprived of access to literacy, the tools of citizenship, denied the right of selfhood by law, philosophy, and pseudo-science, and denied as well the possibility, even, of possessing a collective history as a people,"[117] but also intentionally

conflates the self's individuality with its racial-collective representation in the quest for its deserved recognition, that is, its *Thymos*:
"If the *individual black self* could not exist before the law, it could,
and would, be forged in language, as a testimony at once to the supposed integrity of the black self and against the social and political
evils that delimited *individual and group* equality for all African-
Americans."[118] And this demand for recognition of individual/racial
self-worth also marks the path to empowerment: "The will to power
for black Americans," Gates insists, "was the will to write; and the
predominate mode that this writing would assume was the shaping
of a *black self* in words."[119]

The construction and maintenance of a pridefully worthy black
self is said in some quarters to be a necessary (but not necessarily
sufficient) prerequisite for African American participation in American society. According to this perspective, in the years since Emancipation, blacks have retained one of the debilitating legacies of
slavery—disesteem—and have put forward a less thymoticized self
than they might have.[120] Whether this thymotically disvalued self is
a product of biosocial temperament, genetic constitution, excessive
deracination, or baleful circumstances, the outcome is said to be the
same: diminished capacity to live, work, and enjoy the opportunities available in a more or less open society.

However, excessive thymotic self-assertion presents the opposite
problem: as a feature of a civil society—whether acculturated or
not—a constructed ethnoracial self must also avoid *megalothymia*,
that is, Fukuyama's neologism for the "desire to be recognized as
superior to other people."[121] The thymotically ambivalent black
self is hence caught up in an agonizingly difficult dilemma. If, on the
one hand, it fails to exhibit the kind of self-esteem that Gates, et al.,
believe to be derivable from the authorial ethnoracial empowerment that his deconstruction of black texts will evoke, it will have
acquiesced to an undeserved neocolonial status that impugns its
true value; on the other hand, should it put forward a claim that
overvalues its actual worth and in the process asserts an unworthy
superiority over other individuals or entire peoples, it will have
succumbed before the very racist egoism that its resurrection was
designed to bring to an end.

The avoidance of *megalothymia* has also been recognized—under
a different term of reference, to be sure—as a problem for other
forms of collective ethnoracial group assertion. When, for example,
Marcus Lee Hansen thought he had uncovered a "law of third generation return" in the resurgence of American ethnic consciousness,

he warned against filiopietism and other forms of hagiographic mythopoetic reconstructions of a people's history.[122] But, Hansen took no notice of the support given to megalothymotic white supremacy by the academic as well as popular acclaim given to *Gone With the Wind*, a novelized historical fiction that celebrated the Redemptionist victory over antiracist Reconstructionists in the postbellum South. In fact, he himself hailed the accolades given to Margaret Mitchell's novel, treating them as an exemplification of his "law" and a rightful restoration of southern white ethnoracial esteem.[123]

More recently, in an essay linking men to history, history to myth, and myth to the appropriation of an estimable past, Leonard Barkan has explained how the fact that classical "Rome should come so close to being the model of the historical unconscious demonstrates the persistence of an imagined antiquity as the universal past of (at least Western) humanity."[124] Barkan notes that appropriation of an elaborately embellished antiquity occurs even—one might say especially—among those, like Freud, "whose own ethnic or racial history cannot be traced to Latium." For those who locate the source of their identity in Western culture but for whom the entitlement is unclear, "Rome . . . [Barkan asserts, becomes] . . . a Family Romance."[125]

A similar appropriation of a sublimated history occurs for some of those who seek to establish the rightful portion of group esteem that should descend on contemporary African Americans: the glory that was once Rome's is displaced in favor of that of the ancient kingdom of Songhay, the classical polis of the Ashanti, or the empire of Mali[126]—or, in a recent and even more daring move, in the claim of a "Black Athena," that is, a documented demand that the African philosophic and artistic basis of Greek antiquity, and, by extension, of Western civilization, be given its just due.[127] In their eagerness, spokespersons for the recognition and the restoration of African and Afro-American group dignity risk being accused of *megalothymia*,[128] while their cultural critics are all too often *hypothymic* in their responses.[129] The achievement of a balanced and efficacious *thymos* becomes quite difficult.

These dilemmas, however, are more readily products of modernist thought and less those of the postmodernists. Postmodernism finds its peculiar dilemma in resolving the tensions attending the terms "black"/"self." Derrida's famous essay on race is a philosophical and literary tour de force against South Africa's then operant system of apartheid, but, even in his reply to his politico-economic critics, Derrida did not address those tensions directly or effectively.[130] "Self" is associated with individuality, individualism, and individuation, all signifiers arising out of the medieval era in the Occident during which, so Colin Morris tells us, there occurred the discovery of the individual.[131] Such a discovery did not take place in the Orient or in Africa, according to the researches of Louis Dumont,[132] who has emphasized the role of Christianity in its development[133] and pointed out that "the idea of the individual constitutes a sociological problem."[134] Hence, when European Christianity invaded Africa, it brought the idea of the individualized self along as an uneasy concomitant to its imperialistic, ethnocentric, and racist ideas.[135] Although Africans appropriated this and other Christian ideas in relation to their own needs, one result was that when the collective racially based ideology of black consciousness called *Negritude* arose in the 1930s in Africa,[136] the Caribbean,[137] and, subsequently, to a more limited extent in the United States,[138] it was countered by those blacks who sought to liberate themselves from all collective biocultural constraints and identities in behalf of an irreducible and unenlargeable individuality and an unalloyed self-assertion.[139] The tension between the collective "black" and the individuated "self" remains in stark relief but unrelieved.

Conclusion: Assimilation/Pluralism— From "Difference" to "Allusion"

The discourse on assimilation and pluralism takes a new turn in postmodernist thought. In conventional and modernist discourses—which, it should be noted, are discourses of the sociological discipline, and therefore like other discourses, are worthy candidates for deconstructive analysis[140]—the concepts are typically treated as polarities pointing up two dichotomous metaphors of social structure—respectively, "the melting pot" and the "mosaic." Moreover, each metaphor stands for an ideal toward which a modern society might move at a pace determined by the motility of its norm-engaging institutions. Hence each idealized outcome is regarded as uncompleted in every presentist analysis of the issue.

The metaphoric language in which these ideals are usually expressed tends to conflate ethnic with racial aspects of the problem, confound attempts at exact depiction of the societal structure toward which each is directed, and cover over the forms of coercion and power that make each effective. Hence, the claim that blacks, Hispanics, Asians, and other persons are assimilating in American society, or that they ought to be, must confront the twin issues of the well-established ethnoracial pluralism that exists "beyond the melting pot,"[141] and the hidden hand of white Anglo-Saxon Protestant power that informs and modifies the assimilative process.

The "crucial thing about the melting pot," observed Charles Silberman in 1964, "was that it did not happen."[142] Although a number of sociocultural changes transformed the several peoples living in America so much that their immigrant forebears would not recognize them as dedicated conservers of a mummified Old World culture, Silberman insisted that "the ethnic groups are not just a political anachronism. . . . The WASPs . . . , the Irish Americans, the Italian Americans, the Jewish Americans . . . differ from each other in essential ways." Regarding each of these ethnically distinct peoples as equally serviceable models of emulation for would-be assimilaters, Silberman poses a question: "If Negroes are to assimilate, if they are to integrate with the white American . . . with *which* white American [people are they to accomplish this feat]?" The racial epithet "white" breaks down into its diverse ethnic constituencies. "For in truth," Silberman concludes, "there is no 'white American'; there are only white Americans."[143]

However, Silberman's conventional critique of assimilation does not reach the political dimension of the issue. It is a cardinal point of postmodernist criticism to perceive culture and the discourses and debates on culture as mediations of power relations. In this sense, it is necessary to see how the assimilationist discourse both privileges WASP culture and hides the process whereby that privilege is hegemonically encoded.[144] A fine elucidation, a virtual deconstruction of the latter process, has been presented by Roxana Robinson in an essay reviewing a book of Louis Auchincloss's short stories:

> White Anglo-Saxon Protestants, [Robinson writes], have created an insular and powerful world, and have maintained it by means of an ingenious sociological mechanism. Ethnic outsiders could succeed as themselves in politics and finance, but to succeed in society they had to abandon ethnic outsiderness. Society was tightly and exclusively controlled by WASPs, who permitted little cultural deviation. This meant these newcomers did not assert their ethnic individuality but instead tried for assimilation. Conformity to the prevailing social ethic and marriage into Protestant families meant that other ethnic identities dissipated within a generation or so.[145]

The postmodern project undertaken by such black critics as Henry Louis Gates, Jr., and his followers does much to expose the privileged status of the WASP text on assimilation, but it does not identify nor does it locate the source of social justice in the society to come, that is, the postmodern society. How societal coordination will occur in a society in which all texts are disprivileged, and no particular ethnoracial group exercises ethnoracial control is unanswered. Paradoxically, however, an answer is provided by the ideal society projected in modernist assimilation theory: should unreserved assimilation, acculturation, and amalgamation take place in a market-oriented, industrial society, the normative order would reside in racially integrated classes, and in the policies that accorded with the interests of the oligarchy of power and privilege that the dominant classes had organized. For Marxists, and even for those like Robert E. Park who did not adhere either to the Marxist agenda or to its theory of history, the outcome of ethnoracial assimilation would inaugurate a new conflict, the class struggle.[146]

However, the essential elements of postmodern cultural analysis go beyond these issues, transcending the modernist discourses on both power and culture as they are deconstructing them. Postmodernism overcomes the dichotomies central to Western modernism by imposing *differance* as an intrusion upon them. For the discourse on assimilation/pluralism this promises not only an effort at extracting ethnoracial diversity from its stigmatizing and disvaluing hierarchicalization under the modernist regime of particularistically valorized and selectively privileged WASPishness, but also, and only seemingly paradoxically, a refiguration of the metaphorized ideals of both Crèvecoeur's and Toomer's assimilationism and Kallen's and Bourne's pluralism as *deferrals*, that is, as desiderata put off to a future not yet realized.

However, postmodernism does even more. Its critique is epistemologically ecumenical but distributed over the geo-intellectual map according to the particular ideational locus of each privileged perspective. Thus, Kwame Anthony Appiah observes:

> In philosophy, postmodernism is the rejection of the mainstream consensus from Descartes through Kant to logical positivism. . . . The modernity that is opposed here can thus be Cartesian (in France), Kantian (in Germany), and logical positivist (in America). . . . In political theory . . . postmodernism is the rejection of the monism of Big-M Marxist (though not of the newer little-m marxist) and liberal conceptions of justice. . . . Every perspective [is] essentially contestable from other perspectives.[147]

If we take seriously the utter contestability of perspectives, we may see how the dichotomy of assimilation/pluralism—and of each's respective deferrals—may be dis- and then re-integrated in the acidic solvent of what the classical Italian philologist Gian Biagio Conte calls an "allusion." An allusion is "a poetic dimension . . . created by the simultaneous presence of two different realities whose competition with one another produces a single more complex reality."[148] That single more complex reality is American's not yet fully realized civil society, a society perhaps already beyond the modernist's liberal conception of ethnoracial justice, but, still, a society whose ultimate ethnoracial dimensions are in a problematic state of conflicted deferral.

NOTES

1. Anthony Giddens, *Modernity and Self-Identity: Self and Society in the Late Modern Age* (Standford: Stanford University Press, 1991).

2. Ibid., p. 215.

3. Ibid., p. 211. Emphasis supplied.

4. Rose Laub Coser, *In Defense of Modernity: Role Complexity and Individual Autonomy* (Stanford: Stanford University Press, 1991).

5. Stjepan G. Meštrović, *The Coming Fin de Siècle: An Application of Durkheim's Sociology to Modernity and Postmodernism* (London: Routledge, 1991).

6. Ibid., p. 204.

7. Stephen Crook, "The End of Radical Social Theory? Notes on Radicalism, Modernism, and Postmodernism," in *Postmodernism and Society*, ed. Roy Boyne and Ali Rattansi (New York: St. Martin's Press, 1990), p. 47.

8. Mike Featherstone, "In Pursuit of the Postmodern: An Introduction," *Theory, Culture and Society*, 5:2–3 (June 1988), pp. 195–216, esp. pp. 204–7. See also Barry Smart, "Modernity, Postmodernity, and the Present," in *Theories of Modernity and Postmodernity*, ed. Bryan S. Turner (London: Sage Publications, 1990), pp. 14–30, esp. pp. 25–26.

9. See John M. Ellis, *Against Deconstruction* (Princeton: Princeton University Press, 1989); and Christopher Norris, *What's Wrong with Postmodernism: Critical Theory and the Ends of Philosophy* (Baltimore: Johns Hopkins University Press, 1990), pp. 134–63.

10. Norman Denzin, "*Blue Velvet*: Postmodern Contradictions," *Theory, Culture and Society*, 5:2–3 (June 1988), pp. 461–74; "Reading 'Wall Street': Postmodern Contradictions in the American Social Structure," in Turner, ed., *Theories*, pp. 31–44; *Hollywood Shot by Shot: Alcoholism in American Cinema* (New York: Aldine de Gruyter, 1991); "Whose Cornerville Is It, Anyway?" *Journal of Contemporary Ethnography*, 21:1 (Apr. 1992), pp. 120–32.

11. Norman K. Denzin, "Representing Lived Experiences in Ethnographic Texts," in *Studies in Symbolic Interaction*, vol. 12, ed. Norman K. Denzin (Greenwich, Conn.: JAI Press, 1991), p. 67.

12. Robert E. Park, "Racial Assimilation in Secondary Groups with Particular Reference to the Negro," in *Race and Culture, The Collected Papers of Robert Ezra Park*, vol. 1, ed. Everett Cherrington Hughes, Charles S. Johnson, Jitsuichi Masuoka, Robert Redfield, and Louis Wirth (Glencoe, Ill.: The Free Press, 1950), pp. 206–10.

13. See Harry F. Dahms, "Democracy and the Post-Enlightenment: Lyotard and Habermas Reappraised," *International Journal of Politics, Culture, and Society*, 5:3 (Spring 1992), pp. 473–509.

14. Jean Baudrillard, *America*, trans. Chris Turner (London: Verso, 1988), pp. 15–16.

15. Ibid., pp. 1–2.

16. Ibid., pp. 30, 32.

17. Ibid., p. 83.

18. Ibid., p. 89.

19. Ibid., p. 111.

20. See Stanford M. Lyman, *Militarism, Imperialism, and Racial Accommodation: An Analysis and Interpretation of the Early Writings of Robert E. Park* (Fayetteville: University of Arkansas Press, 1992), pp. 81–135.

21. Baudrillard, *America*, p. 113.

22. Arthur Kroker, *The Possessed Individual: Technology and the French Postmodern* (New York: St. Martin's Press, 1992), p. 143.

23. Ibid., p. 144.

24. Here I draw on David Harvey's discussion in *The Condition of Postmodernity: An Enquiry into the Origins of Cultural Change* (Cambridge: Blackwell, 1990), pp. 44–47.

25. Ibid., p. 45.

26. See Robert E. Park, "The Nature of Race Relations," in *Race Relations and the Race Problem*, ed. Edgar T. Thompson (Durham, N.C.: Duke University Press, 1939), pp. 3–45.

27. Arthur Schlesinger, Jr., *The Disuniting of America: Reflections on a Multicultural Society* (Knoxville: Whittle Books, 1991).

28. Francis Fukuyama, "The End of History?" *The National Interest*, no. 16 (Summer 1989), pp. 3–18.

29. See two works by Fredric Jameson, *Signatures of the Visible* (New York: Routledge, 1990), pp. 226–27; and *Postmodernism, or the Cultural Logic of Late Capitalism* (Durham, N.C.: Duke University Press, 1992).

30. Harvey, *Condition*, pp. 117–18.

31. Neil Postman, *Technopoly: The Surrender of Culture to Technology* (New York: Alfred A. Knopf, 1992).

32. Jean-Francois Lyotard, "Universal History and Cultural Differences," in *The Lyotard Reader*, ed. Andrew Benjamin (Cambridge: Basil Blackwell, 1989), p. 321.

33. Ibid., p. 322.

34. Ibid., p. 321.

35. Ibid., p. 323.

36. Harvey, *Condition*, p. 49.

37. Warren Montag, "What Is at Stake in the Debate on Postmodernism?" in *Postmodernism and Its Discontents: Theories, Practices*, ed. E. Ann Kaplan (London: Verso, 1988), pp. 88–103.

38. Henry Louis Gates, Jr., "Writing 'Race' and the Difference It Makes," in Gates, ed., *"Race," Writing and Difference* (Chicago: University of Chicago Press, 1985), p. 6.

39. Margaret Hodgen, *Early Anthropology in the Sixteenth and Seventeenth Centuries* (Philadelphia: University of Pennsylvania Press, 1964).

40. Ruth Benedict, *Race: Science and Politics* (New York: Viking, 1943).

41. Ashley Montagu, *Man's Most Dangerous Myth: The Fallacy of Race*, 5th ed. (New York: Oxford University Press, 1974).

42. Stanford M. Lyman, "The Race Question and Liberalism: Casuistries in American Constitutional Law," *International Journal of Politics, Culture, and Society*, 5:2 (Winter 1991), pp. 183–247.

43. Quoted in English translation from p. 393 of Jacques Derrida, *Marges de la Philosophie* (Paris: Minuit, 1972) in Jonathan Culler, *On Deconstruction: Theory and Criticism after Structuralism* (Ithaca: Cornell University Press, 1982), p. 141.

44. Herbert Marcuse, *An Essay on Liberation* (Boston: Beacon Press, 1969), pp. 25–28. See the discussion of this and related phenomena in Marvin B. Scott and Stanford M. Lyman, *The Revolt of the Students* (Columbus: Charles E. Merrill Publishing Co., 1970), pp. 56–67.

45. See Winthrop D. Jordan, *White Over Black: American Attitudes toward the Negro, 1550–1812* (Chapel Hill: University of North Carolina Press, 1968). See also Dana D. Nelson, *The Word in Black and White: Reading "Race" in American Literature, 1638–1867* (New York: Oxford University Press, 1992). That the race question is an extension of the Jewish question—especially as that question arose in the century preceding the first voyage of Columbus and the expulsion of the Jews from Spain—both occurred in 1492—is a feature of the challenging and original thesis of Jose Faur, *In the Shadow of History: Jews and "Conversos" at the Dawn of Modernity* (Albany: State University of New York Press, 1992), esp. pp. 1–27.

46. See two works by Lester F. Ward, *Applied Sociology: A Treatise on the Conscious Improvement of Society by Society* (Boston: Ginn and Co., 1906), pp. 205–38; and *Pure Sociology: A Treatise on the Origin and Spontaneous Development of Society*, 2d ed. (New York: Macmillan, 1907; reprint, New York: Augustus M. Kelley, 1970), pp. 108–10. See also the discussion of Ward's thesis in Arthur J. Vidich and Stanford M. Lyman, *American Sociology: Worldly Rejections of Religion and Their Directions* (New Haven: Yale University Press, 1985), pp. 20–35.

47. Charles Johnson, *Being and Race: Black Writing since 1970* (Bloomington: Indiana University Press, 1988), p. 123.

48. See Adam Begley, "Henry Louis Gates, Jr.: Black Studies' New Star," *New York Times Magazine*, section 6 (Apr. 1, 1990), pp. 24–27, 48–50. For two of Gates's essays critically examining the depiction of blacks in earlier

eras, see Henry Louis Gates, Jr., "From Wheatley to Douglass: The Politics of Displacement," in *Frederick Douglass: New Literary and Historical Essays*, ed. Eric J. Sundquist (Cambridge: Cambridge University Press, 1990), pp. 47–65; and "The Trope of the New Negro and the Reconstruction of the Image of the Black," in *The New American Studies: Essays from Representations*, ed. Philip Fisher (Berkeley: University of California Press, 1991), pp. 319–45.

49. Henry Louis Gates, Jr., *Figures in Black: Words, Signs, and the "Racial" Self* (New York: Oxford University Press, 1987), pp. xxii–xxiv.

50. Ibid., p. xxvi. See also Henry Louis Gates, Jr., *Loose Canons: Notes on the Culture Wars* (New York: Oxford University Press, 1992), pp. 3–42, 87–104.

51. Henry Louis Gates, Jr., "Canon-Formation, Literary History, and the Afro-American Tradition: From the Seen to the Told," in *Afro-American Literary Study in the 1990s*, ed. Houston A. Baker, Jr., and Patricia Redmond (Chicago: University of Chicago Press, 1989), p. 21.

52. Ibid., p. 20.

53. Quoted in Ibid., p. 24.

54. Ibid., pp. 24–25.

55. See Clinton M. Jean, *Behind the Eurocentric Veil: The Search for African Realities* (Amherst: University of Massachusetts Press, 1991).

56. Houston A. Baker, Jr., *Afro-American Poetics: Revisions of Harlem and the Black Aesthetic* (Madison: University of Wisconsin Press, pp. 96–97.

57. Ibid., pp. 97, 100.

58. See Jacques Derrida, *Speech and Phenomena and Other Essays on Husserl's Theory of Signs*, trans. David B. Allison (Evanston: Northwestern University Press, 1973), pp. 107–28.

59. Ibid.

60. Jean Toomer, *Cane* (New York: Harper and Row, 1969 [1923]).

61. See James Haskins, *Pinckney Benton Stewart Pinchback* (New York: Macmillan, 1973).

62. Since the republication of *Cane* in 1969, there has been a veritable renaissance in Toomer studies. See, among many, Frank Durham, comp., *Studies in "Cane"* (Columbus: Charles E. Merrill, 1971); Darwin T. Turner, *In a Minor Chord: Three Afro-American Writers and Their Search for Identity* (Carbondale: Southern Illinois University Press, 1971), pp. 1–59; Brian Joseph Benson and Mable Mayle Dillard, *Jean Toomer* (Boston: Twayne Publishers, 1980); Nellie Y. McKay, *Jean Toomer, Artist: A Study of His Literary Life and Work, 1894–1936* (Chapel Hill: University of North Carolina Press, 1984); Cynthia Earl Kerman and Richard Eldridge, *The Lives of Jean Toomer: A Hunger for Wholeness* (Baton Rouge: Louisiana State University Press, 1987); Therman B. O'Daniel, ed., *Jean Toomer: A Critical Evaluation* (Washington, D.C.: Howard University Press, 1988); Rudolph P. Byrd, *Jean Toomer's Years with Gurdjieff: Portrait of an Artist, 1923–1936* (Athens: University of Georgia Press, 1990). Republications of Toomer's works in-

clude, in addition to *Cane*, *The Wayward and the Seeking: A Collection of Writings by Jean Toomer*, ed. Darwin T. Turner (Washington, D.C.: Howard University Press, 1980); and *Essentials*, ed. Rudolph P. Byrd (Athens: University of Georgia Press, 1991).

63. Jean Toomer, "Autobiographical Sketches: The *Cane* Years," in *The Wayward and the Seeking*, p. 121.

64. Ibid., pp. 121–22.

65. Gates, *Figures in Black*, p. 201.

66. Ibid., p. 202.

67. Ibid.

68. Ibid.

69. Ibid.

70. Bernard W. Bell, *The Afro-American Novel and Its Tradition* (Amherst: University of Massachusetts Press, 1987), p. 101.

71. The most important essays of the Frazier-Herskovitz debate will be found in "Part 3: The African Diaspora and Cultural Survivals: The Frazier-Herskovitz Debate," *Intergroup Relations: Sociological Perspectives*, ed. Pierre van den Berghe (New York: Basic Books, 1972), pp. 103–36.

72. See two works by Melville J. Herskovitz, *The Myth of the Negro Past* (Boston: Beacon Press, 1958 [1941]); and *The New World Negro: Selected Papers in Afro-American Studies*, ed. Frances S. Herskovitz (Bloomington: Indiana University Press, 1966), esp. pp. 83–134, 157–98, 321–61.

73. Melville J. Herskovitz, *The American Negro: A Study in Racial Crossing* (Bloomington: Indiana University Press, 1964 [1928]).

74. Quoted in Arna Bontemps "Introduction" to Jean Toomer, *Cane*, p. viii.

75. Ibid., pp. viii–ix.

76. Robert E. Park, "The Conflict and Fusion of Cultures with Special Reference to the Negro," *Journal of Negro History*, 4:2 (Apr. 1919), pp. 111–33. See also my discussion of Park's concept of temperament in Lyman, *Militarism, Imperialism*, pp. 106–12, 132.

77. See Stanford M. Lyman and William A. Douglass, "Ethnicity: Strategies of Collective and Individual Impression Management," *Social Research*, 40:2 (Summer 1973), pp. 344–65; William A. Douglass and Stanford M. Lyman, "L'Ethnie: Structure, Processus, et Saillance," trans. Alain Kihm, *Cahiers Internationaux de Sociologie*, 61 (1976), pp. 197–220; and Stanford M. Lyman, "The Existential Self: Language and Silence in the Formation of Human Identity," in Lyman, *Civilization: Contents, Discontents, Malcontents and Other Essays in Social Theory* (Fayetteville: University of Arkansas Press, 1990), pp. 250–58.

78. Toni Morrison, *Playing in the Dark: Whiteness and the Literary Imagination*, The William E. Massey, Sr., Lectures in the History of American Civilization, 1990 (Cambridge: Harvard University Press, 1992).

79. Ibid., pp. 32, 33.

80. See two works by Bernard Bailyn, *The Peopling of North America: An Introduction* (New York: Alfred A. Knopf, 1986); and *Voyagers to the*

West: A Passage in the Peopling of America on the Eve of the Revolution (New York: Alfred A. Knopf, 1986).

81. Jacques Derrida, *Speech and Phenomena*, pp. 82 n. 8, 129 n. 1.

82. Morrison, *Playing in the Dark*, p. 44.

83. Ibid., p. 45.

84. Ibid., pp. 47–48.

85. Ibid., p. 48.

86. Derrida, *Speech and Phenomena*, p. 142. Emphasis supplied.

87. For the concept of the time track, see Stanford M. Lyman and Marvin B. Scott, *A Sociology of the Absurd*, 2d ed. (Dix Hills, N.Y.: General Hall, Inc., 1989), pp. 35–50.

88. Morrison, *Playing in the Dark*, p. 47.

89. Joel Williamson, *New People: Miscegenation and Mulattoes in the United States* (New York: The Free Press, 1980), p. 195.

90. See Henry Louis Gates, Jr., "Black Demagogues and Pseudo-Scholars," *New York Times*, July 20, 1992, Op-Ed p. All; and the exchange: Tzevetan Todorov, " 'Race,' Writing and Culture," and Henry Louis Gates, Jr., "Talkin' That Talk," in Gates, ed., *"Race," Writing, and Difference*, pp. 370–80 and 402–9. See also Gates, *Loose Canons*, pp. 105–20, 173–93.

91. Henry Louis Gates, Jr., "Talkin' That Talk," p. 405.

92. Herbert Blumer, *Symbolic Interaction: Perspective and Method* (Englewood Cliffs, N.J.: Prentice-Hall, 1969), pp. 1–60.

93. Gates, "Talkin' That Talk," p. 408.

94. See Derrida, *Speech and Phenomena*, pp. 70–87; and Gates, *Figures in Black*, pp. 98–124, esp. pp. 106–7.

95. Henry Louis Gates, Jr., *The Signifying Monkey: A Theory of Afro-American Literary Criticism* (New York: Oxford University Press, 1988), p. 46.

96. Ibid., pp. 51–88.

97. Henry Louis Gates, Jr., "Writing 'Race' and the Difference It Makes," pp. 4, 5.

98. Ibid., p. 6.

99. Ibid., p. 9.

100. Ibid., p. 11.

101. Ibid., pp. 11, 12. See also Gates, *Loose Canons*, pp. 71–83.

102. Gates, "Writing 'Race,' " p. 12.

103. Ibid., p. 13.

104. Ibid., p. 15.

105. Ibid.

106. See two works by George Washington Williams, *History of the Negro Race in America from 1619 to 1880: Negroes as Slaves, as Soldiers, and as Citizens; Together with a Preliminary Consideration of the Human Family, An Historical Sketch of Africa, and An Account of the Negro Governments of Sierra Leone and Liberia* (New York: G. P. Putnam's Sons, 1883; reprint, New York: Bergman Publishers, 1968), 2 vols.; and *A History of the Negro Troops in the War of the Rebellion, 1861–1865, Preceded by a Review of the*

Military Services of Negroes in Ancient and Modern Times (New York: Harper and Brothers, 1887; reprint, New York: Bergman Publishers, 1968).

107. See Darlene Clark Hine, ed., *The State of Afro-American History: Past, Present, Future* (Baton Rouge: Louisiana State University Press, 1986); August Meier and Elliott Rudwick, eds., *Black History and the Historical Profession, 1915–1980* (Urbana: University of Illinois Press, 1986). See also Benjamin Quarles, *Black Mosaic: Essays in Afro-American History and Historiography* (Amherst: University of Massachusetts Press, 1988), pp. 181–213; and John Hope Franklin, *Race and History: Selected Essays, 1938–1988* (Baton Rouge: Louisiana State University Press, 1989), esp. pp. 1–70, 132–52, 267–76, 293–348.

108. James T. Stewart, "The Development of the Black Revolutionary Artist," in *Black Fire: An Anthology of Afro-American Writing*, ed. Le Roi Jones and Larry Neal (New York: William Morrow and Co., 1969), p. 3. Stewart's essay had originally been published in the Winter 1966 issue of *Black Dialogue*.

109. Ibid., pp. 5–6.

110. Ibid., p. 6.

111. Ibid. For the thesis that the black religion of the slave south formed the paradigm of the white Baptist style in America, see Harold Bloom, *The American Religion: The Emergence of the Post-Christian Nation* (New York: Simon and Schuster, 1992), pp. 237–55.

112. Jacques Derrida, "Semiology and Grammatology: Interview with Julia Kristeva," *Positions*, trans. Alan Bass (Chicago: University of Chicago Press, 1981), pp. 25–26.

113. See Charles T. Davis and Henry Louis Gates, Jr., eds., *The Slave's Narrative* (New York: Oxford University Press, 1985).

114. Francis Fukuyama, *The End of History and the Last Man* (New York: The Free Press, 1992), pp. 162–63.

115. Ibid., p. 165.

116. For my critique of Fukuyama on these matters, see Stanford M. Lyman, "The Race Question and Liberalism," esp. pp. 183–87 and 232–35.

117. Henry Louis Gates, Jr., "Introduction: On Bearing Witness," in *Gates*, ed., *Bearing Witness: Selections from African-American Autobiography in the Twentieth Century* (New York: Pantheon Books, 1991), p. 4.

118. Ibid. Emphasis supplied.

119. Ibid. Emphasis supplied.

120. See e.g., Ann Wortham, *The Other Side of Racism: A Philosophical Study of Black Race Consciousness* (Columbus: Ohio State University Press, 1981), pp. 75–142; Shelby Steele, *The Content of Our Character: A New Vision of Race in America* (New York: St. Martin's Press, 1990); and Claude M. Steele, "Race and the Schooling of Black Americans," *The Atlantic*, 269:4 (Apr. 1992), pp. 68–78.

121. Fukuyama, *End of History*, p. 182.

122. Marcus Lee Hansen, *The Problem of the Third Generation Immigrant* (Rock Island, Ill.: Augustana Historical Society, 1938). The essay was

reprinted but retitled as "The Third Generation in America," *Commentary*, 14 (Nov. 1952), pp. 492–500.

123. See Stanford M. Lyman, "Hansen's Theory and America's Black Birthright: The Historical Novel as History and Collective Memory," in *American Immigrants and Their Generations: Studies and Commentaries on the Hansen Thesis after Fifty Years*, ed. Peter Kivisto and Dag Blanck (Urbana: University of Illinois Press, 1990), pp. 126–41.

124. Leonard Barkan, *Transuming Passion: Ganymede and the Erotics of Humanism* (Stanford: Stanford University Press, 1991), p. 16.

125. Ibid.

126. See, e.g., J. C. deGraft-Johnson, *African Glory: The Story of Vanished Negro Civilizations* (New York: Walker and Co., 1954).

127. Martin Bernal, *Black Athena: The Afroasiatic Roots of Classical Civilization, Vol 1: The Fabrication of Ancient Greece, 1785–1985* (New Brunswick, N.J.: Rutgers University Press, 1987); *Vol. 2: The Archaeological and Documentary Evidence* (New Brunswick, N.J.: Rutgers University Press, 1991). See also Ivan Van Sertima, ed., *African Presence in Early Europe* (New Brunswick, N.J.: Transaction Books, 1986).

128. See Jean, *Eurocentric Veils*, pp. 65–99.

129. See, e.g., Columbia University's Professor Henry E. Garrett's denigrating statement about African history and culture quoted in Felix N. Okoge, *The American Image of Africa: Myth and Reality* (New York: Third Press International, 1971), p. 3. For more recent hypothymotic critiques of African Americans see Allan Bloom, *The Closing of the American Mind: How Higher Education Has Failed Democracy and Impoverished the Souls of Today's Students* (New York: Simon and Schuster, 1987), pp. 91–96 et passim; and Michael Vannoy Adams, Charles Junkerman, and Allan Bloom, "Responses to 'The Stanford Mind,' " letters to the editor, *Wall Street Journal*, January 4, 1989, January 6, 1989, January 27, 1989, in *Essays on the Closing of the American Mind*, ed. Robert L. Stone (Chicago: Chicago Review Press, 1989), pp. 366–69. For another example, see Dinesh D'Souza, *Illiberal Education: The Politics of Race and Sex on Campus* (New York: The Free Press, 1991), pp. 94–123.

130. See the exchange between Jacques Derrida, Anne McClintock and Rob Nixon in *"Race," Writing, and Difference*, pp. 329–69.

131. Colin Morris, *The Discovery of the Individual, 1050–1200* (New York: Harper Torchbooks, 1972).

132. Louis Dumont, *From Mandeville to Marx: The Genesis and Triumph of Economic Ideology* (Chicago: University of Chicago Press, 1977).

133. Louis Dumont, *Essays on Individualism: Modern Ideology in Anthropological Perspective* (Chicago: University of Chicago Press, 1986), esp. pp. 23–59.

134. Louis Dumont, *Homo Hierarchicus: The Caste System and Its Implications*, trans. Mark Sainsbury (Chicago: University of Chicago Press, 1970), p. 8.

135. See, e.g., Amos J. Beyan, *The American Colonization Society and the Creation of the Liberian State: An Historical Perspective, 1822–1900* (Lanham, Md.: University Press of America, 1991), pp. 149–64; and Richard Gray, *Black Christians and White Missionaries* (New Haven: Yale University Press, 1990), pp. 1–11, 59–117.

136. See two works by Aimé Cèsaire, *Return to My Native Land*, trans. John Berger and Anna Bostock (Baltimore: Penguin Books, 1969 [1956]), pp. 37–92; and *Discourse on Colonialism*, trans. Joan Pinkham (New York: Monthly Review Press, 1972), esp. pp. 65–79. See also Leopold Sedar Senghor, *The Collected Poetry*, trans. Melvin Dixon (Charlottesville: University Press of Virginia, 1991); Irving Leonard Markovitz, *Leopold Sedar Senghor and the Politics of Negritude* (New York: Atheneum, 1969); and Janet G. Vaillant, *Black, French, and African: A Life of Leopold Sedar Senghor* (Cambridge: Harvard University Press, 1990), pp. 243–71.

137. See O. R. Dathorne, *Dark Ancestor: The Literature of the Black Man in the Caribbean* (Baton Rouge: Louisiana State University Press, 1981), pp. 10, 30, 59, 77, 172–78, 205–09, 220–29, 258–61.

138. For an appreciation, see Bell, *Afro-American Novel*, pp. 115–16; for a critique, see St. Clair Drake, "Hide My Face?—On Pan-Africanism and Negritude," in *Soon, One Morning: New Writing by American Negroes, 1940–1962*, ed. Herbert Hill (New York: Alfred A. Knopf, 1963), pp. 77–105.

139. See Christopher L. Miller, *Theories of Africans: Francophone Literature and Anthropology in Africa* (Chicago: University of Chicago Press, 1990), pp. 196–97; Jacques Maquet, *Africanity: The Cultural Unity of Black Africa*, trans. Joan R. Rayfield (London: Oxford University Press, 1972), pp. 6–7, 13–15. For a fine example from the Cameroons, see Richard Bjornson, *The African Quest for Freedom and Identity: Cameroonian Writing and the National Experience* (Bloomington: Indiana University Press, 1991), pp. 170–237.

140. See Charles C. Lemert, "The Uses of French Structuralisms in Sociology," in *Frontiers of Social Theory: The New Syntheses*, ed. George Ritzer (New York: Columbia University Press, 1990), pp. 230–54. See also Richard Harvey Brown, *Society as Text: Essays on Rhetoric, Reason and Reality* (Chicago: University of Chicago Press, 1987), esp. pp. 97–192; and Brown, ed., *Writing the Social Text: Poetics and Politics in Social Science Discourse* (New York: Aldine DeGruyter, 1992), esp. pp. 39–52, 91–116.

141. See two works by Nathan Glazer and Daniel Patrick Moynihan, *Beyond the Melting Pot: The Negroes, Puerto Ricans, Jews, Italians, and Irish of New York City*, 2d ed. (Cambridge: M.I.T. Press, 1970); and with Corinne S. Schelling, eds., *Ethnicity: Theory and Experience* (Cambridge: Harvard University Press, 1975), esp. pp. 1–266. For an earlier period see Joyce D. Goodfriend, *Before the Melting Pot: Society and Culture in Colonial New York City, 1664–1730* (Princeton: Princeton University Press, 1992).

142. Charles Silberman, *Crisis in Black and White* (New York: Random House, 1964), p. 165.

143. Ibid.

144. See e.g., the three essays on Frederick Douglass's narrative by Robert B. Stepto, Robert G. O'Meally, and Henry Louis Gates, Jr., in *Afro-American Literature: The Reconstruction of Instruction*, ed. Dexter Fisher and Robert B. Stepto (New York: Modern Language Association of America, 1979), pp. 171–232.

145. Roxana Robinson, "It's Not Easy Being a WASP"—a review of *False Gods* (Boston: Houghton-Mifflin, 1992), by Louis Auchincloss, *New York Times Book Review*, sec. 7 (Mar. 15, 1992), p. 8.

146. Park, "Nature of Race Relations," p. 45.

147. Kwame Anthony Appiah, *In My Father's House: Africa in the Philosophy of Culture* (New York: Oxford University Press, 1992), p. 143.

148. Gian Biagio Conte, *The Rhetoric of Imitation: Genre and Poetic Memory in Virgil and Other Latin Poets*, trans. Charles Segal (Ithaca: Cornell University Press, 1986), pp. 23–24.

Index

STANFORD M. LYMAN is Robert J. Morrow Eminent Scholar and professor of social science, Florida Atlantic University. He is the author of *Civilization: Contents, Discontents, Malcontents, and Other Essays in Social Theory* (University of Arkansas Press, 1990), *The Seven Deadly Sins: Society and Evil* (General Hall, Inc., 1989), and *Chinatown and Little Tokyo: Power, Conflict, and Community among Chinese and Japanese Immigrants in America* (Associated Faculty Press, 1986), among other books. In addition to posts held at major universities in the United States, Lyman has served as a Fulbright lecturer in Japan (1981), visiting foreign expert at Beijing Foreign Studies University, China (1986), and a United States Information Agency lecturer in Singapore, Taiwan, Hong Kong, Ghana, Liberia, Nigeria, and the former Yugoslavia. In 1976 he was elected to a lifetime honorary appointment as senior lecturer, Linacre College, Oxford.